MODERN MYSTICS

MODERN MYSTICS

An Introduction

by
Bernard McGinn

A Herder & Herder Book
The Crossroad Publishing Company
New York

A Herder & Herder Book
The Crossroad Publishing Company
www.crossroadpublishing.com

© 2023 by Bernard McGinn

Crossroad, Herder & Herder, and the crossed C logo/colophon are registered trademarks of The Crossroad Publishing Company.

All rights reserved. No part of this book may be copied, scanned, reproduced in any way, or stored in a retrieval system, or transmitted, in any form or by any means, electronic, mechanical, photocopying, recording, or otherwise, without the written permission of The Crossroad Publishing Company. For permission please write to rights@crossroadpublishing.com.

In continuation of our 200-year tradition of independent publishing, The Crossroad Publishing Company proudly offers a variety of books with strong, original voices and diverse perspectives. The viewpoints expressed in our books are not necessarily those of The Crossroad Publishing Company, any of its imprints or of its employees, executives, or owners. Although the author and publisher have made every effort to ensure that the information in this book was correct at press time, the author and publisher do not assume and hereby disclaim any liability to any party for any loss, damage, or disruption caused by errors or omissions, whether such errors or omissions result from negligence, accident, or any other cause. No claims are made or responsibility assumed for any health or other benefits.

Book design by The HK Scriptorium

Library of Congress Cataloging-in-Publication Data
available from the Library of Congress.

ISBN 9780824595258-cloth
ISBN 9780824598594-tradepaper

Books published by The Crossroad Publishing Company may be purchased at special quantity discount rates for classes and institutional use. For information, please e-mail sales@crossroadpublishing.com.

Contents

Preface	vii
Modern Mystics: An Introduction	1
Chapter 1 Charles de Foucauld (1858–1916): Imitating the Life of Nazareth	33
Chapter 2 Thérèse of Lisieux (1873–1897): Mystic of Loving Confidence	62
Chapter 3 Elisabeth of the Trinity (1880–1906): The Praise of Glory	87
Chapter 4 Pierre Teilhard de Chardin (1881–1955): Pan-Christic Mystical Convergence	114
Chapter 5 Edith Stein (1891–1942): "May Your Will Be Done"	149
Chapter 6 Dag Hammarskjöld (1905–1963) Mystic and Public Servant	178
Chapter 7 Simone Weil (1909–1943): Dialectical Mysticism	208

Chapter 8
Henri Le Saux (Swami Abhishiktānanda) (1910–1973):
Mysticism beyond East and West   245

Chapter 9
Etty Hillesum (1914–1943):
Witness to Universal Love   271

Chapter 10
Thomas Merton (1915–1968) and the Renewal
of Contemplation: A Reflection   297

Conclusion   327

Index of Scripture References   331

Index of Subjects   333

Preface

This is a book that might not have been. In 2020, as Covid pervaded the world, I was able to send the manuscript of the ninth and final volume of my history of Christian mysticism, *The Presence of God*, off to the good folk at Crossroad-Herder, who published it in March of 2021. I frankly did not have any plans for the future, except for finishing off some overdue articles. By early 2021, however, I discovered that I was still around despite Covid and that, while diminishing in body due to old age, my mind still seemed to be working. Research in libraries at that time was severely limited, so I turned to thinking about writing something on materials I had mostly on hand, that is, the writings of some modern mystics, figures from the twentieth century who had made notable contributions to the tradition of Christian mysticism. I had been reading some of these people for many decades, as well as collecting their writings. Perhaps I could try to gather my thoughts about *some* of those who had attracted me. I had many of their books and was able to order others online. Given the constraints of the time of Covid, I would do what I could do. The result is what follows.

This is a decidedly personal selection, one that is more modest than what I originally intended. I planned on writing fifteen to twenty short essays on a range of figures—constituting a short book. As I began to write, however, I realized that brief essays would not do justice to these men and women. So, I have gradually whittled down my plans to embrace only ten mystics about whom I could write in some detail, if by no means fully: five men and five women. I have gone back and forth on whom to include, and whom, reluctantly, to exclude. I apologize to those who miss their favorite mystics here—I miss them too.

A note about the limitations of the following essays. They do not pretend to be full studies of their subjects. Rather, they testify to what I have found important in them. The bibliographies attached to each essay, furthermore, are selective and directed to the English-language reader who may be inspired to read more, so many important studies in other languages have been omitted. Note that all citations of texts in these essays follow the format and pagination of the editions cited in the respective bibliographies.

In the course of writing this book, I have been much assisted by the kindness of colleagues and friends, who read the essays and gave me valuable help. Harvey Egan, S.J., of Boston College, who has written so well on mysticism, old and new, read all the essays and was extremely helpful in many ways. Other good friends, especially Patrick Logan, David Tracy, and Peter Tyler, also read some essays and provided useful feedback. Michael Le Chevallier of the Lumen Christi Institute in Chicago loaned me several hard-to-find books of Henri Le Saux. My sincere thanks to each of them. My wife, Patricia, as usual, read all the essays and made numerous suggestions to improve the style and presentation. Finally, thanks, as ever, to the staff at Crossroad-Herder, particularly Gwendolin Herder, Chris Myers, and Julie Boddorf, as well as Paul Kobelski and Maurya Horgan of The HK Scriptorium, who corrected and copyedited, and typeset the manuscript.

Bernard McGinn
July 22, 2022. The Feast of Mary Magdalene the Mystic

Modern Mystics:
An Introduction

The twentieth century has not lacked for strong statements about the importance of mysticism in Christianity. In the second volume (1916) of his monumental eleven-volume *A Literary History of Religious Thought in France from the Wars of Religion down to Our Own Times*, the noted scholar Henri Bremond (1865–1933), included an "Appendix: Notes on Mysticism," in which he stated, "In short, it is not possible to ignore the mystics without disowning the self."[1] Bremond did not consider himself a mystic, but he devoted his life to the study of mysticism. A few years later (1923), another French priest, who was a mystic, Pierre Teilhard de Chardin (1881–1955), wrote to his friend Abbé Breuil, "Mysticism remains the great science and the great art, the only power capable of synthesizing the riches accumulated by the other forms of human activity."[2] Another mystic, the American Cistercian Thomas Merton (1915–1968), wrote to the English student of mysticism E. I. Watkin the following in 1963: "There is no question that it is the mystics who have kept Christianity going, if anyone has."[3] Another noted supporting statement comes from the great German theologian Karl Rahner (1904–1984) in an essay from the 1960s entitled "Christian Living Formerly and Today," where he said, ". . . the devout Christian of the future will either be a 'mystic,' one who has 'experienced' something, or he will cease to be anything at all."[4] So, the mystics cannot be ignored, because they are engaged in the science and art that synthesize all human activity. They are necessary to keep Christianity going, especially in the present era, as foreseen by Rahner and many others. This is not to say that the great mystics are for everyone. David Tracy, reflecting on the fact the William James gave pride of place to mystics and saints in his classic study *The Varieties of Religious Experience* (1902), noted,

"If you want to understand what most of us are like most of the time, then do not choose the 'mystics' and the 'saints' for your analysis. But if you want to understand what human beings can be when they break out of self-centeredness into Reality-centeredness, then reflect, with James, not just on yourself but on the two extreme types: the cognitive extremity of the mystic and the action-transforming activity of the saint."[5]

The growing importance of spirituality in the broad sense, and mysticism in the more restricted sense as the goal of the spiritual path, is also evident in the teaching of the Catholic Church, specifically, in its catechetical documents meant to guide and shape the belief and practice of the faithful. The noun "mysticism" is a modern word, first appearing in the seventeenth century, although mysticism as the search for a deeper experience of God's presence goes back to the beginning of Christianity. Much of what is understood as mysticism today appeared under the rubric of "contemplation" in earlier centuries. Here it is instructive to look at two major catechisms that reflect the growing stress on the mystical element of Christianity in the modern era. *The Catechism of the Council of Trent* was commissioned by the Council to express the truths of Catholic belief, especially (not solely) against the attacks of the sixteenth-century Reformers. Published at the command of Pope Pius V in 1566, it is relentlessly doctrinal, with its four parts dealing with the Apostle's Creed, the Sacraments, the Ten Commandments, and Prayer and the Lord's Prayer. Naturally, mysticism does not appear as a discrete topic, but under "Part IV. On Prayer" there is a treatment of prayer in general, including the main types (petition and thanksgiving), the fruits of prayer, the objects of prayer, and so on.[6] What is surprising to the modern reader is that there is almost no mention of contemplative prayer—the word "contemplation" occurs only twice. The most important appearance is in a passage on the prayer of just persons, who are said to "rise successively from one degree of purity and of fervor in prayer to another, until, at length, they reach that height of perfection, whence they can contemplate the infinite power, beneficence, and mercy of God."[7] Contemplative, or mystical, prayer seems not to have been that important to the authors of the *Catechism*. We can only speculate about this deficiency, but it may have been due to the fact that since the fourteenth century there had been a growing divide between doctrinal theology, on the one hand (the kind represented in the *Catechism*), and spiritual/mystical theology, on the other. The deleterious effects of this divide became increasingly evident in the twentieth century, as pointed out by many of the major theologians of the time (e.g., Karl Rahner, Bernard Lonergan, Hans Urs von Balthasar, and others).

In contrast, *The Catechism of the Catholic Church*, published in 1992 at the command of Pope John Paul II, has a large place for contemplative prayer in its Part Four, "On Prayer."[8] There is also a treatment of mystical union as the goal of "Life in Christ," which comes in Part Three of the work.[9] Section One of Part Three is entitled, "Man's Vocation: Life in the Spirit" (§§1699-2051, pp. 421-95). Chapter Three, Article 2, of this deals with "Grace and Justification" (§§1987-2029, pp. 481-90) and contains a treatment of "Christian Holiness" in which the following description of progress in the spiritual life appears: "Spiritual progress tends toward ever more intimate union with Christ. This union is called 'mystical' because it participates in the mystery of Christ through the sacraments . . . , and, in him, in the mystery of the Holy Trinity. God calls us all to this intimate union with him, even if the special mystical graces or extraordinary signs of this mystical life are granted only to some for the sake of manifesting the gratuitous gift given to all" (§2014, p. 488). Note here the assertion that the call to mystical union is meant for all (an important point given earlier twentieth-century debates), and that mystical union arises from "participating in the mystery of Christ through the sacraments" and involves contact with the mystery of the Trinity. Furthermore, the so-called "special gifts," or "extraordinary signs of the mystical life," such as visions, ecstasies, and paranormal gifts, are not essential but are "granted only to some," and *only* for the purpose of "manifesting the gratuitous gift [i.e., sanctifying grace] given to all." This is a lucid and precise theological description of the nature of mysticism.

Mysticism, of course, was very much a part of the life of the Church in the sixteenth century when the *Catechism of the Council of Trent* appeared, but it was not featured in this doctrinal handbook. By the end of the twentieth century the recent *Catechism* saw that it was necessary to provide correct teaching on the nature of contemplative prayer and mystical union to all the faithful. We might say that the Church's formal teaching had caught up with the claims about the necessity of mysticism reflected in the figures quoted above.

The sixteenth century was full of mystics. We need only note such names as Ignatius of Loyola, Teresa of Avila, and John of the Cross, to realize this. These mystical teachers could look back on fifteen centuries of mystics, from the Fathers of East and West, through the medieval monastic mystics, into the late Middle Ages with a host of mystical figures, both men and women. The seventeenth century was also a great age of mystics, especially in France with figures like Francis de Sales, but also in Italy, Germany, and Spain. But a grave crisis put a check on the development of Catholic mysticism at the end of the seventeenth century. Between 1675 and 1700 a series of inquisitorial proceedings, banning of books, persecutions, and papal decrees condemned many mystical authors as "Quietists," people accused of so stressing interior quiet, passive prayer, and pure love that they undercut the official piety and authority of the institutional Church, and perhaps even the moral law.[10] There were certainly exaggerations and false formulations among some spiritual authors of the time, but the blanket condemnation of "Quietism," its elevation into a dubious heretical "-ism," and the succeeding turn against mysticism were severe blows to the Christian mystical tradition that had been nurtured and developed for a millennium and a half. It was a time of real crisis for mysticism, though fortunately it proved to be a caesura in the story, not a total end.

As a result of this crisis, the eighteenth and nineteenth centuries, at least in the Catholic tradition, represent a nadir, a very low period, in the story of Western mysticism.[11] It is not that there were no mystics (there always are), or that there were no mystical texts written, but the production was meager and not generally impressive. The Quietist condemnations had severed the link between mystical consciousness and serious theological reflection. Most of those considered mystics during this time were female ecstatics and visionaries, who, unlike Teresa of Avila and earlier women mystics, did not produce mystical theology worth pondering. They show; they do not tell.

A Rebirth

The ways of the Holy Spirit are not our ways. The triumph of Enlightenment rationalism and its emphasis on experimental science, accompanied by the internal crisis of Quietism in the Catholic world during the centuries from 1700 to 1900, might well have marked the end of mysticism—a failed aspect of an outmoded religion. As the representative of the Enlightenment, the English Lord Bolingbroke (1678–1751), once said, "All the ways of acquiring a more direct knowledge of the mind of God by archetypal ideas . . . , by the irradiations of mystic theology, or by the inward light of Quakerism, and several more, which the phrenzy of metaphysics, not very distant from that of enthusiasm, has invented, are too ridiculous to deserve the regard of commonsense."[12] Some may still say "Amen" to that, but the history of the past hundred or more years tells a different story. Mysticism is alive and well. It has been growing since the end of the nineteenth century, not only among academics interested in this aspect of religion, but (more importantly) in the lives and practice of believers.

Academic Perspectives

We can begin with a brief look at the development of the academic study of mysticism in the modern era.[13] Serious new engagement with mysticism began at the end of the nineteenth century. In the eighteenth and earlier nineteenth centuries large boring tomes of Scholastic theology were devoted to parsing the intricacies of what was termed "Ascetical and Mystical Theology." The triumph of the Anti-Quietists, such as Bishop J.-B. Bossuet (d. 1704), meant that mysticism was seen as a special grace of God, given only to the very few, and characterized by extraordinary and paranormal gifts. It was to be closely regulated by clerical authority at all times. Furthermore, since these gifts could be easily parodied by demonic forces, much of the study of mysticism during the time was devoted to establishing criteria to determine true from false mysticism. The most extensive work devoted to mysticism in the nineteenth century, the five volumes of J. J. von Görries's *Die christliche Mystik* (1837–1842), written from the perspective of German Catholic Romanticism, illustrates this by its division into two volumes devoted to authentic Catholic mysticism and three further volumes on its demonic counterfeits. Catholic focus on mysticism as the realm of the bizarre and paranormal, however, also attracted some late nineteenth-century nonreligious thinkers, especially psychologists, mostly in France, to the study of ecstatic mystics, whom they often identified as "hysterics." The most important product of this psychological interest was a book still considered a classic, William James's *Varieties of Religious Experience*. Whatever its shortcomings, James's book showed that mysticism was a topic for serious intellectual engagement around the turn of the century.

Parallel to the secular interest in mysticism as an example of abnormal psychology was the new look at mysticism that was part of the triumph of Neoscholasticism in Catholic thought. Pope Leo XIII's encyclical *Aeterni Patris* of 1878 established Thomas Aquinas as the Church's foremost doctrinal authority and an antidote to the corrosive acids of modernity. In their efforts to create a "fortress Catholicism," some Neoscholastic thinkers began to revisit the Catholic mystical tradition to identify the "best" mystics who could serve as touchstones for truth in mysticism the way that Thomas did in doctrine. Teresa of

Avila (d. 1582) was one such figure. Rather more puzzling was how her colleague, John of the Cross (d. 1591), emerged as an equally potent authority. John was controversial in his life; his path to sanctity was slow; and for more than a century he was under suspicion as a kind of Quietist. By the end of the nineteenth century, however, John had become the mystical equivalent of Thomas, a position confirmed by his declaration as a Doctor of the Church in 1926. For much of the twentieth century, Catholic writing on mysticism was measured by the yardstick of Teresa and John. My point here is not to criticize these great mystics, but only to note that the criterion for truth in teaching is not a single person or persons but rather revelation and the general tradition of the faith. Neoscholastic treatments of mysticism, centered mostly in France, were preoccupied with issues left over from the Quietist debates, such as whether all believers were called to mystical prayer, and the difference between acquired and infused contemplation. Significant names were the Sulpician Auguste Saudreau (1859–1942), who defended the universal call to mysticism, and the Jesuit A.-F. Poulain (1836–1919), who denied it. Little of this large literature is much read (or readable) today.

A convenient, if somewhat imprecise, way to sketch the story of twentieth-century study of mysticism is to see it as developing over three generations, although the three periods should not be separated, because some scholars were productive across generations. The first generation (ca. 1900–1940) was notable for important contributions from philosophy and philosophical psychology, although theology, history, comparative religion, and literature were also involved. The center of discussion was France, although the Anglophone world was a secondary nexus. The second generation (1940–1975) began with the break constituted by World War II and its effects on intellectual life and the exchange of ideas. This period did not see as much original philosophical activity, but was a time of historical and theological *ressourcement*, the recovery of aspects of the history of theology and mysticism that had been forgotten or seriously neglected. From roughly 1975 to the end of the century, and, indeed, into the present, the third generation witnessed a flowering of the study of mysticism, but from so many perspectives that it might be termed a "multidisciplinary era." During this period the work of editing and translating classic mystical texts, begun in the second generation, has continued to grow to the extent that we can say that the richness of almost the whole mystical tradition is now available, for the first time, to the general public.

Between 1900 and 1940 numerous French philosophers wrote important works on mysticism. These include Maurice Blondel (d. 1949), whose *Le problème de la mystique* appeared in 1925, and Henri Bergson (d. 1941), especially in his *Deux sources de la morale et la religion* of 1932. In the same year, the Thomist philosopher Jacques Maritain (d. 1973) published his *Distinguer pour unir, ou les degres du savoir*, an analysis of the nature of knowing based on Thomas Aquinas and John of the Cross. The Belgian Jesuit Joseph Maréchal (d. 1944) was both a philosopher and a psychologist. His two-volume *Études sur la psychologie des mystiques* (1926 and 1937) brought together important essays that had begun to appear in 1908. An interest in mysticism flourished among some of the early twentieth-century Catholic thinkers loosely grouped as "Modernists," due to their desire to effect a rapprochement between the Catholic Church and modernity.[14] Some of these figures (Alfred Loisy, George Tyrrell, Ernesto Buonaiuti) were formally condemned by Rome. Others, like Blondel, were not. Among the sympathizers of the movement was Friedrich von Hügel (d. 1925), whose book *The Mystical Element of Religion as Studied in St. Catherine of Genoa and Her Friends* (1908), is one of the classic works in the field.[15] Another was the former Jesuit Henri Bremond, cited above, whose multivolume history of seventeenth-century mysticism deliberately sought to be a literary, not a theological, account in order to avoid Roman censure. Cuthbert Butler (d. 1934), abbot of Downside, was a friend of von Hügel, Bremond, and others in the circle. His *Western Mysticism* (1922) was one of the first books that sought to go back to the older monastic mysticism of the Middle Ages rather than concentrate on the sixteenth-century Spaniards.[16]

In the United States during the first generation, the most important work was done by a group of philosophers and scholars connected with Harvard University, including William James (d. 1910), Josiah Royce (d. 1916), and William Hocking (d. 1966). The Quaker historian of mysticism Rufus Jones (d. 1948) studied at Harvard and taught at Haverford College for many years. There was also work done on mysticism in Germany, Spain, and to a lesser degree in Italy in this first generation.

As early as the 1930s some French and German Catholic scholars had begun intensive study of the patristic and medieval authors often neglected by the Neoscholastics. This was to bear extensive fruit in the post–World War II era as the movement of *ressourcement* picked up steam and began to erode the dominance of the Neoscholastic model for philosophy and theology. The movement had a significant impact on the study of mysticism. This is evident in the fact that a number of the major Catholic theologians active in the period ca. 1940–1980 gave considerable attention to mysticism. The French Jesuit Henri de Lubac (d. 1991) was a pioneer in studying the mystics at the Jesuit House of Studies at Lyon in the 1930s. De Lubac maintained a lifelong interest in mysticism but never wrote the major book he had planned. Between 1959 and 1963, however, he published a four-volume study, *Exégèse médiévale* (three volumes later appeared in English as *Medieval Exegesis*), a wide-ranging treatment of the spiritual/mystical reading of scripture that had been the foundation of the mystical tradition for its first twelve centuries. Jean Daniélou (d. 1974), a student of de Lubac, pursued the investigation of the patristic mystics and was also instrumental in starting the *Sources Chrétiennes* series (1941–), a project that over the decades has produced more than five hundred volumes of editions of religious texts, many mystical, along with translations and learned apparatuses. Another student of de Lubac was the Swiss theologian Hans Urs von Balthasar (d. 1988). During his distinguished career Balthasar wrote many monographs on mystics and incorporated mystical theology into his large theological oeuvre. His greatest contribution came mostly in the third generation through his trilogy consisting of the seven-volume *Herrlichkeit* (1961–1969; English version, *The Glory of the Lord*), the five volumes of *Theodramatik* (1982–1988; English version, *Theo-Drama*), and the three volumes of *Theologik* (1985–1987; English version, *Theo-Logic*). The role of de Lubac in encouraging interest in mysticism is evident also in the career of Michel de Certeau (d. 1986), a Jesuit who began his studies with de Lubac, wrote on Jesuit mystics in the 1960s, but moved on to psychoanalytical, cultural, and postmodern investigations of mysticism in his later works, especially his two volume *Le Fable mystique* (1982, and posthumously 2002). The historical retrieval of mysticism evident from the 1940s benefited from the contributions of many other figures, such as the Benedictine Jean Leclercq (d. 1993), the great scholar of monasticism, as well as historians of French mysticism, such as Louis Cognet and Jean Orcibal.

Along with the historical studies of the second generation there were other significant theological contributions to the investigation of mysticism. A key figure was the German Jesuit Karl Rahner (d. 1984), cited above. In the 1930s, Rahner published some youthful essays on mysticism, but it was not until the 1950s and later that his groundbreaking theological works began to be widely read. Like Balthasar, Rahner never wrote a single book on mysticism, but his view of mystical experience pervades both his general theological works, such as *Grundkurs des Glaubens* (*Foundations of Faith*, 1976), as well as the theological essays found throughout his twenty-three volumes of *Schriften zur Theologie* (*Theological Investigations*).[17] Rahner's many sermons, talks, prayers, and meditations are also a resource for the practical aspects of his view of the role of mysticism in the Christian life.

What I am calling the third generation of the twentieth-century academic study of mysticism (ca. 1975 to present) continued many trends begun in the second generation but also developed new interests. For example, the genre of histories of spirituality began with the first generation with Pierre Pourrat's four-volume *La spiritualité chrétienne* (1917-1928), although this Sulpician priest took a dim view of mysticism. More friendly toward mysticism was the four-volume multiauthor *Histoire de la spiritualité chrétienne* (1960-1966; the first three volumes were translated into English). An ecumenical endeavor, *The Encyclopedia of World Spirituality*, devoted three volumes to Christian spirituality (1985-1989). It was not until the 1990s, however, that the growing interest in mysticism led to the appearance of multivolume histories of mysticism itself. The German medievalist Kurt Ruh (d. 2002) produced the four volumes of his *Geschichte der abendländische Mystik* between 1990 and 1999, covering the patristic and medieval periods. My own *The Presence of God: A History of Western Christian Mysticism* covers the history down to 1700 in nine volumes (1991-2021). A number of single-volume histories of mysticism have also appeared, primarily in German and English.[18] The work of scholars of German literature and culture, such as A. M. Haas, has also contributed much to the study of mysticism in the third generation.[19]

Philosophers continued to show interest in mysticism during the last decades of the past century. Considerable interest was generated by the debates beginning in the 1970s between the "constructivists," like Steven T. Katz, who argued for a variety of mysticisms constructed according the belief systems of diverse religions, and the "essentialists," sometimes referred to as "perennialists" (e.g., W. T. Stace, Robert Forman, et al.), who contended that there was a common, or universal, core to all mystical experience across cultures and religions.[20] Two other tendencies increasingly evident late in the twentieth century deserve note: the role of mysticism in so-called postmodern thought, particularly in France; and what has been called the "apophatic turn." These are by no means discrete phenomena, and, while they are most manifested in philosophy, they are also multidisciplinary in nature, being found in theology, psychology, literary studies, and the like.[21] Postmodernism, perhaps more a "cultural drift" than a definable movement, is a blanket term used to cover recent critics of modernity with its stress on the hegemonic power of rationality and social hierarchies. Many of the heroes of postmodernity, however, like the philosopher Jacques Derrida (d. 2004), rejected the label for themselves. A postmodernist *avant la lettre* was Georges Bataille (d. 1962), an atheist, who nonetheless had a strong interest in female mystics, such as Teresa of Avila and Angela of Foligno, because he believed that their eroticism and excess served as a model for challenging the tyranny of rationality. Bataille's *L'érotisme* (1957; English translation, *Death and Sensuality*, 1962) is one of the most impressive books devoted to the erotic element in mysticism. Other recent French authors often seen as postmodernists who wrote on the mystics include the psychoanalyst Jacques Lacan (d. 1981) and the feminists Simone de Beauvoir and Luce Irigaray.[22]

The importance of apophatic, or negative, theology has been recognized by a number of the major theologians of the mid-century, such as Balthasar and Rahner. In recent decades the "apophatic turn" has become strong across many disciplines, such as philosophy (Derrida and Jean-Luc Marion), literary studies (Kevin Hart), comparative studies (Michael Sells), and theology (Denys Turner).[23] This has led to considerable attention being given to the masters of apophatic mysticism, such as Pseudo-Dionysius, John Scottus Eriugena, Meister Eckhart, the anonymous author of the *Cloud of Unknowing*, Nicholas of Cusa, and John of the Cross. It is important to remember that all Christian mystics make use of both cataphatic (positive) and apophatic (negative) modes of discourse in approaching the mystery of the God who lies beyond all human predication. Still, a fuller appreciation of the necessity of negation has given the contemporary study of mysticism a flavor quite different, say, from the approach to mysticism found in the old Neoscholastic tomes.

The Nature of Mysticism

The issue that immediately confronts anyone writing about modern mysticism is the question, Who is a modern mystic? —that is, how do we identify mystics in the modern world? Implied in this question is the second issue of the extent to which mystics living in the twentieth century may or may not differ from the mystics of the classic Christian mystical tradition that ended at the close of the seventeenth century. Naturally, there will be differences between the mystics of old and the modern mystics, but I believe that, however different some of the modern mystics may be from their forebears, they still can be viewed according to the general heuristic understanding of mysticism I set out in my series *The Presence of God*.

The "General Introduction" to volume 1 of *The Presence of God*, entitled *The Foundations of Mysticism*, briefly discussed the contours of a view of mysticism that I later expressed as follows: "Mysticism is that part, or element, of Christian belief and practice that concerns the preparation for, the consciousness of, and the effect of what the mystics themselves have described as a direct and transformative [encounter with] the presence of God."[24] In several essays I have offered further explanations of this heuristic description.[25] The description emphasizes six aspects of mysticism.

First, "mysticism" (a modern term) is a part, or *element*, of concrete religious traditions, like Christianity, Judaism, Islam, and Hinduism—it is not the *whole*. This is why it is in many ways more correct to speak of the "mystical element" rather than of mysticism itself. It was the contribution of von Hügel in his *The Mystical Element of Religion* to have first underlined this important truth by distinguishing three essential elements in religion (the institutional, the intellectual, and the mystical), elements that are meant to function in harmony but that have not always done so.[26] Seeing the mystical element contextually, that is, as interdependent with the other two main elements, is important for overcoming skewed views of the nature of the mystical that too often treat it in isolation from the other aspects of religion.

The second element of my approach stresses that the mystical aspect of religion involves a total *process*; that is, it is not just some moment or instant in or out of time in which God is attained but involves the whole life of the mystic. Mystics typically prepare for meeting God through acts of asceticism, worship, study, spiritual direction, and the like, although God can sometimes make a sudden and unexpected incursion into a person's life, as in the case of Saul's conversion on the road to Damascus (Acts 9). After this preparation, often involving considerable time, the mystic can receive the grace of a direct encounter with God. This is central to the whole process, but that moment of attainment (temporary; sometimes perhaps more permanent) is not meant to be the end of the process, unless the mystic dies and goes right to heaven. Attaining God is furthermore intended to have an *effect* on the life of the mystic, as well as on how the mystic relates to other people. In other words, the mystical element is meant to be *transformative* of the mystic's life in order to enable him or her to help transform others.

The third element is the term *consciousness*. Most students of mysticism have talked about "mystical experience" and have labored to understand what it is and how it differs from ordinary experience. Experience is a highly contested term among philosophers, but in common parlance it often seems to be used in the sense of *feeling*, or sensation. Mysticism, however, is more than just a new feeling, sensation, or emotion; it involves the whole conscious subject, which is the reason why I prefer the word "consciousness." My use of consciousness does not rule out an important role for experience, although I think that the way most mystics use *experientia* and its equivalents is not so much to indicate an experience *of* something, that is, some kind of sensation (e.g., "I experienced great heat"), but more in the sense of being experienced *in*, that is, coming to possess an intimate knowledge of something (e.g., "He was an experienced wine taster").

"Consciousness," as I am using it here, is a capacious term that refers to the *awareness* that exists on all levels of the subject's intentionality, from its beginning in inner and outer sensation, through the exercise of thinking (attention, reasoning, insight, understanding, affirming), up to the activities of loving, deciding, and acting.[27] My argument is that the whole intentional life of the mystic is transformed by the encounter with God. While in ordinary conscious acts there are two primary aspects—awareness of objects and awareness of self (implicitly or reflexively), in mystical consciousness there also enters in a "co-awareness" of God, which may be more or less direct.[28] This co-awareness, or co-presence, is where the transformation takes place in both our way of loving and our way of knowing—we become more than we usually are in our ordinary consciousness. We come to love God in a higher way by receiving the love of God so that we now can love in a divine way (Rom. 5:5, "God's love has been poured into our hearts through the Holy Spirit that has been given to us"). But our way of knowing God is also changed. First, we come to understand in a deeper way that God cannot be understood—contact with God enhances the mystery rather than lessening it. Second, we gain what many mystics and theologians have spoken of as a "connatural" knowing of God; that is, we do not know *more about* God, but we become aware of God in a new way, as friend knows friend or lover knows lover. Finally, in mystical consciousness we do not know God or love God as an *object*; rather, God's nonobjective co-presence in our intentionality moves us to a higher stage of life. As I summarized in my essay on "Mystical Consciousness": "The mystic therefore both *loves*, consciously and unrestrictedly, on the basis of God's presence in the ground of awareness, and consciously and unrestrictedly *knows and affirms* the horizon of divine unknowability through the practice of *docta ignorantia* [learned ignorance]."[29]

I have emphasized that this consciousness of God is direct or in some way *immediate*. This is the fourth aspect of my description. Is direct contact with God ever possible in this life? Several things need to be noted in addressing this difficult question. First of all, direct does not mean full or complete. Mystics and theologians have always insisted that any contact with God in this life can never be equal to the full, perfect, and eternal contact or vision of God to come in heaven. The second issue is that I use the word "direct" because this is what seems to reflect the language of many of the mystics about how their consciousness of God's presence is of a different order from how they ordinarily know and love God. Finally, I do not intend to take up all the issues involved in the question of how "direct" actually is the heightened nature of mystical contact with God, or the extent to which it may still involve some forms of mediation. I have elsewhere appealed to Bernard Lonergan's notion of "mediated immediacy" as a possible way to address this issue, but a full answer would require more attention than can be given here.

The fifth element of my heuristic description is *presence*. Why do I emphasize contact with God's presence rather than, say, the commonly used term "union"? Union language is based on scripture (e.g., 1 Cor. 6:17; John 15 and 17) and is the most frequent way that mystics have characterized the goal of the mystical path.[30] Nevertheless, union is only one of the ways mystics have described their contact with God. Some mystics, like Augustine, seem to have consciously avoided speaking of union, perhaps because that was the language of pagan philosophical mystics, such as Plotinus. Other mystics have deployed a whole range of terms along with, or even in substitution for, union: the vision of God, contemplation, attaining or touching God, tasting God, endless pursuit of God, radical obedience to God, and many more. I think all these terms can be embraced under the broad category of becoming conscious of the *presence* of God, which is why I highlight presence over union.[31]

Nevertheless, as all who have read the mystics know, many mystics have felt that God seems often more *absent* than present. God not only is experienced as absent, but, more terribly, God sometimes seems to have deliberately abandoned those who love him the most, inflicting on them a sense of dereliction, desolation, and even consigning them to hell, to be eternally separated from him. Presence and absence, then, are paradoxically intertwined terms in mysticism. Among modern mystics, Simone Weil expressed what I would call the philosophical paradox of absence when she said, "Contact with human persons is given to us through the sense of presence. Contact with God is given to us through the sense of absence. Compared with this absence, presence becomes more absent than absence."[32] The Welsh priest-poet R. S. Thomas was more direct, when he said, "Why no! I never thought other than / That God is that great absence / In our lives, the empty silence / Within, the place where we go / Seeking, not in hope to / Arrive or find."[33] These are profound expressions of the sense of the absence of God, but even they may not fully capture the most radical sense of absence as divinely induced torture, something we find in many mystics of the past (e.g., Mechthild of Magdeburg, Angela of Foligno, John Tauler), and also in modern mystics from Thérèse of Lisieux to Mother Teresa of Calcutta. The mystery of the internal suffering and dereliction of the mystics due to God's absence is a reminder that God's ways are not our ways, since the story of salvation centers on Christ's sense of abandonment by his Father on the cross. In that sense, suffering and mystical dereliction are part of the "Christo-mimesis" of the mystical path.

The sixth and final aspect of my heuristic description is more implied than directly stated. In order to be known and become fruitful, the mystical element has to be *expressed* and *written down*. The study of mysticism must begin with the ways in which the mystic strives to communicate the meaning of his or her consciousness of God. We have no real access to the experience of others, however much we may be able to study the kinds of brain waves that seem to accompany the forms of consciousness typical of "mystical states." It is only through verbal, written, and artistic communications that we can come to know what these "states" *meant* to those who underwent them. As an object of study, mysticism is a matter of expression or communication, something that one subject tries to tell to another. Many mystics doubtless never spoke about what they experienced, or only talked about it to a few. Others felt compelled to write their experiences down or, in earlier ages, to dictate them to spiritual advisors and learned scribes. Some expressed them in non-verbal ways.

Insofar as mysticism involves textual mediation, there is obviously a need for the development of a mystical hermeneutic, or art of interpretation. Since this is an art that will vary according to the kinds of mystical texts, it cannot be set out as a rigid set of rules, but some general principles can be discerned. For example, mystical discourse is paradoxical in nature, because almost all mystics admit that God is ineffable and what is ineffable cannot be spoken. Augustine reflected on the general problem of speaking about God in his *De doctrina christiana* 1.6. "Have we spoken or solemnly uttered anything worthy of God?," he begins. "Rather, I feel I have done nothing but wish to speak. If I have spoken, I have not said what I wish to say. How do I know this?

Because God is ineffable [*ineffabilis*]. If what I have said were ineffable, it could not be framed in words, and for this reason God should not be said to be ineffable. . . . When this is said, something is said, and a contradiction [*pugna verborum*] is created. . . . This contradiction is to be passed over in silence rather than resolved in words." So, the horizon of silence and worship limits all God-talk, especially mystical discourse. We cannot *really* talk about God, but the mystic feels that he or she *must* talk about God—a necessary impossibility!

All talk about God, *a fortiori* mystical talk, is a venture, an experiment, a self-effacing artifact. It does not denote God but suggests something that approaches God. Therefore, ordinary modes of speaking will often have to be stretched, transformed, even subverted in mystical discourse, which is far more like poetry than like scientific exposition. Mystical language usually involves verbal strategies, such as the creation of neologisms, the use of paradox, oxymoron, rhetorical excess, and the like. This, of course, is more true of some mystics than of others, but the general drift of speaking about the God who becomes hiddenly present moves in that direction.

One special form of mystical discourse regards the role of negation and the relation between positive (cataphatic) and negative (apophatic) speaking about God. This is one of the three negativities involved in mysticism (Negativity 1); the other two being the negation of desire found in ascetical effort and radical detachment (Negativity 2), and the negation involved in affliction, dereliction, and the loss of God (Negativity 3).[34] Three principles can help in understanding Negativity 1, that is, unsaying God. First, all mystics use both cataphatic (yes-saying) and apophatic (no-saying) expressions—they necessarily imply each other. Therefore, any easy distinction between cataphatic and apophatic mystics is a chimaera. The investigator needs to be attentive to *how* and in what *proportion* the mystic relates positive and negative predication about God. A second principle is that the negative way is generally seen as higher and more adequate, because God is not really like anything we know. Things may have some likeness to God, but God has no real likeness to things. As Thomas Aquinas put it, "We know God as unknown."[35] Finally, what I call "strong" apophaticism or, perhaps better, super-negation insists that God is so far outside our ways of knowing and speaking that he goes beyond yes-saying and no-saying into the realm of above-saying, supereminent predications like *hyperagathon* ("more-than-good"), *hypertheon* ("more-than-God"), *hyperousian* ("more-than-being"). This is the place of silent *docta ignorantia*, as described in the Dionysian *De mystica theologia*.

Some Themes of Modern Mysticism

The mystical tradition can be compared to a great symphony in which different instruments, as well as individual virtuosi players, all are meant to contribute to an effect that goes beyond what any individual member can achieve but which includes all their particular efforts. This is why selecting a few great mystics, such as Teresa and John, as the measure for the whole mystical tradition is wrong-headed.

The sheer variety of mystics shows how difficult it is to construct any adequate typology of Christian mystics up to 1700. From the early martyrs, the catechists and bishops of the Church in the Roman Empire, into the monastic mystics that dominated the period ca. 300 to 1200, the first major strand in Christian mysticism already displays great differences. In the period that I call the "New Mysticism" (ca. 1200–1650), new forms of mystical piety, clerical, religious, and lay proliferated—mendicants, beguines, independent layfolk, as well as the successors of the monks and clerics that dominated up to 1200. There were many varieties of mystics—from ecstatic and visionary mystics to those who warned against seeking such special gifts.

The modern mystics of the twentieth century are no less varied, both in their forms of life and in the content of their teaching. The mystics considered in this book, as pointed out in the preface, constitute a personal selection and are not meant to be anything like a total survey. In terms of their lifestyles and their teaching, some look much like earlier mystics; others will seem new in relation to past mystical traditions. Before looking at the individual mystics themselves, it may be helpful to consider some major themes that appear in many twentieth century mystics to see how these relate to what we find in the "classic" period of mysticism.

Visions and Ecstasy

Many mystics, especially in the medieval and early modern periods, were famous for their visionary experiences, which were often accompanied by ecstasy, that is, being drawn out of ordinary states of consciousness, as well as other forms of paranormal manifestations.[36] The majority of the visionaries were women, but there were also male figures, such as Rupert of Deutz, Francis of Assisi, and Henry Suso. Some visionaries merely recounted what they saw and announced messages sent from God (e.g., Elisabeth of Schönau, Birgitta of Sweden), but many others meditated on their visionary experiences to uncover the theological truths contained in them—think of Hildegard of Bingen in the twelfth century, Mechthild of Magdeburg in the thirteenth, Julian of Norwich in the fourteenth, and Teresa of Avila in the sixteenth. The visionary tradition was ambiguous, because everyone admitted that visions could come from one's own imagination, from diabolical action, as well as from God, so the need for "discernment of spirits" (*discretio spirituum*) was recognized.

The twentieth century saw a number of female visionaries and ecstatics. Let me say a bit about some of these women, because I do not intend to deal with the visionaries in the essays below. Some visionaries have been canonized, for example, Gemma Galgani (1878–1903), and Sister Faustina Kowalska (1905–1938), although we need to remember that canonization does not entail the approval of the private revelations made to any saint. Gemma Galgani's *Autobiography*, *Diary*, and *Letters*, are filled with accounts of her visions, raptures, and spiritual gifts like the stigmata, but are notable for the lack of much theological reflection on the meaning of these mystical gifts. Her writings portray Gemma as the image of what a visionary ecstatic was supposed to look like.[37] Sister Faustina's lengthy *Diary* features a plethora of reports of her ecstasies and her visions of Jesus, Mary, and the saints, as well as her experiences of the Dark Night and even of union with the Trinity. Faustina underwent attacks from the devil and at times endured a sense of being abandoned by God. There is also a reflective character to her writings, one that emphasizes some doctrinal and spiritual teaching, especially on the role of Divine Mercy, the center of her message.[38] Still, the devotion to Divine Mercy that she initiated was controversial, at least early on. On March 6, 1959, the Holy Office issued a Notification forbidding the spread of the devotion, but on June 30, 1978, during the pontificate of John Paul II, who as archbishop of Warsaw had been a strong supporter of the cult, the ban was lifted. Pope John Paul went on to canonize Sister Faustina in 2000, and in 2001 he extended the Feast of Divine Mercy to the entire Church (First Sunday after Easter).[39]

Other female visionaries have had a more disputed reception. A good example is Therese Neumann (1898–1962), a peasant woman from Konnersreuth in Bavaria, who first received the stigmata in 1926. Neumann's extensive visions and her other paranormal gifts (miraculous cures, raptures, inedia, bilocation, levitation, and the stigmata) can be seen as extending a visionary trajectory established centuries before. Her visions deal with the life of Jesus as found in the Gospels and celebrated in the feasts of the liturgical year. They contain a great deal of material added to the biblical account, especially regarding the actions of individuals and such details as what everyone was wearing at each event. (It is almost as if Therese is describing a technicolor movie she has just seen!)[40] To give an example. In a vision of Jesus on the road to Jerusalem and the Passion, Neumann recounts, "The Savior put on his fine yellow robe; it was long, hemmed, and bound with a simple broad girdle. Two men placed the Savior on the animal, one of them lifting him while the other helped from the other side. He did not take the old animal, but rather the young one."[41] Neumann's film-like showings were faithfully recorded by her admirers; others found them products of the hyperactive imagination of a pious person. The local bishop began a process for her canonization, but this has gone nowhere.

Another example of visions that are basically imaginative projections amounting to an almost endless recounting of the life of Christ (fifteen thousand pages in her notebooks), is found in *The Poem of the Man-God* by the Italian visionary Maria Valtorta (1897–1961), a laywoman who was an invalid for much of her life.[42] This collection was supposedly approved by Pope Pius XII in 1948, but the first printed edition (1956–1959) was placed on the *Index of Forbidden Books* at the end of 1959. On January 6, 1960, the Vatican paper *L'Osservatore Romano* attacked the book in an article entitled "A Life of Jesus Badly Fictionalized." Later, the head of the Congregation for the Doctrine of the Faith, Cardinal Joseph Ratzinger, confirmed the disapproval of her works in January 1985.

Along with these four fairly standard seers, the past century saw a number of visionaries of new kinds. One unusual figure was the Swiss married Protestant visionary who wrote under the pseudonym of Joa Bolendas (1917–2005). She left a number of books featuring conversations with a variety of heavenly figures, including songs communicated by the angels. Many of these visions, which have a strong ecumenical character, are recorded in her *Journals*.[43] Joa's early visions, featuring conversations with Christ, Mary, and the saints, fit within standard Christian parameters, but her later conversations broaden out to describe dialogues with a number of individuals she calls "the Risen Ones," the dead who are now filled with the light of Christ. The Risen Ones include individuals she knew in life, as well as anonymous representatives of human types; others are historical personages (Moses, Ramses II, Nietzsche, Galileo, etc.). The nature of these appearances and messages is too eclectic to be easily summarized.

A visionary who deserves a more extended consideration than can be given here is the Swiss doctor and convert to Catholicism, the prolific Adrienne von Speyr (1902–1967), a close associate of the theologian Hans Urs von Balthasar. Together with Balthasar she founded the religious community of the Johannes Gesellschaft.[44] Von Speyr was indeed a visionary, but her showings were of a different nature from the women mentioned above. Like Balthasar, she critiqued psychological or subjective views of mysticism and insisted that her "objective mysticism" was based solely on scripture and the teaching of the Church, and that her visionary experiences were therefore rooted in the Bible and the events of Christ's life, especially the Passion.[45] The major part of her teaching was set forth in a vast series of biblical commentaries she dictated to Balthasar, who was her confidant and spiritual director. The heart of Speyr's mystical vision of God is centered on her novel teaching on the Trinity, what has been called a "radical Trinitarianism" based on the interchange of love among the three Persons as revealed in the life of Christ, especially his death on the cross. Von Speyr's mysticism, which is Marian and Ignatian in background, stresses radical obedience to the Father following the model of Jesus, and not mystical union.[46]

We can say in summary that the trajectory of visionary mysticism, strongly rooted in the tradition, continued on during the twentieth century, sometimes with new accents.

Suffering and Dereliction
This is the second theme worth highlighting. Most readers will have some familiarity with John of the Cross's teaching about the Dark Night in which God purges both the senses and the spirit of all that is created in order to prepare one for union with him. This painful emptying can even extend to a sense of being abandoned by God. The stress on suffering and dereliction was scarcely new with the Spanish Carmelite. Job was an Old Testament model, and the account of Jesus's abandonment on the cross ("My God, my God, why have you forsaken me?") rings down through Christian history. Almost all mystics, ancient and modern, have seen suffering—physical suffering through illness, external suffering by persecution, and mental suffering through doubt and distress—as integral aspects of the mystical path. What I am talking about here, however, is more intense. There have been a number of mystics who underwent the graver trial of dereliction, the feeling of being abandoned by God, even consigned to hell.[47] Several examples of this aspect of mysticism have been seen during the past century.

Thérèse of Lisieux (d. 1897) is a case in point. The original publication of her *Autobiography* downplayed the terrible desolation of the loss of faith she experienced in the last eighteen months of her life, so as not to impede her path to canonization. Today this trial is seen as strong evidence of her role as an exemplary modern mystic. (I will examine this in the chapter on Thérèse below.) Thérèse's contemporary, the lay mystic Elizabeth Leseur (1866–1914), not only struggled with severe illness in her last years but also spoke of undergoing a Dark Night experience. Another religious woman, Marie of the Trinity (1903–1980), experienced psychological difficulties, but also mystical dereliction, hard as the two phenomena may be to distinguish easily. Simone Weil (1909–1943) made the notion of "affliction" (*malheur*) central to her view of how humans deal with living in the face of the mystery of God. Thomas Merton's reflections on "dread" in the mystical path also testify to the feeling of abandonment by God. Finally, the publication of the writings of Mother Teresa of Calcutta (1910–1997) perplexed some Catholics by their witness to her lifelong sense of being abandoned by God. Mother Teresa's example is extreme, but is not different in kind from what had gone before.

Action and Contemplation (the Political and the Mystical)
This third theme is one of the oldest in the history of Christian mysticism—the relation of the active and the contemplative lives. Although the categories of action and contemplation were originally taken over from Greek philosophy, Christians understood the *vita activa* not as civic engagement but as loving outreach to the neighbor, while the *vita contemplativa* was not a philosophical gaze toward the First Principle, but was the desire of the purified heart to see God ("Blessed are the pure of heart for they shall see God," Matt. 5:8). Influenced by the Greek model, however, many early and medieval Christian mystics felt that contemplation and action, while both necessary, could not be realized simultaneously. A person had to oscillate between action and contemplation, between engagement with the world and retreat into contemplative prayer. This is the view put forth by Augustine, Gregory the Great, and Bernard of Clairvaux, to cite just a few. Beginning in the fourteenth century with Meister Eckhart, some mystics challenged this outlook—Why was it not possible to combine action and contemplation, since both are manifestations of divine love? Many later mystics, such as Catherine of Siena, Ignatius of Loyola, and Teresa of Avila, defended the possibility of combining the two, to become *in contemplatione activus*, as was said of Ignatius. Nevertheless, because this fusion seemed to be an ideal difficult to realize, the old dichotomy between action and contemplation lingered on.

One of the signal achievements of twentieth-century mysticism is that almost all of the modern mystics insisted on the necessary unity of action and contemplation—the most effective proof of contemplative love of God was engagement with the world and the neighbor. Loving the neighbor nourished, rather than detracted from, contemplative love of God. Despite the fact that she was an enclosed contemplative nun, Thérèse of Lisieux already made that evident. Other mystics, like Edith Stein, Simone Weil, Teilhard de Chardin, Thomas Merton, and Karl Rahner, created philosophical and theological arguments for the necessary unity of the active and the contemplative dimensions, or what has been called the political and the mystical aspects, of the spiritual life. Teilhard was especially important in his stress on the commitment of the mystic to the evolutionary progress of the cosmos. Dag Hammarskjöld, the great statesman and mystic, expressed the point clearly and succinctly: "In our era, the road to holiness necessarily passes through the world of action" (*Markings*, 108). Naturally, this unification process was spelled out in different ways and was realized in diverse forms in the lives of the mystics—but there was no disagreement on the principle.

Holistic Perspective
Christian mysticism has often been criticized for its attitude toward the body and even material creation in general. It cannot be denied that many earlier theologians and mystics used language about the opposition between the body and the soul that smacked of a quasi-dualism at odds with Christian belief in the goodness of creation. The Pauline opposition (e.g., Gal. 5:17) between the "flesh" (*sarx*) and the "spirit" (*pneuma*) was sometimes mistakenly read as signifying conflict between the body and the soul, rather than the struggle between fallen human nature (the "flesh") and human nature restored in Christ and empowered by the Holy Spirit. Although the inner logic of belief in God incarnate in Jesus necessarily includes the full appreciation of the body and the material universe of which it is a part, this logic was not always realized by past theologians and mystics. Of course, careful study of the mystics of the tradition shows that many had a profound sense of the holistic character of the path to God—it is the entire person who is saved, not just the disembodied self, as the doctrine of the resurrection of the body shows.

Another of the major achievements of twentieth-century mysticism has been that the bifurcated view of human nature and an antimaterial attitude toward Christian perfection have been decisively left behind. This is true of almost all modern mystics and is best seen in those mystics who have mounted detailed arguments for the need of a holistic approach to life before God. In the essays below, particular attention can be given to Edith Stein's mystical anthropology and to the thinking of Teilhard de Chardin, whose arguments for how the heart of matter aims toward a transcendent assumption into spirit on the way toward the divine Omega point is one of the most impressive theological achievements of the century. As Teilhard once put it, "In its dogmas and sacraments, the whole economy of the Church teaches us respect for matter and insists on its value. Christ wished to assume, and had to assume, a real flesh. He sanctifies human flesh by a specific contact. He makes ready, physically, its Resurrection."[48]

The Return of the Apophatic

Another important theme concerns the importance of negation. As mentioned above, the apophatic element of mysticism and its relation to the positive, or cataphatic, dimension, have been long-term features of Christian mysticism. How can we speak about God in any remotely adequate way? Only by applying all the resources of both positive and negative speech, but with some priority being given to negation, was the answer of most mystics who considered the issue. No age has lacked for mystics who laid great stress on the need for "un-saying" God. Nonetheless, the modern crisis of faith, God's seeming withdrawal from the world, has given greater attention to apophaticism than was typical in the preceding centuries, especially those that saw the triumph of the Enlightenment, which sought to subject all things, even God, to positive rational categories.[49] Already in the nineteenth century thinkers like Søren Kierkegaard (d. 1855) protested against the tyranny of a rationalistic God. In the twentieth century this reaction has grown stronger. This "apophatic turn," with its emphasis on the hidden God and the "darkness of God," is evident not only in recent philosophy and theology but also in the broader culture—in poetry and literature, in humanistic studies, in art and music. The turn to "un-saying" is evident in a number of twentieth-century mystics, both those discussed below and others who will not be treated here. Simone Weil is certainly among the most powerful apophatic thinkers of the era, and in theology Karl Rahner (d. 1984) wrote much on the interrelated incomprehensibility of God and of the human person. A more recent and controversial figure, Bernadette Roberts (1931–2017), centered her mysticism on what she called the path to "No-Self," a radical effacement of the subject. Other mystics lived the negative way without explicitly theorizing about it—Charles de Foucauld, Elizabeth of the Trinity, Etty Hillesum, and Mother Teresa, to name but a few.

Crossing Traditions

Another special characteristic of twentieth-century mysticism is what we can call "crossing traditions," or "spiritual hybridity," that is, the effort not only to learn from other religious and mystical traditions, but even in some way to live *within* other traditions.[50] This is a new development, doubtless facilitated not only by the Christian ecumenical movements that began around 1900, but also by the wider ecumenicity that has produced what Ewert Cousins called "global spirituality."[51] Perhaps for the first time in human history individuals and even groups have been able to view other religious traditions as partners and collaborators, not as enemies, in search for God. The desire for sharing with other mystical traditions is evident in some figures identified primarily within the Christian tradition, such as Thomas Merton, who took a great interest in other religions, especially Zen Buddhism. Other figures, who had abandoned Christianity, took their major resources from other traditions. An example can be found in the French literary figure Romain Rolland (1866-1942), who left the Roman Catholicism he was born into; he became fascinated with Hinduism and sought to find a higher unity of all religions in his notion of a mystical "oceanic feeling." Powerful witnesses to this new aspect of mysticism can be found in those Christians who experienced a call to live in the midst of, and even as participants in, other forms of religion. A pioneering figure was Charles de Foucauld (d. 1916), whose desire to live among the Muslim Tuaregs of the Sahara was designed not so much to convert them as to serve as a witness to Jesus in their midst by sharing in their lives. Other examples are found in the mystics who felt called upon to try to effect a concord between Christian and Hindu mystical traditions, however difficult this task might seem. A key figure here is the French monk Henri Le Saux (1910-1973), who went to India, received training as a Hindu monk, and eventually gained renown as a holy man (Swami Abhishiktānanda). His *ashram* in India attracted many Westerners, among them the English monk and mystic Bede Griffiths (1906-1993), who continued working toward the rapprochement of Christian and Hindu mysticism. Other figures, such as Teilhard de Chardin, hoped for a coming unification of the "Way of the East" and the "Way of the West," where the spiritual riches of both traditions would be subsumed into a higher unity. This hope may seem utopian, but we can say that the crossing of mystical traditions represents a new moment in Christian mysticism.

Marginality

Mystics, insofar as they are seeking a deeper awareness of God in their lives, have always been marginal in the sense that most members of society disregard, even when they do not reject, their fundamental commitment to a different, "atopic" life (one that does not fit in the ordinary world). Nonetheless, many mystics have also been pillars of the ecclesiastic establishment—bishops, popes, abbots, religious founders, and canonized saints. This is perhaps not as much of a paradox as it seems, because the routinization of religious institutions frequently has moved those who started on the margins to the center. We have only to think of that great "protest movement" against late antique society that we call monasticism to realize this truth. The monks began as "drop-outs," but they later took on central ecclesiastical and societal roles. The subsequent story of mysticism witnesses the eruption of many marginal groups out of established ecclesiastical and spiritual structures that had become too rigid and their eventual absorption back into these structures. We can note, for example, the appearance of the mendicant friars and the independent beguines in the early thirteenth century. The marginal mendicants became central to the institutional Church, although the beguines did not.

A number of forms of mystical marginality appeared in the past century. Some Catholic mystics deliberately chose lives of marginality, such as Charles de Foucauld in the Near East and Africa, and Teresa of Calcutta among the poorest of the poor in India. Edith Stein illustrates another kind of marginality. This secular Jew who had been an atheist was converted in 1922. Despite her conversion, her death *as a Jew* in 1942 in the gas chambers of Auschwitz, as well as her reflections on sharing in the sufferings of her Jewish people, show her as a figure who suffered as an "outsider," one living on the margins. Simone Weil also lived on the boundary between Judaism and Christianity. She rejected the Jewish religion and even tried to reject being Jewish. Despite her deep attraction to the crucified Christ and many aspects of Catholicism, she felt unable to make the final commitment of baptism. Finally, we have the case of Etty Hillesum (d. 1942), a young Jewish woman who sacrificed herself for the victims of Nazi genocide she encountered in the death camps of World War II. Unlike Stein, who became a Christian, or Weil, who almost seemed to some to be a Christian mystic, Hillesum was a Jewish martyr to a mystical love that went beyond denominational boundaries. Hillesum and others provide striking examples of how many of the mystics of the past century broke the boundaries of traditional denominational categories.

The example of the twentieth-century mystics, both those to be considered below and others who cannot be included here, testifies to the vitality of the mystical tradition in the past century, as well as many possible new directions. Some of the trends these mystics pioneered show great promise for our time, such as "the crossing of traditions," the role of the negative dimension in mysticism, and the increasingly holistic, even cosmic, dimensions of mysticism.[52] But it is certainly too early to tell. What will I offer in what follows are merely some reflections on significant figures of the twentieth century, mystics who revived, reinvigorated, and often challenged inherited mystical traditions. I believe that they give us hope for its future.

Some Mystics of the Twentieth Century

The following chronological list makes no pretense to completeness, nor does it try to answer the difficult question, Who should be counted as a mystic? These are figures known to me whose lives extended into the past century. The major exception is the short-lived Thérèse of Lisieux (d. 1897), whose influence as a mystic is such an important part of the story of twentieth-century mysticism that I have included her here.

1. Andrew Murray (1828–1917)
2. John of Kronstadt (1829–1909)
3. Richard Bucke (1837–1902)
4. Richard Jeffries (1848–1887)
5. Charles de Foucauld (1858–1916)
6. Elizabeth Leseur (1866–1914)
7. Romain Rolland (1866–1944)
8. Silouan the Athonite (1866–1938)
9. Thérèse of Lisieux (1873–1897)
10. Albert Schweitzer (1875–1965)
11. Evelyn Underhill (1875–1941)
12. Gemma Galgani (1878–1903)
13. Elizabeth of the Trinity (1880–1906)
14. Pierre Teilhard de Chardin (1881–1955)
15. Titus Brandsma (1881–1942)
16. Pio of Pietralcina (1887–1968)
17. Edith Stein (1891–1942)
18. Thomas R. Kelly (1893–1941)
19. Catherine de Hueck Doherty (1896–1985)
20. Sophrony Sakharov (1896–1993)

21. Maria Valtorta (1897–1961)
22. Therese Neumann (1898–1962)
23. Howard Thurman (1899–1978)
24. Adrienne von Speyr (1902–1967)
25. Marie of the Trinity (1903–1980)
26. Karl Rahner (1904–1984)
27. Maria Faustina Kowalska (1905–1938)
28. Dag Hammarskjöld (1905–1961)
29. Bede Griffiths (1906–1993)
30. Simone Weil (1909–1943)
31. Henri Le Saux (Swami Abhishiktānanda) (1910–1973)
32. Teresa of Calcutta (1910–1997)
33. Etty Hillesum (1914–1943)
34. Divo Barsotti (1914–2006)
35. Thomas Merton (1915–1968)
36. Joa Bolendas (pseudonym) (1917–2005)
37. Oscar Romero (1917–1980)
38. Silja Walter (1919–2011)
39. Chiara Lubich (1920–2008)
40. John Main (1926–1982)
41. Ruth Burrows (Sr. Rachel, OCD) (1927–)
42. Bernadette Roberts (1931–2017)
43. Gustavo Gutiérrez (1933–)

Mystics in the Arts. When I began thinking about this book, I conceived of the possibility of including poets, musicians, and painters, whose works seemed to me to have significant mystical elements. Alas, I soon discovered that this would be a large task to which I would not be able to commit myself. I hope that others might take up this important challenge. Here is a personal selection.

Poets: Rainer Maria Rilke (1875–1926), T. S. Eliot (1888–1965), David Jones (1895–1974), R. S. Thomas (1913–2000), Paul Celan (1920–1970)

Musicians: Olivier Messiaen (1908–1992), John Cage (1912–1992), Arvo Pärt (1935–), John Taverner (1944–)

Painters and Sculptors: I am conscious that a number of twentieth-century artists might be considered mystics, but I do not have the competence to try to create a list.

Notes

1. I cite from the English version of K. L. Montgomery (London: SPCK, 1930), 432.
2. Pierre Teilhard de Chardin, *Letters from a Traveller, 1923–1925* (New York: Harper, 1962), 87.
3. Letter quoted in *The Hidden Ground of Love: The Letters of Thomas Merton on Religious Experiences and Social Concerns,* ed. William H. Shannon (New York: Farrar, Straus & Giroux, 1985), 583.
4. Karl Rahner, *Theological Investigations VII* (New York: Herder & Herder, 1971), 15.
5. David Tracy, *Dialogue with the Other: The Inter-Religious Dialogue,* Louvain Theological and Pastoral Monographs 1 (Louvain: Peeters, 1990), 30.
6. "Part IV. On Prayer," in *The Catechism of the Council of Trent,* trans. Rev. J. Donovan (Hawthorne, CA: Christian Book Club of America, 1975; reprint of 1829 ed.), 460–83.
7. *Catechism of the Council of Trent,* 467 (contemplation is mentioned also on 482).
8. *Catechism of the Catholic Church* (Rome: Libreria Editirice Vaticana, 1994; English version: Paulist Press, 1994; page numbers refer to this Paulist Press edition.). Article 1 of Part Four, Chapter Three. The Life of Prayer, deals with "Expressions of Prayer" (§§2699–2724, pp. 648–53). The highest expression is "Contemplative Prayer," treated in §§2709–2719, pp. 650–52. See especially §2713.
9. *Catechism of the Catholic Church,* Part Three, "Life in Christ" (§§1691–2557, pp. 421–612).
10. Bernard McGinn, *The Crisis of Mysticism: Quietism in Seventeenth-Century Spain, Italy, and France* (New York: Crossroad, 2021).
11. This is true of Catholic mysticism. The same period was a time of remarkable productivity in Orthodox Christian mysticism, both in Greece and in Slavic lands, as well as in aspects of Protestant mysticism, such as in the Pietist tradition.
12. Henry St. John Bolingbroke, Letters or Essays Addressed to Alexander Pope, in *The Works of the Right Honorable Henry St. John Bolingbroke,* 5 vols. (London: David Mallet, 1754), 5:539.
13. For more on the modern academic study of mysticism, see Bernard McGinn, "The Role of Mysticism in Modern Theology," *Annali di Scienze Religiose* 7 (2014): 373–400; and "L'étude contemporaine de la mystique aux États-Unis," in *L'Université face à la mystique: Un siècle de controverses?,* ed. Mariel Mazzocco, François Trémolières, and Ghislain Waterlot, Sciences des religions (Rennes: Université de Rennes, 2018), 169–81.
14. See C. J. T. Talar, ed., *Modernists and Mystics* (Washington, DC: Catholic University of America Press, 2009).
15. Von Hügel was the friend and spiritual director of Evelyn Underhill (d. 1941), an Anglican theologian who wrote numerous works on mysticism.
16. The second edition of 1926 contains Butler's "Afterthoughts" (ix–lviii), which are a good overview of the Neoscholastic views of mysticism of the early twentieth century.
17. Some representative titles include "Reflections on the Problem of the Gradual Ascent to Christian Perfection"; "The Ignatian Mysticism of Joy in the

World"; "The Experience of God Today"; and "Mystical Experience and Mystical Theology."

18. The most recent is Volker Leppin, *Ruhen in Gott: Eine Geschichte der christlichen Mystik* (Munich: C. H. Beck, 2021).

19. E.g., Alois M. Haas, *Mystik im Kontext* (Munich: Wilhelm Fink, 2004).

20. For an overview, see Richard H. Jones, "Constructivism in Philosophy of Mysticism," *Journal of Religion* 100 (2020): 1-41. Jones rightly argues for considerable confusion in terminology in the debates, noting the differences between "constructivism" and "contextualism," on the one hand, and "essentialism" and "perennialism," on the other.

21. For an overview of some recent approaches, see Louise Nelstrop, Kevin Magill, and Bradley B. Onishi, eds., *Christian Mysticism: An Introduction to Contemporary Theoretical Approaches* (Burlington, VT: Ashgate, 2009).

22. For studies of these and other "postmodern" figures, see Amy Hollywood, *Sensible Ecstasy: Mysticism, Sexual Difference, and the Demands of History*, Religion and Postmodernism (Chicago: University of Chicago Press, 2002).

23. For a sense of how widespread the apophatic turn has been in modern thought, see William Franke, *On What Cannot Be Said: Apophatic Discourses in Philosophy, Religion, Literature, and the Arts*, vol. 2: *Modern and Contemporary Transformations* (Notre Dame, IN: University of Notre Dame Press, 2007).

24. Bernard McGinn, "General Introduction," in *The Foundations of Mysticism*, Presence of God 1 (New York: Crossroad, 1991), xv-xx. The quotation comes from Bernard McGinn, *The Essential Writings of Christian Mysticism* (New York: Modern Library, 2006), xiv.

25. See especially Bernard McGinn, "Mystical Consciousness: A Modest Proposal," *Spiritus* 8 (2008): 44-63.

26. Friedrich von Hügel, *The Mystical Element of Religion as Studied in Saint Catherine of Genoa and Her Friends* (London: J. M. Dent, 1908), vol. 1, chapter 2 (50-82), especially 55-57, 70-76.

27. My thinking about the nature of consciousness in mysticism has been influenced by the thought of Bernard Lonergan, especially in *Method in Theology* (New York: Herder & Herder, 1972), and such essays as "Cognitional Structure" and "Christ as Subject: A Reply," both in *Collection: Papers by Bernard Lonergan* (New York: Herder & Herder, 1972), 221-39, and 175-78.

28. Thomas Merton once used the term "superconsciousness," which is fitting here. See his essay "Transcendent Experience," in *Zen and the Birds of Appetite* (New York: New Directions, 1968), 71-78.

29. McGinn, "Mystical Consciousness," 53.

30. Bernard McGinn, "Mystical Union," in *The Oxford Handbook of Mystical Theology*, ed. Edward Howells and Mark A. McIntosh (Oxford: Oxford University Press, 2020), 404-21.

31. The importance of the category of presence was first highlighted by Joseph Maréchal in his essay "On the Feeling of Presence in Mystics and Non-Mystics," in *Studies in the Psychology of the Mystics* (1927; repr., Albany, NY: Magi Books, 1964), 55-145.

32. Simone Weil, *Notebooks*, 2 vols. (London: Routledge, 1952-1956), 1:239-40.

33. R. S. Thomas, "Via Negativa," in *Collected Poems: 1945-1990* (London: Phoenix, 1996), 220.

34. Bernard McGinn, "Three Forms of Negativity in Christian Mysticism," in *Knowing the Unknowable: Science and Religions on God and the Universe,* ed. John Bowker, Library of Modern Religion 2 (London: I. B. Taurus, 2009), 99–121.

35. Thomas Aquinas, *In Boetium De Trinitate,* I.2, ad 2: "Deum tamquam ignotum cognoscimus."

36. See Bernard McGinn, "Ecstasy in Classic Christian Mysticism," *Lo Sguardo: rivista di filosofia* 33 (2021): 187–213.

37. There is a translation of Gemma Galgani's writings and a study by Rudolph M. Bell and Cristina Mazzoni, *The Voices of Gemma Galgani: The Life and Afterlife of a Modern Saint* (Chicago: University of Chicago Press, 2003).

38. For a translation, see *Blessed Sister M. Faustina Kowalska: Diary, Divine Mercy in My Soul* (Stockbridge, MA: Marians of the Immaculate Conception, 1999).

39. A male canonized ecstatic visionary and stigmatic is St. Pio of Pietralcina (1887–1968).

40. Many of these Gospel visions have been translated by Johannes Steiner, *The Visions of Therese Neumannn* (New York: Alba House, 1976).

41. Steiner, *Visions of Therese Neumann,* 146.

42. There are said to be five volumes, but I have only seen *The Poem of the Man-God,* vol. 1 (Sherbooke, QC: Editions Paulines, n.d.).

43. E.g., *So That You May Be One: From the Visions of Joa Bolendas* (Hudson, NY: Lindisfarne Books, 1997); and *Alive in God's World: Human Life on Earth and in Heaven as Described in the Visions of Joa Bolendas* (Great Barrington, MA: Lindisfarne Books, 2001).

44. For an introduction, see Hans Urs von Balthasar, *First Glance at Adrienne von Speyr* (San Francisco: Ignatius Press, 1981).

45. For a potent example, see her vision of Apocalypse 12, as recounted in Balthasar, *First Glance,* 90–96.

46. A number of translations of von Speyr's books have been published by Ignatius Press.

47. For an overview, see Bernard McGinn, "Suffering, Dereliction and Affliction in Christian Mysticism," in *Suffering and the Christian Life,* ed. Karen Kilby and Rachel Davies (London: T&T Clark, 2020), 55–70.

48. Pierre Teilhard de Chardin, "Cosmic Life," in *Writings in Time of War* (New York: Harper & Row, 1967), 64.

49. See Louis Dupré, "Spiritual Life in a Secular Age," *Daedalus* 111 (1982): 21–31, as well as many of the writings of Michel de Certeau.

50. On this phenomenon, see the essays in the "Symposium on Multiple Religious Belonging," *Spiritus* 15.1 (2015): 75–118.

51. Ewert H. Cousins, *Global Spirituality: Toward the Meeting of the Mystical Paths* (Madras: University of Madras, 1985).

52. I have tried to spell some of this out in Bernard McGinn, "The Venture of Mysticism in the New Millennium," *New Theology Review* 21 (May 2008): 70–79.

Selected Bibliography

Balthasar, Hans Urs von. "Understanding Christian Mysticism." In Balthasar, *Explorations in Theology,* vol. 4: *Spirit and Institution,* 309–35. San Francisco: Ignatius Press, 1995. Brief summary of Balthasar's view.

de Certeau, Michel. *The Mystic Fable: The Sixteenth and Seventeenth Centuries*. 2 vols. Chicago: University of Chicago Press, 1992, 2015. A new theory of mystical language.

Egan, Harvey D. *Christian Mysticism: The Future of a Tradition*. Eugene, OR: Wipf & Stock, 1984. A survey of some classic mystics and reflections on mysticism.

Fanning, Steven. *Mystics of the Christian Tradition*. London: Routledge, 2001. A good one-volume survey.

Howells, Edward, and Mark A. McIntosh, eds. *The Oxford Handbook of Mystical Theology*. Oxford: Oxford University Press, 2020. Thirty-three cutting-edge essays.

Hügel, Friedrich von. *The Mystical Element of Religion as Studied in Saint Catherine of Genoa and Her Friends*. 2 vols. London: J. M. Dent, 1908. Difficult, but important. Von Hügel sets out his theory mostly in chapters 9-15.

Idel, Moshe, and Bernard McGinn, eds. *Mystical Union in Judaism, Christianity and Islam: An Ecumenical Dialogue*. New York: Continuum, 1996; Reprint, London: Bloomsbury, 2016. Essays and discussions.

James, William. *The Varieties of Religious Experience. Centenary Edition*. London: Routledge, 2002. Classic, if controversial.

Katz, Steven T., ed. *Mysticism and Philosophical Analysis*. New York: Oxford University Press, 1978. Essays on the "constructivist" view of mysticism.

Maréchal, Joseph. *Studies in the Psychology of the Mystics*. London: Burns, Oates & Washbourne, 1927. Reprint, Albany, NY: Magi Books, 1964. See especially "On the Feeling of Presence in Mystics and Non-Mystics" (55-145).

Marion, Jean-Luc. *God without Being: Hors-texte*. Religion and Postmodernism. Chicago: University of Chicago Press, 1991. Modern revival of Dionysian apophatic theology.

McGinn, Bernard, ed., *The Essential Writings of Christian Mysticism*. New York: Random House, 2006. An anthology and study of major mystical themes.

———. "Mystical Consciousness: A Modest Proposal." *Spiritus* 8 (2008): 44-63.

———. *The Presence of God: A History of Western Christian Mysticism*. 7 vols. in 9. New York: Crossroad-Herder, 1991-2021.

McIntosh, Mark A. *Mystical Theology: The Integrity of Spirituality and Theology*. Challenges in Contemporary Theology. Oxford: Blackwell, 1998. Good discussion of current theologies of mysticism.

Nelstrop, Louise, Kevin Magill, and Bradley B. Onishi, eds. *Christian Mysticism: An Introduction to Contemporary Theoretical Approaches*. Burlington: Ashgate, 2009.

Scholem, Gershom. "Religious Authority and Mysticism." In *On the Kabbalah and Its Symbolism*, 5–31. New York: Schocken Books, 1996. A comparative study by the great scholar of Jewish mysticism.

Stolz, Anselm. *The Doctrine of Spiritual Perfection*. Milestones in the Study of Mysticism and Spirituality. New York: Crossroad, 2001. On the biblical and patristic basis of Christian mysticism.

Turner, Denys. *The Darkness of God: Negativity in Christian Mysticism*. Cambridge: Cambridge University Press, 1995. Historical and theoretical study.

Underhill, Evelyn. *Mysticism: A Study in the Nature and Development of Man's Spiritual Consciousness*. London: Methuen, 1912. Another classic work in print since its publication.

Chapter 1

Charles de Foucauld (1858–1916): Imitating the Life of Nazareth

Charles Viscomte de Foucauld (1858–1916) lived a life of excess. Everything he did, he did to the utmost. As a young wastrel, he indulged his appetite for food, sex, and pleasure excessively, despite his natural indolence. After his conversion in 1886, he sought to live the Christian life in the deepest possible way. His asceticism became more and more pronounced as time went by. The most rigorous form of recognized religious life at the time was Trappist Cistercianism. He joined a poor Trappist abbey in France but soon transferred to its even poorer offshoot in Syria. Trappist asceticism was not rigorous enough for him, however, so he left and began to live as a hermit devoted to absolute poverty and complete self-denial. Charles was equally excessive in his contemplative life. His devotion to the Blessed Sacrament was legendary. He spent much of his day in silent prayer before the Eucharist. Given this excess, it might seem that Charles was a dour and off-putting figure. Nothing could be further from the case. He was a model of Christian love of neighbor and was treasured by those who knew him, both Catholic and Muslim.

Charles de Foucauld wrote a good deal, composing thousands of letters and many pages of prayers and meditations.[1] Nonetheless, it is the story of his life, even more than his writings, that demonstrates his message of love centered on living in perfect imitation of the hidden life of Jesus at Nazareth—a constant theme of what he said and did. His status as a saint and mystic received official approbation when he was canonized by Pope Francis on May 15, 2022.

The Life of Charles de Foucauld

Part 1: 1858–1886

Charles was born at Strasbourg on September 15, 1858. His father, Viscount Édouard de Foucauld, came from a junior branch of an ancient aristocratic military family. An ancestor, Bertrand de Foucauld, had died defending St. Louis on the Fifth Crusade. Édouard's family had lost their lands and money in the Revolution, however, and he worked as a forestry inspector in Alsace. In 1855 Édouard married the pious Elisabeth de Morlet. They had two children, Charles and his sister Marie, born in 1861. Tragedy soon struck. Édouard experienced a severe psychotic personality change and left the family. Elisabeth visited him and conceived another child, but she died in childbirth in 1864 and Édouard followed her six months later. The two young children were left orphans. Although they were adopted by their maternal grandfather, Colonel de Morlet, the loss of their parents deeply affected them. The aged colonel was kindly toward them but was not skilled at raising young children. A good deal of Charles's wayward youth can be put down to this course of events.

Charles was an intelligent but introverted child, given to outbursts of anger. In 1868 he met the woman who was to be the greatest influence in his life, his older cousin, Marie Moitessier (Marie de Bondy in marriage). Marie had a winning personality and a deep piety, as well as a strong will. Although she was eight years older than he, the two became deeply attached. She remained an inspiration for him, as well as a counselor and at times a critic, down to the end of his life (his last letter was written to her). When Charles made his First Communion in 1872, Marie gave him a copy of Bishop Bossuet's *Elevations on the Mysteries*, a book that was to have an influence on his later conversion. Much happened, however, between 1872 and 1886.

Charles was a quick student but a lazy one. During his years in the Lycée (high school), he gradually lost his faith and began to show signs of the immoderation that marked the next dozen years of his life. Speaking of himself at a later time, he said, "At seventeen, I was all egotism, all impiety, all desire for evil; it was as if I had gone mad" (Antier, 31). His heritage marked him out for a military career. He studied for two years with the Jesuits at Paris (1874–1876), whose strict discipline grated on him. Charles then entered the military academy at St. Cyr in 1876, where he spent the next three years. His escapades almost led to his being dismissed several times, but as an aristocrat and now very wealthy (in 1878 he inherited his grandfather's fortune), he was allowed many liberties. He ate excessively and grew fat (his classmates called him "Piggy"), partied as much as he could, and took a succession of mistresses. Not a promising beginning for a saint. When his regiment was sent to Algeria in 1880, he connived to bring along his latest mistress, Mimi, a forbidden act. He refused to send her home and was eventually cashiered and sent back to France, where he continued to waste his fortune on wine, women, and parties.

The beginning of the turn in the wastrel's life was war. In 1881, when an insurrection broke out in Algeria and his regiment was called into action, Charles abandoned his mistress and sought to be reinstated. After he was allowed back, the fat young lieutenant surprisingly turned out to be a good soldier who won the respect of his men. He also became fascinated with the desert and its peoples, as well as with the Islamic religion. In 1882, he resigned from the army and resolved to explore the unknown parts of Morocco. He spent a year of preparation in Algiers, studying Arabic and reading about North Africa. During the period 1883–1885, disguised as a wandering Jewish peddler and with a Jewish merchant he hired to accompany him, Charles visited and surveyed areas of Morocco's interior that had never before been seen by a European. It was a remarkable feat of exploration that won the young man considerable fame and a gold medal from the Geographical Society of Paris. Still an unbeliever, Charles had settled down enough to contemplate marriage, but his family, who now had control of his finances, did not approve of the woman he had chosen, who had no dowry. Charles acquiesced with sadness and returned to North Africa for further exploration in the Sahara. Back in France in 1886, he worked hard on finishing his book *Reconnaisance au Maroc* (*Surveying Marocco*), and had renewed contact with his cousin, Marie de Bondy, who sought to bring him back to the practice of the faith. He read the Bossuet book she had given him and was much impressed, but still hung back. Marie was a regular penitent of the remarkable parish priest of Saint-Augustin, Abbé Henri Huvelin (1838–1910), perhaps the most famous spiritual director of the age, who counted the philosopher and student of mysticism Friedrich von Hügel among his penitents.[2] On October 30, 1886, Charles went to Saint-Augustin, hoping to meet Fr. Huvelin and to ask him for instructions to help overcome the intellectual difficulties he had with the faith. He was in for a surprise. Huvelin told him, "You are mistaken, my son. What is missing now in order for you to believe is a pure heart. Go down on your knees, make your confession to God, and you will believe."[3] Charles knelt, made his confession, and felt immediate joy and peace. Since he was already fasting, Huvelin told him to receive communion, which brought further joy. Speaking of this surprising conversion in a letter to his friend Henri de Castries, Charles said, "As soon as I came to believe there was a God, I understood that I could not do otherwise than live only for him. My religious vocation dates from the same hour as my faith. God is so great! There is such a difference between God and everything that is not God" (Antier, 104). That vocation, however, was to go through many twists and turns in the last thirty years of his life.

Part 2: 1886–1916

Charles's family maneuvered to get the recent convert safely married, but he would have none of it. His natural bent for all-or-nothing now showed itself. In another letter to Henri de Castries, he said, "While desiring to exhale all that is in me before God and lose myself totally in him, I do not know which [religious] order to choose. The Gospels showed me that the first commandment is to love God with all one's heart and to enclose everything in that love. The first effect of love is imitation" (Antier, 105). But what form would that imitation take? Charles did not wish to become a priest or preacher and was not interested in missionary work. Even at this early stage of his new life, it was humility, poverty, and hiddenness that attracted him: "Thus, I should imitate the hidden life of the poor and humble workman of Nazareth" (Antier, 105). Which order would best allow him this form of imitation? In obedience to Abbé Huvelin, Charles refrained from rushing into religious life. In late 1888 and early 1889, he made a pilgrimage to the Holy Land, visiting Jerusalem, Bethlehem, and Nazareth. In 1889 he also began reading Teresa of Avila, whose life and writings remained a guiding star for the rest of his life. Finally, Charles made up his mind about his future, and in January 1890, he entered the Trappist monastery of Notre-Dame-des-Neiges in the Ardèche region of France, taking the name of Brother Marie-Albéric. Yet Charles found the austere life of this poor Trappist house not sufficiently rigorous, so in July of the same year he was allowed to transfer to the remote and even poorer priory that the Ardèche monastery had established at Cheikhlé near Akbès in Syria in order to pursue his novitiate under the guidance of Dom Polycarpe, the deeply spiritual prior. On February 2, 1892, he made his monastic profession and took simple vows.

For eight years Charles de Foucauld lived the Trappist life, but with increasing dissatisfaction. His restless spirit and his desire for absolute poverty and severe penance made him unfit for any form of organized religious life, at least as then practiced. He was especially unhappy with the mitigation of austerities introduced when three different branches of the Trappists were joined together by Pope Leo XIII in 1892. Recognizing his natural talents, Dom Polycarpe wanted Brother Marie-Albéric to begin studies for the priesthood in 1893, something that did not please him, because it seemed contrary to his calling to live a life of simplicity, abjection, humility, and hiddenness. It was around this time that Brother Marie-Albéric began to think of founding a new religious order that would fulfill his dream of a more perfect imitation of the poverty of Jesus. Writing to Abbé Huvelin he wondered, "Is there no way of forming a little congregation to lead that life, living solely by the labor of its own hands—as did our Lord, who supported himself neither by alms or offerings? Would it be impossible to find a few souls ready to follow our Lord in this . . . ?" He goes on, "A life of prayer and work, not with two kinds of religious [i.e., priests and lay brothers], as there are at Citeaux, but one, as St. Benedict wanted—but not using St. Benedict's complicated liturgy, but long hours of prayer, the rosary, the holy Mass" (*Spiritual Autobiography*, 28). Over the course of the next few years, this dream gradually coalesced into a plan for a form of religious life he first called "The Hermits of the Sacred Heart," and later "The

Little Brothers of Jesus." In June of 1896, Charles wrote down the first form of his *Rules and Directory* for the planned group.

The *Rules and Directory* that Brother Marie-Albéric drew up and sent to Abbé Huvelin in 1896 dismayed the priest, who did not see his spiritual son as a religious founder—"You wish to be a founder? A director of souls? Your regulations are unworkable and have frightened me" (Antier, 139). In his *Rules and Directory*, Brother Marie-Albéric kept to the Benedictine pattern of eight hours of work and eight hours of prayer, as well as seclusion, silence, and a life commitment to one house. He broke with the Benedictine regimen of the daily hours of the Office, replacing them with five hours of adoration before the Eucharist. His recommendations concerning asceticism were so severe that they explain why he was never able to attract any followers during his lifetime. Poverty was to be absolute. His ideal was "[t]o live solely from our manual labor. No gifts, no honoraria for saying Mass. Nothing, absolutely nothing, not in cash, not in kind." Furthermore, "[t]he work shall be of the lowliest kind, that performed by the country's poorest class. . . . This labor shall provide occupation for the body alone, leaving the mind free to meditate and pray while the fingers work" (Antier, 138). The houses of the brotherhood were to be small (eighteen at most), and all the members would be equal. Lay members were not to be ordained, but priests could join. The small communities were to be established in areas where the poor lived and to look like a typical dwelling place, not a fancy monastery.

From 1894 to 1897, Brother Marie-Albéric lived in a state of indecision and inner turmoil. Should he petition to leave the Trappists or try to follow his call for abjection within the confines of the Trappist life? Obedience struggled with the call to radical poverty. Abbé Huvelin at first advised him to remain with the Trappists, but by September 1895, he had come around to approving Brother Marie-Albéric's desire to leave the order and take up a life more suited to the call he had received. Finally, in July 1896, Marie-Albéric asked to be dispensed from his vows but was instead sent to Rome to study theology as preparation for being ordained. During these trying months he sought to surrender utterly to the divine will, whatever might happen. In a meditation from December 1896, he prays, "Poverty, humbleness, penitence—you, O God, know my sole longing is to practice them to the extent and in the exact way you want me to do. But what are that way and degree?" (*Spiritual Autobiography*, 32). After an interview with Dom Sébastian Wyart, the new General of the Trappists, Brother Marie-Albéric unexpectedly received dispensation from his vows on February 14, 1897. He then took private vows of poverty, chastity, as well as one of obedience to the direction of Abbé Huvelin. He then set out for Nazareth and the next stage in his spiritual pilgrimage.

The four years that Charles spent in the Holy Land, mostly in Nazareth, were decisive for his spiritual development. Here he was finally able to live the life of absolute poverty, total abjection, and contemplative prayer before the Eucharist that he had dreamed of. After visiting Jerusalem again, Charles walked to Nazareth, hoping to be taken on as a servant in one of the religious houses there. After an interview with Mother Marie-Ange of the Nazareth community of Poor Clares, he was allowed to live in a little hut outside the convent walls and to function as a gardener and kind of factotum for the nuns, as well as serving the daily Mass at the convent. It was perfect for him. As he wrote in his *Retreat at Nazareth*, "To embrace humility, poverty, renunciation, abjection, solitude, suffering, as did Jesus in the manger. To care not for human grandeur, or rising in the world, or the esteem of men, but to esteem the very poor as much as the very rich. For me to seek always the last of the last places, to order my life as to be the last, to be the most despised of men" (Antier, 152). On Abbé Huvelin's advice, he began to read more mystical literature, including John of the Cross and the *Abandonment to Divine Providence* ascribed to Jean-Pierre de Caussade. He spent as many hours in adoration before the Blessed Sacrament as he could. As Brother Marie-Albéric, Charles had already begun to write down some of his prayers and meditations on scripture. He expanded on this practice at Nazareth and many of his most important spiritual writings, such as the *Retreat at Nazareth* of 1897, and the *Meditations on the Holy Gospels* (1898–1899), come from this period.[4] In 1898, while on pilgrimage to other religious sites in Galilee, he experienced mystical union with Christ. According to an entry in his journal for February 28, he felt "the kiss of Jesus's lips on his face, and Jesus's hand, which he was allowed to hold for a long while." On April 7, another entry says that he felt Jesus's heart beating against his own, so that he was led to exclaim, "Who entered me? Who united with me in a union that has no earthly name, that the mind does not comprehend? In a divine union. You united with me, Lord, by means of a divine miracle and in a supernatural way."[5]

Charles seems to have been satisfied with his own practice of the poverty of life represented by Nazareth, but he still longed to spread the message to others. In July of 1898, Mother Marie-Ange sent him to meet her superior, Mother Elisabeth du Calvaire, abbess of the Poor Clares of Jerusalem. Mother Elisabeth was a formidable person who had already founded a number of religious houses. She saw in Charles, the beggarly ascetic, a "true man of God, a saint in the house." Charles returned to Jerusalem from September 1898 to February 1899, a time during which Mother Elisabeth gradually convinced him that he needed to become a priest in order to serve as the chaplain for her community and possibly establish the new order of his dreams. Once again, Charles was torn between ideals: total poverty and the hidden life, or a more public role as a priest. In 1900 an opportunity presented itself to buy a property on the so-called Mount of the Beatitudes on which he might be able to found his community. At this time Charles, who had been so opposed to ordination a few years ago, reversed course and sought ordination, although the purchase of the property on the Mount of the Beatitudes turned out to be a scam. Later in 1900 he returned to Europe, where he was able to see Abbé Huvelin again, and began to prepare for ordination under the patronage of the sympathetic Bishop Bonnet of Viviers as an independent missionary. Charles was ordained subdeacon and deacon during 1900 (important retreat *Journals* date from this time), and was finally made a priest on June 9, 1901. During the time of preparation for the priesthood, Charles made of number of personal "elections" in the style of Ignatius of Loyola's *Spiritual Exercises.*

During the last few years, Charles's restless mind had begun to turn to North Africa and its need for a Catholic presence. He had come to the realization, as he put it, that "Nazareth was everywhere," so he that he could live his "Nazareth-life" in Africa as well as in the Holy Land.[6] There was certainly a missionary aspect to his new direction, but it was not the active preaching mission such as that represented by the recent order of the White Fathers. Charles, or Brother Charles of Jesus as he now called himself, was initiating what might be called a "mission of presence," that is, a life of serving among the Muslim population of North Africa as a witness to the poverty and love of Jesus Christ for all humans. In the beginning, he hoped that this mission of presence might soon begin to make converts, but after some years he realized that this was not to be the case. He made only two converts in his sixteen years in North Africa—an aged slave woman, and a young slave boy he adopted. Brother Charles did become discouraged from time to time, but he never gave up. He realized that it would take many years, even generations, before Christianity might begin to have an impact on the Islamic population of North Africa (still true today), but this did not mean that witness to the love of Jesus among Muslims was in any way less important. This realization is another of the factors that makes Charles de Foucauld a particularly modern mystic.

In September of 1901, Brother Charles of Jesus arrived back in North Africa under the patronage of Bishop Charles Guérin, the apostolic vicar of the Sahara. Here he was to remain for the last period of his life, although he made a number of trips back to France. In late October, he arrived at the oasis of Beni-Abbès on the northern edge of the Sahara, where he established a hermitage, hoping to attract applicants to his planned congregation who would be willing to live in total poverty in the midst of a non-Christian population. Beni-Abbès also had a garrison of French soldiers, and Charles served the pastoral needs of the troops, some of whose superiors had been his classmates at St. Cyr. Both at Beni-Abbès and later in his hermitage at Tamanrasset deep in the Sahara, Charles remained in close contact with the French military in North Africa.

The connection between Charles de Foucauld and the French occupying forces raises the issue of his relation to colonialism. Charles de Foucauld was a colonialist. It would be foolish to deny this, but it is important to put his colonialism in perspective. As a loyal citizen of France and a former military officer, he had no doubts about the necessity of France's intervention in North Africa. Today, we look back on the interference of France and the other European powers in Africa, Asia, and elsewhere, and rightly see how much suffering and destruction this caused. Charles witnessed and strongly protested against the excesses of colonial rule; but, like most of his European contemporaries, he felt that colonialism in essence was good, even necessary. How could he and his contemporaries have thought this?

The colonial powers of the nineteenth and early twentieth centuries certainly sought to enhance their power and prestige by acquiring empires abroad. They did so, however, under the umbrella of a pacifying and "civilizing" intent. North Africa, especially the Sahara as Charles experienced it, was a vast area plagued by weak government, violence, and endemic slavery. The nomadic tribes of the desert engaged in constant raiding and fighting in armed bands called *rezzous*, which robbed caravans, harried the sedentary population, and often took the inhabitants, especially black people, as slaves. From time to time Jihadist preachers riled up these raiders to wage holy war on Christians. Charles de Foucauld, like almost all Europeans at the time, believed in the necessity of pacifying the desert, encouraging economic development through sedentary farming where possible, and ending the practice of slavery. He protested vigorously against those French leaders who did not act decisively against the slave trade. He emphasized the dignity of all people, Arab and Black, slave and free, as brethren made in the image of God. He also denounced any form of colonialism that sought only economic profit from pacified territories. Charles de Foucauld was a colonialist, but one who stressed only what he thought of as the good aspect of the phenomenon, while attacking many of its evils.

Brother Charles began building his hermitage at Beni-Abbès late in 1901 and was able to celebrate the first Mass there on December 1. He settled down to lead the rigorous life of a "Little Brother of Jesus." Rising each day at 4:00 AM, he prayed for some hours, celebrated Mass, and finished his thanksgiving at 6:00. After a modest breakfast of dates, figs, and coffee, he made an hour adoration of the Eucharist and then worked or wrote letters until about 11:00. A modest dinner was taken at 11:30 and until Vespers at 5:30 PM he prayed before the Eucharist, meditated, and wrote. Supper was at 6:00, and after that he often gave Benediction and a Gospel homily for any soldiers who might be interested. He then said the rosary and Compline and went to bed at 8:00, but rose again at midnight to say Matins and Lauds. He dressed much like the poor Arabs he lived among—a long white robe (but with a belt and rosary), a high tarboosh hat and neck covering against the sun, and sandals. His robe featured the distinctive badge of the Little Brothers, a red heart surmounted by a cross.

When the French first moved into Algeria in 1830, they had outlawed slavery, but the practice still continued in Charles's time and the French generals allowed it. Brother Charles was indignant. In a letter of February 7, 1902, he complained to the abbot of Neiges back in France: "It must be made known to whom it may concern: 'this is not legal.' It is hypocrisy to put on stamps and everything else, 'liberty, equality, fraternity, human rights,' you who fetter slaves and condemn to the galleys those making a lie of what you print on your banknotes.... Voices must be raised so that France will know of this injustice and thievery. I have informed the apostolic prefect. I do not wish to betray my children, to be a bad shepherd" (Antier, 191). Rather, Brother Charles was rapidly being recognized as a good shepherd by his unlikely flock of poor Muslim peasants and rough French soldiers. Although he wished to spend most of his day in contemplation before the Blessed Sacrament, this became more and more difficult as people flocked to his door, asking for help, physical and spiritual. Within a few months, up to a hundred people a day were calling on him. His family and Abbé Huvelin were worried about his declining health under these impositions and urged him to moderate his austerities. By now his neighbors on the oasis were calling him "Khaouia Carlo, the Christian marabout [holy man]."

The ever-restless Brother Charles, beset with so many responsibilities, began to think of moving deeper into the desert, perhaps even to go to Morocco, where there were no priests at all in the hinterland. But Morocco was inaccessible to Westerners, so Charles turned his attention to the Tuareg people of the deep Sahara, nomadic tribes who maintained a degree of independence. In 1903 and 1904, Charles received permission from Bishop Guérin to accompany his friend, Major Henri Laperrine, on a pacification tour of the Sahara to try to restore order to the warring tribes. This gave him greater knowledge of the desert and cemented his desire to move south to live among the Tuareg. Along with Laperrine and his troops, he advanced to the edge of the Ahaggar mountains and believed he had found what he was looking for. In his diary for April 16, 1904, he wrote, "To found in the heart of Tuareg country the sanctuary, the Fraternity of the Sacred Heart of Jesus. . . . I offer my life for the conversion of the Tuareg, of Morocco, all the peoples of the Sahara, all the infidels." But what kind of life would he lead there? On May 17, he queried himself about this and answered, "Imitate Jesus in his hidden life. Be as small and as poor as he. . . . Pray at night, work by day, love and contemplate Jesus unceasingly with all my heart, in poverty, holiness, and love. . . . Letting myself, like a lamb, to be shorn and immolated without resistance or protest; imitating in everything Jesus of Nazareth and Jesus on the Cross."[7] Brother Charles had developed an increasing desire for martyrdom as the ultimate form of the imitation of Christ.

Charles returned to Beni-Abbès on January 24, 1905, but he now had his sights set firmly on Tuareg country. He returned to the Tuareg in May, and on August 13 he settled at the village of Tamanrasset in the Hoggar region. Here, as he wrote to Marie de Bondy, he felt he would be finally able to live in perfect imitation of Christ: "Settle here permanently. The will of the Beloved. I am choosing this forsaken place and I am here to stay, taking as my only example the life of Jesus of Nazareth. May he deign to convert me. To make me to be such as he wishes me to be. Loving him, obeying him, imitating him" (Antier, 234). Under the protection of Moussa ag Amastane, the local Tuareg chief, Charles began to construct a hermitage. Tamanrasset was a poor village at the crossroads of several caravan routes set among the mountains. It had less than a hundred inhabitants—sixty Haratins, or former slaves, a few dozen Tuareg landowners, and a shifting population of shepherds and caravaners. Charles was the only European; the nearest French presence was a small garrison at Fort Motylinski, some thirty kilometers away. He immediately began to improve his knowledge of the Tuareg language and started to compile a French-Tuareg dictionary, a task that occupied him down to 1915 (it eventually contained over two thousand pages).

Life at Tamanrasset followed the same rigorous schedule that Brother Charles had used at Beni-Abbès. Once again, the Christian marabout soon became well known for his acts of kindness in providing food for the hungry and in handing out small gifts to the desperately poor. He did not give up hope that some disciples would come to join him in his far-off desert hermitage. Several times it looked like someone would come, and a Brother Michel did try to live with him for some time, but did not last due to the rigors of the life. At times Charles fell into a depression, especially when his catechumen, the unreliable Paul Embarak, had to be sent away for misbehavior. In those days, without an altar server, a priest could not say Mass. Sick and alone, Brother Charles had reached the depths, his Dark Night, without the consolation of the Eucharist. He had, however, petitioned the Vatican for a dispensation from the need for a server, and in early 1908 this miraculously arrived. He wrote to Abbé Huvelin in February, "Great happiness. Every day I say Mass, it is a new life for me and an infinite grace for this poor country. . . . Alone at the foot of the tabernacle with Jesus so near me day and night. . . . I lack for nothing" (Antier, 261). Charles, however, was not to have the good counsel of Huvelin for long, because the holy priest died in 1910.

By this time Brother Charles of Jesus had come to the realization that he was not going to make converts among the Tuareg or other peoples of the Sahara. He told a visiting military doctor, "I am here, not to convert the Tuareg in a single stroke, but to try to understand and improve them. I am certain the Lord will welcome in heaven those who have led good and upright lives, without their having to be Roman Catholics" (Antier, 266). This, of course, was quite at odds with the official thinking of many Catholic prelates of the time. Charles did, however, continue to seek to spread knowledge of his way of life and to encourage prayer and financial support for evangelizing the Sahara. In 1908 he composed statutes for a pious confraternity he called the "Association for the Evangelization of Peoples without Faith." In 1909 this led to the formation of the renamed "Association of the Brothers and Sisters of the Sacred Heart," a kind of Third Order of laity who pledged personal conversion, aid for the Sahara, and to live a life of imitation of Jesus. On a visit to France in that year, Charles saw Abbé Huvelin for the last time and also had a moving encounter with his beloved cousin, Marie de Bondy, the first in eighteen years. He also had an interview with a young student of Islam, Louis Massignon (1883–1962), who had first written him in 1906. Massignon, like Charles, had lost his faith as a youth, but Brother Charles promised to pray for him, and in 1908 Massignon experienced a remarkable conversion. Although he intended to become a professor of Islamic studies, in his new-found piety Massignon thought seriously about joining Charles as the second "Little Brother." This, alas, was not to be. Although the two remained close and wrote frequently, Massignon could never make a final decision. Nevertheless, Massignon, who became a noted professor of Islamic mysticism, later saw to the publication of the *Rules and Directory of the Little Brothers*.

By June 11, 1909, Charles was back in Tamanrasset. In August he journeyed into the heart of the Ahaggar mountains, finally reaching the Assekrem plateau (almost nine thousand feet), where he hoped to establish a summer hermitage to escape the heat of Tamanrasset. With financial help from friends in France, he constructed the hermitage in 1910 and spent months there in the following year, but the place was so isolated, though spectacularly beautiful, that it proved difficult to maintain and was impossible to live in late in the year due to the cold and wind. Charles had to abandon it in December 1911. He made some more trips back to France in the following years, meeting with Massignon several times. Charles's health was declining, but he still worked away on his French-Tuareg dictionary and other writings describing Tuareg customs.

The fateful year of 1914, which plunged Europe into war, affected even the far-off Sahara. Most of the French troops were sent back to fight on the Western front, and the desert became a more dangerous place. The Turkish Sultan, an ally of Germany, declared a *jihad* in 1914 against the French, Italians, and British. The Italians withdrew from Tripoli, which left this area open to the Senoussi Brotherhood, a fundamentalist Muslim group founded in Mecca in 1840 to oppose European colonialism. In March of 1916, the Senoussi amassed an army under Sultan Ahmoud, moved on the French in Algeria, and took Fort Djanet, which was only 310 miles from Tamanrasset. Since June 1915, fearing the growing unrest, Brother Charles and a group of Haratins had labored to convert his hermitage into a fort, or *bordj*, as a place of refuge for the small community of Haratins and Tuareg at Tamanrasset. In mid-1916, the French commanders left in the Sahara urged Brother Charles to go to Fort Motylinski. He refused to abandon his flock, so the army sent him some rifles and cartridges to store for possible trouble. It was not long in coming. In September, Sultan Ahmoud and the Senoussi forces moved deeper into Algeria intending to assault Fort Motylinski. Brother Charles was by now the most noted Frenchman in the area, so a plot was launched to kidnap him and to hold him for ransom. Rumors flew about that his little fort was filled with gold and treasure. A *rezzou* of thirty-eight raiders set out across the desert to capture Charles. On the way, they recruited one of Charles's community, a man named El Madani, to help betray him. On the evening of December 1, 1916, they approached the *bordj* at Tamanrasset and knocked on the fortified door. Charles, who was expecting troopers with the mail, recognized El Madani's voice. He opened the door and was seized and bound, while the *rezzou* ransacked the little fort. The troopers with the mail did arrive, however, and in the ensuing confusion and fight (the two troopers were killed) the young man who was guarding Charles shot him in the head. His longed-for martyrdom had arrived. Back in December of 1904 he had written, "Unless the grain of wheat falling to the ground dies, it remains alone; if it dies, it brings forth much fruit. I have not died, so I am alone. Pray for my conversion that, dying, I may bear fruit" (Ellsberg, 90).

Charles de Foucauld died a failure—another dead man in a year that saw millions die in the Great War. He was not a success in converting Muslims; he attracted no members to his planned religious community. Like the Jesus he loved so passionately in his long hours before the Blessed Sacrament, however, his subsequent success was remarkable. The novelist René Bazin wrote a life of the desert priest in 1921 that did much to spread his fame. As his spiritual writings became available through the efforts of Louis Massignon and others, the new spirituality found in his plans for the Little Brothers of Jesus and for a parallel group of Little Sisters began to bear fruit. In the 1920s, some French priests in Africa began to try to live according to his model, and in 1933 the young René Voillaume (1905–2003) established the first community of Little Brothers of the Sacred Heart in the Sahara. In 1939, also in the Sahara, Sister Magdeleine of Jesus (Hutin) (1898–1989) founded an uncloistered group of "Little Sisters of Jesus," based on Charles's rules. In the 1950s and 1960s both groups established congregations back in France and have since spread throughout the world. This is not the place to tell the story of the Little Brothers and Sisters of Jesus, who look to Charles de Foucauld as their founder and inspiration, and who have had a real impact on modern Catholicism.[8]

The Message of Charles de Foucauld

There is little that is original in what Brother Charles of Jesus had to say, beyond what we find in the Gospels, which is what makes reading him seem at one and the same time both familiar and startlingly new. He took Jesus seriously and wanted to live as he had. In that sense, Charles's message is biblical through and through. His *Meditations* most often are on texts from scripture, particularly the Psalms and the Gospels. Charles had a simple, but effective, hermeneutic for reading the Bible, as he set out in his *Commentary on Saint Matthew*, where he says, "Then, let us always read the Gospel *lovingly*, as if seated at the feet of the Beloved and hearing us speaking with him."[9] The whole of the Bible, the Old Testament, as well as the New, is a "tender conversation" (*tendre entretien*) which the Beloved has with us. Although he treasured a few spiritual writers, especially John Chrysostom, Teresa of Avila, and John of the Cross, Charles cites them only rarely and does not subject them to close study. His writings are biblical, meditative, prayerful.

The imitation of Christ, as noted above, is the over-arching theme of Brother Charles's life and writings. He continues to challenge us today to try to understand what *imitatio Christi* really means. But one cannot imitate Christ unless one believes in him. For at least a dozen years Charles de Foucauld did not believe in Christ, and his conversion in 1886 led him to think much on the nature of faith.

Faith

In his *Meditation at Nazareth* of November 1897, Charles reflected on his path to faith and conversion in 1886, noting how he would visit churches even when he did not believe. "My mind," he says, "was troubled, in anguish at searching and searching for the truth; I prayed, 'My God, if you exist, help me to know you'" (*Meditations*, as found in *Silent Pilgrimage*, 17). Faith was a gift of God, not the reward of one's own rational effort, as he learned from Abbé Huvelin. In the same *Meditation at Nazareth* he gives a definition of faith as "the gift by which we believe from the bottom of our souls all the dogmas of religion, all the truths that religion teaches us, and therefore the whole content of Holy Scripture and all the teachings of the Gospels: in short, everything the Church proposes for our belief" (*Silent Pilgrimage*, 20). This sounds like a very intellectual approach; but Charles actually stresses much more the effect of faith, that is, how faith is lived. "The soul who lives by faith is full of fresh thoughts, fresh judgments; fresh horizons open up before him. . . . Wrapped round by these new truths of which the world has no inkling, he necessarily starts a new life which the world thinks madness" (ibid.). In his *Meditations on the Gospels*, Charles says, "God's work is faith; holiness is faith; God's will, perfection, glory, what pleases him supremely in us, is faith. . . . Faith in one's heart and faith in one's deeds together make up true, living faith" (*Silent Pilgrimage*, 22). In the *Meditation at Nazareth* he notes that, in the Gospels, when Jesus praises someone it is almost always for his or her faith. He reflects on why this is the case in a long passage that deserves quotation.

> Why was this? Doubtless because although faith is not the highest virtue (charity surpasses it), it is nonetheless the most important, both because it is the foundation of all the others, including charity, and it is the most rare. How wonderful it is to have the faith that inspires the believer's every action. Such faith is supernatural, and strips the mask from the world and reveals God in everything. It makes nothing impossible; it renders meaningless such words as "anxiety," "danger," and "fear," so that the believer goes through life calmly and peacefully, with profound joy—like a child hand in hand with its mother. (Ellsberg, 99)

Such faith, he says, gives the soul the detachment that allows it to see the nothingness of material things; it allows us to pray with confidence. "It puts everything in a new light, revealing people as images of God, to be loved and venerated as portraits of our Beloved, and to be made the recipients of all possible good, and showing us that every other created thing without exception is there to be used as an aid in getting to heaven" (Ellsberg, 100). Finally, for Charles, as for John of the Cross, faith is our main resource in the experience of the Dark Night. As one letter puts it, "Aridity and darkness, everything is painful for me, even telling Jesus that I love him. I must cling fast to the life of faith. If at least I could feel that Jesus loves me! But he never tells me that he does."[10]

The Imitation of Christ

Faith is the foundation of the virtues and the entire life of the Christian, but that faith is realized in our following, our imitation, of the source of faith, Jesus Christ. *Imitatio Christi*, of course, is one of the most pervasive themes in the history of Christian spirituality and mysticism.[11] Few mystics, however, stressed it more than Charles de Foucauld, who gave it his own distinctive twist by his emphasis on the imitation of the life of Nazareth. In a notice from his *Diary* on July 22, 1905, he reflects on how the imitation of Christ, especially of his hidden and poor life in Nazareth, has been his guiding principle. He says:

> Love, obey, imitate—a life of faith, hope, and charity. Love Jesus, obey and imitate him. Obedience will put you into the situation that he wills for you. When his will does not show you clearly that he is willing an alteration in your situation, remain in the *status quo*. But always imitate him. *Without imitation of him, there can be no perfection.* In your own case especially, for imitating him is your vocation, duty and obligation at every moment of your life. Imitation of him has always been your first resolution in all your retreats: *in capite libri* (Heb. 10:7). It stands at the head of your life and gives it its direction. Jesus has put you into the life of Nazareth to stay there forever. (*Spiritual Autobiography*, 166)

Speaking of his decision to enter the Trappists, Charles again noted the connection between love and imitation: "The Gospel showed me that 'the first commandment is to love God with your whole heart' (Matt. 22:37), and that everything had to be enfolded in love. Everyone knows that love's first effect is imitation. Therefore I was to enter the order where I would find the most exact imitation of JESUS. I did not feel I was made to imitate his public life of preaching: thus I ought to imitate his hidden life as a poor and humble workman at Nazareth" (Ellsberg, 38). In a passage from his *Retreat at Nazareth* he portrays Jesus addressing him: "Just take me as a model: do what you think I did and what I would have done. Do not do what you think I should not have done or would not do. Imitate me" (Ellsberg, 56–57). By the time he made his *Retreat for the Diaconate* in 1900, he was sure that this imitation resided in the order he wished to found: "What would God like me to do? That which consists of the greatest love. The greatest love is in the closest imitation. Where shall I find the closest imitation of the life of Jesus of Nazareth? In the order of the Little Brothers of the Sacred Heart of Jesus that I wish to found with other souls" (Antier, 171).

Imitation of Christ is also the source of the love that is directed to our neighbor: "We must give [to others in order] to obey God's oft repeated command; we must obey to imitate him, he who gives so generously, to imitate Jesus who gave so much; we must give because the love of God forces us to carry the love we have for him over to people, his beloved children." He concludes, "Everything we do for our neighbor we do for Jesus himself" (Ellsberg, 95). Imitation constitutes the total life of the follower of Jesus, as Charles says in commenting on Luke 18:22 ("Come follow me"): "Who follows Jesus by taking the same path as he, imitating him in everything, truly seeing him as the path, 'following' him as the apostles followed him in the union of souls which 'followed' his own, . . . 'following' him by sharing and imitating everything in his interior and exterior life—Who does this except the saints?" (Ellsberg, 97-98). Such an imitation will seem foolishness to the world, but Charles says that "we should not blush when we are seen as mad, possessed, importunate, for the love of him, in imitation of him, if he gives us the great grace of such a conformity with him. One thing only should put us to shame: not loving him enough" (Ellsberg, 59). Such imitation must extend to the imitation of Christ's Passion and death. The *Retreat at Nazareth* of 1897 expresses the following wish: "To long for sufferings to give him love for love and imitate him, and not to be crowned with roses whereas he was crowned with thorns, to expiate the sins of mine he has already expiated with such suffering, to share in his work, offering myself with him in sacrifice—though I am nothing—as a victim for the sanctification of humans" (*Spiritual Autobiography*, 94).

Aspects of the Imitation of Christ

The Life of Nazareth

As we have already seen, Brother Charles was fixated on the hidden life of Jesus during his thirty years in Nazareth. It is hard to say where this interest came from, because imitation of Jesus in Nazareth was not a dominant theme in earlier Christian spirituality. In the *Retreat at Nazareth* there are several long passages on the significance of Nazareth and the hidden life. In one Jesus speaks to him of the aspects of his life that he wishes Charles to follow, because, "I have so often called [you] to the vocation of imitating me perfectly and me alone." Jesus wants him to be exactly "what I was during my life at Nazareth, neither higher nor lower." That is, Charles must be a poor working man, living among other poor persons, dressing like them and eating what they eat. Like the poor everywhere, he will be scorned and even persecuted. Despite his inner gifts, he will joyfully accept being thought of as "unlearned, . . . unintelligent, untalented, and ungifted." Everything he does, however, should be done in secret to avoid notice. He will seek out the most humiliating tasks and accept every attack and misunderstanding with joy: "Endure everything with great joy and gratitude to the Lord that gives it, as though it were a most acceptable present from a brother" (*Spiritual Autobiography*, 66–67).[12] The notion of Jesus as his big brother is found in other texts where Charles imagines himself, perhaps nostalgically, as a new member of the Holy Family in its life at Nazareth (e.g., *Silent Pilgrimage*, 56–57).

Several other passages describe in literal fashion the characteristics of the Nazareth-life. Also from the *Retreat at Nazareth* is a passage where Charles prays to Jesus, "My Jesus, you are so close to me: inspire in me the thoughts I should have about your hidden life." In answer, he reflects on the various dimensions of the hidden life of Jesus, which he divides into that part turned to the world, the visible life of the Lord, and "the invisible part [which] was your life in God, a life of unceasing contemplation." So, along with the virtues of poverty, self-effacement, and the like, of Jesus's public life, Charles wishes to imitate his inner life. "Your life," he says, "was one continual outpouring into God, a continual gazing at God, unending contemplation of God at every moment of your life." It was a life of prayer, involving "*adoration*, that is, *contemplation*, that silent adoration which is the most eloquent of prayers." In the second place, it also comprises *thanksgiving*: thanksgiving first for the divine glory, for the fact that God is God, then thanksgiving for the graces he has bestowed on the world and all created things." It also includes a cry for *forgiveness* of the sins committed against God, and finally, *petition*, asking that God might be glorified in all things (Ellsberg, 49–51). The imitation of the life of Nazareth therefore is a total program embracing both the active and the contemplative aspects of spirituality, to use traditional vocabulary.

On May 17, 1906, Charles wrote down fourteen resolutions that he had adapted while making a retreat between Holy Thursday and Easter Tuesday. They summarize his renewed commitment to living the life of Nazareth in the midst of the desert at Tamanrasset. He begins, "1. I must remember to what kind of a life I have been called: the imitation of Jesus at Nazareth; the adoration of the Sacred Host exposed; the silent sanctification of unbelieving peoples by carrying Jesus among them, adoring him and imitating his hidden life." The list continues with resolutions related to Jesus's hidden life: penance; poverty; lowliness; silence; detachment; adoration and interior prayer; zeal for souls; good example, and the like. It closes with, "14. I must remember to let the Heart of Jesus live in my heart, so that it may be no longer I who live, but the Heart of Jesus living in me, as it lived in Nazareth" (Gal. 2:20) (*Spiritual Autobiography*, 170–71).

The Virtues of Nazareth

As the 1906 *Retreat Resolutions*, as well as many other writings, make clear, there are particular virtues and practices that Brother Charles felt were especially manifested in Jesus's hidden life at Nazareth. Prominent among these was poverty. Like Francis of Assisi, whom he much admired, Charles insisted on the most extreme poverty, both for himself and for the Little Brothers he hoped to found. In one of the *Meditations* written at Nazareth he says, "O my Lord Jesus, here is your divine poverty. How greatly I need your direction—you loved poverty so much. Already in the Old Testament you showed your predilection for it. During your life on earth you made it your faithful companion. You left it as an inheritance to your saints." The passage goes on to invoke the saints who lived lives of poverty, such as Teresa of Avila and Mary Magdalene, always a favorite of Charles. It is not just physical, outward poverty that is the ideal. "Total poverty," he says, "is more than this. It is *poverty of spirit* which you, Lord Jesus, said was blessed (Matt. 5:3), that makes every—absolutely every—material thing a matter of complete indifference, so that we can brush everything aside, break with everything, as St. Mary Magdalene did in the holy cave." Such poverty empties the heart, so that God can fill it totally with love for him and love of neighbor (*Spiritual Autobiography*, 62–65).[13]

Closely related to the poverty of spirit that is the complete emptying of self is a trio of related practices: humility, abjection, annihilation. Humility is the traditional foundation of the virtues, and Charles of Jesus saw it as essential to the life of Nazareth. He wrote a meditation on humility in his *Retreat at Nazareth*, where he begins by citing Jesus's text, "Learn of me, for I am meek and humble of heart" (Matt. 11:29), and notes, "You God, made yourself man, and made yourself the lowest of men, a humble workman in that little Nazareth where I have lived, and when you passed from the hidden life to your public life what humility you showed in your words and acts, in your teaching and your example." He goes on to lay out a practical program of the practice of humility comprising being humble in thought, humble in desire, humble in speech, and humble in actions (Ellsberg, 53–56).

The practice of humility also involves abjection, that is, willingly accepting, indeed rejoicing in being an outcast, as Jesus was. In another passage from the *Retreat at Nazareth*, Jesus says to Charles, "One of the reasons for which I made myself poorer than the poorest working man is that I came to teach men to despise honors, . . . and to give an example of complete poverty and the deepest abjection" (Ellsberg, 67). In a *Reflection* written at Beni-Abbès in 1902, Charles says, "I must always be humble, gentle, and ready to serve as were Jesus, Mary, and Joseph at the holy house of Nazareth. To serve others, I need gentleness, humility, abjection, and charity" (Ellsberg, 73).[14] Abjection, a term found in earlier French mysticism, is often paired with the even stronger language of annihilation, at very least a moral annihilation of all self-will, and at times an even stronger understanding as a loss of self. Charles of Jesus employed annihilation language both with regard to Jesus's death on the cross and with regard to our following of him. In his *Retreat Notes* of 1904, echoing John of the Cross, he says, "The most fruitful hour of his [Jesus's] life was that of his greatest abasement and annihilation, that in which he was plunged in suffering and humiliation." In the last letter he ever wrote (to Marie de Bondy on December 1, 1916), he inscribes the following poignant words: "Our annihilation is the most powerful means we have to unite ourselves to Jesus and to save souls; that is what St. John of the Cross repeated in nearly every line" (Ellsberg, 120). In an earlier letter to Marie of 1902, he notes the root of annihilation, the recognition of our own nothingness: "The sight of my own nothingness does not weigh me down: it helps me forget myself and think only of him who is all in all" (*Silent Pilgrimage*, 37).

A person demonstrates true humility, abjection, and annihilation by living in obedience. Once again, Brother Charles turns to the example of Jesus at Nazareth, as recounted in Luke 2:51: "And he went down with them and came to Nazareth and was subject to them." The Savior lived a life of lowliness, labor, poverty, obscurity, and retirement, in which he was subject to Mary and Joseph—"You were *subject to them*—subject as a son is to his father and mother. Your life was one of *submission*, filial submission. You were obedient in every way that a good son is obedient" (*Spiritual Autobiography*, 84). To be sure, Brother Charles realized the tensions sometimes experienced in obedience, as when in the 1890s he wrestled with his obedience to his Trappist superiors and his obedience to the form of life to which God was calling him. He took a vow of obedience to Abbé Huvelin after he left the Trappists, and he remained true to that vow, although he often labored to bring his spiritual director over to his own point of view. In 1898 he imagined Jesus speaking to him as follows: "How perfect my life at Nazareth. . . . [It] was a sermon on *obedience*. . . . How could you, seeing me so obedient to those to whom I owed no obedience, whose sovereign Lord, Creator and Judge I was, refuse a *perfect obedience* to your lawful superiors?" (*Silent Pilgrimage*, 52). In the *Retreat at Nazareth* he provides the key for his understanding of the root of obedience. He asks, "How can I repay God for what I owe him when I have received so much? By love.

By obedience to his will for me in all things—for obedience is the sign of love" (*Spiritual Autobiography*, 57). Or, as he put it in another place, "Obedience is the measure of love: be perfectly obedient in order to have perfect love" (*Spiritual Autobiography*, 156).

Love is the heart of it all—the power at the basis for the other virtues of the Nazareth-life. Charles de Foucauld was a love mystic of a simple but profound kind. He does not theorize about the nature of love but rather sets out love as he sees it in the Gospel. The command to love God above all things is the core of the Gospel, and for Charles this command meant essentially love for Jesus, the Spouse of the soul. Writing to his sister in 1898, he says, "If we love Jesus, we live much more in him than in ourselves, we forget our own affairs and think only of his, and as he enjoys an unspeakable peace and happiness seated at the Father's right hand, we share in the peace and happiness of the Divine Beloved depending on how much we are in love" (*Silent Pilgrimage*, 75). Brother Charles certainly felt such joy, peace, and happiness at times in his life; but, like many other mystics, he also experienced an absence of the feeling of love. Writing to Louis Massignon on July 15, 1916, he provides the following wise counsel: "Love consists not in the feeling that we love, but in wanting to love. We love above all things what we want to love above all things." If we fail and succumb to temptation because our love is too weak, "[l]ike St. Peter, we should weep (Luke 22:62), like him we should repent and humble ourselves—but also like him we should say three times: 'I love you. I love you. You know that despite my weakness and sins, I love you' (John 21:15-17)." We must believe in Jesus's love for us, even if we do not feel it. He concludes, "To feel we loved him and he loved us would be heaven. But heaven is not, except in rare moments and in rare cases, for us below" (Ellsberg, 116). The same message is found in his last letter to his cousin Marie. Noting that we do not always feel that we love Jesus, he says, "But one knows that one wishes to love, and wishing to love is to love. One finds that one doesn't love enough. That's true. One will never love enough," yet we know "that he will never cast out those who come to him" (Ellsberg, 120).

True love of God cannot exist without love of neighbor. Charles's life was singular for its manifestation of Jesus's command to love all humans, after the example of the Good Shepherd. In 1898 he has Jesus speak the following: "I am the Good Shepherd, I am tireless in my search for the lost sheep, I have told you so a hundred times: *Love me!*, because I have shown such love for you, all of you, my sheep, and *love one another*, because your Shepherd loves you all so tenderly!" Jesus continues, "*Help me in my work, do as I do,* do all you can, with me and like me, . . . to bring as many sheep back as possible" (*Silent Pilgrimage*, 81). When he took up the apostolic part of his career, Charles came to see himself as the "universal brother" to all. Writing from Beni-Abbès, he put it this way: "I want to accustom all the inhabitants, Christians, Muslims, Jews and non-believers, to look on me as their brother, their universal brother" (*Silent Pilgrimage*, 43). Brother Charles rooted this notion of universal brotherhood in the fact that all persons—Christians, Jews, and Muslims, believers and unbelievers—have been created in the image of God (Gen. 1:26–27).[15] It is also confirmed by Jesus himself. Writing to Louis Massignon from Tamanrasset, he said, "I do not think there is a Gospel phrase which has made a deeper impression on me and transformed my life more than this one: 'Insofar as you did this to the least of these brothers of mine, you did it to me' (Matt. 25:40)" (*Silent Pilgrimage*, 42). This is why Charles insisted that "the salvation of one's neighbor is as important as the salvation of one's self. *Every Christian must be an apostle.* That is not advice; it is a command—the command of charity" (Ellsberg, 80–81). This point is also expressed in the principle he set forth in 1897: "It therefore follows that if we want to spend our entire life doing the most good to Jesus, we must use our life to do the most good to our neighbor" (Ellsberg, 96).

Love of God and love of neighbor lead to the final form of following Jesus, the imitation of his salvific suffering and death, something prepared for in Nazareth, but not realized until Calvary. Brother Charles's writings recognized the need to imitate the sufferings of Jesus but did not dwell excessively, as some contemporary piety did, on the details of the accounts of the crucifixion. Jesus suffered; so too must we. His notion of the imitation of the cross is closely tied to his thoughts on death, and especially the death of martyrdom. This was, indeed, standard Catholic spirituality, and Brother Charles did get to die a martyr (although some have questioned this because of his political involvement). Once again, I cite just a few texts from many. In the December 1916, letter to Massignon, Charles comments on John 12:24 about the grain of wheat falling to the ground in order to yield a rich fruit, saying, "Jesus saved the world by his cross; by the cross we must continue the work of redemption until the end of time, letting Jesus live in us and make up all that has still to be undergone by Christ. Without the cross there can be no union with the crucified Jesus, no union with Jesus the Savior" (*Silent Pilgrimage*, 48). In a letter of 1909, he reflected on the paradox of the Christian as always experiencing persecution and defeat, but always triumphing with Jesus: "He has conquered the world; like him we shall *always* have the cross, like him we shall *always* be persecuted, like him we shall *always* be defeated in the eyes of the world, like him we shall *always* triumph in fact, and this to the extent of our faithfulness to grace" (*Silent Pilgrimage*, 83).

Charles had nurtured a hope for martyrdom since at least the 1890s, but after he undertook his apostolic work in Africa, this hope became more problematic. On the one hand, he still desired to die a martyr (now a distinct possibility); on the other, he recognized his obligations to his community, nonbelievers as they mostly were. It is clear that he thought a good deal about death and his final union with his Beloved, when he, like Jesus, could say, "Father, into thy hands I commend my spirit" (Luke 23:46). In the "Memento" inscribed in the notebook he carried with him in his last years, he wrote, "Live as though you were going to have to die a martyr today" (*Spiritual Autobiography*, 213).

Prayer and Contemplation

In concluding, it is useful to single out a few other issues in Brother Charles's teaching that are implied in his central concern for the imitation of Jesus at Nazareth and hinted at above, but that need a bit more exposition. Charles, as we have seen, tried to imitate the exterior life of the hidden Jesus, as well as his inner life of prayer. Regarding his interior life, Charles's fundamental desire was to spend most of his day in adoration before the Blessed Sacrament. He continued to try to do so despite his recognition that Christian love demanded he yield to the necessary needs of his flock. Thus, Brother Charles lived a life of both contemplation and apostolic action, although it is true that he experienced some tension between the two. True to his biblical theology, Charles singled out the desert and the mountain as places especially apt for contemplative prayer, as can be seen in his dedication to life in the Sahara and in his mountain hermitage at Assekrem.[16]

Charles de Foucauld left a number of passages on the nature of prayer in his writings.[17] He often puts his teaching in the mouth of Jesus, who says, "Prayer is all intercourse of the soul with God. It is also an attitude of the soul when it contemplates God without words, solely occupied in contemplation, speaking its love with constant regard, though lips are silent and even thoughts are still. *The best prayer is the most loving prayer*" (Ellsberg, 109; see also 105). Thus, Charles adheres to the traditional distinction between verbal prayer and silent contemplation. Above all, he insists that prayer is the expression of love: "*Prayer*, you see, is above all to think of me with loving thoughts, and the more you love, the better you pray" (Ellsberg, 110). He envisaged his Little Brothers as engaged both in vocal prayer and in silent loving contemplation of the Blessed Sacrament. In this he says he is following, once again, the example of Jesus—"If prayer in common is enjoined by him, so is secret and solitary prayer, and in both we have his example" (Ellsberg, 103). In a *Meditation* from 1897, Charles even describes several methods of interior prayer, as well as three modes of prayer for attendance at Mass (Ellsberg, 77). Prayer, particularly silent prayer during the night, is accepting Jesus's invitation to the apostles in the Garden of Gethsemane. Jesus speaks, *"Watch and Pray* (Matt. 26:41). I invite you to spend the night in converse with me. Will you refuse? I ask you to stay awake to contemplate me, to tell me that you love me—to adore me: to pray for all persons: to ask pardon of me for those who are sinning at this moment, and who stay awake for the purpose of sinning" (Ellsberg, 123). Charles also composed a number of striking prayers found throughout his writings. Among these is the "Prayer of Abandonment," which is his expansion on Jesus's last words (Luke 23:46):

> Father, I put myself in your hands; Father, I abandon myself to you, I entrust myself to you. Father, do with me as it pleases you. Whatever you do with me, I will thank you for it. . . . I put my soul into your hands. I give it to you, O God, with all the love of my heart, because I love you, and because my love requires me to give myself. I put myself unreservedly in your hands. I put myself in your hands with infinite confidence, because you are my Father (Ellsberg, 104).

Brother Charles obviously thought that this should be the prayer of all who love God.

The Role of the Eucharist

Charles de Foucauld's devotion to the Blessed Sacrament was evident throughout his life after his conversion. He spent as much of every day as he could in adoration before the Sacrament. A passage from the *Retreat at Nazareth* provides an insight into the nature of these Eucharistic prayers: "Lord Jesus, you are in the Holy Eucharist. You are there, a yard away in the tabernacle. Your body, your soul, your human nature, your divinity, your whole being is there, in its twofold nature. How close you are, my God, my Savior, my Jesus, my Brother, my Spouse, my Beloved!" (Ellsberg, 52). A text from the *Meditations on the Gospels* speaks to the constancy of his adoration: "The Holy Eucharist is Jesus, all Jesus! . . . In the Holy Eucharist you are there, my beloved Jesus, living and whole, as fully as you were in the home of the Holy Family in Nazareth. . . . Oh, let us never leave the presence of the Holy Eucharist for a single moment as long as Jesus allows us to be there" (*Silent Pilgrimage*, 33). Adoration also implies receiving Jesus in communion as often as possible. Again, from the *Retreat at Nazareth*: "Wherever the Sacred Host is to be found, there is the living God, there is your Savior, as really as when he was living and talking in Galilee and Judea. . . . Never deliberately miss Holy Communion. Communion is more than life, more than all the good things of this world, more than the whole universe: it is God himself, it is I, Jesus. Could you prefer anything to me?" (*Spiritual Autobiography*, 99). As he prepared for being ordained, Charles discovered another dimension of his relation to the Eucharist, one as a priest who imitates Jesus in offering himself as a sacrifice to God: "Never does a man imitate our Lord more perfectly than when he is offering the Holy Sacrifice. . . . I must be humble where our Lord was humble, practice humility as he practiced it, and so practice it in the priesthood as he did" (*Silent Pilgrimage*, 34). It would be easy to cite more passages, especially from Charles's *Meditation on Psalm 83* (*Au fil des jours*, 53–59), a consideration of our spousal union with Christ in the sacrament; but these few can suffice to gain some sense of the depth of Charles's Eucharistic devotion.

Oneness with Jesus
We do not go to Charles de Foucauld for extended discussions of mystical union as a topic. Nonetheless, he does speak about different ways of enjoying the presence of the Beloved and becoming united with him. He does not speculate about union; he speaks out of his experience of being one with his Beloved. Among the ways Charles talks about union is through his union with all believers in Christ's Body, the Church. In a letter to Marie de Bondy of 1909 he emphasizes how we are all united with Christ in his Passion: "The royal way of the Cross is the only one for the elect, for the Church, for each individual disciple; it is a law to the end of time: the Church and souls, spouses of the crucified Groom, must share his thorns and carry the Cross with him. The law of love is that the spouse should want above all else to share the life of the Groom" (*Silent Pilgrimage*, 53). In a series of vows he made at Christmas 1903, he spells out the different levels of union he hopes to achieve. "I propose to: strive to unite myself to the material creation by offering all living creatures to God. . . . Strive to remain united and devoted, in my whole spiritual life and apostolate, to the Catholic Church. . . . Strive to be united, in my whole spiritual

life and apostolate, to all the saints in heaven, in purgatory and on earth.... Strive to be united, in my whole spiritual life and apostolate, to the nine choirs of angels and to all they do in heaven... and on earth" (*Silent Pilgrimage*, 82). Above all, however, Brother Charles of Jesus speaks of union in terms of loving oneness with Jesus his Divine Spouse. At times this language seems to reflect the theology of union with the different states of Jesus during his earthly life set forth in the writings of Cardinal Bérulle (d. 1629). Writing to Abbé Huvelin in 1898, he says that he is "dissolving and drowning in the peace" of Jesus's simple way of life at Nazareth, and that his reading of theology is not "distracting him from union with Jesus." Rather, "[m]y interior life is one of union with Jesus at the different stages of his life in this world. Until tomorrow, I shall be at Bethlehem; tomorrow morning I am going to the Temple; tomorrow evening I shall leave during the night for Egypt" (*Spiritual Autobiography*, 109). At times he uses strong language about union, though not in a technical way. In the *Retreat at Nazareth*, for example, Jesus says, "Contemplate me unceasingly and give all the time you can to prayer and holy reading, which will unite you to me and through which I will speak to you as I spoke to my parents and to Mary Magdalene at Nazareth and Bethany.... Let your soul melt into mine, immerse yourself in me, lose yourself in me" (Ellsberg, 66). The melting that Charles speaks of here calls up the image of the union between human spouses and their Divine Bridegroom found often in the hermit's writings. For example, in the *Commentary on Psalm 83* Charles says, "You are so good to have given to the human person this privilege of love, which unites him to you as his Spouse, so that he lives only from you, for you, with you, ceaselessly at your feet as a loving and faithful spouse" (*Au fil des jours*, 53).[18] I close with a passage from the *Retreat at Nazareth*, which also expresses this outlook. Brother Charles writes:

> And he is near me, this perfect Being, who is All Being, who is only true Being, who is all Beauty, goodness, wisdom, love, knowledge, intelligence. Those creatures in whom I admire a reflection of his perfection, ... are outside me, far removed from me, distant and separate, while you, who are Perfection, Beauty, Truth, Infinite and Essential Love, you are in me and around me.... How I am blessed! What happiness to be united so completely to Perfection itself; to live in it, to possess it living in myself! (Ellsberg, 108–9).

Notes

1. According to Antier, 15 (for full citations of works cited by author or short title, see the bibliography at the end of this chapter), Charles left about seven thousand letters and some twelve thousand pages of other writings. His spiritual writings were first collected in the *Écrits spirituels* of 1923. The full *Oeuvres spirituelles de Charles de Foucauld* total sixteen volumes.
2. Huvelin remained Charles's spiritual director for the rest of his life, mostly by way of letters. On Huvelin, see Jean-François Six, "Huvelin (Henri)," in the *Dictionnaire de spiritualité: Ascétique et mystique, doctrine et histoire*, ed. Marcel Viller et al., 17 vols. (Paris: Beauchesne, 1932–1995), 7:1200–1204 (1971); and Robyn Wrigley-Carr, "The Abbé and the Baron—Henri Huvelin's Spiritual Nurture of Friedrich von Hügel," *Studies in Spirituality* 23 (2013): 135–200. Huvelin was a student of French mysticism; see his *Some Spiritual Guides of the Seventeenth Century* (London: Burns, Oates & Washbourne, 1927).
3. Charles left several accounts of his conversion. I cite here from Antier, 100.
4. According to Antier (159), Charles wrote some three thousand pages of *Meditations* at Nazareth during the years 1897–1900.
5. *Écrits spirituels* for February 28 and April 7, as translated in Antier, 159.
6. A letter of July 2, 1905, puts it as follows: "Love Jesus with all your heart . . . and your neighbor as yourself for love of him. The life of Nazareth can be lived everywhere: even there in the place most useful for your neighbor" (Ellsberg, 91).
7. These passages from the *Diary* are translated in Antier, 218.
8. For some information, although not a history, see Antier, 329–34.
9. *Commentary on Saint Matthew* (*Au fils des jours*, 137).
10. Cited in Antier, 157. For more, see the sections devoted to faith in *Silent Pilgrimage*, 16–23; Ellsberg, 96–102; and the *Spiritual Autobiography*, 68–71.
11. For an extensive survey, see É. Cothenet, É. Ledeur, P. Adnès, and A. Solignac, "Imitation du Christ," *Dictionnarie de spiritualité*, 7:1536–1601 (1971).
12. The same text can be found in *Silent Pilgrimage*, 71–73.
13. Charles has a *Meditation on the Beatitudes* from Matthew 5, including "Blessed are the poor in spirit," partly translated in Ellsberg, 93–95, who also provides a series of statements on poverty in 57–62. For another version of the *Meditation on the Beatitudes*, see *Spiritual Autobiography*, 58–62.
14. For more, see Charles's moving prayer on "Holy Abjection" in his *Commentary on Psalm 83* (v. 11b) in *Au fil des jours*, 58–59.
15. On all persons as made in God's image, see the reflection written at Beni-Abbès in 1902: "Every living being, however wicked, is a child of God, an image of God and a member of Christ's body: there must therefore be respect, love, attention, and solicitude for their physical relief, and an extreme zeal for the spiritual perfection of every one of them" (Ellsberg, 74; see also 87–88, and 100).
16. Charles saw Assekrem in terms of the legend of Mary Magdalene, who was reputed to have spent her last years in contemplation on Mount Sainte-Baume in southern France (*Silent Pilgrimage*, 57–61). On the desert as the place of contemplation, see the *Retreat at Nazareth*, where Jesus addresses him: "You must break with all that is not me. Make to yourself a desert where you will be as much alone with me as Mary Magdalene was alone in the desert with me" (Ellsberg, 65).
17. See the selections in *Spiritual Autobiography*, 73–78, as well as Ellsberg, 102–10.

18. In the same collection, see also the *Meditations on Love of the Heart of Jesus* (101–6).

Bibliography

Writings of Charles de Foucauld

French
Oeuvres spirituelles de Charles de Foucauld. Introduction by Msgr. Jacqueline. 16 vols. Paris: Nouvelle Cité, 1974–1997.
There are many other editions and collections. The only one used here is Charles de Foucauld. *Au fil des jours: Nouvelle anthologie des Écrits Spirituels.* Edited by Pierre Sourisseau. Paris: Nouvelle Cité, 1997.
Letters. There are at least eleven volumes of letters to various friends. The only one available in English appears to be *Letters from the Desert* (London: Burns & Oates, 1977).

English. There are several anthologies. Those used here are the following:
Spiritual Autobiography of Charles de Foucauld. Edited and commented on by Jean-François Six. New York: P. J. Kenedy & Sons, 1964.
Silent Pilgrimage to God: The Spirituality of Charles de Foucauld. By a Little Brother. London: Darton, Longman & Todd, 1974.
Charles de Foucauld. Selected and edited by Robert Ellsberg. Maryknoll, NY: Orbis Books, 1999.

Studies. There are many biographies and studies in French, as well as some biographies in English. I have used the following:
Antier, Jean-Jacques. *Charles de Foucauld (Charles of Jesus).* San Francisco: Ignatius Press, 2022 (French original, 1997). The most recent biography available in English. Despite the author's penchant for inventing dialogue, this is a useful study with much citation from the letters.
Graef, Hilda. "VI. Charles de Foucauld." In Graef, *Mystics of Our Times,* 127–52. Garden City, NY: Doubleday, 1962.
Huvelin, Abbé. *Some Spiritual Guides of the Seventeenth Century.* Translated by Joseph Leonard. London: Burns, Oates & Washbourne, 1927. Contains some of Huvelin's spiritual discourses. The "Introduction" (ix–lxxvii) has a sketch of Huvelin's life and his relationships with Baron von Hügel and Charles de Foucauld.
Voillaume, René. *The Need for Contemplation.* Denville, NJ: Dimension Books, 1972. Meditations by Foucauld's foremost disciple.
Wrigley-Carr, Robyn. "The Abbé and the Baron: Henri Huvelin's Spiritual Nurture of Friedrich von Hügel." *Studies in Spirituality* 23 (2013): 135–200.

CHAPTER 2

St. Thérèse of Lisieux (1873–1897): Mystic of Loving Confidence

Sister Thérèse of the Child Jesus and of the Holy Face (1873–1897), to give her full name in religion, is not an ordinary saint or a typical mystic. Pope Pius XI, who canonized her in 1925, is reputed to have said that she was the most important saint of the modern world! Not an easy reputation to live up to. It is clear that, within a few years of her death, largely on the basis of the 1898 publication of a revised version of her personal journals under the title *The Story of a Soul*, this obscure Carmelite nun achieved worldwide fame and became known for many acts of healing, both physical and spiritual. Her reputation has continued to spread over the century since her canonization, as is evidenced not least by the success of the world tour of her relics in 1997, the centenary of her death.

For some older Catholics, like myself, who grew up in the 1940s and 1950s, Thérèse was an off-putting figure—a saccharine image bedecked with flowers and representing a form of nineteenth-century French bourgeois piety that seemed alien. A typical example of a "plaster saint" (Balthasar, 102). A large part of this discomfort was due to "the politics of sanctity" by which Thérèse's sister, Mother Agnes, as prioress of Lisieux edited and altered her texts to make her look more like the standard image of a female saint to facilitate her path to canonization. This constructed image began to be questioned in the years after 1945, when researchers first gained access to the surviving manuscripts of her writings and began to produce critical editions, a process not complete until the 1990s. During these decades, new evaluations of the saint appeared, primarily in French, but also in many other languages. As I read this literature and continued to study her writings, I began to get a very different picture of Thérèse—a much more original, more audacious, more daring, even revolutionary figure than the "plaster saint." Although some aspects of her life and writings continue to be troubling (to me at least), such as her self-absorption,[1] and the strange dynamics of her family (the Martins) that followed her into the convent, this young, sick, sheltered nun advanced a striking mysticism that broke with much of the superficial piety of the three prior centuries and boldly addressed themes that were to be central in the emerging modern world. Although her language often reflects her background, Thérèse's message reversed the nineteenth-century quasi-Jansenist spirituality based on fear of God, intense acts of asceticism, the necessity of satisfaction for sin, and the like, with a mysticism of loving confidence, or trust, in God's merciful love.

But was Thérèse of Lisieux really a mystic? Some interpreters have denied that she was a mystic,[2] but this is due to a failure to appreciate the broad contours of what constitutes a mystic, especially in the modern world, as discussed in the introduction. If we take mystics, especially female mystics, to be ecstatic visionaries gifted with paranormal experiences, such as the stigmata and the like, then Thérèse is not a mystic. She deliberately rejected such gifts. In her *Last Conversations* (DE) to Mother Agnes, she says, "You will remember that it's 'my little way' not to desire to see anything. You know well what I've said so often to God, to the angels, and to the saints: 'My desire is not to see them here on earth.'"[3] But if a mystic is essentially someone who stands as a model of profound love of God and devoted love of neighbor—and teaches others this message—then Thérèse is certainly a great mystic. The Carmelite is particularly striking not only in her absolute confidence in God's love for us, but also for her insistence on the reciprocity of love between humans and the Divine Lover. Writing to Sister Marie of the Sacred Heart (her eldest sister) in September 1896, she says that Jesus has taught her the "science of Love" contained in the book of life, exclaiming, "I desire only this science. Having given all my riches for it, I look upon this as having given nothing, just as the spouse in the sacred canticles" (Sg. of Sgs. 8:7). . . . I understand so well that it is only love that can make us pleasing to God [so] that this love is the only good that I have ambition for." But God *needs* our love too, as the letter goes on to say. "He has no need of our works but only of our *love*, for this same God, who has no need to tell us if He is hungry, did not hesitate *to beg* for a little water from the Samaritan woman. He was thirsty. . . . But when he said, 'Give me to drink' (John 4:7), it was the love of his poor creatures that the Creator of the universe was asking for. He was thirsty for love."[4] That is why I have described Thérèse as a mystic of loving confidence. As she lay on her deathbed in mid-1897, the last words she was able to write in the document called Manuscript C of *The Story of a Soul* said the same thing: "It is not because God, in his anticipating Mercy, has preserved my soul from mortal sin that I go to him with confidence and love [*par la confiance et l'amour*]."[5] It was, of course, because God had shown her that this was the only way to attain him. As we will see below, love is *the* major theme of the Carmelite from Lisieux, but Thérèse's understanding of love is characterized by a distinctive emphasis on confidence, trust, and hope in the goodness of the loving God (O'Connor, 143–51). As she put it in Letter 197 (September 1896) to her sister Marie, "It is trust [*confiance*] and only trust that must lead us to love."[6] In her *Last Conversations* with her sister Céline on July 22, when asked about what attracts her to heaven, she answered, "Oh! it's Love! To love, and be loved, and to return to the earth."[7]

Some Aspects of the Life of Thérèse Martin

Born in 1873, Thérèse was the ninth and last child of a devout couple Louis Martin (1823–1894) and Marie-Azélie (Zélie) Guerin (1831–1877), both of whom had originally aspired to join religious orders. Four children died in infancy; five girls survived. The oldest was Marie (1860–1940), who entered Carmel in 1886, becoming Sister Marie of the Sacred Heart. It was she who first suggested that Thérèse write down the reminiscences of her childhood that became Manuscripts A and B of *The Story of a Soul*. The second daughter was Pauline (1861–1951), who played a key role in Thérèse's life. When Zélie died of breast cancer in 1877, Pauline took over as Thérèse's second mother. Pauline entered the Lisieux Carmel in 1882, taking the name of Agnes of Jesus. Thérèse was devastated and promptly became ill. As Mother Agnes, Pauline was the prioress of the community for some of the years that Thérèse was there and for many decades after her death. Thérèse left the manuscript of *The Story of a Soul* to her for editing and publication. The third daughter was Léonie (1863–1941), a difficult child, who struggled with a religious vocation but eventually wound up entering the Sisters of the Visitation in 1899. Céline (1869–1959), later Sister Geneviève of St. Teresa, was Thérèse's closest companion growing up and remained so during her life, as frequent letters show. Although Céline lived in the world for a time, taking care of Mr. Martin, who suffered illness and dementia during his final years, Thérèse eventually persuaded her to enter Carmel. Thérèse herself, the last child, was born on January 2, 1873. The deep piety of Louis and Zélie Martin, as well as the way they nurtured the spiritual lives of their children, led them to being declared saints by Pope Francis on October 18, 2015, the first husband and wife to be canonized together.

The world of the Martin sisters and their father, revealed in numbing detail in *The Story of a Soul* and in countless letters, so different from that of anything that contemporary families, however pious, might experience today, has invited many psychological interpretations, Freudian and non-Freudian. It is not my purpose to review or to try to evaluate these. Thérèse, as the favored child both of her father and her sisters, grew up pampered, sickly, hypersensitive, and stubborn. She found it difficult to relate to children or adults outside the family circle. *The Story of a Soul* paints a portrait of a girl and young woman of almost excessive piety. I cannot tell the whole story here, but will focus on only a few incidents that were spiritual turning points in her brief life.

A revealing early incident (probably 1877) shows little Thérèse's desire for total perfection. Once, when confronted by her sister Léonie with a basket full of dresses and asked to choose a favorite one, Thérèse said, "I choose all!," and took the whole basket. She reflects, "I understood that to become *a saint* one had to suffer much, seek out always the most perfect thing to do, and to forget self." Although sanctity necessarily seems to involve choosing among sufferings, the mature Thérèse takes this incident as a model for her approach: "Then, as in the days of my childhood, I cried out: 'My God, *I choose all!*' I don't want to be a *saint by halves*, I'm not afraid to suffer for You, I fear only one thing: to keep my *own will*; so take it, for 'I choose *all*' that You will!"[8]

In 1882, when her sister Pauline entered the Lisieux Carmel, Thérèse decided that she too would become a Carmelite. The loss of Pauline seems to have precipitated a severe illness, psychological and physical, in the young girl. She was cured on Pentecost, May 13, 1883, by a vision of the Blessed Virgin associated with a statue of Our Lady of Victories. With three of her sisters, Thérèse was praying fervently to Mary to take pity on her in her illness. "All of a sudden," she says, "the Blessed Virgin appeared *beautiful* to me, so *beautiful* that never had I seen anything so attractive; her face was suffused with an ineffable benevolence and tenderness, but what penetrated to the very depths of my soul was the '*ravishing smile of the Blessed Virgin*'"[9] This visionary account, quite rare in her writings, became a "spiritual trial" for her. Her sister Marie was allowed to tell the other Carmelite nuns about the miraculous apparition, and on the next visit to the Carmel Thérèse was peppered with questions about what Mary looked like to the extent that she felt a profound humiliation and self-loathing. This may help in understanding her subsequent aversion to mystical visions and special experiences.

A third incident took place in 1886. Thérèse had experienced a loving union with Jesus at the time of her First Communion on May 8, 1884. Soon, however, she underwent a long trial of spiritual scruples and "extreme touchiness." She was relieved of this by what she calls "the grace of my complete conversion" while returning home from Midnight Mass in 1886. At this time Jesus changed her heart to the extent that "Thérèse [speaking in the third person] had discovered once again the strength of soul which I had lost at the age of four and a half [her mother's death], and I was to preserve it forever! . . . I felt *charity* enter into my soul, and the need to forget myself and to please others." She says that this influx of grace "began the third period of my life, the most beautiful and the most filled with graces from heaven."[10] The young girl had been converted from a self-centered life to one marked by thirst for helping other souls after the model of Christ on the cross.

The next two years of Thérèse's life were consumed by her desire to enter the Lisieux Carmel, although she was several years below the canonical age of sixteen. Her father supported her and some of the local ecclesiastical authorities were brought around. During this time Thérèse experienced moments of spiritual, perhaps even mystical, exaltation,[11] as well as inner trials, one of which she says was a three-day "painful martyrdom," which she describes as, "The dark night of the soul! I felt I was all alone in the garden of Gethsemane like Jesus, and I found no consolation on earth or from heaven. God himself seemed to have abandoned me."[12] During this time she also did much spiritual reading, especially of *The Imitation of Christ*, which was a major resource for her during the rest of her life. On pilgrimage to Rome with her father in November 1887, she even presented her petition to enter Carmel to Pope Leo XIII, who advised her to do what the religious superiors told her, but said that she would certainly enter if God willed it. Eventually the local bishop gave permission for the uncanonical entry and on April 9, 1888, Thérèse entered the Carmel at Lisieux.

Thérèse's few years in this convent were remarkable mostly in retrospect. Without the evidence of *The Story of a Soul* and her many letters, she would probably have gone down in history as a grave marker in the convent's cemetery. She was a modest and self-effacing nun, who sought to be of service to all the other members of the community, no matter how difficult they were. The two prioresses she served under, the aristocratic and imperious Mother Marie de Gonzague (1831–1904), and Mother Agnes of Jesus (her sister Pauline), both favored her and gave her positions of some authority, especially as acting mistress of novices. The poems and plays she began writing in 1893 were popular with the other nuns. Although scarcely great literature, these provide another source for her inner life. Thérèse was strongly influenced by the suffering-centered piety of the Jesuit Almire Pichon (1843–1919), to whom she made a general confession and who remained her spiritual director. He went so far as to declare to her that she had never committed a mortal sin, perhaps not the wisest spiritual advice.

In the convent, Thérèse's reading broadened. Around 1890, when she first gained access to a French version of the Old Testament, she was especially struck by the "Suffering Servant" passages in Isaiah. She also began an intensive reading of John of the Cross, of whom she says, "Ah! How many lights have I not drawn from the works of our holy Father, St. John of the Cross! At the ages of seventeen and eighteen I had no other spiritual nourishment; later on, however, all books left me in aridity and I'm still in that state."[13] She also refers to John in many letters (e.g., LT 108, 109, 135, 137, 154, 188, 221, 245). Although Teresa of Avila's works were well known to the Carmelite nuns, at that time John of the Cross was less familiar.

During her brief years in the Lisieux Carmel Thérèse does speak, if often in veiled ways, of some of her spiritual graces. Although she had taken the name of Sister Thérèse of the Child Jesus out of her devotion to littleness, she soon developed an attachment to the Face of Jesus veiled on the cross, a devotional practice popular among the Carmelite nuns of the time. "Ah!," she says, "I desired that, like the Face of Jesus, 'my face may be truly hidden, that no one on earth would know me' (Isa. 53:3). I thirsted after suffering and I longed to be forgotten."[14] On her reception of the habit on September 8, 1890, she expanded her name in religion to Thérèse of the Child Jesus and the Holy Face. She describes this as "her beautiful wedding day" to Jesus, one on which she experienced peaceful joy and a sense of being united to her celestial Spouse "in the bosom of eternal happiness." Although she continued to receive inner graces, all was not easy. "At this time," she says, "I was having great interior trials of all kinds, even to the point of asking myself whether heaven really existed"—a harbinger of things to come.[15] In 1894, she entered into a stage of more total surrender to Jesus. "And now I have no other desire except *to love* Jesus unto folly. My childish desires have all flown away. . . . Neither do I desire any longer suffering or death, and still I love them both; it is *love* alone that attracts me . . . . Now, abandonment alone guides me. I have no other compass."[16] She glosses this by quoting St. John of the Cross (*Spiritual Canticle*, stanzas 26 and 28).

During 1895 and 1896, Thérèse gradually outgrew her early fairly conventional spirituality that Conrad De Meester has described as that of a "spiritual merchant," one who performs acts of love and devotion to win God's favor and gain heaven (De Meester, 43–55). She began to realize a deeper and more radical view of acceptance and abandonment to God's loving action. Ceasing to worry about her own imperfections and failings, and releasing or abandoning herself to God's love marked the beginning of Thérèse's deepest level of spirituality. This is evident in many of her letters, but especially in an event of Trinity Sunday (June 9) of 1895, when she received a powerful grace that enabled her to understand better than ever before how much Jesus desires to be loved. As a consequence, she wrote down an "Act of Oblation to Merciful Love," which she convinced Céline to take along with her. This is a significant document about her teaching on the relation of divine love and justice. She begins, "O My God! Most Blessed Trinity, I desire to *Love* You and to make You *Loved*, to work for the glory of Holy Church by saving souls on earth and liberating those suffering in purgatory. . . . I desire, in a word, to be a saint, but I feel my helplessness and I beg You, O my God!, to be Yourself my *Sanctity*." Here the apostolic, even priestly, dimension of Thérèse's spirituality comes to the fore. It was to grow exponentially in her last years. The Carmelite proceeds to offer God the merits of all the saints and angels, especially the merits of the Blessed Virgin. She wants to console God for the ingratitude of the wicked and thanks him for her being allowed to share in the sufferings of Christ. She boldly prays, "I hope in heaven to resemble You and to see shining in my glorified body the sacred stigmata of Your Passion!" As she nears heaven, she says that she does not depend on her own merits or works but asks "to be clothed in Your own *Justice* and to receive from Your *Love* the eternal possession of Yourself. I want no other *Throne*, no other *Crown,* but You, my Beloved!" She concludes with the following oblation:

> In order to live in one single act of perfect Love, I OFFER MYSELF AS A VICTIM OF HOLOCAUST TO YOUR MERCIFUL LOVE, asking You to consume me incessantly, allowing the waves of *infinite tenderness* shut up within You to overflow into my soul, and that thus I may become a *martyr* of Your *Love,* O my God! May this martyrdom, after having prepared me to appear before You, finally cause me to die. . . . I want, O my *Beloved,* at each beat of my heart to renew this offering to You an infinite number of times, until the shadows having disappeared I may be able to tell You of my *Love* in an *Eternal Face to Face!*[17]

A passage from her *Last Conversations* records Thérèse's reflections about an experience of the fire of love she received on the occasion of the "Act of Oblation." She says, "I was seized with such a violent love for God that I can't explain it except by saying it felt as though I were totally plunged in fire. Oh! What fire and what sweetness at one and the same time! I was on fire with love, and I felt that one minute more, one second more, and I wouldn't be able to sustain this ardor without dying."[18] She says this experience enabled her to understand what some of the saints (e.g., Teresa of Avila) had said of such states, but it was a unique event in her life.

The story of Thérèse's inner life during later 1895 and much of 1896 is found in Manuscript B of *The Story of a Soul,* which she was asked to write by her oldest sister, Marie. The theme of God's merciful love, what she calls her "*little*" doctrine," is here given an in-depth analysis. Thérèse begins by saying that she is not "swimming in consolations," because "my consolation is to have none on earth." Jesus was teaching her in secret, not by books but by inward instruction in "*the science of LOVE.*"[19] The road to the furnace of Divine Love is "the *surrender* of the little child who sleeps without fear in its Father's arms." The themes of surrender, gratitude, and total love here emerge as the essence of Thérèse's teaching. She tells her sister about a dream she had on the night of May 9–10, 1896, in which the Venerable Anne of Jesus, the Spanish foundress of the French Carmelite nuns, appeared to her and consoled her about her approaching death. This is a prelude to a prayer to Jesus about the vocations she aspires to. She wants to be a "*Carmelite, Spouse, Mother,*" all quite ordinary desires; but Thérèse goes further in a daring way: "I feel the *vocation* of THE WARRIOR, THE PRIEST, THE APOSTLE, THE DOCTOR, THE MARTYR. Finally, I feel the need and desire of carrying out the most heroic deeds for *You, O Jesus.*"[20] She explains how she would like to fulfill each of these vocations, realizing the paradox that she, the littlest soul, desires things that "are *greater* than the universe." The reading of Paul (1 Cor. 12–13) gives her deeper insight into these many vocations. She wishes to see herself in all the ministries of Christ's Mystical Body, and realizes that this is possible only through charity. "I understood that LOVE COMPRISED ALL VOCATIONS, THAT LOVE WAS EVERYTHING, THAT IT EMBRACED ALL TIMES AND PLACES . . . IN A WORD THAT IT WAS ETERNAL! Then, in the excess of my delirious joy, I cried out: O Jesus, my Love . . . my *vocation*, at last I have found it. . . . MY VOCATION IS LOVE."[21]

To fulfill her vocation of love demanded that Thérèse recognize that it is her very lowliness alone that makes her worthy to become the victim, or holocaust, of Divine Love. In pursuing this thought, she calls upon a theme popular with the Spanish mystics of the sixteenth century and the French mystics of the seventeenth century: "Pure Love" (*pur amour*). She says, "O my Jesus! I love You! I love the Church, my Mother! I recall that the *smallest act of* PURE LOVE *is of more value to her than all other works together* [here she quotes John of the Cross, *Spiritual Canticle*, stanza 29.2]. But is there PURE LOVE in my heart? Are my measureless desires only a dream, a folly? Ah! If this be so, Jesus, then enlighten me, for You know I am seeking only the truth."[22] So, she does not depend on herself as the measure of the purity of love, but only on Jesus whose gift it is.

If Thérèse was not able be ordained a priest, nor fated to go work in the missions, she did have the opportunity to share in the priestly and missionary activities of two young priests who were put under her prayer ministry as her "spiritual brothers." On October 17, 1895, she began correspondence with the seminarian Maurice Bellière (1874–1907), destined for missionary work in North Africa. Her many letters of spiritual counsel and support to him, as well as his responses to her, are a wonderful example of a spiritual friendship and provide valuable insight into her teaching.[23] On May 30, 1896, she was given a second spiritual brother, Adolphe Roulland (1870-1930), a missionary to China with whom she also had an extensive and revealing correspondence.

On the night of April 2-3, 1896, Good Friday, Sister Thérèse experienced her first hemoptysis, the coughing up of blood that was the sign of her tuberculosis, the dread disease of the nineteenth century. It was to kill her in a short eighteen months. More troubling to the young nun was the sudden descent on Easter Sunday, April 5, into a state of inner desolation, "the trial [*épreuve*] of darkness," that was to be her fate for the rest of her life. Many previous mystics had undergone such times of dereliction, desolation, and loss of faith in heaven and even God (see McGinn). Thérèse would have been familiar with John of the Cross's teaching on the "Dark Night," but her own experience of dereliction does not seem to follow John's account. She does not, for example, use the phrase "Dark Night," but has her own vocabulary for her trial: storm, struggle, torment, tunnel, fog, night, wall, temptation. We know about this trial and the last events of her life primarily through Manuscript C of *The Story of a Soul*, which Thérèse was ordered to write by Mother Marie de Gonzague at the beginning of June of 1897. There is also considerable information in the *Last Conversations*, mostly taken down by her sister Mother Agnes between April 6 and September 30, 1897.

Thérèse's trial primarily focused on faith, but faith understood as confidence in God's goodness. The essential passage comes at the beginning of Manuscript C and there are brief references later in this text.[24] The trial of faith is also mentioned in the *Last Conversations* and is hinted at in some of the later letters (e.g., LT 213, 254, 258). Thérèse commences the account in Manuscript C by reminding Mother Agnes that she has suffered much throughout her life. This particular trial, however, is paradoxically also a "great grace." The trial is twofold: first, the incident of her first coughing up of blood; and then the more difficult loss of a sense of faith. When her faith was living, she had never been able to understand people who had no faith, she says, but then at Easter Jesus revealed this terrible reality to her. She says, "He permitted my soul to be invaded by the thickest darkness, and that the thought of heaven, up until then so sweet to me, be no longer anything but a cause of struggle and torment." This trial would be lifted only when God so willed, and that hour never came prior to her death. Thérèse says the experience is impossible to describe, but she provides a comparison of a fog-filled country where people cannot even perceive the light of the sun. These are the unfaithful sinners, whom now Thérèse welcomes as her brothers and with whom she wishes to eat the "bread of sorrow."

"She is resigned to eat the bread of sorrow as long as You desire it," she says to Christ. "She does not wish to rise up from this table filled with bitterness at which poor sinners are eating until the day set by You."[25] Thérèse had come to experience the tortured lostness of the damned. When she tries to remember her long-held hope for heaven, the fog around her descends more deeply and she cannot even discern the Homeland. She hears the voices of sinners mocking her: "Advance, advance; rejoice in death which will give you not what you hope for but a night still more profound, the night of nothingness." No wonder that she tells Mother Agnes that she will not write about it any longer, lest she blaspheme.

Thérèse's descent into darkness, scarcely mentioned in the creation of the plaster image of the "Little Flower," has emerged as a key aspect of her mysticism in recent decades.[26] Some have interpreted Thérèse's trial as a total loss of faith, but it is rather, I think, a loss of all *feeling* of faith and *hope* for heaven. She says that, while she does not have *the joy of faith*, "I am trying to carry out its works at least." She continues by noting that she still "runs towards my Jesus" and professes her readiness to serve him, because she knows that "[t]he more interior the suffering is and the less apparent to the eyes of creatures, the more it rejoices You, O my God!" Above all, she "WANTS TO BELIEVE." Thérèse, then, did not totally lose the spirit of faith, as she later tells Agnes: "Since the time He permitted me to suffer temptations against the *faith*, He has greatly increased the *spirit of faith* in my heart."[27] Regarding her frequent temptations against faith, she says, "I undergo them under duress, but while undergoing them I never cease making acts of faith."[28] Thérèse saw her trial of faith, however personally painful, as redemptive for others, but this did not relieve her inner agony. Her only hope during this time was to rely on love—constantly repeating to Jesus that she loved Him, no matter what. Thérèse was confined to the infirmary on July 8, 1897. She suffered excruciating pain throughout July and August. After much suffering, she died on Thursday, September 30, about 7:30 PM.

Throughout her short life Thérèse had promised to continue her work of intercession on earth after her death. This certainly seems to be the case, as one looks at the success of her writings and story. I note just a few of the milestones. As early as 1899–1901 miraculous cures were reported due to her intercession. In 1910, a Diocesan Tribunal was established to examine her cause for canonization. The Roman cause was initiated by Pius X in 1914. She was beatified by Pius XI in 1923 and canonized in 1925. In 1927, she was declared co-patron of the missions. Between 1937 and 1954, a vast basilica in her honor was erected in Lisieux. In 1980, Pope John Paul II made a pilgrimage to her shrine, and the same pope elevated her to the ranks of the Doctors of the Church on October 19, 1997—the third woman to be so honored. The pope hailed her as a "reference point" for Catholic understanding of revealed truth, noting how her "Little Way" was based on "the profound love of truth as the center and heart of the Church."

Thérèse's Teaching

Although Hans Urs von Balthasar speaks of Thérèse's "existential theology" (Balthasar, 54–80), it is important to remember that Thérèse was not a theologian in any technical sense, despite her role as a Doctor of the Church. She did show, however, that the "profound understanding of spiritual things given to the saints" is a major source for teaching of both pastoral and theological significance (John Paul II, apostolic letter "Divini Amoris Scientia"). Although the Carmelite read and cited some important mystical works (*The Imitation of Christ*, Teresa of Avila, and John of the Cross), the essential source of her teaching was the Bible.[29] At one stage, she confessed that even very beautiful spiritual books left her cold. She goes on: "In this helplessness, Holy Scripture and *The Imitation* come to my aid; in them I discover a solid and very *pure* nourishment. But it is especially the *Gospels* that sustain me during my hours of prayer."[30] In the Gospels certain texts were especially appealing to her, such as the parable of the Prodigal Son (Luke 15:11–32) and Jesus's Priestly Prayer (John 17). In the Old Testament she was drawn to the Isaian texts on the Suffering Servant (Isaiah 53, 66) and the Song of Songs, which she cites seventy-seven times. The biblical basis of Thérèse's thought and her lack of formal theological training mean that she presents her insights not by way of explicit doctrines, careful distinctions, or analysis of theological concepts, but through images and symbols taken from the Bible and everyday life to which she often gives her own special meaning. Many of these are common images, such as flowers, birds, toys, boats, grains of sand; others are more unusual, such as the table of sinners and the elevator that raises little souls quickly to heaven.

Thérèse of Lisieux is often associated with her teaching on the "Little Way." Although she herself used the phrase rarely (she does refer to going to heaven by "a little way that is very straight, very short, and totally new),"[31] the expression reflects a common theme in her writings—its stress on littleness, humility, lowliness, and utter dependence on God in the way a small child depends on its parents. References to and images of her littleness crowd her writings, especially *The Story of a Soul* and the Letters. The most popular is her frequent self-referencing as a "little flower" (*petite fleur*) or, in a double diminutive, as a "little flowerlet" (*petite fleurlette*). But there are a host of other images of littleness, such as the rather cloying descriptions of herself as the "little toy of Jesus" (LT 34, 36, 74, 76, 78, 79), as well as the "little grain of sand" (LT 45, 49, etc.), the "little lamb" (e.g., LT 54–56, etc.), the "little reed" (LT 49), the "little bird" (LT 197), and the "little brush" for painting (Ms. C, trans., 235). She is also a "little dew drop": "To be His, one must remain little, like a drop of dew! . . . Oh! how few are the souls who aspire to remain little in this way!"[32] Writing to her sister Léonie in 1893, she says, "Dear little Sister, do not forget to pray for me during dear little Jesus's month; ask Him that I remain always little, *very little!*"[33] These homely images, however, should not blind us to the true meaning of Thérèse's littleness. As De Meester puts it, "Littleness signifies profound humility and self-forgetfulness, truth and openness to God's grace" (87).

To become little is to become a child—an important theme of the Gospel. Oddly enough, Thérèse does not turn to New Testament texts about becoming like a child to enter the kingdom of heaven (Matt. 18:2–10; Mark 10:13–16) but uses two Old Testament passages: Proverbs 9:4 ("Whoever is a little one, let him come to me"), and Isaiah 66:12–13 ("As a mother caresses her child, so I will comfort you"). Despite her often sentimental language (a feature of her age and upbringing), to become a child does not mean to be childish; rather, the language points to an attitude of total surrender to God's love and mercy. This emerges in a letter that is one of the most important expressions of her understanding of the Little Way. Writing to her oldest sister, Marie, on September 17, 1896 (LT 197; trans., *Letters,* 2:998–1000), she says that her desires for martyrdom are nothing in themselves. What gives her "the unlimited confidence I feel in my heart" is rather accepting all consolation or the withdrawal of consolation as equally coming from God. "Dear Sister, . . . I really feel that it is not this at all [i.e., her desire for martyrdom] that pleases God in my little soul; what pleases Him is *that He sees me loving my littleness* and my *poverty*, the blind hope I have in His mercy." Later on she emphasizes, "I beg you, understand your little girl, understand that to love Jesus, to be his *victim of love*, the weaker one is, without desires or virtues, the more suited one is for the workings of this consuming and transforming Love." Being poor in spirit means not to seek God as great souls do, but as little souls, in their lowliness and nothingness. "Ah! Let us remain *very far* from all that sparkles, let us love our littleness, let us love to feel nothing, then we shall be poor in spirit, and Jesus will come to look for us, and *however far* we may be, He will transform us in flames of love." Striking an essential note, she tells Marie, "It is confidence [*confiance*] and nothing but confidence that must lead us to Love." This is the essence of the Little Way, something that Thérèse says is meant for all. According to a saying recorded in the *Last Conversations*, she saw the Little Way as the essence of her mission: "I feel that I'm about to enter into my rest. But I feel especially that my mission is about to begin, my mission of making God loved as I love Him, of giving my little way to souls."[34]

Closely associated with the Little Way and the acceptance of our lowliness and imperfection is one of Thérèse's most original modern images, the elevator to heaven. (She and her family had been fascinated by seeing elevators on a trip to Paris.) Heroic saints like Teresa and John of the Cross, she says, laid out the stages of the soul's ascent to God, but this is beyond "little souls" like hers. She says, "I wanted to find an elevator which would raise me to Jesus, for I am too small for the rough stairway of perfection." Searching the Bible for hints of such an elevator, she seized on Proverbs 9:4 mentioned above: "*Whoever is a LITTLE ONE,* let him come to me." Joining this text with Isaiah 66:13 about the mother caressing and caring for her children, the Carmelite nun emphasized the Christological meaning of the elevator image: "The elevator which must raise me up to heaven is Your arms, O Jesus! And for this, I had no need to grow up, but rather I had to remain *little* and become this more and more."[35]

Reflections on her littleness are found throughout Thérèse's late writings. In a letter to Abbé Bellière of April 1897, Thérèse glories in her state as a "little soul," or "a poor flower without splendor," and therefore different from the great souls, or "roses," that adorned Carmel in the past. She knows that those who have been forgiven much are under the obligation to love more (Luke 7:47), "so," she continues, "I take care to make my life an act of love, and I am no longer disturbed at being a *little soul*; on the contrary, I take delight in this."[36] In another letter from June 1897, late in her illness, she tells Sister Martha of Jesus: "Do what you *can*; detach your heart from the *worries* of this earth, and above all from creatures, and then be sure that Jesus will do the *rest*. . . . Above all, let us be *little*, so little that everybody may trample us underfoot."[37] The same message is found in a June letter to her sister Céline: "So let us line up humbly among the imperfect, let us esteem ourselves as *little souls* whom God must sustain at each moment. . . . YES, it suffices to humble oneself, to bear with one's imperfections.

That is real sanctity!"³⁸ Almost three hundred years before, Francis de Sales had advocated a spiritual attitude based on our acceptance of our own weakness and confidence in God's mercy. The humble Carmelite of Lisieux heightens the Salesian message.

The Little Way is the way of Jesus. He is the goal, the path, the motive force of the whole enterprise. Thérèse often speaks to and about "God," but she mostly seems to mean Jesus. The language of God as Trinity is relatively rare in her writings. Her desire, as she says in a number of places in Manuscript C, is "only to please Jesus."³⁹ It is a phrase found throughout her writings. Thérèse's devotion to the entire life of Jesus is well seen in Poem 24, "Jesus, My Beloved, Remember!," thirty-three stanzas reviewing the course of the life of Jesus and Thérèse's reactions to it.⁴⁰ Nevertheless, the nun's devotion to Jesus is anchored primarily in the beginning and end of Jesus's life, that is, in the Infant Jesus and in Jesus dying on the cross. She speaks of the happy inspiration that moved her to take the name "Sister Thérèse of the Child Jesus" and, while talking about her Christmas conversion, says, "On that night when He made Himself subject to our weakness and suffering for love of me, He made me strong and courageous, arming me with His weapons."⁴¹ The Child Jesus and the childlike Thérèse were made for each other. Still, the Carmelite also had a profound devotion to Christ on the cross, especially his bloody face. After her entry into the convent, she notes, "Until my coming into Carmel, I had never fathomed the depths of the treasures hidden in the Holy Face.... Ah!, I desired that, like the Face of Jesus, 'my face may be truly hidden, that no one on earth would know me' (Isa. 53:3). I thirsted after suffering and I longed to be forgotten."⁴²

A particularly poignant expression of Thérèse's desire for martyrdom with Jesus is found in a letter to Céline of October 1889, where in a strong outburst, she announces, "Ah, let us understand His *look*! There are so few who understand it.... Let us make our life a continual sacrifice, a martyrdom of love, in order to console Jesus. He wants only a *look*, a *sigh*, but a look and a sigh that are for *Him alone*!"⁴³ For Thérèse, the best way to attain to Jesus is not to try to climb up to where he is in celestial glory, but to descend into our littleness and thus compel him to come down to fill us. Again writing to Céline (LT 137 of October 1892), she cites Luke 19:15 about Jesus telling Zacchaeus to come down from the tree to prepare a dwelling for him:

> Well, Jesus tells us to descend.... Where, then, must we descend?
> ... What Jesus desires is that we should receive Him into our hearts.

No doubt they are already empty of creatures, but, alas, I feel mine is not empty of myself, and it is for this reason that Jesus asks me to descend.... He, the King of Kings, humbled Himself in such a way that His face was hidden (Isa. 53:3), and no one recognized Him, and I too want to hide my face; I want my Beloved alone to see it.[44]

In an earlier letter to Céline, thinking about the need for suffering in the present, she came to the following insight: "I have found the secret of suffering in peace.... The one who says *peace* is not saying joy, or at least *felt* joy.... To suffer in peace it is enough to will all that Jesus wills.... To be the spouse of Jesus we *must* resemble Jesus, and Jesus all bloody. He is crowned with thorns!"[45]

Because the Carmelite was such a holistic thinker, it is difficult to distinguish, let alone separate out, the major themes of her teaching. There can be no artificial distinction between what may be more "theological" and what is more "pastoral, or practical." Everything she wrote has both theological and pastoral consequences if we go beyond the sometimes cloying surface of her presentations. On virtually every page of her works, love and its many ramifications emerge as her constant preoccupation. Thérèse's message about love is not a speculation about the nature of love, or the kind of consideration about the relation of love and knowledge that many previous mystics engaged in. It is a meditation on what it means to say that God is Love (1 John 4:16) and how the love between God and humans is meant to work in practice. For Thérèse, love and hope, confidence and trust, are different words for the same dynamic reality.

Throughout her writings Thérèse talks about love as the center of her life, but her understanding of the meaning of love deepened over time. At one place in Manuscript A she says, "Now I have no other desire except *to love* Jesus unto folly.... Neither do I desire any longer suffering or death, and still I love them both; it is *love* alone that attracts me."[46] In a response to her sister Marie, who had asked her if she thought her illness would lead her to heaven, she says, "I do not count on illness, it is too slow a leader. I *count only on love.*"[47] Thérèse's mature theology of love is marked by a number of breakthroughs that are evident in Manuscripts B and C of *The Story of a Soul*, as well as in her late letters. *First*, she came to understand that no matter how much she tried to love the infinite God, it would never be enough. A passage in Manuscript C is revelatory here. She starts by saying that her only desire has been to love God, but, "Your Love has gone before me, and it has grown with me, and now it is an abyss whose depths I cannot fathom." Thérèse would love to fill that abyss herself, but she cannot.

"For me to love You as You love me, I would have to borrow Your own Love, and only then would I be at rest."[48] But Jesus has done just that. He gives us his own love, not on the basis of our merits, or efforts, or good deeds, but precisely according to our littleness, our openness to receiving his love. Therefore, and this is the *second* development, we must love Jesus by means of his own love acting in us. This teaching is also found in Poem 41 of late 1896, entitled, "How I Want to Love." Stanza 2 says, "It's Your love, Jesus that I crave. / It's Your love that has to transform me. / Put in my heart Your consuming flame, / and I'll be able to bless You and to love You. / Yes, I'll be able to love You and bless You / As they do in Heaven. / I'll love You with that very love / With which You have loved me, Jesus Eternal Word."[49]

Third, Thérèse discovered that the love of Christ acting within us is the love that enables us to fulfill the second great commandment of the law of love, love of neighbor. Addressing Mother Agnes, she notes, "This year, dear Mother, God has given me the grace to understand what charity is; I understood it before, it is true, but in an imperfect way." She says that the true meaning of "Love your neighbor as yourself" is found "on almost every page of the Gospel," but it clearly comes out in Jesus's address to his disciples at the Last Supper. "When He knew the hearts of the disciples were burning with a more ardent love for Him who had just given Himself to them in the unspeakable mystery of his Eucharist, this sweet Savior wished to give them a *new commandment*. . . . 'A new commandment I give you that you love one another: THAT AS I HAVE LOVED YOU, YOU ALSO LOVE ONE ANOTHER'" (John 13:34–35).[50] So, we are no longer just to love our neighbors *as we love ourselves*; we are to love them with the same infinite love with which they are loved by Jesus.

A *fourth* discovery, noted above, was Thérèse's recognition that Jesus *needs* our love; he is thirsty for it. Writing to her cousin Marie Guerin as early as 1890, she notes that love is the path to perfection and that Jesus alone can understand the profundity of love. More daringly she goes on: "Console Jesus, make Him *loved* by souls. . . . Jesus is sick [with love], and we must state that the sickness of love is healed only by love! . . . Marie, really give your whole heart to Jesus. He is thirsty for it, He is hungry for it. Your heart, that is what He longs for. . . . How does one dare to speak of one's poverty when Jesus makes Himself like his fiancée."[51] A *fifth* discovery was the sense of the infinite and unending power of love. To put this in the language of Gregory of Nyssa and some other mystics, love is *epektetic*, that is, it stretches out forever (Phil. 3:16), and while it finds its satisfaction in attaining the Lover, it always yearns for more. In 1889, Thérèse already associates such yearning with suffering: "I know another spring [i.e., other than the creaturely spring]; it is the one at which, after one has drunk, one is still thirsty, but with a thirst that is not panting. It is very sweet on the contrary, because it has something satisfying in it, and this spring is the suffering that is known to Jesus alone!"[52] Toward the end of Manuscript C, however, it is love itself that is epektetic: "I ask Jesus to draw me into the flames of his love, to unite me so closely to Him that He lives and acts in me. I feel that the more the fire of love burns within my heart, the more I shall say: *Draw me*" (Sg. of Sgs. 1:3).[53] There is much more on love throughout Thérèse's writings, especially in the Letters (e.g., LT 143, 258, 263, etc.), as well as some of the poems (e.g., Poem 17), but this should be sufficient to grasp the essentials of her teaching.

An important theme flowing from Thérèse's doctrine of divine love is the relation of God's justice and mercy. Much of the quasi-Jansenist piety of the time placed great emphasis on satisfying God's justice by acquiring merits through good actions. Practitioners of this spirituality lived in a state of constant fear regarding the ultimate expression of divine justice at the last judgment. Thérèse more and more distanced herself from such a program of doom and gloom, not only through her actions but also through her reflections on the relation of justice and mercy. Basically, the Carmelite sees no difference between the two. Reflecting on Psalm 117:1 ("God's mercy endures forever"), she rejoices in what God has done for her:

> To me He has granted His *infinite Mercy*, and *through it* I contemplate and adore the other divine perfections! All of these perfections appear to be resplendent *with love*, even His Justice (and perhaps this is even more so than the others) seems to me clothed in *love*. What a sweet joy it is to think that God is *Just*, i.e., that He takes into account our weakness, that He is perfectly aware of our fragile nature. What should I fear then?[54]

Closely associated with love, both in Thérèse and in earlier mystical traditions, are the themes of abandonment and detachment. In Poem 52 ("Abandonment Is the Sweet Fruit of Love"), we read, "Love is the name / Of this ineffable tree, / And its delectable fruit / Is called Abandonment" (stanza 3). Later comes, "Abandonment alone brings me / Into your arms, O Jesus. / It alone makes me live / The life of the Elect" (stanza 7).[55] To surrender utterly to love, to give up our own feeble attempts to love and let God's love take over in us, is the deepest form of abandonment and self-surrender. A powerful image Thérèse used for such total abandonment is that of the unpetaling of flowers, especially roses, as in Poem 51 ("An Unpettaled Rose"). Stanza 3 reads, "The rose in its splendor can adorn your feast, / Lovable Child, / But *the unpettaled rose* is just flung out / To blow away. / *An unpettaled rose* gives itself unaffectedly / *To be no more.* / Like it, with joy I abandon myself to You, / Little Jesus."[56] Abandonment is another aspect of the Little Way, as we are told at the end of Manuscript B: "O Jesus! Why can't I tell all *little souls* how unspeakable is your condescension? I feel that if I found a soul weaker and littler than mine, which is impossible, You would be pleased to grant it still greater favors, provided it abandoned itself with total confidence to Your Infinite Mercy."[57] The language of detachment is more rare in Thérèse, although the reality is always present in her insistence that God's "blow of love" to the soul is designed to free us from all that is creaturely (LT 94).[58]

Thérèse insisted that love of Jesus is inseparable from love of suffering. From an early age, she was enamored of suffering. Speaking of her First Communion, she says, "I felt born within my heart a *great desire* to suffer, and at the same time an inner assurance that Jesus reserved a great number of crosses for me."[59] Of her first five years in the convent she says, "Jesus made me understand that it was through suffering that he wanted to give me souls, and my attraction to suffering grew in proportion to its increase."[60] Her letters are filled with discussions of suffering and invitations to her correspondents to accept the way of suffering. Sometimes her language expresses the kind of morbidity that characterized so much nineteenth-century piety. Writing to Mother Agnes about joy, she says, "O no! no joy.... Joy is to be found only in suffering and in suffering without any consolation!"[61] This view would rightly be puzzling to many today. Poem 45, "My Joy," written in January 1897, echoes this. She says, "My joy is to love suffering. / I smile while shedding tears. / I accept with gratitude / The thorns mingled with the flowers" (stanza 2).[62] Nonetheless, we must remember that Thérèse saw suffering through a Christological lens. Just as the Redeemer expressed his love for us by his suffering and death on the cross, so too, the soul who truly loves him not only accepts but welcomes suffering as the road to union with him. In this matter a distinction is important. Much of what Thérèse says about suffering echoes the kind of "dolorist," even at times masochist, theology of her times. Nevertheless, the deepening insights of her last years into the true nature of love allowed her to overcome, or at least qualify, the worst features of the traditional picture of suffering as punishment for sin. In one of her last letters to the Abbé Bellière she says, "I feel it, we must go to heaven by the same way, that of suffering united to love. When I shall be in port, I shall teach you, dear little Brother of my soul, how you must sail the stormy sea of the world with the abandonment and the love of a child who knows His Father loves Him and would be unable to leave Him in the hour of danger."[63] So, suffering is connected not so much to sin as to love, the confident love of a child toward her Father, who will never abandon her or allow suffering to defeat her. Eventually, especially in her last days, Thérèse came to realize that it was not suffering in itself that was the way to God, but perfect abandonment to God's will, whether that involves suffering or not. Toward the end of Manuscript A this becomes clear in a passage already cited above: "Neither do I desire any more suffering and death, and I still love them both: it is *love* alone that attracts me. . . . I desired them for a long time; I possessed suffering and believed I had touched the shores of heaven. . . . Now abandonment alone guides me. I have no other compass!"[64]

There are many other aspects of Thérèse's message that cannot be touched on here, such as her doctrine of prayer, her teaching on time and eternity, her reflections on the Eucharist, and her teaching on Mary (see her important Poem 54, "Why I love You, Mary"). I hope the above analysis, however, is sufficient to highlight the basic contours of her thought, as well as the originality of the Carmelite's Little Way. Thérèse presents us with a mystical spirituality that eschews all heroic actions and insists that mysticism is open to all believers. It is also a mysticism based on absolute devotion to truth, "a sanctity without illusions." As she once put it in *The Story of a Soul*: "I am seeking only the truth."[65] Thérèse's mysticism is far removed from the dominant conception of mysticism of her time, one focused on paranormal and miraculous experiences—visions, levitations, inedia, stigmata, and the like. It also does not involve rigorous, often almost inhuman, feats of asceticism. She knew that she was suffering enough from her illness and inner trial. She dismantled the basic structure of the merit-based theology that had dominated so much Christian spirituality for centuries (Balthasar, 237–70). Her message broke with the Jansenist theology of fear and dread that pervaded most of nineteenth-century France because of her emphasis on a message of optimism and loving confidence in God. It is fair to say that, in her last years, Thérèse largely rejected, or at least forgot about, hell (Balthasar, 354–58). How could the loving God condemn most humans to eternal punishment? The same is true with regard to purgatory, that bugbear of so much modern Catholicism, and even of heaven, at least as conceived of as a place of peaceful repose after the strenuous activity of this life (Nevin,

293-95). Thérèse's heaven is a sharing in God's infinite mercy (e.g., LT 263), a place of ceaseless apostolic action for those still on earth—the eternal proclamation of the Little Way.

For Thérèse, sanctity consisted not in extraordinary actions but in the sanctification of the everyday, the little acts of love and compassionate understanding she tried to practice in her convent and that could be performed by any Christian, inside or outside the religious life. Although she does not discuss theoretical issues, it is also evident that she saw no division between acts of contemplative prayer and apostolic action. Prayer for her is the deepest and most fruitful form of action, because it always takes place in the context of the Mystical Body of Christ (Balthasar, 190-201). In all these ways, and many others, Thérèse of Lisieux, while seemingly conventional, was actually a revolutionary mystic who was prophetic of much to come in the decades after her death. We hail the humble Carmelite nun as a Patron of France, Patron of the Missions, and Doctor of the Church, and more. Why not also proclaim her the Patron Saint of the movement for women priests?

Thérèse was, to be sure, still caught in the rigid doctrinal categories and bourgeois piety she grew up in, but at the same time her struggle to overcome these constraints is evident. The combat was perhaps never fully resolved, but in her final months, despite the veil of pious obfuscation in much of what we read about her, her sharing in the suffering and desolation of Christ on the cross and her conviction that she must "eat at the table of sinners" produced a strong rejection of much of the moralism and negativity of the piety of her time. Thérèse was a great saint of the modern world, not just because she was chronologically modern, but because her teaching was open to much that expresses the "modernist turn" (Ulanov in Sullivan). Among the many paradoxes of the Little Flower was the contrast between the constructed image of her as a "plaster saint" and the reality of her challenge to so many aspects of traditional teaching and spiritual practice. The paradox remains, but the *real* Thérèse deserves our continuing respect, attention, and engagement.

Notes

1. Kathryn Harrison refers to her "characteristic monomania" (76). For full titles and publication information of works cited by author or short title, see the bibliography at the end of this chapter.

2. E.g., Balthasar, 333-40; Nevin, 288-89.

3. DE (ed., 1007; trans., 55; see also trans., 134, 143). The same view is also found in Ms. A, trans., 157.

4. LT 196 (ed., 550-51; trans. *Letters,* 2:994-95).
5. Ms. C (ed., 285; trans., 259).
6. LT 197 (ed., 552; my trans.; see also LT 261).
7. DE (ed., 1152; trans., 217).
8. Ms. A (ed., 84-85; trans., 27)
9. Ms. A (ed., 116-17; trans., 65-66).
10. Ms. A (ed., 141-43; trans., 98-99). See also LT 201.
11. See, for example, the experience with Céline that she compares to the Ostia experience of Augustine and Monica (*Confessions* 9.10) in Ms. A (ed., 147-48; trans., 103-4).
12. Ms. A (ed., 153; trans., 109).
13. Ms. A (ed., 210; trans., 179).
14. Ms. A (ed., 189; trans., 152). See also LT 80.
15. Ms. A (ed., 205; trans., 173).
16. Ms. A (ed., 210; trans., 178).
17. Pri. 6 (ed., 662-64; trans. *Prayers,* 53-55).
18. DE for July 7, 1896 (ed., 1027; trans. *Last Conversations,* 77).
19. Ms. B (ed., 219; trans., 187).
20. Ms. B (ed., 224; trans., 192).
21. Ms. B (ed., 226; trans., 194).
22. Ms. B (ed., 229; trans., 197).
23. The letter exchange is discussed by Ahearn.
24. Ms. C (ed., 240-44; trans., 210-14). See also Ms. C (ed., 248-49, 277; trans., 219, 240).
25. On the "table of bitterness" image, see Nevin, 203-6, 322-23, and 333-34.
26. See Balthasar, 339-44; De Meester, 77-85; Six, 25-34, 52-54, 170-73, 193-96; Nevin, 295-316.
27. Ms. C (ed., 248; trans., 219).
28. DE (ed., 1178; trans. *Last Conversations,* 258).
29. On Thérèse and the Bible, see Balthasar, 81-96.
30. Ms. A (ed., 210-11; trans., 179).
31. Ms. C (ed., 237; trans., 207).
32. LT 141 (ed., 461; trans. *Letters,* 2:784). See also LT 142-43.
33. LT 154 (ed., 484; trans. *Letters,* 2:836; see also LT 173, 178).
34. DE (ed., 1050; trans. *Last Conversations,* 102).
35. Ms. C (ed., 237-38; trans., 207-8). For other mentions of the elevator, see LT 229, 258, and *Last Conversations,* 49.
36. LT 224 (ed., 584; trans. *Letters,* 2:1085).
37. LT 241 (ed., 598; trans. *Letters,* 2:1117).
38. LT 243 (ed., 599; trans. *Letters,* 2:1122).
39. E.g., Ms. C (trans., 208, 215, 218, etc.).
40. PN 24 (ed., 692-700; trans. *Poetry,* 121-31).
41. Ms. A (ed., 141; trans., 97).
42. Ms. A (ed., 189; trans., 152).
43. LT 96 (ed., 399; trans. *Letters,* 1:588).
44. LT 137 (ed., 452-53; trans. *Letters,* 2:762).
45. LT 87 (ed., 553; trans. *Letters,* 1:552).
46. Ms. A (ed., 210; trans., 178).

47. LT 242 (ed., 599; trans. *Letters*, 2:1121).
48. Ms. C (ed., 282; trans., 256).
49. PN 41 (ed., 726; trans. *Poetry*, 173).
50. Ms. C (ed., 249; trans., 219; see also trans., 220–21, 225–26, and 228–29).
51. LT 109 (ed., 415; trans. *Letters*, 1:641–42).
52. LT 75 (ed., 371; trans. *Letters*, 1:501).
53. Ms. C (ed., 283; trans., 257).
54. Ms. A (ed., 211; trans., 180; see also LT 226 and 263).
55. PN 52 (ed., 745–48; trans. *Poetry*, 205–8).
56. PN 51 (ed., 744–45; trans. *Poetry*, 203–4).
57. Ms. B (ed., 232; trans., 200).
58. For more on abandonment and indifference in Thérèse, see Balthasar, 304–24.
59. Ms. A (ed., 127; trans., 79).
60. Ms. A (ed., 187; trans., 149; see also trans., 157, 173, 181, 217, etc.)
61. LT 76 (ed., 373; trans. *Letters*, 1:504).
62. PN 45 (ed., 733–34; trans. *Poetry*, 185–86).
63. LT 258 (ed., 615; trans. *Letters*, 2:1152; see also LT 253).
64. Ms. A (ed., 210; trans., 178).
65. Ms. B (ed., 229; trans., 197). See Balthasar, 43–53.

Bibliography

Thérèse wrote a good deal and the literature on her is voluminous. This is just a selection.

Sources

French

Sainte Thérèse de L'Enfant-Jésus et de la Sainte-Face. *Oeuvres Complètes*. Paris: Éditions du Cerf, 1997. The indispensable and massive edition of her writings (over 1,500 pages). These have been translated into English by the Institute of Carmelite Studies (ICS) in Washington, DC. The ICS versions are not without error and need to be checked in places.

English

Story of a Soul: The Autobiography of Saint Thérèse of Lisieux. Translated by John Clarke, OCD, 3rd ed. (Washington, DC: ICS, 1996). Translates all three parts: Ms. A (written in 1895), an account of her early years; Ms. B (finished in September 1897), which summarizes her teaching on the Little Way; and the unfinished Ms. C of June 1897, an essay on love of neighbor. There are really two versions of the autobiography: (a) the original text as written by Thérèse and now available in the critical edition; and (b) Mother Agnes's altered *The Story of a Soul*, first published in 1898 and still available in older printed versions. I use the sigla A, B, C for the three parts.

Letters of St. Thérèse of Lisieux, vol. 1: *1877–1890*; vol. 2: *1890–1897*. Translated by John Clarke, OCD (Washington, DC: ICS, 1982, 1988). Contains Thérèse's 266 letters (numbered LT), as well as 202 letters written to her (numbered LC).

Her Last Conversations (Deniers Entretiens). Translated by John Clarke, OCD (Washington, DC: ICS, 1977). Some scholars (e.g., Jean-François Six) have denied the authenticity of these accounts written down and edited by Mother Agnes, but most continue to use them, albeit with caution. Cited as DE.

The Poetry of Saint Thérèse of Lisieux. Translated by Donald Kinney, OCD (Washington, DC: ICS, 1996). There are 54 major poems (PN) and 8 supplementary poems (PS).

The Prayers of Saint Thérèse of Lisieux. Translated by Aletheia Kane, OCD (Washington, DC: ICS, 1997). 21 Prayers; cited as Pri.

Studies

Ahearn, Patrick. *Maurice and Thérèse: The Story of a Love*. Garden City, NY: Doubleday, 1998. A popular account of Thérèse's relationship with one of her spiritual sons.

Balthasar, Hans Urs von. *Two Sisters in the Spirit: Thérèse of Lisieux and Elizabeth of the Trinity*. San Francisco: Ignatius Press, 1992. This uses the 1970 version of Balthasar's work, rather than the early 1950 text. Despite some quirks (e.g., Balthasar's obsession over whether Thérèse thought she was without sin), this remains the best theological account of the saint's message.

Combes, André. *The Spirituality of St. Thérèse: An Introduction*. New York: P. J. Kenedy, 1950. Somewhat hagiographical, but still an important study.

De Meester, Conrad. *With Empty Hands: The Message of St Thérèse of Lisieux*. Washington, DC: ICS, 2002. De Meester made important contributions to the study of Thérèse in French, but this seems to be his only book in English.

Egan, Harvey D. "Thérèse of Lisieux (1873–1897)." In *Soundings in the Christian Mystical Tradition*, 307–12. Collegeville, MN: Liturgical Press, 2010.

Furlong, Monica. *Thérèse of Lisieux*. London: Virago Press, 1987.

Gaucher, Guy. *The Story of a Life: St. Thérèse of Lisieux*. San Francisco: Harper & Row, 1987. The best life of Thérèse.

Görres, Ida F. *The Hidden Face: A Study of St. Thérèse of Lisieux*. New York: Pantheon, 1959. An old, but still valuable, portrait of the saint with many psychological insights.

Guitton, Jean. *The Spiritual Genius of Saint Thérèse of Lisieux.* Ligouri, MO: Ligouri Publications, 1997. A brief analysis of some key themes.

Harrison, Kathryn. *Saint Thérèse of Lisieux.* New York: Penguin Books, 2003. A lively outsider account, marred by some dubious Freudian interpretations.

McGinn, Bernard. "Suffering, Dereliction and Affliction in Christian Mysticism." In *Suffering and the Christian Life*, edited by Karen Kilby and Rachel Davies, 55–70. London: T&T Clark, 2020.

Nevin, Thomas R. *Thérèse of Lisieux: God's Gentle Warrior.* Oxford: Oxford University Press, 2006. A detailed and often penetrating study, but marred by attacks on other interpreters and a debatable view of the saint's final months.

O'Connor, Patricia. *In Search of Thérèse.* London: Darton, Longman & Todd, 1987. A short, but insightful, introduction.

Six, Jean-François. *Light of the Night: The Last Eighteen Months in the Life of Thérèse of Lisieux.* Translated by John Bowden. Notre Dame, IN: University of Notre Dame Press, 1996. A polemical and controversial, but still important, account of Thérèse's final trials.

Sullivan, John, ed. *Experiencing St. Thérèse Today.* Carmelite Studies 5. Washington, DC: ICS, 1990. A collection of essays, including Barry Ulanov, "Thérèse and the Modern Temperament" (157–75).

CHAPTER 3

Elizabeth of the Trinity (1880–1906): The Praise of Glory

Elizabeth of the Trinity (1880–1906), a French Carmelite of the Dijon convent, is less well known than her contemporary Thérèse of Lisieux but shows some remarkable similarities to the slightly older mystic, whose *Story of a Soul* she had read. Like Thérèse, Elizabeth died young after great suffering. However, she is not just an imitator of Thérèse. Elizabeth had a distinctive mystical message, which emphasizes some themes that are not much developed by Thérèse, such as the infinity of God, the indwelling of the Trinity, predestination in Christ, and a theology of adoration expressed in the phrase "the praise of his glory" (Eph. 1:6 and 12). Although she wrote less than the Carmelite of Lisieux, she left a substantial corpus of letters, some short treatises, and 123 poems. Her path to official ecclesiastical recognition was slow. She was beatified on November 25, 1984, and canonized by Pope Francis on October 16, 2016.

As I hope to show in what follows, there can be no question that Elizabeth of the Trinity was an important mystical author. Did she also receive mystical graces? Again, if one mistakenly thinks of mystics as primarily visionaries and the recipients of various miraculous gifts, like the stigmata, Elizabeth is not a "mystic." She makes no claims to miracles.[1] She does, however, sometimes speak of experiences of contemplative rapture and union with God. In her *Journal* under February 20, 1899, she recounts a retreat during which she was reading Teresa of Avila's *Way of Perfection*. Praising the saint's teaching on infused contemplation, she says:

> I recognized there the moments of sublime rapture to which the Master deigned to raise me so often during that retreat, as He has done since then too.... After those ecstasies, those high raptures, during which the soul forgets everything and sees only its God, how hard and trying ordinary prayer seems! How painfully one must toil to unite all one's powers! How much it costs and how difficult it seems![2]

Such passages are rare, but it is hard to doubt, especially in reading her letters and other works, that Elizabeth based her teaching on a deep interior sense of God's presence. Like many of the great mystics, she does not speak much *about* her own experiences, but rather fashions her message *out of* these experiences. The theological weight of her teaching guarantees her a place in any list of modern mystics.

Life and Works

Elizabeth Catez was born at an army encampment at Avor on July 18, 1880, to Joseph Catez (1832–1887), a soldier, and Marie Rolland (1846–1927). Both parents were quite devout, but her father's death when she was only seven meant that her strict mother exercised the greatest influence on her upbringing. Madame Catez shared the Jansenist-influenced piety of much nineteenth-century French Catholicism, and Elizabeth, again like Thérèse, only gradually freed herself from this gloomy spirituality.[3] Throughout her life, Elizabeth (nicknamed Sabeth) was very close to her only sibling, Marguerite (nicknamed Guite), who was two years younger.

In 1882, the family moved to Dijon in Burgundy, where Elizabeth was to live most of her life. Sabeth was a precocious and pious child, but she also was strong-willed and had a fierce temper. As early as 1888, Elizabeth told Canon Angles, a family friend with whom she stayed close, about her desire to become a nun, a conviction that disturbed her mother. Elizabeth's formal education was limited, but she showed aptitude for music and spent many years as a student at the Conservatory of Dijon as a promising pianist. At Elizabeth's First Communion on April 19, 1891, she experienced a deep outpouring of love for Jesus dwelling in her heart, an event she later described in one of her poems (P 47).[4] The Catez family lived just around the corner from the Dijon Carmel, and on the day of her communion she visited the Carmel for the first time and met the prioress, Mother Marie of Jesus, who encouraged her vocation. As a teenager, Elizabeth, who had mastered her childhood anger and tantrums, continued to long for Carmel, being nourished by her reading of Teresa of Avila. Madame Catez, not willing to lose her, insisted that she needed to wait until the age of twenty-one to make a final decision. During this time, Elizabeth enjoyed a rich social life and took the customary vacations of the French bourgeoisie, but devotion to prayer continued to be central to her, as can be seen from the many letters and poems that date from before her entry into the convent. Some of her most beautiful poems, such as "Pentecost" (P 54), come from this period. Elizabeth also engaged in apostolic activity in her parish, giving religious instruction to the local youth. In 1900, she came under the influence of Fr. Irenée Vallée, the prior of the Dominican house at Dijon, whose sermons she heard and whose spiritual direction she followed for several years.[5] As she prepared for her entry into Carmel, Elizabeth began writing a *Journal*, or *Diary*. Its entries (January 30, 1899, to January 27, 1900) offer a rare insight into her inner spiritual experience at this early stage of her development.[6] In 1899, Elizabeth had been given a copy of Thérèse of Lisieux's just-published *Story of a Soul*, a book that was to be a major influence on her.

The Carmel of Dijon was the third oldest in France, founded by Mother Anne of Jesus, the disciple of Teresa of Avila, in 1605. Dispersed during the French Revolution in 1780, the nuns returned in 1866 and moved into a new convent in 1868. This was the establishment that Elizabeth Catez asked to enter. Permission was granted, and she entered the community on August 2, 1901. A few days later, Elizabeth filled out the customary "Questionnaire" for postulants, which gives us an insight into her thinking as she began her life as a Carmelite. She gives brief answers to fifteen questions. Among the most revealing are the following: No. 1: "What is your ideal of sanctity? To live by love." No. 2: "What is the most rapid way to reach it? To make myself very little and to release myself without return." No. 3: "Which male saint do you love the most? The Beloved Disciple who reposed on his Master's heart." No. 4: "Which female saint do you love the most? Our Holy Mother Teresa because she died of love." No. 9: "Can you give a definition of prayer? The union of the one who is not with Him who is." No. 12: "What dispositions would you like to have before death? I want to die of love and to be buried in the arms of Him whom I love." No. 14: "What name would you like to have in heaven? The Will of God."[7]

Elizabeth's five years as a Carmelite were even shorter than those of Thérèse of Lisieux. Even though the main lines of her spirituality were largely set before her entry, the convent years saw a considerable development in her teaching. Most of this was due to her intensive prayer life, but she also profited from meditation on scripture,[8] especially John and Paul, as well as the reading of mystical authors. She had already read Teresa, Thérèse, and Catherine of Siena before her entry into Carmel; she now added John of the Cross and other mystics like Angela of Foligno and Jan van Ruusbroec to the list. Elizabeth was not a great reader, but she certainly profited from these figures, whom she often quoted.[9] Her convent life was fairly uneventful. She received the Carmelite habit on December 8, 1901, and made her full profession on January 11, 1903. The various retreats conducted each year gave her the opportunity for deeper reflection on the mysteries of the Christian life. She was under the guidance of Mother Germaine of Jesus, the prioress of the Dijon Carmel. A sign of her deepening mystical theology was the noted prayer, "O my God, Trinity whom I adore," composed on November 21, 1904. Another witness to a significant development in her spiritual life was her "discovery" of the Pauline phrase "in praise of his glory." In Ephesians 1:11–12, the apostle says, "we are called as predestined according to his purpose . . . that we may be in praise of his glory, we who previously hoped in Christ" (*ut simus in laudem gloriae suae qui ante speravimus in Christo*). Elizabeth's attention was first drawn to the phrase by a conversation with another nun that appears to have taken place in the summer of 1903. By early 1904 (see L 191), Elizabeth was already citing the phrase in her letters, and she soon came to identify herself as "the praise of glory" (keeping the Latin accusative form, *laudem gloriae*). As many students of her writings have noted, *laudem gloriae* is the best expression for the mature phase of her spiritual journey.

In Lent of 1905, Elizabeth experienced the first symptoms of Addison's disease, a then incurable endocrine illness. She was soon relieved of some of the ordinary obligations of the Carmelite life, but the progress of the disease was relentless. At the end of March 1906, she entered the infirmary. Although weak and in pain, she used her time in the infirmary to write her four most important brief treatises, as well as many letters. The first treatise, from early August, is the ten-day retreat called *Heaven in Faith*, intended for her sister Guite.[10] She was now a married woman with two small children, but Elizabeth saw her mystical message as applicable to all, not just enclosed men and women. The second work was the short, more ascetical tract, *The Greatness of Our Vocation*, written in September to a close friend, Françoise de Sourdon (nicknamed "Framboise"), to help her discern a vocation to the Carmelite life.[11] The most important of these final works was the *Last Retreat*, written in late August at the request of Mother Germaine that she write down a few of her "spiritual insights."[12] This is perhaps the saint's single most important text. Finally, the last work is the short but moving *Let Yourself Be Loved*, a kind of spiritual testament she wrote for Mother Germaine in late October.[13] Elizabeth was fading fast. On October 31, she received the last sacraments for the second time, and on November 1 she made her last communion. She died on November 9.

Elizabeth's writings are not large. Her *Journal* and four treatises have already been mentioned. Letters form by far the greatest part of her writings (abbreviated as L with number). There are 342 of these in the critical edition, all with excellent introductions and annotations. The first 83 were written before her entry into Carmel and are not available in English; the Carmel letters can be found in *The Complete Works*, volume 2. In addition, she wrote 123 poems, 72 of which predate her entry into Carmel. There are translations of some of these.[14] Elizabeth's poetry seems mostly didactic (at least to me), but some pieces rise to a level of real spiritual intensity. Seventeen of the saint's brief miscellaneous pieces were later collected and given the name *Personal Notes (Notes Intimes)*.[15]

Mystical Teaching

Like Thérèse of Lisieux, Elizabeth of the Trinity had no formal theological training. Even her access to the Bible was limited, since Catholics of that time did not read the full Bible very much. Most of Elizabeth's knowledge of the sacred text came from the contemporary French prayer book, the *Manuel du Chrétien*, which contained the whole New Testament, some Old Testament texts, especially the Psalms, and the *Imitation of Christ*. Nevertheless, Elizabeth shows a remarkable insight into key doctrines of the faith, discoveries that should be put down to the enlightenment of grace rather than her own efforts or genius. We may call Elizabeth a theologian, not in an academic sense, but as someone who conveys contemplative wisdom. Here I shall try to give a brief summation of the key themes of her mystical teaching as an introduction to further reading of this French Carmelite.

Laudem Gloriae: The Theme of Loving Adoration

All Christian mystics, in one way or another, can be described as mystics of love, following 1 John 4:16, which says, "God is love and he/she who abides in love abides in God and God in him/her."[16] The centrality of God as love in Elizabeth's writings is unmistakable, but it is necessary to spell out the distinctive aspects of the Carmelite's view of God's love and our response to it in order to appreciate the originality of her thought. A phrase that Elizabeth loved was to describe God as "all love" (*ce Dieu tout Amour*: L 57, 58, 94, 95; P 57). She also speaks of God as "the Being that is Love" (L 330). She seized on a text from Ephesians 2:4 ("He has loved us exceedingly"), a passage she refers to no fewer than thirty-six times. Another characteristic of her view of love is to describe herself as "the prisoner of love" (e.g., L 97, 108, 111, 116, 137, 198, 209, 243, 303; P 74, 203), or "the victim of love" (L 57). To love is to desire to become one with the Beloved, and so union language as found in the Bible (e.g., 1 Cor. 6:17, John 17:21) occurs often in her writings. Elizabeth does not seek to define love or analyze its stages, as many earlier mystics had, rather, she tells us how she has experienced it.

Perhaps the best way to understand Elizabeth's view of love is to study the expression she came to use so much, her self-description as the *laudem gloriae*, a phrase she found in her favorite epistle, that to the Ephesians. Elizabeth uses the phrase some sixty-six times in her letters and treatises.[17] The first chapter of Ephesians emphasizes the theme of God's loving predestination of all those who have been adopted as his children through Jesus Christ. The purpose of this predestination is what Elizabeth focused on. According to Ephesians 1:6, this is, "Unto the praise of the glory of his grace, in which he has graced us in his Beloved." In Ephesians 1:12, the same purpose is rendered as, "that we may be unto the praise of his glory, we who beforehand hoped in Christ." The young nun discovered in this phrase the meaning of her life, that is, to become a total act of loving adoration to the divine glory as the goal of all things. "Adoration," as she once put it, "can be defined as the ecstasy of love" (*Last Retreat*, no. 21).

The earliest appearance of the expression is in a letter written to the soon-to-be-ordained Abbé Chevignard on January 25, 1904 (L 191). The missive is a meditation on passages from Ephesians, in which Elizabeth says that "in his magnificent epistles, Saint Paul preaches nothing but this mystery of the charity of Christ." She concludes with the prayer, "Let us unite to make Him forget everything by the strength of our love, and let us be, as Saint Paul says, 'the praise of His glory.'"[18] Loving union alone makes us into what we were created to be—the praise of God's glory. Again writing to Abbé Chevignard in late November 1905, she meditates on a series of Pauline passages on love and sacrifice: "Let us ask Him to make us true in our love, to make us sacrificial beings, for it seems to me that sacrifice is only love put into action: 'He loved me, He gave Himself for me' (Gal. 2:20)."[19] She then begs for the Abbé's prayers: "On December 8th (since you are a high priest), would you consecrate me to the *power of His love* so that I may in truth be 'Laudem Gloriae' that I read in Paul and I understood that it was my vocation even now in exile while awaiting the eternal Sanctus."[20]

One of the most penetrating uses of the motif in Elizabeth's letters is found in L 269, written to her sister Guite in April 1906. The sick Elizabeth is already thinking about her death. Using an image taken from Thérèse of Lisieux, she describes Christ as the divine eagle: "But, you see, at times it seems to me that the Divine Eagle wants to swoop down on His little prey and carry her off to where He is into dazzling light."[21] This light is her true dwelling place, "the bosom of the Trinity." The letter expands on the Trinitarian dimension of the *laudem gloriae* motif, thus connecting with another major theme of Elizabeth's spirituality. She invites Guite to "Live within Them in the heaven of your soul," where "the Father will overshadow you" (Matt. 17:5), "the Word will imprint in your soul, as in a crystal, the image of his beauty," and "the Holy Spirit will transform you into a mysterious lyre, which, in silence, beneath His divine touch, will produce a magnificent canticle to Love; then you will be 'the praise of His glory' that I dreamed of being on earth." She continues, "You will take my place. I will be the 'Laudem Gloriae' before the throne of the Lamb; and you, the 'Laudem Gloriae' in the center of your soul; we will always be united, little sister. Always believe in Love." Love aims at embracing our vocation of becoming "lost in the Furnace of love" (*me perdre dans le Foyer d'amour*), living in Love and glorifying Love on earth and in heaven.[22] Love is the motivating force that makes it possible for Elizabeth to fulfill her vocation as the *laudem gloriae*. Not only Elizabeth's letters, but also her poems, are filled with references to the "praise of glory" (e.g., P 94, 100, 115, 120, and 122).

In *Heaven in Faith*, Elizabeth of the Trinity expands on the meaning of being the "praise of glory" in the course of her Second Prayer of the Tenth and Last Day of the retreat.[23] She begins by citing Ephesians 1:11-12. How, she asks, do we realize our vocation and become "Praises of Glory of the Most Holy Trinity?" The answer is found in becoming totally transformed into the Three Persons. "In Heaven each soul is the praise of the glory of the Father, the Word, and the Holy Spirit, for each soul is established in pure love and 'lives no longer its own life, but the life of God'" (citing John of the Cross, *Spiritual Canticle*, stanza 12.8). The soul then knows God as God knows it (1 Cor. 13:12). Again referring to John of the Cross, Elizabeth says that the soul's intellect becomes the divine intellect, its will the divine will, and its love the love of God (*Spiritual Canticle*, stanza 38.3). As a result of this transformation, which is begun in this life but completed in heaven, the soul becomes "a perfect praise of Glory" (no. 42). The following paragraphs (nos. 43-44) explain further the meaning of being a praise of glory. "A praise of glory is a soul that lives in God, that loves Him with a pure and disinterested love, without seeking itself in the sweetness of this love" (no. 43). Next, "A praise of glory is a soul of silence that remains like a lyre under the mysterious touch of the Holy Spirit so that He may draw from it divine harmonies." Employing two more of her favorite images, Elizabeth goes on: "A praise of glory is a soul that gazes on God in faith and simplicity; it is a reflector of all that He is; it is like a bottomless abyss into which He can flow and expand; it is also like a crystal through which He can radiate and contemplate all His perfections and His own splendor."[24] Finally, she says, "a praise of glory is one who is always giving thanks. Each of her actions, her movements, her thoughts, her aspirations, at the same time that they are rooting her more deeply in love, are like an echo of the Eternal Sanctus" (no. 43). She concludes, "In the heaven of her soul, the praise of glory has already begun her work of eternity" (no. 44). So, there is no essential difference between the praise of glory on earth and in heaven, but only in the degree of intensity. This is a key aspect of the message of Elizabeth, as well as of Thérèse of Lisieux, namely, that we can already begin to live the life of heaven here below, if not perfectly.

The Indwelling of the Trinity

As is clear from what was said above, becoming the "praise of glory" is not a human achievement; it is a realization of the action of the Three Persons of the Trinity in the depths of the soul. As befits her name,

Elizabeth of the Trinity is one of the most Trinitarian mystics of the modern period, not in the sense that she contributes to abstract speculation on the mystery of the Three-in-One, but that she lives the inner life of the Trinity and tries to lift the veil (as best she can) on how she has experienced her participation in the Triune God. All Christian mystics are by definition Trinitarian, but some (think of William of Saint-Thierry, Bonaventure, Hadewijch, Eckhart, Ruusbroec, John of the Cross, etc.) feature the Trinity more than others. Elizabeth belongs to this group. Before turning to what she has to say about the Trinity itself, however, it is important to consider her doctrine about the infinity of God.

Divine infinity, or limitlessness, has been a major theme of Christian mysticism since the days of the Fathers. Although some theologians have had little to say about it, the greatest, like Aquinas and Duns Scotus, made God's infinity central to their thinking, as did mystics such as François Fénelon. Elizabeth of the Trinity speaks over and over again about divine infinity in a highly personal way. She also makes use of mystical images, especially of God as ocean, that suggest the mystery of the One who is beyond all boundaries.[25] Hans Urs von Balthasar has seen "Limitlessness" as an essential feature of her thought and expresses the relation among three primary components of Elizabeth's mysticism as follows: "Because limitlessness is a Thou, and the Thou is limitlessness, movement into infinity must be a movement of worship. Predestination is the framework, limitlessness the destination of this movement; adoration its essential content, action, fullness and significance."[26]

Elizabeth does not provide theoretical analyses of what it means to call God infinite, but her frequent references to the infinite show that she experienced God as measureless and unbounded throughout her life. The divine infinity also is the root of another of her favorite images for God, the scriptural witness to God as an all-consuming fire (Deut. 4:24 and Heb. 12:29 are often cited). A few examples of the use of infinity found in her letters are revealing. In L 109 (February 16, 1902) she tells her sister, "Ah! If we could only raise the curtain, what a beautiful horizon we would see on the other side! It is the Infinite, that is why it expands every day."[27] Again to Guite in 1902 (L 117): "Isn't it good to be close to Him? He is my Infinite, in Him I love, and am loved, and have everything. A close and profound union." Union with the Infinite is also expressed in L 133, written to a friend in August 1902: "So she [the soul] *hungers for silence* that she may always listen, penetrate deeper into His Infinite Being. She is identified with Him she loves, she finds

Him everywhere; she sees Him shining through all things." Infinity calls up not only the image of the ocean (see L 129, L 332), but also of the endless desert, another mystical symbol for God as infinite (L 156). Love is also seen as infinite (L 192), and Elizabeth speaks about "infinite adoration" (L 202). Souls can "penetrate the Infinity of God, and there, in that silence and calm where He Himself is, there hear what flows from One to the Other" (L 203). In a late letter (L 298 of July 16, 1906), she picks up on the theme of the double abyss, used by Angela of Foligno, understanding the Psalm text "Abyss calls out to abyss" (Ps. 41:8), as referring to the divine abyss of mercy and the soul's abyss of misery. She tells Guite, "I love to lead you above what dies, into the bosom of Infinite Love."[28]

The Infinite Love and Oneness that is God is also the God who is Trinity. In Letter 332, written shortly before her death to Marthe Weishardt, a former novice of Carmel, Elizabeth compresses a number of her essential themes into a short summary, among them God as "exceeding love," living "in the night of faith," and union with God. Her attention is focused on what is soon to come, "that first meeting with the Divine Beauty." She goes on, "Thus I will flow out into the Infinity of Mystery and contemplate the wonders of the Divine Being. . . . He has united us so closely! Let us hide ourselves in eternal silence, may our simple gaze upon Him separate us from everything and fix us in the unfathomable depths of the mystery of the Three, while we await the Bridegroom's 'Veni.'"[29] Another powerful late text (September 1906) is Poem 115, which the editor entitled "I plunge into the Infinite."[30] The poem begins with the image of the nun's launching her small boat on the "immense ocean bearing me." Then, waves overwhelm "the flimsy skiff," waves that are the torrents of the Trinity. "The Trinity's embrace—opening now! / In this I found my center, deep in the divine abyss. / Not at the water's edge, you'll see me now. / I dare to plunge into the Infinite—my heritage is there. / My soul has its repose in that immensity; / It lives there with 'its Three' as in eternity / . . . . That 'Praise of Glory' may the story's ending tell." To plunge into the infinite ocean of the Divinity is also to be immersed or swallowed up in the three Persons of the Trinity.

It would be easy to cite a host of texts on the Trinity, what Elizabeth called "my Trinity" (L 288), from her relatively sparse writings.[31] All those who have written on the Carmelite have noted this central aspect of her thought.[32] Letter 185, for example, shows the influence of John of the Cross on her doctrine of union with the Three Persons.[33] "Carried away in the "great vision of the Mystery of mysteries," she cites "our blessed Father Saint John of the Cross" (*Spiritual Canticle*, stanza 39.4) about how God leads the saints "to the divine summits where union is made perfect between Him and the soul who has become His bride, in the mystical sense of the word." Here the soul, according to John, enters into the inner life of the Three Persons: "The Holy Spirit raises it to so wonderful a height that He makes it capable of producing in God the same spiration of love that the Father produces in the Son and the Son in the Father, the spiration that is the Holy Spirit Himself!"

Elizabeth's brief "Prayer to the Trinity" ("My God, Whom I Adore," of November 21, 1904), provides a good summary of her Trinitarian teaching.[34] This piece shows that the deeper she penetrated into God as infinity, the more she came to realize that this infinity was the dynamic interaction of Father, Son, and Holy Spirit, as seen in how God's Trinitarian reciprocity gives itself to be shared in by humans. The structure of the "Prayer to the Trinity," which features a host of biblical references, is in five parts. It begins with an invocation to the Trinity: "O my God, Trinity, whom I adore, help me to forget myself entirely that I may be established in You as still and as peaceful as if my soul were already in eternity." Then, perhaps surprisingly, it turns to Christ, not the Father: "O my beloved Christ, crucified by love, I wish to be a bride for Your Heart; I wish to cover You with glory. I wish to love You . . . even unto death." I would suggest that the invocation to Christ is placed here because it is only the God-man who makes the Trinitarian mystery known to us. The third part specifically addresses the Eternal Word who has taken on flesh in Jesus. "O Eternal Word, Word of my God, I want to spend my life in listening to You. . . . Then, through all nights, all voids, all helplessness, I want to gaze on You always and remain always in Your great light." Then, in part 4, Elizabeth turns to the other two divine Persons. First, she addresses the Holy Spirit: "O consuming Fire, Spirit of Love, 'come upon me' (Luke 1:35), and create in my soul a kind of Incarnation of the Word: that I may be another humanity for Him in which He can renew His whole mystery."[35] Here Elizabeth is invoking the Spirit to enable her to serve not just as a worthy *imitation* of Christ, but as a true *co-redeemer*, because of her status as a new manifestation of Christ's human nature. (The boldness of such claims by Elizabeth, and also by Thérèse of Lisieux, have often been toned down by some of their supporters.) At the end of part 4, the Carmelite prays to the Father: "O Father, bend lovingly over Your little creature; 'cover her with Your shadow' (Matt. 17:5), seeing in her only the 'Beloved in whom You are well pleased'" (Matt. 3:17). The prayer concludes in part 5 with another impassioned plea to the Trinity: "O my Three, my All, my Beatitude, infinite Solitude.[36] Immensity in which I lose myself. I surrender myself to You as Your prey. Bury Yourself in me that I may bury myself in You until I depart to contemplate Your light in the abyss of Your greatness."

The appearance of the term *abyss* here, frequent throughout her works,[37] ties the Carmelite mystic to one of the traditional themes of Western mysticism, found in Angela of Foligno, Ruusbroec, and John of the Cross, among others.[38] As noted above, she also uses the theme of the "double abyss" of the unknowable immensity of God and our own emptiness. In Poem 118 ("Who is Like to God") of late September 1906, we read, "Let us cast ourselves into the depth of the 'double abyss' / The immensity of God and our own nothingness, / Our praise of Him then mounts higher, / So that we can render glory to the Lord Omnipotent."[39]

For Elizabeth, the Trinity is not a doctrine to be admired from afar but is a life to be lived, specifically through the indwelling of the Three Persons in the center of the soul. The Carmelite, possibly under the influence of Fr. Vallée, strongly emphasized Trinitarian inhabitation, or what may be more rightly called the "reciprocal indwelling" of the Trinity in the soul and the soul in the Trinity. Writing to Canon Angles two months before her entry into Carmel, she says, "This presence of God is so wonderful! I love to find Him deep within me, in the heaven of my soul, for He never leaves me. God in me, I in him, that is my life! It is wonderful to consider that but for the vision, we already possess Him as the blessed do in heaven. . . . I have a great love for the mystery of the Blessed Trinity. It is an abyss in which I lose myself."[40] During her last illness (June 10, 1906), she sounds a similar note in writing to Germaine de Gemeaux: "Oh! how our soul needs to draw strength in prayer, . . . especially in that intimate heart-to-heart in which the soul flows into God and God flows into it to transform it into Himself. . . . Our souls meet and are 'but one' in the Heart of Jesus, in the Holy Trinity."[41] At the time of her First Communion Elizabeth learned that her name meant "House of God," another manifestation of the indwelling theme (see L 107). She also found the theme of indwelling in the Bible, in texts such as John 14:23, in which Christ says that he and the Father "will come and make our dwelling" in whoever loves him and keeps his word, as well as John 15:9 ("Remain in my love"), and John 17:21, where Jesus prays, "that all may be one, as You, Father, in me, and I in You, and that they may be one in Us."

The Trinity dwells within the depths of the soul, what Elizabeth, following Teresa of Avila and John of the Cross, called "the center of the soul" (*centre de l'âme*). Writing to Madame de Bobet in early 1906, she says, "Oh yes, may the God who is all love be your unchanging dwelling place, your cell, and your cloister in the midst of the world; remember that He dwells in the deepest center of your soul as if in a sanctuary where He wants always to be loved to the point of adoration."[42] The depths/center of the soul is also described as an *abyss* that God hollows out to make his residence. In Letter 190 Elizabeth puts it this way: "I rejoice at spending the day close to my Bridegroom. I have such a hunger for Him. He hollows out abysses in my soul, abysses He alone can fill, and to do that He leads me into deep silence that I never want to leave again."[43] The abyss in the soul is also conceived of as the abyss of humility, as she says in *Heaven in Faith*, no. 37, citing Ruusbroec, "It seems to me that to be plunged into humility is to be plunged into God, for God is the bottom of the abyss. That is why humility, like charity, is always capable of increasing."[44] Elizabeth of the Trinity has no formal anthropology, but she provides an important witness to the action of God in the depths of the soul.

Christology and Pneumatology

All Three Persons of the Trinity are active in the soul, but the Word and the Holy Spirit are sent into the world on the missions that effect salvation. Elizabeth has significant teaching about the nature and effect of these missions.

The Eternal Word comes into history as Jesus Christ, the God-man, whom Elizabeth loves as her Spouse and follows as her model in taking up the cross and suffering. Elizabeth's foundational relation to the Savior and Redeemer is that of predestination. Many observers have noted the importance of predestination in the Carmelite's thought, but we need to note that predestination for Elizabeth is not just an abstract theological teaching but is a lived relation—the Father predestines us to be his children in and through Jesus Christ. Along with Ephesians 1:4–6, Elizabeth's favorite text for God's predestination is Romans 8:29, where Paul says, "Those whom God foreknew he also predestined to be conformed to the image of his Son, in order that he might be the firstborn within a large family." She cites this passage twenty-six times. Elizabeth understands the image to which we are predestined to be conformed to the image of the Crucified One: "Those who march on this way of sorrows are those 'whom He foreknew and predestined to be conformed to the image of His divine Son,' the One crucified by love!"⁴⁵ Predestination, Elizabeth realizes, is not just to make the soul into a reproduction of Christ, but also "to transform and divinize it" (L 231). Predestination is Christological, Passion-centered, and divinizing.

Elizabeth wrote a number of poems for the Feast of Christmas (P 23, 45, 75, 86, 88, 91, 96). These provide a useful starting point for a consideration of her devotion to Jesus.⁴⁶ P 86 hymns God's Son, "the Splendor of the Father," as come down to earth to become Elizabeth's divine Spouse: "God's Son, His Splendor fair, / Incarnate now, this morn / In you. With Mary there / Embrace God, newly-born— / For . . . yours He is!"⁴⁷ P 88 describes the purpose of the Incarnation and Nativity as giving Elizabeth the opportunity to love Christ (*Amo Christum* is the poem's refrain), and even to become a co-redeemer with him: "In me, a house that God is living at, / This Jesus Christ, Divine Adorer there, / Takes me to souls, as to the Father . . . / Co-Savior with me Master, here! / . . . For this I ought to disappear— / I lost in Him, with Him as one."⁴⁸ P 96 also stresses the theme of becoming a co-redeemer because of her intense love of the "little child" who is really the invisible God. "I have lost everything for his love, / And what my soul desires / Is to hold Him more each day. / I wish to know him, / My Christ and my Redeemer, / So that I may conform my whole being / To the image of my Savior."⁴⁹

The love that Elizabeth has for Jesus, as befits a daughter of Teresa of Avila, is essentially a spousal love. In her *Diary* for Good Friday, March 31, 1899, she records how her mother got excited about a possible marriage proposal for her, observing, "Ah, my heart is not at all free; I can no longer dispose of it because I have given it to the King of kings. I hear the voice of My Beloved in the depths of my heart: 'If you follow Me, you will have suffering and the Cross. But also what joys, what sweetness I will make you taste in these tribulations. . . . I want your heart, I love it. I have chosen it for Me. Keep your heart for Me!'"⁵⁰ A good summation of Elizabeth's view of the meaning of being a bride of Christ is found in NI 13 ("Being a Spouse of Christ"), dating from the middle of 1902.⁵¹ Elizabeth understands the relation of the bride and the Divine Bridegroom, as Bernard of Clairvaux had (see *Sermon on Song of Songs* 83), as one of total mutuality: "To be a bride means to be given as He gave Himself; it means to be sacrificed as He was, by Him, for Him. It is Christ making Himself all ours and we becoming 'all His'! To be a bride means to have all rights over His Heart." Being a bride is to be totally focused on love—"to have eyes only for Him, our thoughts haunted by Him, our heart wholly taken over." As a result, the soul enters into all his joys and shares all his sadness. But there is more: "It means to be fruitful, to be a co-redeemer, to bring souls to birth in grace, to multiply the adopted children of the Father, the redeemed of Christ, co-heirs of His glory." Elizabeth's bold claims about sharing in Christ's redemptive activity are again to the fore.[52] Finally, being a bride is both ecstatic and deifying: "To be taken as a bride, a mystical bride, means to have ravished His heart (Sg. of Sgs. 4:9) to the extent that . . . the Word pours Himself out in the soul as in the bosom of the Father with the same ecstasy of infinite love! It is the Father, the Word and the Spirit possessing the soul, deifying it, consuming it in the One by love. It is the marriage, the stable state, because it is the indissoluble union of wills and hearts." Deifying indwelling is not a one-way street from God to human, but an intimate relation in which we are ecstatic to the Word and the Word to us. The theological depth of this teaching amply demonstrates the remarkable penetration of the young Carmelite.

Being a spouse of Christ is being married to the God-man whose life culminates in his suffering and death for the redemption of humanity. As with Thérèse of Lisieux, the need for suffering haunts Elizabeth's writings early and late. Although at times her expressions take on an almost morbid character, the fundamental thing to grasp about her teaching is its Christological nature—our union with Jesus calls on us to share in his sufferings ("to complete what is lacking in Christ's afflictions": Col. 1:24, cited ten times by Elizabeth). A text in her *Journal* (March 31, 1899) says, "O my God, in union with Jesus crucified I offer myself as a victim. . . . I want to live with you [Holy Cross], die with you, according to the example of my Beloved Spouse; yes, I want to live and die crucified!"[53] Again and again in her letters, Elizabeth testifies to her desire to suffer and die with Christ.[54] For example, in Letter 268, written to Madame de Sourdon, she says, "God has made me understand in His light what a treasure suffering is, and we will never understand enough the extent to which He loves us when He gives us trials; the cross is a token of His love!"[55] In Letter 300, written to her mother in the midst of her illness, she tells her not to be sad over her sufferings. "I don't feel worthy of it; think now, to have a share in the sufferings of my crucified Bridegroom, and to go with Him to my passion to be a redemptrix with Him."[56] Again to her mother (September 9, 1906): "The bride belongs to the Bridegroom, and mine has taken me, he wants me to be another humanity for Him in which He can suffer for the glory of His Father, to help the needs of His Church."[57] Later in September, she again writes to her mother: "More and more I am drawn to suffering; this desire almost surpasses the one for Heaven, though that was very strong. Never has God made me understand so well that suffering is the greatest pledge of love He can give to His creature. Oh, you see, with each new suffering I kiss the Cross of my Master." Then she quotes a passage she found in Angela of Foligno, which she often returned to in her late letters. "In speaking of Jesus Christ, one saint wrote: 'Where, then, did He dwell but in suffering?,' and David sang that this suffering was as immense as the sea" (actually Lam. 2:13). She concludes this touching letter by reminding her mother, "I'm keeping a rendez-vous with you in the shadow of the Cross to learn the science of suffering. Your happy daughter."[58] Suffering with Jesus on the cross was a constant in the life of Elizabeth of the Trinity.[59]

Although less often treated, Elizabeth, given her Trinitarian outlook, also has important reflections on the role of the Holy Spirit.[60] The best access to Elizabeth's view of the place of the Holy Spirit comes in her early poem "Pentecost" (P 54, from May 29, 1898).[61] The Holy Spirit is the Spirit of Love, so the poem opens with the invocation: "With your pure and burning flames, / Holy Spirit, deign to enkindle my soul; / Consume it with divine love, / O You whom I invoke each day." The Holy Spirit is the agent of our transformation, so the second stanza addresses, "Spirit of God, brilliant light, / You fill me with your favors, / You inundate me with your sweetness, / Burn, annihilate me completely!"[62] In the third stanza Elizabeth thanks the Spirit for giving her the vocation to interior union with God. Then she asks the Holy Spirit to help her long for the vision of Jesus, who is "my love, my divine Friend." The last stanza emphasizes the Trinitarian aspect: "Holy Spirit, Goodness, supreme Beauty! / O You whom I adore, You whom I love! / Consume with your divine flames, / This body and this heart and this soul! /This bride of the Trinity / Who desires only to do your will!" There is much more that could be said about the Holy Spirit, especially about the seven Gifts, but the basic parameters of Elizabeth's teaching are well expressed in this poem.

Living the Mystical Life

I will treat other aspects of the teaching of Elizabeth under this broad heading and primarily through an analysis of her *Last Retreat* of August 1906, which constitutes her attempt to write down and order her final "spiritual insights" at the request of Mother Germaine.[63] Elizabeth chose the model of a sixteen-day retreat composed of meditations on a host of biblical passages (almost 150), centering on the theme of adoration.[64] This is what it means to be the *laudem gloriae*.[65] Adoration, according to Elizabeth, is rooted in our becoming one with Christ and with the indwelling of the Trinity in the soul. In the course of the sixteen days Elizabeth makes considerable use of the mystical authorities she has been reading, notably Ruusbroec and John of the Cross.[66] Many of the themes we have already considered appear here, but there are other features not yet touched on.

The First Day begins from the perspective of divine predestination and the bride's concentration on Christ alone. "Nescivi," that is, "I no longer knew anything," as the bride in the Song of Songs says (Sg. 6:1), indicates the attitude that "the praise of glory" must adopt in penetrating the divine abyss, that is, knowing nothing but Christ. Elizabeth goes on, "When I am wholly identified with this divine Exemplar, when I have wholly passed into Him and He into me, then I will fulfill my eternal vocation.... I will be the unceasing praise of his glory, Laudem gloriae eius" (no. 1). Mary alone has penetrated into "the depths of the mystery of Christ," but, "[t]his Mother of grace will form my soul so that her living child will be a living, 'striking' image of her first-born, the Son of the Eternal" (no. 2). As a good Carmelite, Elizabeth had great devotion to Mary and her role in salvation history. According to the Litany of Loreto, Mary is the *Janua Caeli* (Gate of Heaven), and this title features prominently in the *Last Retreat* and elsewhere.[67]

The Second Day (nos. 3–5) introduces a number of themes that pervade Elizabeth's writings, especially silence, singleness of eye (i.e., intention), and the necessary role of faith. The Carmelite Rule says, "In silence will your strength be" (Isa. 30:15), and for Elizabeth silence was integral to her life and mysticism, something that can be seen in her Letters (e.g., L 136, 142, 165, etc.). As she says in L 136, "Love silence and prayer, for that is the essence of the Carmelite life."[68] Silence is needed in order to attain singleness of intention: "To keep one's strength for the Lord is to unify one's whole being by means of interior silence, to collect all one's powers to 'employ' them in 'the one work of love,' to have this 'single eye' (Matt. 6:22) which allows the light to enlighten us" (no. 3; see also nos. 21, 26, 27, 39). This is "the one thing necessary" (Luke 10:42), namely (citing Catherine of Siena), that "'the eye of her soul enlightened by faith' recognized her God beneath the veil of His humanity; and in silence, in the unity of her powers, 'She listened to what He told her'" (Luke 10:39) (no. 4). Such a soul "thus simplified and unified, becomes the Throne of the Unchanging One, since 'unity is the throne of the Holy Trinity'" (a quote from Ruusbroec). In her Letters, Elizabeth had defined faith as "the face-to-face in darkness" (e.g., L 165). Like John of the Cross, she always insisted that here below God can only be found in the darkness of faith, a point that comes up often in the *Last Retreat* (nos. 5, 10, 11, 16, 25, 34, 36).

The Third Day (nos. 6–8) concerns predestination and presence. Citing two of her favorite Pauline texts on predestination (Eph. 1:11–12 and 1:4), she concludes (no. 6) that, "in order to fulfill worthily my work of Laudem Gloriae, I must remain 'in the presence of God' through everything'; and that is not all, because the Apostle tells us, 'in charitate,' that is, in God" (citing 1 John 4:16). The practice of remaining in the presence of God is another important spiritual exercise for Elizabeth, both here (nos. 23, 31), in her letters, and in NI 17 ("The Constant Visit of God," in *Oeuvres*, 915–16). She says that she relates all this "to the beautiful virtue of simplicity, of which Ruusbroec says, 'It gives the soul the repose of the abyss.'" The motif of the divine abyss, also found in the letters, appears here and in nos. 21, 43, and 44. In the repose of the abyss, the blessed "contemplate God in the simplicity of His essence," and are transformed from brightness to brightness (2 Cor. 3:18). We can share in this occupation of the blessed when "we cling to God in simple contemplation," something similar to what Adam had before the Fall, so that God can see all his perfections and beauty reflected in the soul "as through a pure and flawless crystal." She goes on, "The soul by the simplicity of the gaze which it fixes on its divine object, finds itself set apart from all that surrounds it, set apart also and above all from itself" (no. 8). Elizabeth does not set out a detailed doctrine of contemplation in the *Last Retreat* (but see also nos. 17 and 43), although she certainly witnesses to the practice of an advanced form of simple contemplation. It should also be noted here that, for Elizabeth as for Thérèse of Lisieux, there is no opposition or tension between contemplation and action. She told Abbé Chevignard, "Don't you find that in action, when we are in Martha's role, the soul can still remain wholly adoring, buried like Magdalene in her contemplation, staying by this source like someone who is starving; this is how I understand the Carmelite's apostolate, as well as the priest's."[69]

The Fourth Day (nos. 9–11) is a further meditation on the role of dark faith. If we want to be open to illumination from God, "we must extinguish every other light," so that the Lamb who reigns in heaven is our only light. This is the "beautiful light of faith," which seems like darkness to us because all our powers must be put into darkness and emptiness (no. 10). The "Praise of Glory" must be like Moses, who was "unshakable in his faith" (Heb. 11:27). When we are absorbed in faith (Heb. 11:1 is cited), we should be indifferent to whether we are in darkness or in light, in enjoyment or not. We are above all God's consolations, "going beyond everything to be united with Him whom we love" (no. 11, again citing Ruusbroec).

The Fifth Day (nos. 12–14) also starts in heaven, citing Apocalypse 7:9, 14–17, about the adoration of the blessed. Elizabeth again wants to show us how we can participate in the celestial worship while still in this life. The souls in heaven have already shared in "the annihilation of Christ" and been transformed and conformed to the image of the Incarnate Word (no. 12). The only way that we can come to partake of this transformation here below is by sharing in Christ's Passion, which allows him "to associate His bride in His work of redemption," expressing the co-redemptrix theme we have seen elsewhere (no. 13).

The Sixth Day of the Retreat (nos. 15–16) also commences in heaven with the citation of Apocalypse 14:1–4, the Lamb standing on Mount Sion being worshiped by throngs of the saved. Elizabeth interprets these souls as models for our own stripping away of all things, natural and supernatural, and our willingness to die daily for Christ (1 Cor. 15:31). This is the "blessed death in God" that enables the soul to cry out, using one of the Carmelite's favorite Pauline texts, "I live now, no longer I, but Christ lives in me" (Gal. 2:20). The Seventh Day (nos. 17–19) commences with another reference to heaven, citing Psalm 18:1 on the heavens telling the glory of God, but now identifies that heaven with the soul awaiting the heavenly Jerusalem. Such a soul, following the Psalm text, "passes on the message from day to day" (Ps. 18:3), that is, obeys all God's decrees, so that "by the depth of its interior gaze [it] contemplates its God through everything in that simplicity which sets it apart from all else" (no. 17). Such a soul also announces the message from "night to night" (Ps. 18:3), which the Carmelite interprets as offering all her faults and sufferings to God mingled with the blood offering of the Savior (no. 18). Finally, Psalm 18:5 with its reference to "tent pitched for the Sun" is read as the soul's emptiness as a fitting receptacle for the divine Bridegroom (no. 19). Elizabeths's personalized mystical reading of scripture is evident here.

The Eighth Day (nos. 22–24), also beginning with the Apocalypse (14:8, 10–11), reprises themes already seen: the depths of God; the abyss of nothingness; adoration and silence. Ruusbroec and John of the Cross are cited. The Ninth Day (nos. 22–24) highlights the theme of deification that had appeared mostly implicitly thus far. Citing Genesis 1:26 on God making humans in his image and likeness, Elizabeth says, "It is always the desire of the Creator to identify and to associate His creature with Himself! St. Peter says, 'that we have been made sharers of the divine nature'" (2 Pet. 1:4) (no. 22). Elizabeth says that this is possible only if we walk in God's presence, that is, journey with God alone in the strength of his right arm (Luke 1:51). This means stripping off the old man (Eph. 4:22), and taking up our cross and following Christ (Matt. 16:24). This is the death proclaimed by the Lord (1 Cor. 15:54), which Elizabeth expresses by having Christ say to her, "O soul, my adopted daughter, look at Me and you will forget yourself; flow entirely into My Being, come and die in Me that I may live in you!" (no. 24).

On the Tenth Day (nos. 25–26) Elizabeth takes the Gospel command, "Be perfect as your heavenly Father is perfect" (Matt. 5:48), to mean that we should live like the Father "in an eternal present." But how is this possible here below? Only by way of being "alone, set apart, stripped of all things" and "destroyed and freed from self-will" (John of the Cross, *Spiritual Canticle*, stanza 40.2). Thus, she can become "a daughter of God, a spouse of Christ, a temple of the Holy Spirit" (no. 25). Such a soul must also be a "great solitary," just as God is "the great solitary." She must live in beautiful interior silence, free from the passions, and be at peace in "the sleep of the powers" (see Teresa, *Life* 16). The total stripping and abandonment of self Elizabeth counsels here is a hallmark of Carmelite mysticism (no. 26). The Eleventh Day (nos. 27–28) continues to develop the theme of inner silence and solitude, where the word of God can be truly heard. It is not enough, however, just to hear the word; "we must also keep it," if we wish to have the Trinity come to dwell in us (no. 28).

The following three days are Christological, that is, they are meditations on how we come to union and even identification with Jesus. The Twelfth Day (nos. 29–31) starts by quoting John 1:14, "The Word was made flesh and dwelt among us." We can ascend to God only by following in the footsteps of the One who descended, the Incarnate Word. Like Paul, we must seek the knowledge of the "mystery which is Christ . . . , the knowledge of the love of Christ Jesus" (Eph. 3:19) (no. 29). No. 30 features a tissue of Pauline quotations on the role of the Redeemer, while no. 31 expresses Elizabeth's total trust in Jesus to overcome her failings and "fill me with Himself," so that she can say, *Mihi vivere Christus est!* ("For me, to live is Christ," Phil. 1:21). The Thirteenth Day (nos. 32–35) is a series of considerations of more Pauline texts on our relation to Christ. These include: (1) What it means "to restore all things in Christ" (Eph. 1:10); and (2) How we are "to walk in Jesus Christ, be rooted in Him, built up in Him, strengthened in faith, growing more and more in Him through thanksgiving" (Col. 2:6–7). Her analysis of these Pauline imperatives takes up nos. 33–35.

Finally, the Fourteenth Day (nos. 36-39) is a summary of Elizabeth's Christological mysticism. She begins once again with her key doctrine of our predestination in Christ "to become the praise of His glory," citing the familiar texts from Ephesians 1. We fulfill this vocation by relying on the "justice that comes from God through faith." Elizabeth says, "What I want is to know Him, to share in His sufferings, to become like Him in His death" (no. 36). In order to have Christ living within us (Phil. 1:21 and Gal. 2:20 are cited), we must be transformed into Jesus Christ, and "study this divine Model so as to identify myself so closely with Him that I may unceasingly reveal Him to the eyes of the Father" (no. 37). Elizabeth says that she must both immolate herself along with Jesus, and also always follow "his decrees, whether exterior or interior." Then, she will become, along with Him, "the great praise of glory to the Father" (no. 38). She must also imitate Christ by going into the hour "of humiliation and of annihilation," that is, the Passion. "And when the hour of abandonment, of desertion, and of anguish comes, the hour that drew from Christ the loud cry, 'Why have You abandoned Me?' (Matt. 27:46)," then she will still remember prayers of consolation, and hopes that "drinking the dregs of 'the cup prepared by the Father' (John 18:11), will find a divine sweetness in its bitterness" (no. 39). It was surely this hope that sustained the Carmelite in her final difficult months.

The final two days of *Last Retreat* are Mariological and Trinitarian. In the Fifteenth Day (nos. 40-41) Elizabeth says that, after Jesus Christ himself, it was only Mary who responded fully to the divine election and gave "great praise of glory to the Holy Trinity." This was because of her perfect inwardness and her total humility (no. 40). "The Queen of Virgins is also the Queen of Martyrs," so we learn from Mary how to suffer along with Christ "in the great work of redemption." When Elizabeth herself will have said her *"consummatum est"* (John 19:30), "it is again she, 'Janua caeli,' who will lead me into the heavenly courts" (no. 41). The Sixteenth Day (nos. 42-44) begins with the nun's longing for these heavenly courts, citing Psalms 41:1-2, 83:3, and 61:2-3. Like Zacchaeus in the Gospel (Luke 19:5), Jesus invites Elizabeth to hurry down so that he can come to her house today. Where is this house? "Into the innermost depths of my being; after having forsaken self, withdrawn from self, been stripped of self, in a word, *without self*" (no. 42). The "house" where the Trinity dwells and has communion with each other and with her "is in living in the bosom of the tranquil Trinity, in my interior abyss, in this 'invincible fortress of holy recollection,' of which St. John of the Cross speaks" (*Spiritual Canticle*, stanza 40.3).

These are the "interior courts," where the soul contemplates God and eventually "dies and flows into Him" (no. 43). The *Last Retreat* concludes (no. 44) with a hymn-like evocation of that "'Spacious place,' of which the Psalmist sings" (Ps. 17:2), which is nothing else but the Trinity itself. The soul rises beyond every joy and pain, beyond even itself, "until it has penetrated *into the interior* of Him whom it loves and who Himself will give it 'the repose of the abyss.'" Here the soul will live like the Trinity itself in an eternal present, "'adoring Him always because of Himself' (Ps. 71:15), and becoming by an always more simple, more unitive gaze, 'the splendor of His glory' (Heb. 1:3), that is, the unceasing praise of glory of His adorable perfections."

These closing lines of the *Last Retreat* demonstrate the center of Elizabeth's message of the *laudem gloriae*, as well as its foundation in a deep integrative reading of the Bible, especially of Paul. The *Last Retreat* is the longest and most developed of all Elizabeth's writings, which is why I thought it was necessary to give it an extended analysis. But I will close by noting something that does not appear in the *Last Retreat*, that is, the way that Elizabeth, like Thérèse of Lisieux, insisted that her mission would continue after her death. Not only would she find in heaven the fullness of her vocation as the "Praise of Glory," but she would also prolong her work as intercessor and co-redeemer for those left behind on earth. This aspect of her life, alluded to often above, is well expressed in one of her last letters (L 335), where she says, "I think that in Heaven my mission will be to draw souls by helping them go out of themselves to cling to God by a wholly simple and loving movement, and to keep them in this great silence within that will allow God to communicate Himself to them and transform them into Himself."[70] Elizabeth of the Trinity is a major witness to the mystical theme of deification.

Notes

1. Philippon, *Spiritual Doctrine*, 161. For titles and publication information of works cited by author or short title, see the bibliography at the end of the chapter.
2. *Journal Lundi 20 févier 1899 (Oeuvres*, 816–17); trans. Philippon, *Spiritual Doctrine*, 9. Elizabeth seems to be using the word *extase* here in a broad sense.
3. Moorcroft, 17–18.
4. The *Poésies* are in *Oeuvres*, 918–1006, and will be abbreviated with P and number.
5. On Fr. Vallée, see C. De Meester, "En quel sens peut-on dire que l'influence du Père Vallée sur Élisabeth de la Trinité a été 'incontestable'?," in Clapier, *Élisabeth de la Trinité*, 165–96.

6. Elizabeth's *Journal* is in *Oeuvres*, 800-889. There is no full English translation to the best of my knowledge.

7. The "Questionnaire" is NI (*Oeuvres*, 903-4; my trans.).

8. See Jean-Michel Grimaud, "Ouvrir les Écritures avec Élisabeth de la Trinité: Les sources pauliniennes et johanniques de sa pensée théologique," in Clapier, *Élisabeth de la Trinité*, 15-52; also Celia Kourie, "Understanding Paul: The Insights of Dom Columba Marmion and Elizabeth of the Trinity," *Studies in Spirituality* 14 (2004): 36-47. Important for Elizabeth's use of scripture is the "Annexe II: Table des Références Bibliques," in *Oeuvres*, 1074-82. For an example of Elizabeth's exegetical skill, see L 239. The letters (L plus a number) are found in *Complete Works*, vol. 2.

9. On Elizabeth's relation to earlier mystics, see the essays on Ruusbroec, Teresa of Avila, John of the Cross, and Thérèse in Clapier, *Élisabeth de la Trinité*, 53-164.

10. *La Ciel dans la Foi* (*Oeuvres*, 90-127); translation, *Heaven in Faith*, in *Complete Works*, 1:85-120.

11. *La Grandeur de Notre Vocation* (*Oeuvres*, 130-39); translation, *The Greatness of Our Vocation*, in *Complete Works*, 1:121-30. Elizabeth wrote no fewer than twenty-six letters to her beloved Framboise over eight years.

12. The *Dernière Retraite* is found in *Oeuvres*, 142-88; translation, *Last Retreat*, in *Complete Works*, 1:131-73.

13. *L'Aisse-Toi Aimer* is in *Oeuvres*, 190-98; translation in *Complete Works*, 1:179-82.

14. The *Poésies* are in *Oeuvres*, 918-1006, and will be abbreviated with P and number. There are translations of twenty poems in Bancroft. In addition, there are some partial translations in De Meester, *Light Love Life*.

15. *Notes Intimes* in *Oeuvres*, 892-916, abbreviated as NI with a number.

16. Not surprisingly, this was one of Elizabeth's favorite texts, being cited twenty-eight times in her writings.

17. Some comparisons will show the importance of the Ephesians text. Elizabeth's favorite Old Testament text is Deuteronomy 4:24 (*Dominus Deus tuus ignis consumens est*, "the Lord your God is a devouring fire" [12x]), although various passages from Psalm 90 are cited fourteen times. What is surprising is that the Song of Songs is used only twelve times. Her favorite Gospel is the Gospel of John (especially John 7:10 [9x]; 13:1 [10x]; 15:9 [10x]; and 17:21-24 [9x]). The Pauline Epistles are her most cited texts, with Romans used 62 times, 1 Corinthians 46x, 2 Corinthians 34x, Galatians 38x, Philippians 32x, Colossians 56x, and Ephesians no fewer than 172x.

18. L191 (*Oeuvres*, 528; trans. *Complete Works*, 2:145).

19. Galatians 2:20 is another favorite Pauline text for Elizabeth, being cited twenty-four times.

20. L 250 (*Oeuvres*, 634-35; trans. *Complete Works*, 2:232-33). See also L 256 and 260.

21. Thérèse of Lisieux used the image of God as an eagle swooping down on her as "his prey" in the *Story of a Soul* (Ms. B; trans., 197-98). Elizabeth employed the image even before her entry into Carmel (e.g., L 41) and returned to it frequently in her Carmelite writings (e.g., P 77, P 83; L 125, L 169, and L 171 (prey of love), and L 270.

22. L 269 (*Oeuvres*, 673-74; trans. *Complete Works*, 2:264-65). The *laudem gloriae* appears in many of Elizabeth's late letters; see L 220, 231, 232, 244, 274, 277, 284, 288, 294, 298, 299, 306, 307, 310, 319, 329, 332, 336, etc.

23. For this text, see *Heaven in Faith*, nos. 41-43 (*Oeuvres*, 125-26; trans. *Complete Works*, 1:111-13).

24. The image of the soul as a crystal is found in many mystics Elizabeth knew well, including Teresa of Avila and John of the Cross. See also L 131, and *Last Retreat*, no. 8.

25. Referring to God as the limitless ocean into which the soul pours itself is a much-used motif in Christian mysticism. See McGinn, "Ocean and Desert." For some uses in Elizabeth, see L 110, 177, 190, 292, 293, and P 115.

26. Balthasar, 438. Balthasar treats each of these themes in detail in sections entitled "Predestination" (385-419), "Limitlessness" (420-37), and "Adoration" (438-62).

27. The quotations in this paragraph are from *Oeuvres*, 391, 403, 421, 548, and 725; trans. *Complete Works*, 2:39, 47, 62, 161, and 305.

28. A number of other letters also mention divine infinity; e.g., L 132, 158, 182, 184, and 164. It is curious that this theme is not emphasized in the four late treatises.

29. *Oeuvres*, 789; trans. *Complete Works*, 2:357.

30. P 115 (*Oeuvres*, 1057-58; trans. Bancroft, 50-52). P 85 also talks about the Infinite.

31. The earliest mention of the Trinity is in P 54. It is also found in P 57, 74, 80, 104, 110, and 115. Among the letters, see especially L 57, 58, 62, 94, 130, 172, 183, 185, 208, 269, 273, 277, 278, 284, and 332. See also *Heaven in Faith*, nos. 2, 14, 27, 31-32, 39, and 41; *Last Retreat*, nos. 1, 2, 5, 21, 25-26, 28, 31, 40, and 43-44.

32. See Philippon, *Spiritual Doctrine*, "Chap. III. The Indwelling of the Blessed Trinity" (46-80); Balthasar, *Two Sisters*, 467-76; and a number of essays in Clapier, *Elisabeth de la Trinité*, especially Jean-Philippe Houdret, "Élisabeth ou l'envahie des Trois: Se devotion pour la Trinité" (241-64); and "Le Mystère trinitaire dans les écrits d'Élisabeth de la Trinité" (265-91).

33. L 185 of November 1903, is in *Oeuvres*, 517-18; trans. *Complete Works*, 2:135-37.

34. The text is NI 15 with extensive notes (*Oeuvres*, 907-13; trans. *Complete Works*, 1:183-91). The prayer uses language and motifs taken from Catherine of Siena's "Prayer to the Trinity" (*Dialogue*, chap. 167; also used in L 115), and Thérèse of Lisieux's "Act of Oblation," 68-69 (see above, 30).

35. This evokes the mystical motif of the Birth of the Word in the soul (see also L 187; P 75, 86, and 91).

36. On the unusual motif of the divine "Solitude," see also *Heaven in Faith*, no. 22; *Last Retreat*, no. 26; and the discussion of Houdret, "Le Mystère trinitaire dans les écrits," 287 n. 20.

37. The abyss motif appears in many letters; see, e.g., L 62, 125, 185, 190, 208, 288, 292 (based on Ruusbroec), 298, and 316. It is also found in the poems, often as the "abyss of Love"; see P 93, 101, 106, 109, and 115. See also *Heaven in Faith*, nos. 3, 7, 11, 21, 22, 31, 32, 35, 36, 37, 40, 43; *Greatness of Our Vocation*, nos. 2, 5; and *Last Retreat*, nos. 1, 7, 21, 43, 44.

38. On the background, see McGinn, "Lost in the Abyss."

39. P 118 (*Oeuvres*, 1060-61; my trans.); see also P 120.

40. L 62 (*Oeuvres*, 312; trans. Philippon, *Spiritual Writings*, 34-35).

41. L 278 (*Oeuvres*, 691; trans. *Complete Works*, 2:278).

42. L 261 (*Oeuvres*, 651; trans. *Complete Works*, 2:246). For more references to the center of the soul, see L 239, 241, 252, 269, 274, etc., See also *Heaven in Faith*, no. 32.

43. L 190 (*Oeuvres*, 526; trans. *Complete Works*, 2:143). See also L 249 and 288.

44. *Oeuvres*, 122; trans. *Complete Works*, 1:109.

45. *Heaven in Faith*, no. 30 (*Oeuvres*, 118; trans., *Complete Works*, 1:107). See also *Last Retreat*, nos. 1, 37, and 41; L 231, 240, 249, 300, 304, 307, 308, 312, 315, 324; and P 93, 105, and 106.

46. One aspect of her Christology that will not be taken up here is her devotion to the soul of Christ, on which see Philippon, *Spiritual Doctrine*, 110-12.

47. P 86 (*Oeuvres*, 1015; trans. Bancroft, 58-59).

48. P 88 (*Oeuvres*, 1018; trans. Bancroft, 64).

49. P 96 (*Oeuvres*, 1034; my trans.).

50. *Journal*, no. 124 (*Oeuvres*, 871; trans. *Light Love Life*, 54). For more on the bridal theme, see, e.g., L 99, 143, 149, 151, 154, 155, 156, 159, 162, 169, 194, 198, 207, 209, 224, 236, 243, 249, 274, 276, 283, 294, 297, 303, 306, 309, 316, 323a, and 332. See also such texts as *Last Retreat*, no. 13.

51. NI 13 is found in *Oeuvres*, 904-6. There is a partial translation in *Light Love Life*, 102, which I have adopted and expanded.

52. On co-redemption in Elizabeth, see Balthasar, 480-82.

53. *Journal 31 Mars* (*Oeuvres*, 872-73; my trans.).

54. See Philippon, *Spiritual Doctrine*, 116-21; Balthasar, 434-37.

55. L 268 (*Oeuvres*, 672; trans. *Complete Works*, 2:263).

56. L 300 (*Oeuvres*, 729-30; trans. *Complete Works*, 2:309).

57. *Oeuvres*, 748; trans. *Complete Works*, 2:325.

58. L 314 (*Oeuvres*, 757-58; trans. *Complete Works*, 2:332-33). Elizabeth cites Angela's saying about Jesus living in suffering also in L 113, 114, 311, 312, 315, and 324.

59. Along with the many references to suffering in the letters (e.g., L 129, 135, 147, 163, 195, 207, 216, 248, 258, 259, 263, 295, 301, 308, 311, 312, 313, 315, 317, 318, 320, 323, 324, 326, 329, 331, etc.), see P 46 and 113.

60. See Philippon, *Spiritual Doctrine*, "Chap. VIII. The Gifts of the Holy Spirit" (154-88); and Balthasar, 472-78.

61. P 54 (*Oeuvres*, 966-67; trans., *Light Love Life*, 54).

62. Elizabeth uses the term "annihilate," dear to many French mystics, a number of times (see, e.g., *Last Retreat*, nos. 12, 13, 39).

63. The English translation (*Complete Works*, 1:141-73) is accompanied by an important "Introduction" by De Meester (131-40).

64. My count of the scriptural citations in the *Last Retreat* is indicative of Elizabeth's general use of the Bible. In the Old Testament, Psalms is the preponderant source (44x), with Genesis, Exodus, Lamentations, Isaiah, Song of Songs, and Hosea appearing a few times. In the New Testament, she cites the following: Matthew (8x), Luke (15x), John (20x), Acts (1x), 1 John (4x), 1 Peter (4x), 2 Peter (1x). James (1x), and the Apocalypse (9x). Paul, as might be expected, is cited often (over 90 times in all): Romans (11x), 1 Corinthians (5x), 2 Corinthians (5x),

Galatians (6x), Ephesians (28x), Philippians (7x), Colossians (16x), 1 Timothy (2x), and Hebrews (11x).

65. *Laudem gloriae* occurs in sixteen of the text's forty-four paragraphs (nos. 1, 6, 7, 8, 9, 10, 14, 19, 20, 25, 35, 36, 38, 40, 42, 44).

66. John of the Cross is cited about seventeen times (nos. 1, 2, 3, 5, 7, 8, 15, 19, 21, 26, 28, 31, and 43), with Ruusbroec being used thirteen times (nos. 1, 3, 4, 5, 7, 10, 20, 21, 25, 28, and 44). Catherine of Siena is mentioned twice (nos. 4, 5), as is Teresa of Avila (nos. 23, 26).

67. For more on the role of Mary, see Philippon, *Spiritual Doctrine*, "Chap. VI. *Janua Caeli*" (122-34).

68. L 136 (*Oeuvres*, 426; trans. *Complete Works*, 2:65).

69. L 158 (*Oeuvres*, 467; trans. *Complete Works*, 2:96). See also L 183. Balthasar stresses this point (428-31, 480).

70. L 335 (*Oeuvres*, 792; trans. *Complete Works*, 2:360).

Bibliography

There is a considerable literature in French on Elizabeth of the Trinity, but I mention only a few items. For an overview of editions and studies, see Conrad De Meester, "Élisabeth de la Trinité (1906-2006): Un siècle d'écritures, d'éditions, de commentaires. Quelques annotations," in *Élisabeth de la Trinité: L'aventure mystique. Sources, expérience théologale, rayonnement*, edited by Jean Clapier, 663-715. Recherches carmélitaines 5. Toulouse: Carmel, 2006.

Sources

French

Elisabeth de la Trinité. *Oeuvres completes*. Edited by Conrad De Meester. Paris: Les Éditions du Cerf, 1996. Over 1,000 pages with excellent introductions and notes.

English

Elizabeth of the Trinity. *The Complete Works*, vol. 1: *General Introduction, Major Spiritual Writings*. Translated by Sr. Aletheia Kane. Washington, DC: ICS, 1984. The Introduction by De Meester is important.

Elizabeth of the Trinity. *The Complete Works*, vol. 2: *Letters from Carmel*. Translated by Anne Englund Nash. Washington, DC: ICS, 1995.

[Volume 3 of *The Complete Works: Diary – Personal Notes – Letters of Her Youth - Poems* appears not to have been published.]

M. M. Philippon, ed. *Sister Elizabeth of the Trinity: Spiritual Writings*. New York: P. J. Kenedy & Sons, 1962. A selection of excerpts, especially from the letters. Includes some passages from the early letters.

Alan Bancroft, trans. *Barb of Fire: Twenty Poems of Blessed Elizabeth of the Trinity and Selected Passages from Blessed Columba Marmion OSB.* Leominster: Gracewing, 2001.

Studies

Balthasar, Hans Urs von. *Two Sisters in the Spirit: Thérèse of Lisieux and Elizabeth of the Trinity.* San Francisco: Ignatius Press, 1992. The best theological account.

Clapier, Jean, ed. *Élisabeth de la Trinité: L'aventure mystique. Sources, expérience théologale, rayonnement.* Recherches carmélitaines 5. Toulouse: Carmel, 2006. A valuable collection of twenty-nine essays.

De Meester, Conrad, and the Carmel of Dijon, eds. *Light Love Life: A Look at a Face and a Heart.* Translated by Sr. Aletheia Kane. Washington, DC: ICS, 1987. A life of Elizabeth in picture and text.

Kourie, Celia. "Understanding Paul: The Insights of Dom Columba Marmion and Elisabeth of the Trinity." *Studies in Spirituality* 14 (2004): 37–47.

McGinn, Bernard. "Lost in the Abyss: The Function of Abyss Language in Medieval Mysticism." *Franciscan Studies* 73 (2014): 273–89.

———. "Ocean and Desert as Symbols of Mystical Absorption in the Christian Tradition." *Journal of Religion* 74 (1994): 155–81.

Moorcroft, Jennifer. *He Is My Heaven: The Life of Elizabeth of the Trinity.* Washington, DC: ICS, 2001. A helpful introduction.

Philippon, M. M. *The Spiritual Doctrine of Sister Elizabeth of the Trinity.* Westminster, MD: Newman Press, 1948. Old and in some ways outdated, but still useful. Includes translations of some important texts.

CHAPTER 4

Pierre Teilhard de Chardin (1881–1955): Pan-Christic Mystical Convergence

Preface

On December 23, 1954, the French Jesuit Pierre de Teilhard de Chardin (1881–1955), living in exile in New York under the orders of the Jesuit General, told his friend and fellow Jesuit Pierre Leroy, "I can tell you that now I am constantly living in the presence of God."[1] Teilhard's last years were difficult, but his deep faith and abiding sense of God's presence did not flag at the end.

Teilhard's thought centered on mystical contact with God, but mysticism for him was not the mysticism of the tradition, much as he respected aspects of it. Teilhard was primarily interested in the cosmic function of mysticism, although he did not reject a role for personal mystical experience. In his essay "My Fundamental Vision," he says, "Mysticism is the need, the science and the art of attaining simultaneously, and each through the other, the universal and the spiritual. To become at the same time, and by the same act, one with the All through release from all multiplicity or material gravity."[2] Mysticism is thus a form of spiritual energy that effects centration and unification (Laird, "Diaphanous Universe," 217). Teilhard often spoke of the "New Mysticism," which would subsume the earlier mysticisms of both "the Way of the East" and "the Way of the West." At times, he talked of a "mysticism of evolution," or a "mysticism of science," and on other occasions he emphasized more Christian terms, such as a "Pan-Christic" mysticism ("Heart of Matter," 47). Above all, he insisted that the coming mysticism would necessarily be rooted in the materiality of the universe, but in a conception of matter as directed toward being subsumed by *esprit* (spirit/mind) on the way to the goal of ultimate convergence he called the "Omega Point." The Omega Point was not an abstraction, but was the center of the forces of personality and consciousness that had already appeared in history in the person of Jesus Christ, who is still present in the universe in the *material* manifestations of bread and wine in the Eucharist. Christ's cosmic universality had yet to be fully realized, but in taking on flesh God had "committed" himself to bringing the process of evolution to its grand fulfillment in the Omega. From one perspective, Teilhard's mysticism appears as a profound realization of the cosmic Christology of Paul (e.g., 1 Cor. 15:28; Col. 1:15–17; 2:10; 3:11; Eph. 1:10, and 21–23; Rom. 8:22–24, texts he often cited); from another, he was sometimes criticized for going beyond Christianity in the direction of some form of pantheism.

Part of the problem in evaluating Teilhard comes from the fact that he disclaimed being a theologian. He was educated in the "hard" sciences, first of all as a geologist and then as a paleontologist. He always spoke of himself as a scientist who was trying to present the "phenomena" he observed. Having rejected the narrow Neoscholasticism of his Jesuit training, Teilhard sometimes had harsh things to say about "theologians," even friends like Henri de Lubac, whom he faulted for not fully embracing his cosmic evolutionary perspective.[3] Nonetheless, Teilhard's writings have important theological implications, which he insisted were founded on scripture, especially the Pauline and Johannine teaching about the Universal Christ. Along with many other interpreters, I think of Teilhard as fundamentally a mystic, that is, someone gifted with a *vision* and committed to pursuing *union with God* as the meaning of life. Teilhard, however, was not a visionary in the sense of a person who claimed to have received special manifestations of Jesus, Mary, or the saints. His vision was an experiential insight into the divine heart of reality, especially material reality giving rise to spirit and consciousness. His sense of "mystical union" is not so much that of an individual's uniting with God, but rather a belief in the convergence of the whole universe of persons with the Divine Omega in a union that unifies, personalizes, and differentiates all at the same time. "Differentiating union" is a leitmotif of Teilhard's thought. The Jesuit's mysticism is hard to compare with other forms. It is also difficult to gauge his knowledge of Christian mystical literature,[4] since he rarely cites sources or appeals to anything more than generic terms like "the mystics."[5] Teilhard's view of mysticism was "scientific" and future-oriented.

Some of the peculiarities of Teilhard's thought are due to temperament. As a geologist, he was concerned with the "deep history" of the billions of years of the universe and the planet, but he had less interest in human history, except in the broadest lines.[6] One of his noted self-descriptions expresses it this way: "I am a pilgrim of the future on my way back from a journey made entirely in the past" (*Letters from a Traveller*, 101). Pierre Leroy said, "He had little interest in the peoples of the earth and their history. What drew him was nature in all its richness and diversity."[7] Writing to his cousin in 1935, Teilhard said, ". . . the past and its discovery had ceased to interest me. The past has revealed to me how the future is to be built, and preoccupation with the future tends to sweep everything else aside" (*Letters from a Traveller*, 207). Later, in a *Journal* entry for 1948, he admitted, ". . . instinctively and against my principles I love Nature more than Man. I love Man only as a natural (cosmic) phenomenon, as an integrated part of Nature."[8]

Life and Writings[9]

Pierre Teilhard de Chardin was born at Sarcenet in the Auvergne region of France on May 1, 1881, the fourth child of eleven of an old family of local gentry. Both his parents were devout, and his father had scientific interests that certainly influenced the young Teilhard. From an early age, Teilhard was fascinated with the sheer "materiality" of objects, like stones and pieces of metal. Beginning in 1892 he was educated by the Jesuits, so it is no surprise that the young man joined the order in 1899. Due to the French anticlerical laws, Teilhard received much of his Jesuit training in England, first on the island of Jersey (1900–1904) and then at the Jesuit theologate at Hastings in Sussex (1908–1912), where he was ordained in 1911. It was during these years that he read Henri Bergson's *Creative Evolution* (1907), a book that confirmed his view that evolution was not just another scientific theory, but was the central law of the modern view of the universe. Between the two periods in England, Teilhard taught at the Jesuit school in Cairo. In all these locations, his passion for geological and paleontological research grew, so that when he returned to Paris he began doctoral studies in these disciplines under the noted scientist Marcellin Boule during 1912–1914.

In 1914, Teilhard was called up to serve in World War I, which turned out to be a decisive event in his life. From 1914 to 1918, he served not as a chaplain but as a stretcher-bearer in order to be closer to the frontline troops. He saw some of the bloodiest fighting of the desperate trench warfare but miraculously escaped unharmed (many Jesuit friends and two of his brothers were killed). What is most astonishing is that it was during the years 1916–1919 that Teilhard began to write some essays (often while sitting in the trenches) that tried to capture his view of the world, in both its cosmic and mystical aspects. Although not published until much later, these sixteen often lyrical pieces express many of the essential features of his thought.[10] Like some others who served at the front, Teilhard experienced the war, despite its horror, as a profound human experience of the vast forces engaged in the evolutionary process, as he recounts in his 1917 essay "Nostalgia for the Front" (*Heart of Matter*, 167–81).

When Teilhard was demobilized, he returned to Paris to gain his doctoral degree with the highest honors in 1922. A brilliant career in French academia seemed in the offing. Alas, it was not to be. His original views, none yet published, were beginning to elicit opposition, first among his fellow Jesuits, and then in Rome, where the authorities still entertained suspicions of anything new as tainted with the "modernism" condemned by Pius X in 1907. (Teilhard always denied that he was in any way a modernist.) His Jesuit superiors decided it would be best to get him out of Paris and the French Catholic intellectual world in which he was becoming famous, so they convinced him to accept an invitation from a fellow Jesuit and paleontologist, Emile Licent, to go to China and help him in his research. On April 1, 1923, Teilhard set sail for China, not knowing that he would spend the better part of the rest of his life there (1923–1946). Although China remained his base, Teilhard traveled widely, returning to Paris a number of times but also visiting Ethiopia, India, Indonesia, Burma, and the United States.[11] During Teilhard's first China trip (1923-1924), an unnamed colleague stole a copy of a private essay he had written on original sin and deleted it to Rome.[12] As a result, the new and conservative Jesuit General ordered him to sign a retraction of his views, which he reluctantly did. He was also forced to give up his teaching in Paris. In June of 1928, he was even ordered to stop all his theological and philosophical work.

Along with World War I, Teilhard's time in China was defining for his life, but in a strange way, because while he learned much about China's geology and paleontology, he was curiously impervious (even hostile) to Chinese culture, history, and religion. It was during the 1920s in China that Teilhard developed the ideas set forth in his wartime writings. While on a paleontological expedition to the Ordos desert near Mongolia in 1927, he reworked his essay "The Priest" (1918) into the striking prose-poem, "The Mass on the World," a Eucharistic meditation on the evolution of the Total Christ. During the same time, he gradually perfected his mystical masterpiece *Le Milieu Divin*. In the midst of the lockdown period of the war between Japan and China, he completed his central philosophical-scientific work, *The Phenomenon of Man* (or *The Human Phenomenon*) during the years 1938-1940. Teilhard held out hope for years to get permission to publish these works, but he was continually rebuffed by the Jesuit and curial authorities.

The often fascinating details of Teilhard's life in China have been well detailed in his many biographies, notably his role in the discovery of *Homo sinanthropus* ("Peking Man") in 1931, which first catapulted him onto the world stage.[13] He also participated in the difficult "Yellow Crossing," an automobile expedition across Asia in 1931-1932. Teilhard's ongoing geological and paleontological discoveries began to give him a worldwide reputation, at least in scientific circles

Teilhard's time in China (largely in Beijing) also reveals an important aspect of his personal life. Teilhard had a number of close male friends, but he said he found it easier to be intimate with women and insisted that a man could not find intellectual and personal fulfillment without a deep relationship to a woman. For him, such relationships were powered by sexual attraction as the human aspect of the powers of aggregation rooted in matter, but in its highest and most potent form the attraction of male and female was not to involve sexual expression, but was intended to sublimate the power of sexuality into the higher evolutionary stage of chastity. Teilhard wrote several essays setting forth his unusual views.[14] His cousin Marguerite was one of his "soulmates" (my word), and there were several other women with whom he was spiritually intimate. In 1929 in Bejing, he met the most potent realization of this relationship in the person of Lucile Swan (1887–1965), a divorced American sculptor. They fell deeply in love.[15] For years they saw each other every day and they exchanged many letters when he was traveling.[16] Lucile became a sounding board for many of his ideas, and she helped him with his writings (how much is unclear). Teilhard conceived of their relationship as an *amour à trois* ("three-way love") in which his love for Lucile and hers for him would lead them both closer to God and to their "real" selves. In one of his letters he says, "Let us converge, you and me, courageously and happily, toward the new face of God which attracts both of us.—For this fascinating task of discovery I *need* you,—and I shall always do my utmost for helping you."[17] Lucile's love, also real and deep, included the desire for physical expression, something that Teilhard, faithful to his vow of chastity, could not give. Lucile thought that Teilhard's position was contradictory, given his stress on the importance of materiality. She once upbraided him, "You will say that you deny only one part of human love but I think you are evading the question, for the physical is not only a very important but an essential part for the race" (Lu, "Love as Energy," 80). Teilhard never really understood this, and some of the things he has to say about sex reflect the negative stereotypes of the Catholicism of his time. This difference put a great stress on their relationship and brought them both much pain. Although they never broke their bond, the relationship was cooler and more distant in Teilhard's last decade.

During the Second World War, Teilhard was cut off from Europe, and letters were sparse. He continued his laboratory work on the numerous specimens he had collected in China. After the war, he was permitted to return to France, where he began to publish scientific articles, give lectures, and receive awards. Teilhard revised *The Phenomenon of Man* and sent it to Rome in hopes of getting permission to publish it. In June of 1947, he suffered a major heart attack, which affected his health for the rest of his life. In 1948 he was invited to come to Rome to discuss his work with the new Jesuit General, Fr. Jean-Baptiste Janssens, but he realized that he would never be allowed to publish and that he would be forbidden to accept the prestigious position he had been offered at the Collège de France. Finally, in 1951 he was allowed to accept a research position in paleontology at the Wenner-Gren Foundation in New York. Although his health was fragile, Teilhard took a number of trips to South Africa to work with the paleontologists whose discoveries of new forms of early man were revolutionizing the field. He was even able to visit France one last time in 1954. Teilhard continued to write bold and original essays down to the end, which came through a sudden stroke on the evening of Easter Sunday, April 10, 1955. He was buried in the Jesuit cemetery at St. Andrews-on-Hudson, far from his beloved Auvergne.

During his lifetime, some of Teilhard's friends had urged him to leave the Jesuits in order to gain more intellectual freedom. His reply, as found in a letter he wrote to Fr. Janssens in 1951, was indicative of his unwavering loyalty: "I fully understand that Rome may have its reasons for believing that in its present form my vision of Christianity is premature and incomplete.... It is on this important point of exterior fidelity and docility that I wish to particularly assure you ... that, despite certain appearances, I am determined to remain 'a child of obedience.'"[18] Teilhard did receive a reward for his "*exterior* fidelity," if in a roundabout way. Not long before his death, he left his extensive writings, many of them already circulating in the *samizdat* form used by Russian political dissidents in the same years, to a non-Jesuit literary executor, Jeanne Montier. Starting in 1957, his works began to appear in French and soon in many other languages. Within a few years Teilhard reading groups, Teilhard societies, Teilhard lectures and courses, as well as a plethora of books and articles, had come on the scene. Despite his growing fame, there was still opposition, as reflected in the fact that in 1962 the Holy Office issued an admonition warning seminary professors of the dangers of his thought and that of his followers. Despite (or because of) the warning, Teilhard continued to be widely read and discussed. Today, almost seventy years since his death, Teilhard appears less well known, but he remains an important presence in the theology and spirituality of the twenty-first century, despite the ultra-traditionalist Catholics who continue to view him as a dangerous figure.

Teilhard's Thought

It would be tempting to try to write only about Teilhard's views on mysticism, but that is impossible. For Teilhard, it is "all one"; that is, his views about evolution and about Christian belief and mysticism are all intertwined. Despite the fragmentation of his writings, there is a comprehensive character to what he wrote—it comes from a central vision. I will try to do some justice to this holism by setting out Teilhard's thought under three categories, though these naturally overlap: (1) Evolution in General; (2) Evolution and Christ; and (3) Evolution and Mysticism.

Evolution in General

Teilhard claimed that his soul felt caught "*between two absolutes*: that of experience (the Universe) and that of Revelation (transcendent God)" (*Heart of Matter*, 207). Nevertheless, these "two stars," or sources, must eventually be coordinated (*Heart of Matter*, 214-15, 218-19).[19] Teilhard is not always very clear about the relation of science and religion. In one place he says that "Science (which means all forms of human activity) and Religion have always been for me one and the same thing" (*Heart of Matter*, 198), but an earlier statement was more nuanced: "Religion and evolution should neither be confused nor divorced" (*Writings in Time of War*, 87). In any case, Teilhard wrote mostly from the perspective of his phenomenological experience of the universe,[20] not from an overtly religious stance. He saw his fundamental vocation as bringing together the modern discovery of evolution with the truths of revelation. Writing to Pierre Leroy in 1954, he said, "By embracing Evolution in order to save it, the Christian message would be incarnated and saved by Evolution" (*Letters from My Friend*, 198).

In *Phenomenon of Man* the Jesuit highlights the essential role that evolution plays in modern thought: "Is evolution a theory, a system or a hypothesis? It is much more: it is the general condition to which all theories, all hypotheses, all systems must bow and which they must satisfy henceforward if they are to be thinkable and true" (*Phenomenon*, 218). Furthermore—and this is what is new and distinctive of Teilhard's view of evolution—the evolutionary imperative embraces both the materiality of the universe (its "without") and its "within," that is, the interior dimension by which matter strives toward consciousness. As he put it toward the end of *Phenomenon*: "To make room for thought in the world, I have needed to 'interiorize' matter: to imagine an energetics of the mind; to conceive a noogenesis rising upstream against the flow of entropy; to provide evolution with a direction, a line of advance and critical points; and finally to make all things double back upon someone" (289). This is where many evolutionary scientists, for whom only matter is real, part company with the Jesuit. On the other side, the notion of the universe as a dynamic process aimed at ever-higher levels of organization, both material and mental/spiritual, was far from the static world of unchanging essences that dominated Catholic theology for centuries. This was the source for the lifelong opposition Teilhard encountered among the Jesuit authorities and in the Roman curia, which still has echoes today.

The Phenomenon of Man was Teilhard's attempt to spell out the details of his new view of evolution. He insisted that the book was not an exercise in metaphysics or theology, but a scientific treatise dealing with the *whole* phenomenon of man (*Phenomenon,* 29). The "phenomenal" approach is basically an attempt to "see," that is, to provide a vision of the nature of man.[21] The book has four parts: *"Pre-Life: Life: Thought—three* events sketching in the past and determining for the future (*Survival*) a single trajectory, the curve of the phenomenon of man" (34). The first part sets out a number of the laws or principles that control the evolutionary process both before and after the appearance of life. Teilhard's argument is that the earth as a physical entity has to contain not only a "without" (i.e., the successive material layers of barysphere, lithosphere, hydrosphere, atmosphere, stratosphere; see *Phenomenon,* 181–83), but also a "within," that is, "a reserve . . . that appears in definite *qualitative* and *quantitative* connections with the developments that science recognizes in the cosmic energy."[22] Thus, he identifies two basic forms of energy: the *tangential* or physical energy, which concerns the "without" of things and necessarily involves entropy, or winding down; and *radial, axial,* or spiritual energy, which concerns the "within" of things, which is the power of *convergence* that on its higher levels is realized in consciousness and eventually in universal love, or "amorization" (*Phenomenon,* 64–66). Teilhard was led to his view on the importance of both the "without" and the "within" and the concomitant two forms of energy by what has been called "the great reversal," or "upward reversal," in his thought that took place gradually during the second decade of the twentieth century. This is reflected in his poetic essay "Cosmic Life" (1916). Here he speaks of his early temptation to immerse himself in sheer matter in a pantheistic way, something that was "reversed" by his growing recognition that life called him to a more difficult and higher path. "Faith in life saved me . . . [that is] the belief *that there is an absolute direction of growth,* to which both our duty and our happiness demand that we should conform."[23] In his later essay "How I Believe" (1934), he also reflected on the reversal, saying, "It was thus that the mirage of nature finally faded from my sight. . . . I witnessed a reversal of the values. The world does not hold together 'from below' but 'from above'" (*Christianity and Evolution,* 113). What this means is that evolution is the process by which the "without" of matter moves "within," becoming interiorized in consciousness in general, then in reflective consciousness (human thought), and finally in the universal consciousness of Omega, understood as "the ultimate center and focus of personality and consciousness" ("Christ the Evolver," 143).

Teilhard's view of evolution is universal and teleological in the sense that it has a direction. That direction follows what Louis Savary has called "the law of attraction-connection-complexity-consciousness," or what Teilhard briefly referred to as "complexity consciousness."[24] The simplest things are *attracted* to each other to form *connections*. These connections gradually grow more *complex* as we move up the scale of being from atoms to molecules to material objects like stones and then on to cells and to the various forms of life.[25] The "law of complexification," as Teilhard called it, governs all the levels of evolution, although its working is more evident in animals than in inanimate things.[26] When living things become complex enough to develop nervous systems and sensation, we are on the way to the emergence of consciousness, which, when it becomes self-reflective, is called thought (*Phenomenon*, "Book Three: Thought," 161-233). This is what Teilhard called "hominization."[27] He admits that most biologists do not agree that life has a direction, that it is going anywhere (*Phenomenon*, 141-43), but his emphasis on the necessary relation between the *without* and the *within* of things, especially with regard to the differentiation of the nervous system in animals, gives him the "Ariadne's thread" that demonstrates that consciousness is, indeed, the goal of evolution ("Ariadne's Thread," *Phenomenon*, 142-46). To be sure, evolutionary progress is not a straight or simple line forward; it takes place by what Teilhard calls "groping," that is, directed chance. Many lines in the evolutionary process do not work out, but the complexity and number of lines eventually find the way forward.[28]

"Complexity consciousness" necessarily involves two other linchpins of Teilhard's understanding of evolution—centration and convergence. In book 1 he says, "In sum, all the rest of this essay will be nothing but the story of the struggle in the universe between the unified *multiple* and the unorganized *multitude*: the full application of the great *Law of complexity and consciousness*: law that itself implies a psychically convergent structure and curvature of the world" (*Phenomenon*, 61). It is not until "Part Four: Survival" (235-98), which treats the development of the noosphere (sphere of thought) toward the Omega Point ("the Prime Mover ahead," 271), that centering and convergence come to the fore.[29] "The universe," says Teilhard, "is a collector and conservator, not of mechanical energy, as we supposed, but of persons." Omega is the "one possible point of definitive emersion—that point at which, under the synthesizing action of personalizing union, the noosphere . . . will collectively reach its point of convergence—at the 'end of the world'" (*Phenomenon*, 272). But what is the "end of the world?" Teilhard later says, "The end of the world: the wholesale internal introversion upon itself of the noosphere, which has simultaneously reached the uttermost limit of its complexity and centrality" (*Phenomenon*, 287). The Jesuit holds that this is "[n]ot an indefinite progress, which is a hypothesis contradicted by the convergent nature of noogenesis, but an ecstasy transcending the dimensions and framework of the material universe" (*Phenomenon*, 289). From the Christian point of view, as Teilhard notes in his theological "Epilogue: The Christian Phenomenon," there is full agreement between the scientific view of the "universe fulfilling itself in a synthesis of centers" and the Pauline teaching about "God, the Center of centers," the final vision of Christian dogma (*Phenomenon*, 294).[30]

The Phenomenon of Man and Teilhard's other writings lay out the stages of evolution. As noted above, Teilhard spoke of layers in the development of the physical world. Far more important were the stages of universal evolution, beginning with physical cosmogenesis, moving upward to biogenesis, then to anthropogenesis, and finally to the noogenesis that would culminate in the Omega. All of these may be said to be expressions of the overall development of "Christogenesis," or even "Theogenesis."[31] As he put it in another context, "Christ is the term of *even the natural* evolution of living being; evolution is holy" (*Writings in Time of War*, 59).

The term "biosphere," the source of "biogenesis," was created in the late nineteenth century, but Teilhard seems to have invented "noosphere" and "noogenesis" in the 1920s on the basis of the Greek *nous*, or mind.[32] The noosphere was one of the great innovations in Teilhard's thought, playing a large role in the *Phenomenon*, as well as in his other late writings.[33] The emergence of man and the noosphere that human self-reflection creates were the core of Teilhard's new understanding of evolution. This is why he gladly adopted Julian Huxley's depiction that "Man . . . is nothing else but evolution become conscious of itself" (*Phenomenon*, 220, 225), and even to assert, "We are evolution" (231). For Teilhard, however, evolution does not come to a screeching halt with the emergence of human beings and the formation of the noosphere. The way forward, that is, horizontal progress by increasing convergence, is also the road upward toward the Total Christ, because human destiny involves both earth and heaven (*Heart of Matter*, 53). In a telling phrase Teilhard says, "Man is not the center of the universe as once we thought in our simplicity, but something much more wonderful—the arrow pointing the way to the final unification of the world in terms of life" (*Phenomenon*, 223).

The final part of *Phenomenon*, prophetic of what Teilhard thought was coming, goes beyond noogenesis by suggesting an emerging level of evolution featuring "the Hyper-Personal" (*Phenomenon*, 254–63), or some kind of "super-mankind," as he put it elsewhere. This is the realm of the triumph of unifying love (*Phenomenon*, 264–67), and the preeminence of the "Omega Point" (*Phenomenon*, 267–72). The "ultra-human," and its "hyper-personalization," remain somewhat vague in Teilhard's thought, as perhaps they must, since they can only be imagined and not yet observed.[34] These terms are obviously connected with what he called in other contexts "the Super-Christ."[35] Such hopes are an integral aspect of Teilhard's universalistic evolutionary perspective but contain problematic and perhaps troubling implications. Can the historical Christ ever be left behind? Teilhard would say no, but does his thought sometimes seem to suggest otherwise?[36]

Evolution and Christ

Even a brief picture of Teilhard's view of evolution makes it clear that, for the French Jesuit, the phenomenological investigation of nature necessarily points the way to the theological truth that Jesus Christ is not only the goal but the meaning of the evolutionary process.[37] Teilhard considered it his vocation to show the inner conformity between modern science and the truths of salvation, *as seen from an evolutionary perspective*. For most of Teilhard's scientific colleagues, this effort was a chimera, while for many of his theological contemporaries, it was a noble hope, but one difficult to achieve. Nonetheless, Teilhard's efforts to show that the Total Christ constitutes the meaning of evolution produced one of the most striking Christologies of the twentieth century.

Teilhard's perspective was scientific and phenomenological, not theological, but theology was bound to creep in to many of his discussions. Several of his essays explicitly address the relation of his evolutionary thought to essential Christian doctrines.[38] Given his outlook, Teilhard was necessarily a strong proponent of the development of doctrine. As he once put it, "truth, even revealed truth, can be preserved only by being continually enlarged" ("Mystical Mileau," 140). Hence, the application of evolution to fundamental Christian doctrines could not but provide new ways of understanding old truths. According to Teilhard, there are four fundamental Christian doctrines—Creation, Fall, Incarnation, and Redemption, which he sees as "universal and cosmic events."[39] These doctrines are all one from the viewpoint of evolution, and can therefore be incorporated into the wider category of "Pleromatization," which he developed out of Saint Paul.[40] For Teilhard, Creation and Fall need to be considered together as part of one evolutionary process. Creation is God's free act and may be understood as the beginning of the process of unification—*creari est uniri* (to be created is to be united).[41] It is also "Creation from nothing" (*creatio ex nihilo*), the unimaginable nothingness of pure dispersion (not a "thing" or substratum).[42] Creation is therefore not a one-time "event" in the past but, as some other Christian thinkers have held, a "continuous Creation" (*creatio continua*), involving what Teilhard called constant "creative transformation."[43] Teilhard's revision of traditional teaching on the Fall, original sin, and the nature of evil is even more challenging, although not without some precedents, such as in John Scottus Eriugena. Basically, the Jesuit rejects the mythic notion of an original Edenic state of paradise, or an imaginary historical Fall of the "First Couple," noting the internal incoherence of such views. In the early 1920s he already put forth the daring view that "original sin expresses, translates, personifies, in an instantaneous and localized act, the perennial and universal law of imperfection which operates in mankind *in virtue* of its being '*in fieri*'" [i.e., "in process"] ("Some Possible Historical Representations of Original Sin," 51). That is to say, the Fall is the condition of continuing dispersal in the universe and in human life—it is a state, not an act. As he put it in a later essay, the Fall "'qualifies' the actual medium in which the totality of our experience develops" ("Christ the Evolver," 149). The implications of this reversal are stunning. Teilhard says that "the intellectual problem" (*not* the individual moral problem) of evil disappears. "In this picture," he continues, "physical suffering and moral transgression are inevitably introduced into the world not because of some deficiency in the creative act but by the very structure of participated being: in other words they are introduced as the *statistically inevitable by-product* of the unification of the multiple" ("Reflections on Original Sin," 196). Teilhard discussed evil and sin in a number of his writings, but even his friend Henri de Lubac thought that his teaching in these areas needed more nuancing and development.[44]

Teilhard's treatment of Incarnation and Redemption is also novel and challenging, though not unexpected. For Teilhard, God's ongoing engagement with the world necessarily implies *incarnatio continua*. God becoming man is not just a "one-off" event, but is (and has been) an active presence throughout the whole course of evolution. For Teilhard, a proper understanding of the Incarnation entails the

Christian transposition of the "fundamental pantheist tendency" in the right direction. "If in his interpretation of the process of the Incarnation," he says, "a Christian adopts an eminently justifiable point of view which rests on organic and physical analogies, then nothing in the world any longer subsists permanently for him apart from the unifying influence of Christ. Throughout the whole range of things Christ is the principle of universal consistence: *'In eo omnia constant'* ('In him all things hold together': Col. 1:17)" ("Pantheism and Christianity," 71). Christ brings together the natural and supernatural centering actions: "The Incarnate Word could not be the supernatural (hyper-physical) center of the universe if he did not function *first* as its physical, natural center. Christ cannot sublimate Creation in God without progressively raising it up by his influence through the successive layers of matter and spirit" (ibid.). Such a realistic view of the mystery of the Incarnation, says Teilhard, has decisive implications for many aspects of Christian belief: the understanding of charity; the obligation of doing everything for God; salvation and damnation; the imitation of Christ; and our understanding of Mass and Communion. This last was to be spelled out in detail in his "Mass on the World." His essay "Suggestions for a New Theology" sets out one of the important implications of his new understanding of the Incarnation—we can no longer think of only two aspects of Christ, the "Man-Jesus" and the "Word-God." No, a third aspect needs to be added to the theandric complex: "the mysterious super-human person constantly underlying the Church's most fundamental institutions and most solemn dogmatic affirmations: He in whom all was created."[45]

The universal and physical understanding of the Incarnation redounds into a changed view of Redemption. Briefly put, the old static view of Redemption had seen it as the attempt to overcome original sin and had therefore emphasized Christ's action as one of expiatory reparation. From the evolutionary perspective in which original sin is the by-product of the process of unification that is being gradually overcome through Christ's universal work of bringing all things together, the outlook shifts. Hence, Teilhard emphasizes a synthesized view of Redemption as involving two poles: the negative aspect of expiatory reparation and a positive one of "reconstruction or re-creation."[46] As he says, "The complete and definitive meaning of Redemption is *no longer only* to expiate: it is to surmount and conquer" ("Christology and Evolution," 85). Teilhard's take on the great mysteries of Christian faith is not entirely new, but has echoes with earlier theologians who advanced a Cosmic Christology. Nevertheless, by inserting these doctrines into the process of evolution, Teilhard changed the standard theological trajectory to give new depth to our understanding of the fundamentals of Christian faith.[47]

The Cosmic Christ and the centrality of Christ's presence in the sacrifice of the Mass are characteristic teachings of Teilhard. Rather than assemble a host of passages, it may be more useful to analyze a few central texts. Teilhard had written about the Cosmic Christ since his days in the trenches in World War I (e.g., "Cosmic Life"; "Christ in the World of Matter"), and especially in his *Le Milieu Divin* of 1927. Two late essays attempt to summarize and clarify his views: "The Heart of Matter" (1950), and his last piece, "The Christic" (1955).

The chapter on "The Heart of Matter" (*Heart of Matter*, 15–79) is a quasi-autobiographical attempt to lay out his life over sixty years, in his words: "to show how, starting from the point at which a spark was first struck, a point that was built into me congenitally, the World gradually caught fire for me, burst into flames; how this happened all *during* my life, and *as a result of my whole life*, until it formed a great luminous mass, lit from within, that surrounded me" (15). This transfiguration was the result of the interplay of three universal circles: the Cosmic, the Human, and the Christic. "The Cosmic, or the Evolutive" circle (16–29) is rooted in the psychological disposition that Teilhard calls "the Sense of Plenitude," or the appetite for "some Unique all-sufficing and necessary reality" (16). The Jesuit recounts how his early concerns with the nature of Matter, Life, and Energy were transformed by reading Bergson's *Creative Evolution* and by his recognition that Matter and Spirit "were no longer two things, but two *states* or aspects of one and the same cosmic Stuff" (26). The second circle is "The Human, or the Convergent" (29–39), the gradual discovery of what Teilhard came to call the "noosphere." Finally, "III. The Christic, or the Centric" (39–61) deals with "the Consistence of the Universe, in the form of Omega Point, that I now hold, concentrated . . . into a single indestructible center, WHICH I CAN LOVE" (39). Teilhard says that, as a Catholic, he already believed in Christ as this universal focal point, although, "I think that my inner [scientific] exploration would have led me to the same spiritual peak" (ibid.). The "spark" that had fallen upon him through his study of evolution, *"was to attain centricity by being amorized*; that spark came to me through my mother: it was through her that it reached me from the current of Christian mysticism and both illuminated and enflamed my childish soul" (41). Teilhard describes the spark in terms of four aspects: "The Heart of Jesus" (40–44), "The Universal Christ" (44–49), "The Divine Milieu" (49–52); and "Towards the Discovery of God" (52–55). He says, "It was the decisive emergence of this 'pan-Christic' mysticism, finally matured in the two great atmospheres of Asia and the War, that was reflected in 1924 and 1927 by *The Mass on the World* and *Le Milieu Divin*" (47). Later, he notes, "Thus I reached the Heart of the universalized Christ coinciding with the heart of amorized Matter" (49). The Cosmic, the Human, and the Christic spheres meet and open up a new domain, the Centric, where the universal operation displays two sides—"the *constructive* and the *destructive*; and when Christ is installed at the Omega Point it is both these two sides that are covered and permeated by a flood of unitive force. In one great surge, Cosmogenesis becomes personalized, both in the things which it adds, which *centrify us for Christ* and the things it subtracts, *which draw us out of our own centers onto him*" (53). Creative union is drawing us toward the *God of the Ahead*, who is one and the same as *the traditional God of the Above*, and the *Ultra-human*, a true *Super-Christ*, in all the radiance of *Super-Charity* (53–55). Teilhard ends the essay with a moving "Prayer to the Ever-Greater Christ" (55–58).[48]

Apparently not quite satisfied with his 1950 essay, Teilhard returned to his Pan-Christic mysticism in "The Christic" of 1955, completed a month before his death. Writing to a friend in February 1955, he was unsure how the piece would work out in comparison with what he had already said, and it is hard to see if anything new is really put forth. The work consists of an "Introduction: The Amorization of the Universe," and a "Conclusion: The Promised Land," with four brief main sections.[49] The "Introduction" returns to Teilhard's theme of vision, his "perception of a *Cosmic Convergence* and a *Christic Emergence*," in which, "I saw the Universe becoming amorized and personalized in the very dynamism of its own evolution" (82–83). He insists, perhaps more than ever, on the properly Catholic character of the amorization process, because it fulfills the "three following characteristics of the incarnate Christian God." These are: "1. Tangibility in the experiential order," in Jesus's historical birth within the process of evolution; "2. Expansibility in the cosmic order," through the operative power of the Resurrection; and "3. . . . assimilative power in the organic order," based on the gathering of all persons into the Body of Christ (89). The "Christified Universe" consists of a double movement—the consummation of the universe by Christ, and the consummation of Christ by the universe (91–94). Teilhard's "vision" of "The Religion of the Future" at the end of his life remains fully orthodox in intention: "As I said before, it is still, and will always be, Christianity: but a 're-born' Christianity, as assured of victory as it was in its infancy" (99). In a poignant conclusion, Teilhard asks himself if he is the only person ever to have seen this wonderful vision, or whether he is "the dupe of a mirage on my own mind." But three "waves of evidence" that sweep up from his inner being counteract that doubt. Teilhard's unflinching inner conviction of the truth of his vision leads him to conclude, "Truth has to appear only once, in one single mind, for it to be impossible for anything ever to prevent it from spreading universally and setting everything ablaze" (102). Teilhard obviously was prepared to be that "one single mind."

Teilhard's Pan-Christic evolution is also Eucharistic—God's physical presence in the sacrament is the sign and the motive source for the unification of all things in the Total Christ. The Jesuit's prose-poem "The Mass on the World" is among his best-known works, a piece so striking that commentary might seem superfluous, but a few reflections may inspire the reader to pick it up again (or even for the first time).[50] As in his early essay "The Priest," written in the trenches of World War I, and now in the vast solitudes of the Ordos desert in 1927, Teilhard found himself without the material realities of bread and wine to consecrate the Body and Blood of Christ in the sacrifice of the Mass. "Since once again, Lord—though this time not in the forests of Aisne but on the steppes of Asia—I have neither bread, nor wine, nor altar, I will raise myself beyond these symbols, up to the pure majesty of the real itself; I, your priest, will make the whole world my altar and on it will offer you all the strivings and sufferings of the world" (19). The work follows the structure of the Mass. "The Offering" (19–21) presents all humanity, with its "labors" (the bread) and its "sap," or sufferings (the wine), to God. The Consecration of the elements of bread and wine into the Body and Blood of Christ is effected by the descent of divine fire in two parts ("Fire over the Earth," 21–23, and "Fire on the Earth," 23–29). "This is my Body" consecrates the springing up and growing of all life, while "This is my Blood" consecrates "every death-force" (23). The consecration of the bread and wine symbolizes, or rather "effects" in the sacramental sense, the two essential forces of evolution—the positive and the negative.

The section on "Fire on the Earth" signifies not only the new humanity but also how "at the touch of the supersubstantial Word the immense host which is the universe is made flesh" (24). The universe is therefore a "diaphany," a veil through which we can see Christ, so Teilhard prays: "Lord Jesus, 'in whom all things subsist,' show Yourself to those who love You as the higher Soul and the physical center of Your creation" (25).[51] The third major action of the Mass, "Communion," follows (29–32). Teilhard reverses the usual polarity about receiving Christ, insisting that the fire of consecration consumes us: "What I must do, when I have taken part with all my energies in the consecration which causes its flames to leap forth, is to consent to the communion which will enable it to find in me the food it has come in the last resort to seek" (29). The "fiery bread" that God offers us is "the seed of all that is to develop in the future," and the wine is the acceptance of the diminutions of suffering and even death, "the *excentration*" necessary to attain full union (30–31). The final section of "The Mass on the World" is entitled "Prayer" (32–37). Here Teilhard, after repeating an old Jesuit prayer for mystical annihilation,[52] creates his own petition to Jesus, the Lord whom "the twofold mystery of this universal consecration and communion" has revealed to him. He hymns the Risen Jesus as both the Sacred Heart (a devotion dear to him) and as the glorious Christ of the Apocalypse (34). Christ is now seen as "the universal *milieu* in which and through which all things live and have their being" (35, echoing Acts 17:28). Teilhard says he now feels that he is "approaching that central point where the heart of the world is caught in the descending radiance of the heart of God" (35–36). Finally, he accepts his vocation as one chosen to proclaim "the innumerable prolongations of Your incarnate Being in the world of matter; I can preach only the mystery of Your flesh, You the Soul shining forth through all that surrounds us" (37).

Evolution and Mysticism

"Mysticism" is a frequent word in Teilhard's vocabulary. For Teilhard, mysticism, as noted above, can be best understood as the cosmic yearning (*erōs*) for the whole, that is, the fundamental force that moves conscious minds toward unification.[53] In one place he speaks of "the sense of the Whole, which is the life-blood of all mysticism" ("How I Believe," 123); in another, he talks about the "fundamental mystical demand" (*Activation of Energy*, 222 n. 3). In the passage cited in the "Introduction" to this volume, Teilhard claimed that mysticism is "the great science and the great art" that synthesizes all human forms of knowing; and in another passage he said, "Without mysticism, there can be no successful religion" (*Toward the Future*, 40). The essay "The Mysticism of Science" (1939) claims that "in the unanimous movement carrying it [the thinking earth] towards new horizons of knowledge, humanity is only supported, and can only be supported, by mysticism."[54] "The Mystical Milieu" (1917) puts it more strongly: "it is for the mystic to carry out the task of taking possession of the world at that point where it escapes from other men and to effect the synthesis. . . . The mystic was looking for the devouring fire which he could identify with the Divine that summons him from all sides: science points it out to him" (*Writings in Time of War*, 129). This essay closes by praising the historical "great mystics," such as St. Francis and Angela of Foligno, for understanding "the full depth of the truth that *Jesus must be loved as a world*" (*Writings in Time of War*, 148). For Teilhard, mystics, both in the tradition and today, are the foremost engines of evolution (Laird, "Diaphanous Universe," 217–25).

Teilhard insists that evolution, at least on the level of the noosphere, must be "mystical." How does this universalized understanding of mysticism relate to previous Catholic conceptions? It seems that Teilhard "de-individualized" without "de-personalizing" previous Christian views,[55] at the same time that he "universalized" mysticism's Christological component in line with his reading of Paul. Just as his view of evolution was new and controversial to many scientists, his position on mysticism was a challenge to twentieth-century theologians.

Teilhard's view of mysticism as evolutionary means that, like the universe, mysticism must continuously evolve.[56] It cannot remain static. The coming "New Mysticism" that Teilhard envisaged was therefore necessary to the very nature of mysticism. There are a number of concomitants of the Jesuit's evolutionary view of mysticism. First, despite his recognition of the role of the "diminishments" inscribed in the process of evolution, Teilhard was fundamentally optimistic. "Everything that happens is adorable," was a phrase he often cited. Second, as Thomas King has noted,[57] Teilhard was primarily a positive, or cataphatic, mystical theologian, although like all mystics he recognized the need for both affirmation and negation in speaking about God. Finally, Teilhard's mysticism fuses the material and the spiritual dimensions in a new way. "Holy Matter" is no longer the enemy of spiritual progress but its engine. Matter will, indeed, become "spiritualized," but for Teilhard materiality is the necessary way to the God who took on *physical* reality in the Incarnation.

If mysticism is the yearning for the whole and the desire for unification, the issue of pantheism emerges, as it did for Teilhard's critics.[58] Does the Jesuit teach, or at least imply, that all things are God and that God is all? Teilhard did not shy away from the word "pantheism." In his early autobiographical paper "My Universe" (1918), he says, "The tendency to pantheism is so universal and persistent that there must be in it a soul (a naturally Christian soul) of truth which calls for 'baptism'" (*Heart of Matter*, 207). To explain the difference between false forms of materialistic pantheism and the good "baptized pantheism" he sometimes spoke of as "Christian pantheism," "spiritual pantheism," or the "pantheism of differentiation," Teilhard wrote an important paper on "Pantheism and Christianity" in 1923 (*Christianity and Evolution*, 56-75). Here the Jesuit is concerned not with distancing Christianity from pantheism, as so many have done, but with narrowing "that gap between pantheism and Christianity by bringing out what one might call the Christian soul of pantheism or the pantheist aspect of Christianity" (56). The "feeling of the importance of the Whole" that is the root of pantheism is natural to humanity and has found expression in poets, philosophers, and mystics throughout history. The magnificent modern revelation about the nature of the universe, according to Teilhard, "has operated on the mystical tendencies to unity and union which are common to mankind of all ages, and has thereby directed a great surge of worship towards the world" (64). The "Passion for the Whole" is the most active part of the "natural mysticism of which Christian mysticism can only be the sublimation and crowning peak" (65). The Christian transposition of the fundamental pantheist tendency takes its clue from St. Paul's picture of the pleroma as the consummation of the universe. This leads to understanding Christ's mystical body in a far more organic and physical way than the customary moral meaning given it by the theologians (67-70). "Without falling back on monism," says Teilhard, "there are, in fact, plenty of ways of conceiving of a 'graduated' type of union for the pleroma . . . , such that, without losing any of their subsistence and personality, the elect would be *physically* incorporated in the organic and 'natural' whole of the consummated Christ" (70). Thus, Christ as the principle of universal consistence (Col. 1:17) fulfills the natural pantheist tendency toward total union. "One single thing is being made" is a perfectly Christian phrase, as long as the one single thing is the Body of Christ in which the individual members are unified in their differentiation. This is the God in whom "we live, and move, and have our being" (Acts 17:28), and of whom Paul spoke in 1 Corinthians 15:28: "God will be all in all."

Teilhard's views on Christian pantheism are based on his thoughts on what he saw as the two essential forms of the spirit that ground the different types of mysticism of the world religions. A key essay for framing his thoughts on the evolution of the forms of mysticism is found in "A Clarification: Reflections on Two Converse Forms of the Spirit" (*Activation of Energy*, 215-27). These two forms are analogous to the isotopes found in modern physics; that is, they are closely related, but still distinguishable, forms of psychic energy. Teilhard claims that a great degree of clarity will be introduced into our interior religious experience if we recognize the distinction between "*two* forms of spirit, ... the spirit of identification, and the spirit of unification; or, if the terms be preferred, the spirit of fusion and the spirit of 'amorization'" (217-18). The yearning for unity, or "cosmic sense," that is at the root of religion and mysticism means that when persons have effected a "deep breakthrough into the domain of religious forces," they invariably feel themselves "drifting towards a mysticism of the monist or pantheist type" (219). Teilhard then argues (rigidly, I think) that there can be *only* two solutions to the issue of "contact of communion with the Whole of the other that surrounds us. . . . The one involves relaxation and expansion, the other tension and concentration" (ibid.). Unity through "relaxation" is the effort "*to become all things and all persons . . .* and is the first gesture of every nascent pantheism" (220). It is achieved through a "de-centration" of the self in the All. Unity through "tension," on the other hand, does not seek a common foundation through "de-centration," but looks for "the form of a universal peak of concentration, which is arrived at through a super-centration of human consciousness" (221). "True union does not fuse: it differentiates and personalizes" (222). These "two isotopes of the spirit," both inexpressible, look much alike, but are in reality very different. Thus, we have a "pantheism of identification, at the opposite pole from love: 'God is all.' And we also have a pantheism of unification, beyond love: 'God all in all'" (223). Teilhard contends that the convergent nature of the universe shows that only the latter form of pantheism is correct. On this basis, the remainder of the essay sets out a typology of mysticism. "*In the eastern* (or Hindu) *quarter*, there is no doubt but that, from the very beginning, the ideal of diffusion and identification has been dominant" (224). *The Marxist quarter* tries to develop the spirit of centration, but fails. Finally, two things must be said about *the Christian quarter*. First, by virtue of its structure, Christianity adheres to a "pantheism of differentiation" with "God finally becoming *all in all* within an atmosphere of pure charity ('*sola caritas*')." Second, however, the "centric and centrifying character of the movement" in Christianity cannot be "considered as having yet been perfectly defined, either in its mystical expression or in its dogmatic formulation" (225). Christianity must jettison its "Aristotelian" and "juridical" conception of the universe to embrace a convergent evolutionary viewpoint that will foster a new "Mysticism of the West." The coming "new mysticism, at once fully human and fully Christian," must reject outworn orientalism and juridical Christianity. Teilhard says it can only emerge "with the help of a new form of psychic energy in which the personalizing depth of love is combined with the totalization of what is most essential and most universal in the heart of the stuff of the cosmos and the cosmic stream—and for this energy we have as yet no *name!*" (227).[59] So, there is an apophatic dimension in Teilhard.

Several of Teilhard's essays discuss the two forms of mysticism under the rubric of the "Road of the East" and the "Road of the West," as well as their role in the coming "New Mysticism."[60] These papers and others raise the question of the Jesuit's attitude to other religions. Frankly, Teilhard's position, despite his praise for elements of Eastern religions (especially Hinduism), is curiously outdated, nonecumenical, even "colonialist." Although Ursula King (*Teilhard de Chardin and Eastern Religions*) has shown that he knew more about Eastern religions than has been commonly thought, I confess to finding Teilhard's thought in this area problematic.[61] Teilhard showed little respect for either Judaism or Islam, considering them evolutionary dead ends.[62] Despite his years in China, he was generally dismissive of Chinese religion and mysticism. It was only with respect to Hinduism and especially Vedanta that Teilhard did some serious reading and expressed admiration. In *Phenomenon of Man* he laments the fact that India did not develop a modern science, but "allowed itself to be drawn into metaphysics, only to become lost there." But he goes on, "India—the region *par excellence* of high philosophic and religious pressures: we can never make too much of our indebtedness to the mystic influences that have come down to each and all of us in the past from this 'anticyclone'" (209). The characteristics of the "Way of the East" and its mysticism, however, are negative: the suppression of multiplicity; seeking the universal essence under all; the relaxation of efforts toward differentiation; and a union of identification without love.[63] Teilhard contrasts this picture with the "Road of the West," which "replaces immersion in a substratum-God, a God of non-tension, by the anticipation of a God who is center and peak, a God who is tension," and is thus able to establish "complete coherence between the various spiritual values which the wisdom of the East found it impossible to reconcile" ("Spiritual Contribution of the Far East," 142). Thus, "love regains its dignity as the supreme spiritual energy, and at the same time the human person has its irreplaceable and incommunicable essence restored" (143). To be sure, "the philosophico-mystical choice" that Teilhard argues for here is not yet *clearly* expressed in the West, but the West is the *necessary* starting point for the confluence of East and West in the dawning "New Mysticism." What are we to make of these vague generalities?

Of course, as Ursula King argues, Teilhard is thinking in terms of "ideal types;" but ideal types are meant to help us understand current and future realities, and I confess to finding Teilhard's ideal types not only unhelpful but counter-productive, because his negative and unnuanced views about other religions and their mysticisms would seem to serve more as an obstacle than as an aid to his hopes for a coming ecumenical New Mysticism.

What will the New Mysticism look like? It is hard to be sure. Teilhard's *tertia via*, or third way, as he expressed it, will be "a communion with God through the earth"; that is, it will embrace both the traditional search for God *and* the concern for the development of the universe, the lack of which Teilhard saw as one of the deficiencies of most Christian mysticism.[64] This latter aspect may well come from the contemporary humanist "Neo-Mysticism" that Teilhard sometimes spoke about. It is harder to see what exactly the contribution of the "Road of the East" may be. It seems to be only an outmoded union of identification. The central role of Christianity, of course, is that it is the religion that already recognizes the "unity of convergence" in Christ (Paul's *plērōma*), divinization by sublimation, and the centrality of love and the person. In his "Suggestions for a New Theology," Teilhard centered his remarks about the coming mysticism on the theme of the love of evolution, something he seemed to think could not come from the "Road of the East."[65]

The essence of Teilhard's view of mysticism is found in his *Le Milieu Divin*, a book remarkable for its succinctness and depth.[66] Writing to his cousin in November 1926, he said, "I have finally decided to write my book on the spiritual life. I mean to put down as simply as possible the sort of ascetical and mystical teaching that I have been living and preaching so long. I call it *Le Milieu Divin*.... I want to write it slowly, quietly—living it and meditating on it like a prayer" (*Letters from a Traveller*, 133-34). Later, writing to a friend, he said, "*Le Milieu Divin* is precisely me" (de Lubac, *Religion of Teilhard*, 27). I will give a brief analysis of the work noting three important mystical themes: the role of action and suffering; the need for both attachment and detachment; and union with Christ. The "divine milieu" signifies not only the context of life but the very "atmosphere" of all living. It is "the vision . . . of Christ as the *All-in-everything*; of the universe moved and com-penetrated by God in the totality of its evolution" (*Milieu*, 153). It is not exactly God, but is rather the interpenetration of the human and the Divine in the process of Christogenesis (Laird, "Diaphanous Universe," 217, 234). Teilhard says he wrote the book not so much for believers as for "waverers" in order to show them that "the most traditional Christianity . . . can be interpreted so as to embrace all that is best in the aspirations of our times" (11). These waverers are those moderns who wonder if the Christ of the Gospels is becoming lost in our new and expanding view of the universe. The book is not a formal treatise, but what he calls "a simple *description* of a *psychological evolution* observed *over a specified interval*" (12). Like so much of Teilhard's writing, it is "a way of teaching how to see" (15; also 29, 123), that is, to discern "the true God, the Christian God," throughout the diaphanous universe.[67]

At the end of his brief "Introduction," Teilhard sets out the rationale for the structure of the work: "Since in the field of experience each man's existence can be properly divided into two parts—what he does and what he undergoes—we shall consider these two parts in turn: the active and the passive." Having investigated "the two halves of our lives, . . . it will remain for us to make an inventory of the wonderful properties of this *milieu* which is all around us" (16). Hence the three sections: "Part One: The Divinization of Our Activities" (19-47); "Part Two: The Divinization of Our Passivities" (49-95); and "Part Three: The Divine *Milieu*" (97-143). There is also a brief "Epilogue: In Expectation of the Parousia" (145-53).

In part 1, Teilhard treats our activities, which may be of growth (i.e., development) or of diminishment, that is, disordered activities or sins. His primary concern is with the former, that is, the traditional doctrine of the sanctification of action. Teilhard rejects the view that human action has no value apart from the intention that directs it (23-27). Rather, he advances a syllogistic argument to prove that all good human endeavor cooperates to complete the world in Christ.[68] Hence, salvation/divinization is found in uniting love of God and love for the world: "Now we unite ourselves with Him in the shared love of the end for which we are working; and the crowning marvel is that, with the possession of this end, we have the utter joy of discovering His presence once again" (35). This is the divine plan for the universe: "By virtue of the Creation, and still more, of the Incarnation, *nothing* here below is *profane* for those who know how to see" (38). The Incarnate God did not come to diminish our vocation to the fashioning of ourselves through dedicated action (43). Nonetheless, Teilhard is aware that a debilitating fixation on one's own actions can sidetrack their real purpose. Hence, part 1 ends with a section on "Detachment through Action" (44-47), arguing that the Christian believes, "It is God and God alone whom he pursues through the reality of created things," so that he "is at once the most attached and the most detached of men"

(46). Here Teilhard picks up on a key mystical theme of the tradition—the need to be detached *from our own desires and possessiveness*, while being totally attached to God and God's love for the world.[69]

Part 2, "The Divinization of Our Passivities," shows the Jesuit's awareness of the importance of ascetical practice and mystical emptying in Christian tradition (see John of the Cross). Since the believer knows that in the final act that will unite him or her to God there is an utter disproportion between the two terms of the union, he recognizes that "he has to receive rather than give," that is, "he . . . must lose himself in God" (51). Although we tend to focus more on our activities, "in the reality of things the passive is immeasurably the wider and deeper part" (52). Or, as Teilhard put it, "We undergo life as much as we undergo death, if not more" (54). There are two kinds of passivities: the passivities of growth, by which even favorable forces inevitably have some negative consequences; and the passivities of diminishment, which may be either *internal* (e.g., natural failings, intellectual and moral weaknesses, etc.), or *external*, such as disease, defeat, illness, and death. Teilhard describes the two forms of passivities as "The Two Hands of God," and provides a detailed analysis of the passivities of diminishment (58-74). In this section death, a major preoccupation of Teilhard's thought, is emphasized: "Death is the sum and consummation of all our diminishments," an evil both physical and moral (61).[70] Nevertheless, "We must overcome death by finding God in it," which we can do by recognizing that Christ has conquered death. "The function of death," says Teilhard, "is to provide the necessary entrance into our inmost selves. . . . It will put us into the state organically needed if the divine fire is to descend upon us" (69). Hence, in the moving prayer that ends this section, "Communion through diminishment" (69-70), Teilhard summarizes his final hope with the words: "*Teach me* to treat my death as an act of communion."

As a conclusion to parts 1 and 2 of *Le Milieu Divin*, Teilhard adds remarks on three themes under the heading, "Some General Remarks on Christian Asceticism." Two of these are traditional: "Attachment and Detachment" (77-84), and "The Meaning of the Cross" (84-89). In "Attachment and Detachment," he returns to the theme of union as the goal: "Your essential duty and desire is to be united to God. But in order to be united, you must first of all *be*–be yourself as completely as possible" (78). Teilhard was able to absorb important aspects of Christian mysticism, while also recasting them in a new light. The final section is pure Teilhard: "The Spiritual Power of Matter" (89-95), a title scarcely conceivable before him. "Matter," according to Teilhard, "is the common, universal, tangible setting, infinitely shifting and varied in which we live." It has both a negative and a positive polarity, so we must pray to Christ to help us transform the negative aspect in order to embrace the positive: "Teach us, Lord, how to contemplate the sphinx without succumbing to its spell.... By virtue of Your suffering Incarnation disclose to us, and then teach us to harness jealously for You, the spiritual power of matter" (90).

The final part of the book brings together many threads already seen. Here Teilhard reprises his teaching on the nature of *Le Milieu Divin* and the Christocentric and eucharistic dimensions of our final union with God. There are three sections. The first deals with "The Attributes of the *Milieu Divin*" (100–109). Teilhard says that the divine *milieu*, characterized by a series of *coincidentia oppositorum*, is the way in which "God reveals Himself everywhere, beneath our groping efforts, *as a universal milieu*, only because He is the *ultimate point* upon which all realities converge" (101). God is the center who fills the whole sphere. Teilhard invites his readers "to leave the surface, and, without leaving the world, [to] plunge into God. There, and from there, we shall hold all things and have command of all things" (103). The mystic who makes this plunge will avoid "the reefs on which mystical ardor has often foundered," namely, pantheism, illuminism, and paganism (103–7). "Christianity alone saves ... the essential aspiration of all mysticism: *to be united* (that is to become the other) *while remaining oneself*" (104; see also 108). Christian mysticism unites all the forces of the soul into "an inexpressible and unique inward attitude, ... a permanent and lucid intoxication" that could be called "passionate indifference" (a phrase Eckhart would have liked). "To reach these priceless layers," Teilhard concludes, "is to experience, with equal truth, that one has need of everything, and that one has need of nothing" (109).

The second section (110–18) concerns the identification of the divine *milieu* with the "Universal Christ and Great Communion." Teilhard begins, "Let us examine step by step how we can validate to ourselves this prodigious identification of the Son of Man and the divine *milieu*" (111). Four steps show how the active center, the living link, and the organizing soul of the pleroma must be "Christ dead and risen *qui replet omnia, in quo omnia constant*" (111–12). Hence, the divine *milieu* is the omnipresence that assimilates us into the Body of Christ. "As a consequence of the Incarnation, the divine immensity has transformed itself for us into *the omnipresence of christification*" (112). Teilhard sees his "realist" notion of the Mystical Body as realized in the "great sacramental operation" of the Mass and Communion that is actually one single event that has been developing throughout history (113–15). The section closes with a long prayer (115–18) that begins with Eucharistic devotion and proceeds to a plea to be absorbed in the adoration of Jesus as Pantocrator.

The lengthy third section (118–43) is entitled "The Growth of the Divine *Milieu*." Here Teilhard describes the coming of the divine *milieu* (119–32), individual progress in the divine *milieu* (123–33), and collective progress in the divine *milieu* (133–47). In this final section on the communion of saints and charity, the theme of divinization becomes strong. Each person constitutes "a particular center" (134) for "the divinization of the whole world" (135). At the very end, Teilhard clarifies by saying, "To divinize does not mean to destroy, but to sur-create."[71] The divinization contained in love of neighbor is the engine of the fullest mystical union, the union of all humans in the One Christ. Hence, divinization is just another way of expressing the "union that differentiates" (Laird, "Diaphanous Universe, 226–28). As Teilhard puts it, "One single operation is taking place: the annexation to Christ of his chosen; one single thing is being made: the Mystical Body of Christ. . . . In a real sense, only one man will be saved: Christ, the head and living summary of humanity. . . . In heaven we shall contemplate God, but, as it were, through the eyes of Christ" (136). Thus, "Christian charity . . . is nothing less than the more or less conscious cohesion of souls engendered by their communal convergence *In Christo Jesu*" (137). Put in another way, "The only subject ultimately capable of mystical transfiguration is the whole group of mankind forming a single body and a single soul in charity" (138).[72]

Conclusion

Le Milieu Divin expresses the grandeur of the Jesuit's mystical vision more than any other work. Of course, Teilhard was rarely comfortable with any single expression of his thought, but constantly returned to his basic insights to refine and examine them from new perspectives. His thinking was always evolving. I have laid emphasis on the newness of Teilhard's view of mysticism. Nevertheless, there is much that tied the Jesuit to the two thousand years of the story of Christian mysticism. In closing, I would like to lift up two central points of connection with tradition. First, Teilhard was one of the greatest Christological mystics, a true successor (if in a different key) to his French predecessor, Cardinal Bérulle (d. 1629). Many readers may think of Teilhard as a supreme intellectual, a great scientific thinker, which he was. But for Teilhard, it was the power of love that was the engine of evolution and our coming ultimate unification in Christ. Mysticism, and indeed all human history, was the "history of universal love."[73]

Notes

1. Leroy, *Letters from My Friend*, 209. For full titles and publication information for works cited by author or short title, see the bibliography at the end of the chapter.

2. Teilhard de Chardin, "3. Mysticism," in "My Fundamental Vision" (*Toward the Future*, 199–205; quotation from 199). See also his definition of mysticism in "My Intellectual Position": "The whole of Evolution being reduced to a process of union (communion) with God, [whereby] it becomes, in its totality, loving and lovable in the innermost and most ultimate of its developments" (*Heart of Matter*, 144).

3. The criticism of de Lubac is in a letter to Jeanne Montier cited in T. M. King, *Teilhard's Mass*, 133. See also the May 1953 letter to Leroy about the "Roman" theologians, of whom he exclaims, "I'm completely done with Theologians!" (*Letters from My Friend*, 172).

4. Teilhard did have some knowledge of Origen; see Lyons, *Cosmic Christ*. He also mentions Gregory of Nyssa, Augustine, Francis, Angela of Foligno, and Teresa, but only in passing.

5. Teilhard certainly read mystics like John of the Cross and Eckhart, but also criticized them for confusing the two forms of union, unity through relaxation and unity through tension (*Activation of Energy*, 225). Teilhard knew some modern theorists of mysticism, including his fellow Jesuit, Joseph Maréchal. Nevertheless, I find little evidence that this reading had much effect on his view of mysticism.

6. See *Phenomenon of Man*, book 3, chapter 2, where only a few pages (202–11) deal with the broad picture of the evolution of human societies.

7. Leroy, "The Man," in *Letters from a Traveller*, 23.

8. Quoted in Nicole Schmitz-Moormann, "Aspects of Teilhard's Legacy," in Salmon and Farina, *Legacy of Pierre Teilhard de Chardin*, 117.

9. There are many biographies. The richest source of information is Claude Cuénot, *Teilhard de Chardin*. For a sketch, see John Grim and Mary Evelyn Tucker, "Teilhard de Chardin: A Short Biography," in Fabel and St. John, *Teilhard in the 21st Century*, 15–25.

10. The essays are collected in *Writings in Time of War*. In addition, Teilhard's letters from the war period, mostly written to his cousin and deep spiritual friend Marguerite Teillhard-Chambon (1880–1959), provide insights into his thinking in this period; see *Making of a Mind*.

11. Teilhard's travels and his observations on what he saw are set out in *Letters from a Traveller*.

12. This essay is "A Note on Some Possible Historical Representations of Original Sin," in *Christianity and Evolution*, 45–55.

13. See Aczel, *Jesuit and the Skull*.

14. Teilhard's writings on the feminine and chastity include a strong Marian component; see the prose poem, "The Eternal Feminine" (1918), in *Writings in*

Time of War, 191–202; and "The Evolution of Chastity" (1934), in *Toward the Future*, 60–87. For a study, see de Lubac, *The Eternal Feminine*. I will not take up this aspect of his thought here.

15. There are several studies: Ursula King, "The Letters of Teilhard de Chardin and Lucile Swan: A Personal Interpretation," in Fabel and St. John, *Teilhard de Chardin in the 21st Century*, 44–56; and Bosco Lu, "Love as Energy according to Teilhard de Chardin," *Fu Jen International Religious Studies* 1 (2007): 63–90.

16. See Thomas M. King and Mary Wood Gilbert, eds., *The Letters of Teilhard de Chardin and Lucile Swan* (Washington, DC: Georgetown University Press, 1993).

17. Cited in Lu, "Love as Energy," 78 n. 61.

18. Leroy, *Letters from My Friend*, 106.

19. On the "two stars," see T. King, *Teilhard's Mysticism of Knowing*, 62–65 and 124–27.

20. Teilhard's appeals to "phenomenology" are to general scientific observation, not to the special phenomenological philosophy pioneered by Edmund Husserl and his followers.

21. On *Phenomenon* as an exercise in "seeing," not abstract knowing, see T. King, *Teilhard's Mysticism of Knowing*, 43–48.

22. *Phenomenon*, book 1, chapter 2, "The Within of Things" (53–66; quotation from 54). Book 1, chapter 3, "The Earth in Its Early Stages" (67–74) deals with both the "without" and the "within."

23. "Cosmic Life," in *Writings in Time of War*, 14–71; quotation from 31–32. On the importance of the reversal to Teilhard's thought, see de Lubac, *Religion of Teilhard*, chapter 15; T. King, *Teilhard's Mysticism of Knowing*, 7–20 and 29–30; and Egan, "Pierre Teilhard de Chardin," 265–66.

24. Savary, *Teilhard de Chardin: The Divine Milieu Explained*, 29–33 and 43.

25. *Phenomenon*, "Book Two: Life" (75–160) discusses this in detail.

26. On the "law of complexification," see *Phenomenon*, 43, 48, 61, 64, 66, 87, 300–301, and 306–8.

27. *Phenomenon*, 180: "Hominization can be accepted in the first place as the individual and instantaneous leap from instinct to thought, but it is also, in a wider sense, the progressive phyletic spiritualization in human civilization of all the forces contained in the animal world."

28. *Phenomenon*, 280: "If life has been able to advance, it is because, by ceaseless groping, it has successively found the points of least resistance at which reality yields to its thrust."

29. On Omega in the *Phenomenon*, see especially "The Attributes of the Omega Point" (267–73), which discusses four attributes: autonomy, actuality, irreducibility, and transcendence.

30. Some might object that Teilhard is making the Pauline notion of Christ as center the term and goal of a purely "natural" evolution. In 1942, Teilhard took up this issue in his essay "Christ the Evolver," where he suggests that the Omega Point of science and the centrality of the revealed Christ coincide *materially* but maintain some *formal* distinction (*Christianity and Evolution*, 144–48).

31. See de Lubac, *Religion of Teilhard*, 226–38, for a summary.

32. On the background, see U. King, *Teilhard de Chardin and Eastern Religions*, 388–92.

33. For some key passages on the noosphere, see *Phenomenon*, 181-83, 214, 285-88, and 297.

34. The use of these terms is found throughout Teilhard's writings; see, e.g., the early "Cosmic Life," in *Writings in Time of War*, 38, 44, 46; and the late *Heart of Matter*, 55.

35. The expression "Super-Christ" is found in *Heart of Matter*, 55, where it is followed by the "Prayer to the Ever-Greater Christ" (55-58).

36. See, for example, de Lubac's reflections on some of Teilhard's passages on Christogenesis, whose intention he finds acceptable but which he also describes as "expressed with insufficient care" (*Religion of Teilhard*, 65-66, 105, 161, 202-3, etc.).

37. Much has been written about Teilhard's Christology. One of the best surveys is Christopher Mooney, *Teilhard de Chardin and the Mystery of Christ*. For a brief account, see Egan, "Pierre Teilhard de Chardin," 284-90, and 295-97.

38. See especially the following essays in *Christianity and Evolution*: "A Note on Some Possible Historical Representations of Original Sin" (45-52); "Christology and Evolution" (76-95); "Christ the Evolver" (138-50); "Introduction to the Christian Life" (151-72); and "Christianity and Evolution: Suggestions for a New Theology" (173-86).

39. On the four basic doctrines, see "A Note on Some Possible Historical Representations of Original Sin," 53-54; and "Christianity and Evolution," 182-83.

40. Paul refers to the *pleroma* in a number of texts, e.g., Eph. 1:23, 3:14, 4:10 and 13; Col. 1:19 and 2:9.

41. In some places (e.g., *Christianity and Evolution*, 178) Teilhard talks about developing a metaphysics of *unire* rather than *esse* (*esse = plus plura unire*).

42. On Creation in Teilhard, see "Christology and Evolution," 82-86; and "Introduction to the Christian Life," 153-57. There is a discussion in de Lubac, *Religion of Teilhard*, 195-200.

43. Teilhard argued this as early as 1920 in his essay "On the Notion of Creative Transformation," *Evolution and Christianity*, 21-24.

44. On evil, see, e.g., *Le Milieu Divin*, 45-68; *Phenomenon of Man*, 311-13; "The Spiritual Energy of Suffering" (*Activation of Energy*, 247-49); and "How I Believe," 31-32. For de Lubac's judgment, see *Teilhard de Chardin: The Man and His Meaning*, 103-5.

45. "Christianity and Evolution," 179-80. Teilhard surely does not mean that the third aspect is a new "person," despite his unclear language—the Total Christ is a neglected aspect of the *one* person who is both God and man.

46. "Christ the Evolver," 144-47; and "Christology and Evolution," 79-86.

47. Several of the essays in *Christianity and Evolution* spell out in more detail how the new evolutionary view allows deeper understanding of the articles of belief, especially the "Introduction to Christian Life," which discusses the Trinity, the Divinity of the Historic Christ, Miracles, Original Sin and Redemption, Hell, the Eucharist, Catholicism and Christianity, and Christian Holiness. The brief treatment of the Trinity here ("Introduction," 157-58) is one of the Jesuit's few considerations of the Trinity—a rather significant lacuna.

48. Teilhard does not really end here, but he tacks on a "Conclusion. *The Feminine, or Unitive*" (58-61) and then an "Appendix" (61-91) consisting of some of his early writings from World War I.

49. "The Christic" is found in *Heart of Matter*, 80–102. The four sections are: The Convergence of the Universe; The Emergence of Christ; The Christified Universe; and The Religion of Tomorrow.

50. "The Mass on the World" is in the *Hymn of the Universe*, 17–37. There is a commentary in T. King, *Teilhard's Mass*.

51. In this section Teilhard mentions a theme that recurs in his writings, that is, how the Catholic vision of the Total Christ both absorbs and corrects three mistaken views of the universe: the absorption of the monist/pantheist; the tangible divinity of the pagan; and the uncontrolled "mystical impulsions" of the quietists (26–27).

52. Teilhard repeats this prayer several times in his writings. His other uses of annihilation show he took the term in a moral sense—the cancelling of the selfish ego (see *Le Milieu Divin*, 82 n. 1, 118; and T. King, *Teilhard's Mass*, 116–19).

53. Henri de Lubac (*Religion of Teilhard*, 84–88) identifies the two poles of his friend's view of mysticism as the "sense of Plenitude" and the "sense of Unity." T. King (*Teilhard's Mysticism of Knowing*, 4–7) founds Teilhard's mysticism in his notion of the "Cosmic Sense."

54. "The Mysticism of Science" (*Human Energy*, 163–81; quotation from 165). This somewhat neglected essay sketches the history of research and science as a progression of forms of mysticism, culminating in the present contrast between the materialist "religion of science" without love and Christianity as the "exemplary [loving] form of the religion of science" (180).

55. On the distinction between individuality which disperses and personality which converges, see *Phenomenon of Man*, 263.

56. U. King, *Teilhard de Chardin and Eastern Religions*, 11–12, 111, 204–6.

57. T. King, *Teilhard's Mysticism of Knowing*, 6–7.

58. Pantheism is a modern term, first used around 1700 by the English deist John Tolland. A number of Teilhard interpreters have wondered why he did not use "panentheism" ("God being *in* all things"), a word invented in the early nineteenth century, but Teilhard appears not to have known the word. On Teilhard and pantheism, see de Lubac, *Religion of Teilhard*, 154–60.

59. A number of other essays treat of the two forms of mysticism; see, e.g., "Some Notes on the Mystical Sense" (*Toward the Future*, 209–11). See U. King, *Teilhard de Chardin and Eastern Religions*, 211–15.

60. See "The Road of the West: To a New Mysticism"; and "The Spiritual Contribution of the Far East: Some Personal Reflections," both in *Toward the Future*, 40–59, and 134–77.

61. For a critique, see Egan, "Pierre Teilhard de Chardin," 277–84.

62. See the stunning rejection of Islam and Judaism in "How I Believe" (*Christianity and Evolution*, 121 n. 8).

63. "Road of the West," 42–45; and "Spiritual Contribution of the Far East," 134–41, which discusses India, China, and Japan.

64. Teilhard distinguished three mystical ways: the first way of "communion with earth"; the second of "communion with God"; and the New Mysticism of "communion with God through the earth." See the texts and discussion in U. King, *Teilhard de Chardin and Eastern Religions*, 213–21.

65. "A New Mystical Orientation: The Love of Evolution," *Christianity and Evolution*, 183–86.

66. On the nature of the book, see de Lubac, *Religion of Teilhard de Chardin*, chapter 3 (20–27). There is a commentary by Savary, *The Divine Milieu Explained*.

67. Teilhard's emphasis here and elsewhere on the importance of seeing and perception implies a theory of contemplation, which, however, he did not make explicit (Laird, "Diaphanous Universe," 228–33).

68. The syllogism is set out on 27, and developed on 27–34

69. Teilhard treats detachment not only in 44–47, but also in 77–84, 108, and 132. See also "The Priest" (*Writings in Time of War*, 212–13). Closely related to detachment in the mystical tradition is the theme of resignation, which Teilhard also discusses ("True Resignation," in *Le Milieu Divin*, 70–74).

70. Death is a constant theme in *Le Milieu Divin*; see 57, 59, 65, 67, 68–70, 81, 83, 90, 100, 107, 117, 128, 138. De Lubac says that "there would be no exaggeration in presenting the whole body of his [Teilhard's] work as one long meditation on death" (*Religion of Teilhard de Chardin*, 48).

71. *Le Milieu Divin*, 152. "Sur-creation" (120, 152), like "sur-animation" (37, 95, 100, 112, 127, 135), are Teilhardian neologisms for the excess energy generated in the pleroma.

72. Teilhard closes the third section with a "Prayer for Love of Neighbor" (138–40). There is a brief fourth section (140–43) on the outer darkness and the possibility of lost souls.

73. See "B. Love. The Historical Product of Human Evolution," in *Human Energy*, 155–60.

Bibliography

The French edition of Teilhard's writings contains 11 volumes of scientific works and 13 volumes of other writings.

Works Used in Chronological Order

Many of Teilhard's writings touch on mysticism. Here I mention only those used in this essay.

"Cosmic Life" (1916). In *Writings in Time of War*, 13–71. New York: Harper & Row, 1967

"Christ in the World of Matter: Three Stories in the Style of Benson" (1916). In *Hymn of the Universe*, 39–55. New York: Harper & Row, 1965.

"The Mystical Milieu" (1917). In *Writings in Time of War*, 117–52. An early version of *Le Milieu Divin*.

"Nostalgia for the Front" (1917). In *The Heart of Matter*, 167–81. San Diego: Harcourt Brace Jovanovich, 1965.

"The Priest" (1918). In *Writings in Time of War*, 203–34. An early version of *The Mass on the World*.

"My Universe" (1918). In *The Heart of Matter*, 196–208. A later and larger version, "My Universe" (1924), is in *Science and Christ*, 37–85. New York: Harper & Row, 1968.

"The Great Monad" (1918). In *The Heart of Matter*, 182-95.
"The Eternal Feminine" (1918). In *Writings in Time of War*, 191-202. An early version of "The Evolution of Chastity."
"The Spiritual Power of Matter" (1919). In *Hymn of the Universe*, 59-71.
"Notes on the Physical Union between the Humanity of Christ and the Faithful" (1920). In *Christianity and Evolution*, 15-20. New York: Harcourt Brace Jovanovich, 1969.
"A Note on Some Possible Historical Representations of Original Sin" (before 1922). In *Christianity and Evolution*, 45-55.
"Pantheism and Christianity" (1923). In *Christianity and Evolution*, 56-75.
Le Milieu Divin (1927). London: Collins, 1960.
"The Mass on the World" (1927). In *Hymn of the Universe*, 13-37.
"The Road of the West: To a New Mysticism" (1932). In *Toward the Future*, 50-59. New York: Harcourt Brace Jovanovich, 1975.
"Christology and Evolution" (1933). In *Christianity and Evolution*, 76-95.
"The Evolution of Chastity" (1934). In *Toward the Future*, 60-87.
"How I Believe" (1934). In *Christianity and Evolution*, 96-132.
"Human Energy" (1937). In *Human Energy*, 113-62. New York: Harcourt Brace Jovanovich, 1971.
"The Phenomenon of Spirituality" (1937). In *Human Energy*, 93-112.
"The Mysticism of Science" (1939). In *Human Energy*, 163-81.
The Phenomenon of Man (1938-40). New York: Harper, 1959.
"Christ the Evolver" (1942). In *Christianity and Evolution*, 138-50.
"Introduction to the Christian Life" (1944). In *Christianity and Evolution*, 151-72.
"Christianity and Evolution: Suggestions for a New Theology" (1945). In *Christianity and Evolution*, 173-86.
"The Spiritual Contribution of the Far East: Some Personal Reflections" (1947). In *Toward the Future*, 134-47.
"Reflections on Original Sin" (1947). In *Christianity and Evolution*, 187-98.
"My Fundamental Vision" (1948). In *Toward the Future*, 163-211.
"My Intellectual Position" (1948). In *The Heart of Matter*, 143-44.
"A Clarification: Reflections on Two Converse Forms of Spirit" (1950). In *The Activation of Energy*, 215-27.
"The Spiritual Energy of Suffering" (1950). In *The Activation of Energy*, 244-49.
"Some Notes on the Mystical Sense" (1954). In *Toward the Future*, 209-11.
"The Christic" (1955). In *The Heart of Matter*, 80-102.
The Activation of Energy (1963). San Diego: Harcourt, 1978.
"The Heart of Matter" (1965). In *The Heart of Matter*, 12-79.

Letters

About 2,600 of Teilhard's letters survive. A number contain important reflections on his view of mysticism. The volumes used here are the following:

The Making of a Mind: Letters from a Soldier-Priest (1914–1919). New York: Harper & Row, 1961.
Letters from A Traveller, 1923–1955. New York: Harper, 1962.
Letters from My Friend Teilhard de Chardin. Edited by Pierre Leroy, SJ. Translated by Mary Lukas. New York: Paulist Press, 1976. Letters from 1948 to 1955.

Works about Teilhard de Chardin

There are many bibliographies and biographies. I mention only works I have used.

Aczel, Amir D. *The Jesuit and the Skull: Teilhard de Chardin, Evolution, and the Search for Peking Man.* London: Penguin, 2007. An account of Teilhard's life and his role in the discovery of *Homo sinanthropus.*
Cuénot, Claude. *Teilhard de Chardin: A Biographical Study.* Baltimore: Helicon, 1965. A full biography.
Fabel, Arthur, and Donald St. John, eds. *Teilhard in the 21st Century: The Emerging Spirit of Earth.* Maryknoll, NY: Orbis Books, 2004. A collection of essays.
Haught, John F. *The Cosmic Vision of Teilhard de Chardin.* Maryknoll, NY: Orbis Books, 2021.
King, Thomas M. *Teilhard's Mass: Approaches to "The Mass on the World."* New York: Paulist Press, 2005.
———. *Teilhard's Mysticism of Knowing.* New York: Seabury, 1981. An insightful study.
King, Ursula. *Teilhard de Chardin and Eastern Religions: Spirituality and Mysticism in an Evolutionary World.* New York: Paulist Press, 2011. Contains a useful "Annotated Study Guide" to everything "Teilhardian" (363–415).
Lubac, Henri de. *The Eternal Feminine: A Study on the Poem of Teilhard de Chardin, Followed by Teilhard and the Problems of Today.* New York: Harper and Row, 1971.
———. *The Religion of Teilhard de Chardin.* New York: Desclee, 1967. One of the best analyses.
———. *Teilhard de Chardin: The Man and His Meaning.* New York: Hawthorn Books, 1965. Primarily apologetic.

Lyons, J. A. *The Cosmic Christ in Origen and Teilhard de Chardin: A Comparative Study.* Oxford Theological Monographs. Oxford: Oxford University Press, 1982.

Mooney, Chistopher. *Teilhard de Chardin and the Mystery of Christ.* Garden City, NY: Doubleday, 1968.

Mortier, Jeanne, and Marie-Louise Auboux, eds. *Album.* New York: Harper & Row, 1966. A richly illustrated life.

Salmon, James, and John Farina, eds. *The Legacy of Pierre Teilhard de Chardin.* Mahwah, NJ: Paulist Press, 2011. Essays.

Savary, Louis M. *Teilhard de Chardin: The Divine Milieu Explained.* New York: Paulist Press, 2007.

Individual Essays

Egan, Harvey D. "Chapter Seven. Pierre Teilhard de Chardin." In Egan, *Christian Mysticism: The Future of a Tradition,* 260–302. Eugene, OR: Wipf & Stock, 1984.

Laird, Martin. "The Diaphanous Universe: Mysticism in the Thought of Pierre Teilhard de Chardin." *Studies in Spirituality* 4 (1994): 206–35. An excellent summary.

Lu, Bosco. "Love as Energy according to Pierre Teilhard de Chardin." *Fu Jen International Religious Studies* 1 (2007): 63–90.

CHAPTER 5

Edith Stein (1891-1942): "May Your Will Be Done"

Preliminary Remarks

Edith Stein, whose name in the Carmelite Order was Sister Teresa Benedicta of the Cross, was born in 1891 and died in 1942, so she lived longer than the other two Carmelites treated here. She differed from Thérèse of Lisieux and Elizabeth of the Trinity in important ways. To begin with, she was Jewish, the fact that determined her tragic end as a victim of the Holocaust, despite her conversion to Catholicism in 1922. Second, Edith had an extensive education and became an accomplished philosopher, a favored disciple of Edmund Husserl (1859-1938), the father of the phenomenological method.

Her education in Catholic thought was deep, but selective, because it was acquired only later in life. Nonetheless, her mental powers helped her to create original readings of Augustine, Pseudo-Dionysius, Thomas Aquinas, and the Carmelite masters, especially Teresa and John of the Cross.[1] Finally, Thérèse and, to a lesser extent, Elizabeth spoke about their own experiences of God. Edith, on the other hand, was reticent about her inner life, in line with the passage from Isaiah 24:16, *secretum meum est mihi* ("My secret is mine"—long a favorite text for mystics).[2] Edith's sense of the need for silence about important aspects of her life is evident in the 1925 letter she wrote to her friend Fritz Kaufmann, with whom she had experienced a break since 1919. She apologizes for her own role in this misunderstanding, but then reflects a bit on "the pitiable state" she had been in during those days. Now, she says, "I have found the place where there is rest and peace for all restless hearts. How that happened is something you will allow me to be silent about today. I am not reluctant to speak about it, and, at the right time, will surely do so with you also, but it has to 'come about'; it is not something about which I can 'report.'"[3] We need to remember that the mystical life, by definition, is a silent and hidden life, so Edith Stein's silence itself may be taken as a sign of her mysticism.

There are, nonetheless, a few passages in her writings that reflect on her inner states. Even before her conversion, Edith seems to have enjoyed at least one experience that can be described as mystical. In her early essay "Sentient Causality" (1919) she talks about having "a state of resting in God [as] something completely new and unique." It is different from the "cessation of activities from the lack of lifepower," which is "dead silence." Rather, it is "a feeling of being safe, of being exempted from all anxiety and responsibility and duty to act. And as I surrender myself to this new feeling, new life begins to fill me up." This is not something that comes from her, but it becomes "operative within me without my asking for it. The sole prerequisite for such a mental rebirth seems to be a certain receptivity."[4] After her conversion, a letter of February 12, 1928, to the Dominican nun Callista Kopf is also revealing. Stein says that she thought at first that she would have to give up serious scholarly work after becoming a Catholic, but that "gradually I realized that something else is asked of us in this world and that, even in the contemplative life, one may not sever connection with the world. I even believe that the deeper one is drawn into God, the more one must 'go out of oneself'; that is, one must go to the world in order to carry the divine life into it." This can be successful, however, only if "one finds, first of all, a quiet corner in which one can communicate with God as though there were nothing else, and that must be done daily."⁵ Edith, however, does not describe her daily communications with God any further.

With such reticence about her inner life, as well as the fact that her major writings are dense philosophical and philosophical-theological treatises, is it possible to consider Edith a significant modern mystic? My response reflects points made in the "Introduction." First, mysticism certainly includes (and often features) personal accounts of consciousness of God's presence, but such narratives are not the essence, or formal feature, of mysticism as the search for transformative encounter with God. Edith Stein's writings display her continued search for God in ways that go beyond autobiographical narrative. Second, the mystical element comes to speech in diverse ways, not least in what may seem on first reading to be dry and speculative discourse. In this sense, I find some of Edith's "academic" works often more mystical than her popular "pious" writings on hagiography, although these should not be ignored. Nevertheless, Edith Stein as a philosopher-mystic presents a number of problems that cannot be taken up here, especially how to understand the relation between her developing philosophical agenda and her inner mystical insights (for more, see Tyler, *Living Philosophy of Edith Stein*). This is a part of the mystery of Edith Stein that has continued to attract investigators from many disciplines.

Introduction: *Fiat Voluntas Tua*

One way to describe the core of Edith Stein's mystical teaching is to reflect on the Gospel imperative: *Fiat voluntas tua* ("May Your will be done"), a phrase found in both Mary's response to the invitation to become the Mother of God (*fiat mihi secundum verbum tuum*; Luke 1:38) and in the Our Father (Matt. 6:10). Stein's life was marked by a deep conviction that we must put ourselves in God's hands and "let his will be done." As she and her sister Rosa were being taken away from their Carmelite convent in August of 1942 to be sent to Auschwitz, it is reported that she was heard to say, "Come, Rosa, we are going for our people." This submission to God's will as a member of his chosen people is also seen in remarks she made in letters from July and August written under the looming threat of deportation and extermination. On July 29, writing about efforts to get her and her sister to safety in Switzerland, she said she "would not be sad if it did not come," and, "I will accept whatever God arranges." In a letter written from the detention barracks at Westerbork in the Netherlands on August 4, she even dwells on the good side of what God's will has brought: "Now we have a chance to experience a little how to live purely from within."[6]

Fiat voluntas tua was not just a truth realized under threat of death, but was a major motif of Edith's life—the only way to the goal of union with God was giving over the self to him in a total fashion. For Christmas of 1935 Edith composed a meditation on "The Mystery of Christmas," one of her most powerful spiritual texts.[7] The Carmelite reviews the economy of salvation revealed in the birth of Jesus, emphasizing the centrality of giving up the self to God's will. "Only then," she says, "will trust in God stand firm when it includes a willing acceptance of all and anything from the hand of God. After all, He alone knows what is good for us." She continues, "This, 'Thy will be done!' in its fullest meaning must be the guiding line of the Christian life." Nevertheless, we are often unsure about what God's will for us actually entails, as we wander in the dark night of estrangement and even seeming abandonment by God (says this student of John of the Cross), so, "Can we say 'Thy will be done' even if we have no certainty of what God wants of us?" In the midst of such trials we have no recourse except to trust in our Redeemer and in his intention to bring us to union with him. "So, whoever daily says in his heart, 'Thy will be done,' can confidently trust that he will not fail to do God's will even when he lacks actual certainty of it."

For Edith Stein, the spiritual practice of the *Fiat* is rooted in God's predestinating plan for the universe, as can be seen in the concluding section of her *magnum opus*, *Finite and Eternal Being*.[8] After analyzing the nature of Christ's lordship over all things and the formation of his universal Mystical Body, she argues that this cosmic structure depends on a double *fiat*: Mary's "may it be done unto me" at the Incarnation, and the Word's acceptance to be born into human nature seen in the *fiat voluntas tua* that the Second Person addresses to his Father. She argues that just as the self-giving of the parents and their generative will prepare for the existence of the child, so the child's growth depends on the mother's "dedication to the task of motherhood." She continues, "The paradigm of this is the *Fiat!* . . . of the Mother of God. This *Fiat!* enunciates her loving self-surrender to God and to the divine will. . . . And must we not further assume that the Son of Man, . . . accepted from his mother's love not only the flesh and blood needed for the forming of this body, but also for the nourishment of his soul?" Just as all humans were judged guilty by God in Adam and Eve, our redemption demands "a second pair that were not included in his judgment: the *new Adam* and the *new Eve*—Christ and Mary. He heard their *Fiat voluntas tua!* and *Fiat mihi secundum verbum tuum!* They are the true parents and the true paradigms of a humankind that is united with God and in God. . . . The resurrected Christ, the King of glory, is the paradigm and head of the human race—the end form to which every human is ordained and from which it receives its meaning."[9]

In Stein's letters we see how often her spiritual advice is based upon *fiat voluntas tua*, the need to surrender to God. To give but three examples. Writing to a woman troubled by doubts as she prepared for baptism, Edith tells her that, "without any kind of human assurance, you place yourself totally in God's hands, then all the deeper and more beautiful will be the security attained."[10] To another distressed soul she says, "Before all else I would like to tell you to lay all care for the future confidently in God's hands, and allow yourself to be led by Him entirely, as a child would."[11] Speaking of her own condition in 1939 with the growing Nazi threat, she declares, "My basic attitude since I've been here [the Cologne convent] is one of gratitude. . . . At the same time I always have a lively awareness that we do not have a lasting city here [Heb. 13:14]. I have no other desire than that God's will be done in me and through me. It is up to Him how long He leaves me here and what is to come then."[12] Edith's confidence in surrendering to God is also reflected in a passage in FEB where she considers the coherence of her life in terms of what is "planned and meaningful" and what seems "accidental and meaningless." Nonetheless, we often see in retrospect that the accidental was far more important than what we had carefully planned. She says, "In other words, what did not lie in *my* plan lay in *God's* plan. And the more often that such things happen to me the more lively becomes in me the conviction of my faith that—from God's point of view—nothing is accidental." Therefore, "for the all-seeing eye of God [there is] a perfect coherence of meaning" (FEB, 113). To be sure, there is scarcely a mystic who has not spoken of the necessity of total surrender to God's will—it is an integral aspect of Christian belief. My point is that this core spiritual value is manifest in Edith Stein in an eminent way.

Life and Writings

Edith Stein was born into a large Jewish family in Breslau in 1891, the last of seven children. Her father died when she was two, but her devout and capable mother, Auguste, took over the family business and raised the children. In 1933, under the growing Nazi threat and soon before entering the convent, Edith wrote a revealing autobiographical work, *Life in a Jewish Family*, which was both an attempt to provide an empathetic portrait of a Jewish family as a protest against anti-Jewish propaganda, and an expression of her own attempt to show how important her Jewish roots were to her developing personhood.[13] Edith had a deep attachment to her mother, even after her conversion created a painful rift between them. Although she excelled as a student, she gave up school at the age of fifteen at the same time that she abandoned the practice of Judaism. Her restless and inquiring mind, however, soon led her back to school, and from 1911 to 1913 she studied psychology at the University of Breslau. Dissatisfied with the empirical direction of contemporary psychology, she switched to the University of Göttingen and from 1913 to 1915 studied philosophy under the direction of Edmund Husserl, the dominant philosopher of the age.[14] She became a prominent figure in the circle of brilliant students gathered around "the Master" (as she always called Husserl). With the onset of World War I Edith, a loyal German, worked for five months as a nurse in a Red Cross hospital. In 1916 she returned to the university, this time at Freiburg, where Husserl had relocated. Here she triumphantly defended the dissertation that became her first book, *On the Problem of Empathy*, a phenomenological exploration of our relationship to the feelings of others.

From 1916 to 1918, Edith worked as Husserl's assistant, helping him put his papers and uncollected writings in order, an almost impossible task, since the Master was disorganized and did not offer her much help. Having given up that post, she continued her philosophical work and tried to find a university teaching position, a very difficult endeavor for a woman at that time. This was a difficult period in her life (1919–1922), but the agnostic Edith seems to have also been gradually gaining an appreciation for religion and the spiritual life. This dramatically culminated in her conversion to Catholicism. Edith spent the summer of 1921 at the house of her friends Theo and Hedwig Conrad-Martius, and here one evening she picked up the *Life* of Teresa of Avila and become so engrossed in it that she read all night. It was a moment of truth. In a 1933 letter to Fritz Kaufmann informing him of her entry into the convent she says, "I entered the monastery of the Carmelite nuns here last Saturday and thus became a daughter of St. Teresa, who earlier inspired me to conversion."[15] During the latter part of 1921, Edith tutored herself in Catholicism and was baptized on January 1, 1922, much to the pain and disappointment of her family and many friends.

From the time of her conversion, Edith felt called upon to enter the Carmelite Order, but her new Catholic acquaintances and clerical advisors cautioned against this for the present. Instead, she began to teach and soon also to give public lectures on many issues, especially relating to education and the role of women in society. From 1923 to 1931, she taught at the Dominican Teacher's College of Saint Magdalena in Speyer, where, under the guidance of the Jesuit philosopher Erich Przywara, she translated Thomas Aquinas's *Disputed Questions on Truth* and John Henry Newman's *Idea of the University*. At this time she began an intensive study of Aquinas, and later also turned to Duns Scotus and the Dionysian corpus, although, as she admits, her knowledge of Scholasticism and Catholic theology was sporadic.[16] Beginning in 1928, she often visited the Benedictine Abbey at Beuron, a center of liturgical study, where she took the Archabbot Raphael Walzer as her spiritual director. The electoral triumph of the Nazis and the beginning of the attacks on the Jews in 1933 meant that Edith could no longer continue her career as a teacher and lecturer. Edith already sensed the peril the Jews were in and, on April 12, 1933, she wrote a letter to Pope Pius XI, asking him to speak out against the Nazi regime. Her changed situation gave her the opportunity to turn her mind again to Carmel. At this point she briefly lifts the veil on her prayer life. On Good Shepherd Sunday (April 30, 1933), while attending a day of prayer, she tells us, "I went there late in the afternoon and I said to myself, 'I'm not leaving here until I have clear-cut assurance whether I may now enter Carmel.' After the concluding blessing had been pronounced, I had the assurance of the Good Shepherd."[17] She was admitted to the Cologne Carmel on the eve of the Feast of Saint Teresa, October 15, 1933. Her mother was devastated by this decision.

Edith Stein felt immediately at home as a Carmelite. After six months, she became a postulant ("one asking for acceptance"), taking the name Teresa Benedicta of the Cross. She made her final vows as a nun in 1938 after the requisite five years. Two personal losses came to Sister Teresa in these years. The first was the death of her mother on September 14, 1936. The nun says at the very time of her mother's passing (as she later found out) she had had a strong experience of her mother at her side while she was renewing her monastic profession.[18] In April 1938, her "beloved Master" Edmund Husserl died. Writing to a Benedictine nun, Sister Teresa said, "I am not at all worried about my dear Master. It has always been far from me to think that God's mercy allows itself to be circumscribed by the visible church's boundaries. God is truth. All who seek truth seek God, whether this is clear to them or not."[19]

Edith's intellectual gifts were recognized by the Carmelites, who encouraged her in the writing of her most important book, *Finite and*

Eternal Being. An Attempt at an Ascent to the Meaning of Being. In this massive and dense ontological analysis, finished in 1938 but not published until 1950, the Carmelite tried to combine the phenomenological method of philosophical investigation of Husserl with the teaching of Thomas Aquinas, both philosophical and theological. Whether the project was entirely successful or not, FEB is a monument in twentieth-century Catholic thought. Sister Teresa Benedicta's final major work was written under the shadow of increasing Nazi persecution of the Jews and the looming tragedy of World War II. For her own safety in 1939 Sister Teresa was allowed to transfer to the Carmel at Echt in the Netherlands. Here, with the encouragement of her new superior, she began bringing together her many years of reading and meditating on John of the Cross in written form, a book she called *The Science of the Cross* (*Kreuzeswissenschaft*), composed between 1940 and 1942.[20] She had just finished the book when the new Nazi rulers of the Netherlands ordered the arrest of all Jews, including converts to Christianity. She and her sister Rosa, a Carmelite third-order, were taken on August 2, kept in a transit camp for a few days, put on a train to Auschwitz, and murdered on August 9.

It was only after the end of the War that the Carmelites became sure of Edith's fate and the effort to collect and publish her writings got under way. So too did the cause for her canonization. She was beatified in 1987 and canonized in 1998 by Pope John Paul II, who also declared her a co-patroness of Europe in 1999. Stein's path to sanctity was not without controversy, since some Jewish groups noted that she was executed as a Jew (not a Catholic nun) and that her canonization might be seen as an attempt to divert attention from the fundamental meaning of the Holocaust as an attack on Judaism. Other individuals and groups have labored to show how Edith Stein can serve as a bridge between Catholics and Jews.[21]

Edith Stein wrote a good deal, as the twenty-eight volumes of the *Edith Stein Gesamptausgabe* (*Collected Works*) show. I have already mentioned some of her most important works in this sketch, but will not discuss her entire corpus here. English translations of the most significant works exist and are listed in the bibliography at the end.

Major Themes of Edith Stein's Mysticism

I cannot give a full account of the thought of Edith Stein here, especially of her contributions to philosophy. What follows is a survey of her mystical teaching with reflections on its roots in her theology and philosophy. I also will not treat her writings on women, political theory, and education.

The Search for Truth

Before and after her conversion, Edith Stein's dominant life purpose was the search for truth, as can be seen in her remark about Husserl cited above—"all who seek the truth seek God."[22] This hunger, evident throughout her life, led her to conversion to Catholicism and then to the need to reflect on the relation of the truth claims of the philosophy in which she had been trained and the revealed truths she had accepted. Her long essay on Pseudo-Dionysius, "Ways to Know God," contains an important account of the relation of reason and faith.[23] She says that "in all genuine knowledge of God it is God Himself who draws near to the knower, although His presence may not always be felt as it is in experiential knowledge. In natural knowledge He draws near in images, works, and manifold effects; in faith by making Himself known personally through the Word." Furthermore, "God wishes to let Himself be found by those who seek Him. Hence He wishes first to be sought." Natural revelation is not clear or unambiguous, however, so that it leaves us with the incentive to seek for the further truth found in the "supernatural revelation [that] answers the questions raised by natural revelation." She goes on, "Faith is a gift that must be accepted," in which "divine and human freedom meet." But faith is not final. "As dark and lacking the evidence of insight, faith awakens a yearning for unveiled clarity; as mediated encounter it awakens a longing for an immediate encounter with God."[24] Such encounters can be found in this life in moments of mystical experience, but will only be completed in the beatific vision.

On this basis, Stein constructs a theory of the relation of reason and faith, of philosophy and theology, set out in her essay "Husserl and Aquinas," and also discussed at the beginning of FEB.[25] "Husserl and Aquinas," originally written as a conversation between Stein's "Master" and the great Catholic doctor, investigates the agreement and divergences between the phenomenological method of rational investigation and the Thomistic approach (at least as Stein understood it) that employs both reason and revelation to search for the truth about God and the world.[26] Stein's study of Thomas had led her to see the limits of phenomenology, which she expresses in the voice of Thomas as arguing that faith "in fact is not a specifically philosophical issue, but one marking the bounds of natural reason and at the same time the bounds of a philosophy based on purely natural reason" (15). Hence, continues Thomas, "there is *a material dependence of philosophy on faith*," as well as a "*formal dependence of philosophy on faith*," in that philosophy must absorb the truths of faith and use them as the final criteria by which to gauge all other truths (17–18). According to Stein, Thomas "assembled, ordered, and shifted" the knowledge of his time, not in order to create a "philosophical system," but to make "a philosophy for life" (26–27), just as she herself was seeking to do in a new environment. Thomas's ontology centers on God as the First Truth and therefore has a "theocentric orientation," whereas Husserl's transcendental phenomenology "posits the subject as the start and center of philosophical inquiry" and has an "egocentric orientation" (28–33). Thus, "Husserl seeks the 'absolute' starting point in the immanence of consciousness; for Thomas it is faith," that is, "God and his relation to creatures" (61–62).

The same position is discussed from a wider perspective of the history of philosophy in Part I of FEB, specifically with regard to the possibility of the existence of a "Christian philosophy," a question much discussed at the time.[27] Stein argues that Thomas did advance such a Christian philosophy in which "it is the task of philosophy to harmonize those propositions at which it has arrived by using its own devices together with the truths of faith and theology," without, however, becoming theology (FEB, 23). This was the task she set herself to in her *magnum opus*. She pursued this in conversation with Thomas Aquinas, but not as a Thomist. She at times mistook Thomas's position, and she explicitly disagreed with him on a number of points.[28] In fine, for Edith Stein there are two forms of philosophy: the phenomenological method based on reason alone, but a reason that soon runs up against its own limits; and higher Christian philosophy, or metaphysics, that she speaks of in a letter "as a grasp of the whole of reality through an inclusion of revealed truth, therefore grounded on philosophy *and* theology."[29]

The Meaning of Being

As a "phenomenological ontologist," Edith Stein was concerned with the meaning of being in the most general sense, as can be seen in her characterization of the FEB as "unabashedly comprehensive."[30] The work contains a detailed treatment of the major themes of metaphysics: being and essence; being and becoming; potency and act; matter and form; substance; the ego; and so on. She begins by hailing Thomas Aquinas as having gone beyond Aristotle by distinguishing between being (*ens/esse*) and essence (*essentia/ousia*) (FEB, 4). Only in God are the two identical (FEB, 41, 335-42), whereas in all other beings they differ. Also like Thomas, she roots this truth in God's self-revelation in Exodus 3:14, "I am who *I am*" (FEB, 342-46). Nevertheless, God is not immediately known to us, so we must begin the philosophical search from the fact of our own existence: "Whenever the human mind in its quest for truth has sought an indubitably certain point of departure, it has always encountered the inescapable *fact of its own being or existence*" (FEB, 35).

We are conscious of our being as subject to change, passing from potency to act, a change that begins to reveal *the idea of pure being* and therefore to point to the need for the *"analogia entis* as indicative of the relationship existing between temporal and eternal being" (FEB, 37-38; see also 46). The beings that we experience are composed of being and essence,[31] potentiality and actuality, as well as matter and form.[32] Matter for Stein has two meanings: first, that which fills and presents itself in space; and, second, that which is capable of formation and "permits further formation" (FEB, 244). Form, or structure, is also double, since Stein distinguishes between essential form (*Wesensform*), or "what makes this formed matter a thing of such and such specific qualities" (FEB, 214), and pure form, or the ideal or limit (essentiality) which something seeks to approximate. Form and matter form an intrinsic unity in keeping with the unifying character of Stein's ontology. Finally, Stein's thought places great stress on the nature of the "I" (*Ich/ego*), which she again distinguishes into the "Pure I" (*reine Ich*) and "I, the Person." The "Pure I" is the source of the many acts of the existential ego, "that pure being which is by itself and in itself" (FEB, 55). The "I, the Person," on the other hand, does not possess the fullness of being of the "Pure I"; rather, it is "the *person* as a conscious and free I," which is "*free* because it determines its life out of its own self in the form of *free acts*" (FEB, 376). This "I" is incommunicable (FEB, 343). Again, the "I" is not something purely spiritual, but is the whole human being: "The human ego, in short, is not only a *pure ego*, not only a spiritual ego, but also a bodily ego" (FEB, 367).

Edith Stein's analysis of the being of the "I" as *a being thrown into existence* (*ins Dasein geworfen*—an expression made famous by Heidegger) went in a very different direction from Heidegger's position. She says, "We are forced to conclude that the being of the ego, as a constantly changing living present, is not autonomous but *received* being. It has been *placed into existence* and is sustained in existence from moment to moment" (FEB, 54). This implies that the analysis of *Dasein* inevitably leads to the conclusion that there must be a Necessary Being that causes and sustains all that exists—a version of Thomas's Third Way (STh, Ia, q. 3, a. 2). Stein deliberately contrasted Heidegger's notion of the anxiety to death of *Dasein* to her own conviction that in *Dasein* the ego accepts its limited existence with a security similar to that of a baby carried in its mother's arms (FEB, 57–58).

Edith Stein's general ontology leads directly to her anthropology, which, although philosophical in character, also builds on truths revealed in faith.[33] The human being is a unified substance comprising body and soul, but on a deeper level Stein's anthropology is not dual but tri-form, because the human consists of body-soul-spirit (FEB, 244–46).[34] "These three basic forms demarcate three different *realms* of actual being, albeit not in an exclusive way, but in such a way that 'the individual formations *within* these realms are in their turn subject to the dominating formative power of these three classes,' determined and modified in each instance by the principle class of category."[35] Thus, the realm of body is that of nature, where Stein distinguished between merely corporeal body (*Körper*) and living body (*Leib*), that is, ensouled body. All living bodies have souls, although these differ in plants, animals, and humans. The human soul is a person, a soul that can say "I" because of its inherent freedom. The human soul, then, is the inner part of the whole physical-spiritual organism. As such, soul has a threefold activity, as *receiving* from the outside, *assimilating* what it has received, and *responding* (FEB, 467). But there is a double aspect to the soul. In its life-giving role it is a "body-bound being," but soul is also open to God, and as a "God-centered-being" it is more properly called spirit (*Geist*).[36] Spirit is a "genus of existence" that is "non-spatial, invisible, and intangible" (FEB, 217), the realm of thinking, willing, and feeling. It is characterized by freedom and the ability to receive the divine life into itself.[37]

God as Trinity

God's necessary and perfect being is infinitely beyond our own being, and Stein followed Thomas (and Dionysius) in adhering to a rigorous apophaticism concerning what can be said about God. Nevertheless, we can make certain true, if never comprehensive, statements about God through the use of the "analogy of being" (*analogia entis*), about which her mentor Father Przywara had said much. Parts III–VI of FEB work out these relations between the divine and finite modes of being in detail, including a long treatment of the transcendental terms. For our purposes, however, it is the second half of Part VI, where Edith treats the First Being of God and the divine inner and outer relations (FEB, 335-54), as well as the whole of Part VII, on "The Image of the Trinity in the Created World" (FEB, 355-468), that are of the most importance. In line with her notion of ontology as involving both truths given by reason and those available through faith, she subjects many "revealed doctrines," such as the Trinity, to a philosophical analysis.

Stein's teaching on the Trinity is so central to her work that Marian Maskulak has spoken of her philosophy as a form of "Trinitarian Ontology."[38] It involves both traditional theological notions taken from Augustine and Aquinas (e.g., substance/essence, relation, hypostasis, person) and original developments in which she argues for the image of the Trinity in the entire created world—pure spirits (i.e., angels), inanimate things, nonpersonal animated beings, and in a special way in human beings, both in their natural spiritual life as persons and in the supernatural indwelling of the Trinity they enjoy. (Had she been more conversant with the broad tradition of Catholic theology, she would have found valuable resources for this universal view of the role of the Trinitarian image in theologians like Bonaventure, Meister Eckhart, and Nicholas of Cusa.) Three sections of the FEB deal with the Trinity.[39]

The first is FEB, Part III, Section 12, "Essential and Eternal Being" (105-20). Here Stein argues that the Lord of being not only gives all being but also all meaning, finding this revealed in John 1:1 (*En archē ēn ho Logos*), which she renders as, "In the beginning was meaningful existence." This text, as well as Paul's passage on all things subsisting in divine Wisdom (Col. 1:17), provides a model of how revealed truth acts correlatively with philosophical inquiry.[40] The Logos is a real essence, the *divine* essence that is called meaning, that is, intellectual meaning. "The actual being of the intellect is *life* and *living understanding*, that is, God as pure act" (FEB, 107-8). Stein then asks if it is possible, even intellectually, "to separate the essential being of the Logos [i.e., the divine being] from its actual being, as it is possible in the case of finite natures?" Her answer is that this seems possible on the basis of the creedal formula that the Father generates the co-eternal Son: "What is *generated* is the *second person*, and the being that the Son receives can thus not be the essential being of the divine nature, but must be its *actual being* in the second Person" (FEB, 108). In a dense argument, Stein suggests that, properly understood, such a mode of understanding essential being might provide a valid foundation for an ontological (i.e., a priori) proof of God's existence, but, given the divine incomprehensibility, she is doubtful of both a priori proofs (e.g., Anselm) and a posteriori proofs (e.g., Thomas). She does, however, proceed to a lengthy investigation about how the inseparability of essential and actual being in God, along with the form of separability suggested in Trinitarian theology, casts light on the philosopher's investigation of finite being (FEB, 111–20).

Another section of FEB (Part VI, Section 5 [348–51]) deals briefly with the comparison of the external relationship of the Creator to creation and the internal relations in the Trinity. According to the creed, the Son is generated co-eternally from the Father as his perfect image. In the created realm, all images differ from what they image, whereas in God, Father and Son are one God. How is this so? God is spirit, as are we, so in our self-knowledge, imperfect as it is, we can find an analogy. Our self-consciousness is an immediate awareness of self that is nonetheless dark and indefinite. God's self-knowledge is also immediate, but is clear and encompasses his entire infinite being. But how can this generated perfect likeness be a person without compromising the unity of the divine nature? "Divine being-a-person," says Stein, "is the archetype or paragon of all finite being-persons" (FEB, 349). A finite "I" can confront a "You," that is, "another I," and can enter into understanding with the other, forming a "we . . . in which we experience the oneness of a plurality of persons" that still maintains personal individuality. In God, however, "[t]he Three Persons have their entire essence or nature in common, so that there remains only the diversity of Persons as such. There is thus a perfect unity of the we, such as can never be attained by any community of finite persons" (FEB, 350). Stein seeks to find models for this "higher unity than that of the I," and does so first of all by exploring the unity of the *love* by which "divine love must be the being-one of a plurality of persons" in mutual self-giving. There is no newly originating being in the Trinity, but "it is the *one* divine being, simultaneously given and received, since giving and receiving pertain to divine being as such" (FEB, 351). A second model, or analogy, is found in *life*, since God's being is life. This movement of life is not a finite generation, "but it is an eternal movement within the self, an eternal self-drawing or self-creating out of the depths of God's own infinite being, an infinitely generous giving of the eternal I to an eternal Thou, and a correspondingly eternal and ever-renewed self-receiving and self-giving. . . . The cycle of the intra-divine life completes and closes itself in the Third Person who is gift, love, and life."[41]

Much the longest of Edith Stein's considerations of the Trinity is found in Part VII of the FEB on "The Image of the Trinity in the Created World" (355–467). Here I can comment only on a few basic aspects of her novel treatment of the doctrine. In the first section ("Person and Hypostasis," 355–59), she discusses the analogical internal relations of the Three Persons, that is, generation and spiration, as well as the difference between hypostasis and person. In order to try to grasp what we can of the mystery of "the Being-in-three-Persons" of the Trinity, Stein embarks on a more complete analysis of the nature of spirit (Section 2, "Person and Spirit," 359–63). The essence of this section is the argument that the archetype of spirit (*Geist*) is the triune God: "The spirit in its purest and most perfect actualization is found in the total self-giving of the divine Persons, a self-giving in which each person totally divests itself of its nature [*Wesen*] and yet totally retains its nature, in which each person is totally within itself and totally within the others" (FEB, 360). On this basis, Part VII proceeds with a long treatment of "The Human 'Being-Person'" (FEB, 363–78) and the persons of created pure spirits, that is, angels (FEB, 380–417). The stage is then set for the major purpose of Part VII, the discussion of the image of the Trinity in the whole created world, not just in the human person as previous theologians had held (e.g., Augustine and Aquinas).

The role of the Holy Spirit is central to Stein's argument. "God is *love* and that love is a free self-giving of an I to a Thou, and a union of both in a We" (FEB, 419). "When Son and Father love each other, their mutual self-giving is simultaneously the free act of the Person of *Love*." Because "love is *life* in its highest perfection, love is being which eternally gives itself without suffering any diminution, and it is thus infinite fecundity. The Holy Spirit is therefore the *gift* as such: not merely the mutual self-giving of the Divine Persons to one another, but the self-giving of the deity *ad extra*" (FEB, 420).[42] This self-giving "on the outside" is necessarily Trinitarian. The self-giving of the Trinity *ad extra* is also ecstatic, as Stein learned from Dionysius (*Divine Names* 4). In a letter from 1938, she says that the Trinity is personally present on every level of the spirit world: "It is not his unapproachable majesty that God communicates to us through his messengers [angels], but rather his overflowing love. It is their bliss just as it will be ours (and already is to some extent), to be allowed to cooperate in God's dispensing of graces."[43]

Each of the three divine Persons has a distinctive role in created reality. God's Wisdom, the Logos, foresaw all things and is the archetype of "the determinateness of all creaturely essences or natures, the eternal paradigm of everything they are destined to be." God's creative will and "life-imparting love" give each creature "their *power of being* or the *power* of unfolding their essence or nature," so that the Holy Spirit "is the archetype of all creaturely life and efficacious action," along with the "spiritual radiance of their essence or nature which is a property even of material structures." Third, "in the standing-upon-itself of every independent actuality . . . we may see an image of the Father as the primary unconditioned principle." Stein concludes, "Then the entire structure of created existents ('that which is') turns into an image of the Triune Deity" (FEB, 420).

Edith Stein then examines the Trinitarian image on each level of created existence—inanimate corporeal things, non-personal animate things, and finally in humans with some comparison with angels. The long Section 9 (FEB, 427–64) emphasizes that the image of the Trinity is found in the whole human being consisting of body-soul-spirit. In order to grasp it properly, it is necessary to explore the deep interiority, or center, of the soul, where God's activity can be felt. The "masters of the *inner life* of every age" experienced this. "They were drawn into the innermost center of their being by some force stronger than the entire external world, and they thus experienced the breaking through of a new, mighty, superior life—a life supernatural and divine" (FEB, 443). Citing Augustine and John of the Cross, Stein says, "Mystical infused graces impart to the soul an experience of what faith teaches on the indwelling of God in the soul" (FEB, 444). Thus, the image of the Trinity in the human being can be said to exist on two levels, as noted above. Stein discusses the *natural image* of the Trinity by way of an examination of Augustine's triadic formulae from his *De Trinitate* and through her own exploration of the nature of love (FEB, 448–57). The *supernatural image* is realized in the divine indwelling in the *soul* through grace, particularly in the threefold formative power of the soul as body-soul-spirit. Here the soul, which "draws from its own sources and molds itself in body and spirit," is the image of the Father, while the *body* images the Son as the "circumscribed expression of the essence, and the *spiritual life* is the image of the Holy Spirit" (FEB, 463). While the whole universe has a Trinitarian structure, the human spirit is a special image of the Trinity. She summarizes, "The human spirit—even on the purely natural level—is an image of God in a much greater sense than are other created things and beings, because the human being is a person and as such capable not only of involuntary and unconscious stepping forth from itself, but of living a free and conscious spiritual life" (FEB, 464).

Christ and the Cross

We have already noted the central role of the Logos as the archetype of all meaning in the universe. The Logos also took on human nature in Jesus Christ in order to redeem humans and the universe from the fragmentation and destruction wrought by Adam's sin. For Edith Stein, the truth of human life was to be conformed to Christ in his Mystical Body through the "Science of the Cross."

The process of being "formed into Christ" is interpersonal. For Stein, our relation to Jesus Christ is a form of empathy, that is, "an experience which an 'I' has of another 'I'." Even in *On the Problem of Empathy*, the book she wrote in her atheist days, she held that empathy is "how humans comprehend the psychic life of their fellows." Yet more, "Also as believers they comprehend the love, the anger, and the precepts of their God in this life; and God can comprehend people's lives in no other way."[44] Our empathetic understanding of Jesus is not merely intellectual knowing, but is meant to change our lives by bringing us closer and closer to the "mind of Christ" (1 Cor. 2:16).[45] Many things contribute to this process: reading the scriptures; reception of the sacraments, especially the Eucharist; and the life of prayer, both the public prayer of the liturgy and the many forms of contemplative silent prayer. Stein wrote on all these issues. Her essay on the Beatitude "Blessed are the Poor in Spirit" (Matt. 5:3), is an example of an in-depth analysis of the mystical meaning of a single biblical text, which concludes by saying, "The soul who has learned to look into one's own heart finds God most surely within himself. This inner way is the way of all the mystics" (Teresa and Augustine are cited).[46]

The Eucharist was also of great significance in Stein's life, as her many hours of prayer before the sacrament show, and as is evident in a number of her writings.[47] Her essay "On the Prayer of the Church" is a study of how the liturgical prayer of the Church, which she learned to appreciate especially at Beuron Abby, as well as private contemplative prayer after the example of Jesus, is necessary in a person's progress toward union with God.[48] There can be no opposition or tension between the two, because "[a]ll authentic prayer is prayer of the church." Stein's high evaluation of prayer is seen in a passage from the long essay she wrote on Teresa of Avila. "Prayer," she says, "is the highest achievement of which the human spirit is capable. But it is not merely a human achievement. Prayer is a Jacob's ladder on which the human spirit ascends to God and God's grace descends to people."[49] Prayer is not a part-time occupation, and perseverance in prayer is necessary for everyone. A letter from 1931 puts it as follows: "God leads each of us on an individual way; one reaches the goal more easily and more quickly than another. We can do very little ourselves, compared to what is done to us. But that little bit we must do. Primarily, this consists before all else of persevering in prayer to find the right way, and of following without resistance the attraction of grace when we feel it. . . . But one may not set a deadline for the Lord."[50]

The central practice for attaining conformity with Christ is sharing in his cross, or living "the Science of the Cross," something evident from Edith Stein's choice of her name in religion, Teresa Benedicta of the Cross.[51] The Science of the Cross, which Stein found admirably set forth in John of the Cross, is more practical than speculative: "If we speak of a *Science of the Cross* this is . . . no mere theory. . . . It is, indeed, a known truth, a theology of the Cross, but it is living, actual and active truth: it is placed in the soul like a seed, strikes root and grows, giving the soul a certain character and forming it in all it does or leaves undone" (SC, 1). Associating her new phrase with the traditional mystical theme of "the science of the saints," Stein notes, "If a saintly soul assimilates the truths of the faith, they become the science of the saints. If the mystery of the Cross becomes its inner form, it grows into the Science of the Cross" (SC, 2). For Stein this science is what John of the Cross learned in his life and set forth powerfully, although not systematically, in his mystical works. The Science of the Cross, for Stein, is the loving acceptance of suffering and even death as the sovereign way to God—*Fiat voluntas tua!* She puts it this way: "Faith offers it [the soul] Christ, poor, humble, crucified, forsaken on the Cross even by his Divine Father. In his poverty and desolation the soul recognizes its own. . . . Christ accomplished his greatest work . . . in the utmost humiliation and annihilation on the Cross." Thus, the soul realizes "that it, too, must be led to union with God through annihilation, a 'living crucifixion'" (SC, 89).

A number of Stein's letters and shorter writings repeat the same message. The key for her is to realize that, when we suffer with Christ, we cooperate with him in the work of redemption. In a letter from 1932, she says, "When we are united with the Lord we are members of the Mystical Body of Christ: Christ lives on in his members and continues to suffer in them. And the suffering borne in union with the Lord is his suffering, incorporated in the great work of salvation and fruitful therein."[52] Writing to the same correspondent in 1933, she consoles her, "I want to wish you very much patience in your suffering and the ultimate consolation that I have often had to point out to you: that the way of suffering is the surest road to union with God."[53] As the 1930s drew on, Stein came to see the suffering of the Jewish people more and more in terms of the suffering of Christ. Reflecting on her name in religion in a letter of 1938, she tells another nun, "By the cross I understand the destiny of God's people which, even at this time, began to announce itself. I thought that those who recognized it as the cross of Christ had to take it upon themselves in the name of all. Certainly, today I know more of what it means to be wedded to the Lord in the sign of the Cross. Of course, one can never comprehend it, for it is a mystery."[54] Edith's sense of the impending tragedy of the Jews and her own involvement in the fate of her people is reflected in the dialogue she wrote in 1940, "A Night Conversation," in which Queen Esther visits Edith's Mother Superior and discusses her role as the protector of the Jewish people.[55] A number of Stein's meditations, prayers, and poems also witness to the special place that the cross, especially the exalted cross lifted up as the sign of redemption, played in her life.[56]

To be joined to Christ on the cross is to become a member of his Mystical Body, a theological theme of great meaning for Edith Stein. As the Logos stands as the source and archetype of all meaning at the beginning of the unfolding of creation, so too the total Christ, head and members, is the goal of universal development of the world. Part VIII, Section 3.3, "The Unity of the Human Race. Head and Body. *One Christ*" (FEB, 510–27) is the central text on this aspect of Stein's thought. The holistic drive of Stein's philosophy is evident here, because, for her, Christ's Mystical Body extends beyond the believing Christians who constitute its core, to move out to the whole of humanity, and even the entire created universe, which had also been affected by Adam's Fall. By their *Fiat!*, as noted above, Christ and Mary overcome the damage wrought by the Fall of Adam *and Eve*. Christ, as free from all sin, possessed the "total plenitude of humanity," and therefore, even on the natural level, all humans are oriented toward him, so that "the fullness of humanity is actualized in a dual manner in the person of Christ and in the entire human race" (FEB, 524). This conception of the Mystical Body, says Stein, aids in the understanding of the meaning of human individuality—another illustration of her metaphysics that embraces both reason and revelation (FEB, 526). The narrow sense of the Body of Christ, restricted to the human level, yields to the "broader sense," which includes the angels, as well as the natural world: "As the entire subhuman nature was implicated in the Fall of Man, it is also to share in the restoration of man wrought by redemption" (FEB, 527). Therefore, "Christ is the head of creation in its totality" (ibid.).

The Mystical Life

Edith Stein, as already noted, did not talk much about her inner consciousness of God, but mysticism as direct contact with God played a significant role in her life and writings. Stein's view of mysticism is essentially Carmelite, the product of her long engagement with John of the Cross, and also with Teresa of Avila and to a lesser extent Thérèse of Lisieux.[57] She realized, of course, that there were many forms of Christian mysticism (she had a good knowledge of Augustine and Dionysius), but from the time of her first reading of Teresa she felt drawn to the contemplative life realized in Carmel. She described the Carmelite life to her friend Roman Ingarden as follows: "Our task is to love and to serve. . . . It is impossible for us to despise the world and humanity. We have not left them because we hold them worthless, but to be free for God."[58] Her enclosed life of prayer, silence, and penance was not a selfish flight from the world, but an opportunity to represent all humanity before God in a special way. In that sense she, like many other modern mystics, thought that any strong opposition between contemplation and action was artificial. I noted above her remark that "the deeper one is drawn into God, the more one must 'go out of oneself'" to carry the divine life into the world (Letter 45). True to John of the Cross, she conceived of the Carmelite life as one of climbing Mount Carmel (Letter 152), although she admitted that she herself was still "way down at the foot of the mount" (Letter 316).

As befits a Carmelite follower of Teresa and John, Edith Stein's view of mysticism centers on union with Christ in mystical marriage. Nevertheless, her reading of Dionysius enabled her to locate "mystical experience" (*Erlebnis*) within a broad understanding of modes of knowing God. Stein distinguished between "religious experience" and "mystical experience." In a 1927 letter to Ingarden, she says, "I believe we can and we must speak of *religious experience*. However, it is not a matter of a 'direct intuition' of God. That is possible only in totally exceptional cases (in ecstasy and the like) for which, however, a strict proof is never possible, as with *genuine* revelation." Religious experience is seeing in events of nature and the lives of people things that point to God. "It is not necessary," she goes on, "that we come to a correct proof of religious experience before the end of our lives. However, it is necessary that we come to a decision for or against God. . . . That is the wager of faith. The way leads from faith to understanding, not the other way round." She concludes by telling him, "Where the actual experience is missing, we have to get it from the testimonies of the religious. . . .

According to my experience the most impressive come from the Spanish mystics, Teresa and John of the Cross."[59] So, the witness of the mystics, even for those who have not enjoyed mystical experience, is vital for Stein's view of the life of faith.

Stein says more about the nature of mystical experience and mystical theology in her essay on Dionysius, "Ways to Know God," which reflects on the ascending stages of knowing God.[60] Stein rightly notes that, for Dionysius, *theology* is not an academic discipline but is holy scripture itself, whose authors are the "theologians," who "*speak of God* because *God has taken hold of them* or *God speaks through them*." Hence, "the various 'theologies' distinguished from 'mystical theology' . . . are not disciplines or fields, but *different manners of speaking about God* and—expressed in them—*different ways or manners of knowing God* (or not-knowing him); *mystical theology* itself represents the *highest stage*" (87).[61] Her basic concern in this essay is with the "Symbolic Theology" by which we know God really, but imperfectly, through the created things that both reveal God in their similarity, but also more strongly veil him in their "yet greater dissimilarity." The symbolic theologian makes use of symbols and images to witness to God on the basis of his awareness of God, which can have three sources: natural knowledge; faith (the 'ordinary' way of supernatural knowledge); and supernatural experience (the 'extraordinary' way of supernatural knowledge) (97). The supernatural experience of the prophet, for example, rests on an inner certainty or feeling of God's presence. "We call this the *experience* [*Erfahrung*] of God in the most proper sense. It is the core of all mystical living experience [*Erlebnis*]: the person-to-person encounter with God" (104). This feeling of God's presence is "the core of all mystical experience," but since it is mediated, it is only the lowest stage of the mystical life. "There are various degrees and transitions between this feeling and the summit of 'infused contemplation,' the lasting union with God" (106). The symbolic theology based on faith leads the way upward to mediated experience of God and, if God grants, "to the highest summit, to Oneness with the One" (110).[62] Stein's other references to mystical experience (e.g., SC, 138) should be seen in light of this general analysis. On the basis of this understanding, Stein can also say that "it is possible to understand the writings of the mystics without . . . being a mystic" ("Ways to Know God," 129), but she insists that leading a "mystical life" demands a higher experience that is often hidden. In *Hidden Life*, 110, she notes, "The greatest figures of prophecy and sanctity step forth out of the darkest night. But for the most part the formative stream of the mystical life remains invisible." This means that "the decisive turning points in world history are substantially co-determined by souls whom no history book ever mentions," a bold claim about the importance of mystics. The path to the full mystical life is arduous. True to her master, John of the Cross, she sees "the unification of knowledge, memory and love" as merely the beginning of the transformation that can be achieved only through the active and passive nights of the spirit. "The strong hand of the living God himself must intervene to free the soul from the snares of all created things and draw it to Himself. This intervention is the dark, mystical contemplation" (SC 87–88).

Edith Stein discusses some other themes well known in the history of mysticism, such as the notion of "pure love," which she found in John of the Cross (e.g., Letter 311). Her major concern, however, is with the highest stage of mystical experience, which she, following Teresa and John, named the union of "spiritual or mystical marriage." The most extensive treatment, as might be expected, is found in the SC. Here Stein engages in a detailed analysis of John's treatment of union with the Trinity from the *Spiritual Canticle* and the *Living Flame of Love*, and a less successful attempt to show that John and Teresa always presented the same message (in her time Carmelite "orthodoxy" smoothed over any differences between the "founders"). Stein held that God calls all people to union with him, but she also insisted, following Teresa and John, that the highest form of union, spiritual marriage, was a special grace different in kind from sanctifying grace.[63] Of course, union is an analogous term, so the universality of the call does not necessarily contradict a special higher gift given only to some.

Following John's *Ascent of Mount Carmel* 2.5, Stein analyzes the saint's three modes of union with God: God's substantial dwelling in all created things; God's indwelling by grace in the human soul; and "the transforming, divinizing union through perfect love."[64] Stein admits that in this text John seems to see a difference only in degree, not in kind, between the second and third modes, but she argues that, on the evidence of Teresa's *Interior Castle*, as well as other passages in John, there is really a difference in kind. All forms of "indwelling" are found only in "personal-spiritual being," because it presupposes "free acceptance by its recipient" (126). The second mode of union is open to many; the third is special to the few: "In fact only a small number of chosen ones attain to an experimental apprehension of the Triune God in their soul. A larger number is led by an enlightened faith to a living knowledge of this indwelling and to a loving communion with the three Persons in pure faith" (127). A rather tortuous comparison of John and

Teresa follows. While John admits that mystical experience begins at lower levels in the soul's ascent, Stein argues that "there is an essential difference between the mystical marriage and the utmost that can be achieved by grace and will" (130). The same Triune God is present in all three modes of union, but the reception is diverse. Indwelling demands from both sides an interior being "capable of receiving another being within itself," so that a unity is achieved without a loss of independence (132). In the purification of the grace-filled Dark Night the human will enters more and more deeply into the divine will, but this is different from the passive purification effected by "the consuming divine fire of love," which is a new and higher mode of indwelling. This is reflected in the difference between faith and contemplation.[65] So, the loving surrender of the soul to God in mystical marriage is different from the soul's previous unconditional surrender to the divine will. It is different in *knowledge*, because the soul comes to know God in a new way, and it is different from the point of view of *will*, because it is a union with the heart of God and the three Persons of the Trinity. She summarizes, "In the bridal surrender not only is one's own will subordinated and conformed with the divine one, but the divine surrender is also received" (135). In this divinizing union of mystical marriage, "the soul can now give *more* to God than it is in itself: it gives God to himself in God" (ibid.; John's *Living Flame* 3.78 is cited).[66] But the total surrender to God in the darkness of faith that God, in his own way, may reward with the gift of marital union is inseparable from its archetype, Christ's surrender on the cross: "Thus, the bridal union of the soul with God is the end for which the soul was created, bought by the Cross, accomplished on the Cross, and sealed with the Cross for all eternity" (SC, 207).

Edith Stein never claimed to have enjoyed the gift of mystical marriage, although she analyzed it with profundity. That she did experience some form of union with God is, nonetheless, clear from a few places in her writings, such as the poem, at once Eucharistic and Trinitarian, entitled "Ich bleibe bei euch . . ." ("I remain with you . . ."). I cite only a few stanzas: "In the heart of Jesus, which was pierced, / The kingdom of heaven and the land of earth are bound together. / Here is for us the source of life. / This heart is the heart of the Triune Divinity, / And the center of all human hearts / That bestows on us the life of God. / It draws us to itself with secret power, / It conceals us in itself in the Father's bosom / And floods us with the Holy Spirit." Then the poem switches to a reflection on the reception of Christ in the Eucharist: "Your body mysteriously penetrates mine / And your soul unites with mine: / I am no longer what I once was."[67]

Notes

1. On Edith Stein's writings and for full titles and publication information of works cited by author or short title, see the bibliography at the end of this essay.

2. On Edith's reluctance to speak of her inner experiences, see Koeppel, *Edith Stein: Philosopher and Mystic*, 72-73, 132; and Mosley, *Edith Stein: Woman of Prayer*, 8, 13, and 72.

3. Letter 38a, *Self-Portrait in Letters*, 47.

4. "Sentient Causality," *Philosophy of Psychology and the Humanities*, 84-85. On this text, see Maskulak, *Edith Stein and the Body-Soul-Spirit*, 124-26.

5. Letter 45, *Self-Portrait in Letters*, 54.

6. These are from some of her last letters, Nos. 339 and 340, as found in *Self-Portrait in Letters*, 350-51.

7. "The Mystery of Christmas" has been translated by Hilda Graef, *Writings of Edith Stein*, 24-31. I will cite from the precis in Koeppel, *Edith Stein: Philosopher and Mystic*, 15-23.

8. *Finite and Eternal Being* (hereafter FEB), "Part VIII. The Meaning and Foundation of Individual Being," section 3.3, "The Unity of the Human Race. Head and Body. *One* Christ" (510-27).

9. "Unity of the Human Race," 517-18; see also 526.

10. Letter 105 of 1931, *Self-Portrait in Letters*, 105.

11. Letter 181, *Self-Portrait in Letters*, 185.

12. Letter 300, *Self-Portrait in Letters*, 309. Many other letters reflect the spirituality of the *fiat*; e.g., Letters 52, 76, 89, 102, 223, and 306.

13. At the beginning of *Life in a Jewish Family*, Stein says, "What I shall write on these pages is not meant to be an *apologia* for Judaism. . . . I would like to give, simply, a straightforward account of my own experience of Jewish life as one testimony to be placed alongside others" (28). For the context of the work, see Brenner, *Writing and Resistance*, 76-84.

14. Stein's notion of phenomenology was based on the earlier, "more realist" thought of Husserl, not his later work, which she criticized as "idealist." In her lectures, *Introduction to Philosophy on a Phenomenological Basis*, she says, "Phenomenology is a science of pure consciousness, which is not a member but a correlate of the world, and the field in which absolute insights are to be gained in pure and faithful description." See Maskulak, *Edith Stein and the Body-Soul-Spirit*, "The Phenomenological Approach" (24-33; quotation from 25). See, more fully, MacIntyre, *Edith Stein: A Philosophical Prologue, 1913-1922*, especially chapters 5, 9-10, 12-13 and 17.

15. Letter 158a, *Self-Portrait in Letters*, 161. On her conversion, see MacIntyre, *Edith Stein*, 167-69, 172-75.

16. A number of Stein's letters reflect on the limitations of her knowledge of Scholasticism; see, e.g., Letters 117, 184, 213, and 224.

17. "How I Came to the Cologne Carmel," in Batzdorff, *Edith Stein: Selected Writings*, 19.

18. Letter 266, *Self-Portrait in Letters*, 274-75.

19. Letter 259, *Self-Portrait in Letters*, 272.

20. *The Science of the Cross* (hereafter SC) may be off-putting to some, because a large part of the book consists in extensive quotations from John's writings, which

is understandable at the time when not much of him was available in German. Nonetheless, the work is filled with deep insights into the Carmelite's mystical teaching, and there are also important sections relating to her own thought, notably the reflections on "The Science of the Cross" (1, 9, 19ff., 23ff., 121ff., 131ff., and 208), and the section, "The Soul in the Realm of the Spirit and the Senses" (114-40). There are three main parts to the book: "Part I. The Message of the Cross," on how John encountered the cross in his own life; the long "Part II. The Doctrine of the Cross," which exegetes John's four mystical treatises; and "Part III. The Imitation of the Cross," basically a hagiography showing how John lived the cross. Stein frequently mentions studying John of the Cross in her letters, e.g., Letters 168, 198, 311, 324, 327, 335, and 336.

21. On the controversy, see Herbstrith, ed., *Never Forget: Christian and Jewish Perspectives on Edith Stein*.

22. The importance of the search for truth for Edith has been noted by many investigators; see Mosley, *Edith Stein*, 3-15; and the selections in Sullivan, *Edith Stein: Essential Writings*, "3. Searching for Deep Truth" (80-93).

23. "Ways to Know God: The 'Symbolic Theology' of Dionysius the Areopagite and Its Objective Presuppositions," in *Knowledge and Faith*, 83-134.

24. "Ways to Know God," 113-14; see also 101-2.

25. For a good discussion, see MacIntyre, *Edith Stein*, chapter 17; also Maskulak, *Edith Stein and the Body-Soul-Spirit*, 33-40.

26. "Husserl and Aquinas: A Comparison," in *Knowledge and Faith*, 1-63. The original dialogical form of the essay had to be rewritten as an objective article for Husserl's *Festschrift* at the request of the editor, Martin Heidegger.

27. FEB, "Part I. Introduction: The Inquiry into Being" (1-29); see also 119-20, 239-44, and 380-84.

28. Stein disagreed with Thomas on such issues as (1) the principle of individuation (FEB, 340, 471-503); (2) the existence of "spiritual matter" in the angels (FEB, 391, 409-11); (3) the image of the Trinity as existing in all creation (FEB, 417-20); and (4) memory as a distinct power of the soul (FEB, 436-37).

29. Letter 126 to her friend Hedwig Conrad-Martius of November 13, 1932, *Self-Portrait in Letters*, 126. Edith seems to think that this was Thomas's view of metaphysics, but the Dominican held that metaphysics was a purely natural philosophical discipline. Stein's view is actually closer to that of Bonaventure, who held for a form of "Christian metaphysics" that makes use of both reason and revelation.

30. Letter 228, *Self Portrait in Letters*, 239. For a summary of her ontology, see Maskulak, *Edith Stein and the Body-Soul-Spirit*, "Chapter 3. Stein's Ontology and Anthropology" (47-89).

31. Stein distinguished between the nature or *essence* (*Wesen*) and essentiality (*Wesenheit*). The former is used in two ways: "(1) to designate the specific determinateness conceivable as a universal, and (2) to designate that which makes an individual what it is" (FEB, 395-96). Essentiality is the archetype or pure form that is independent of the actual object (FEB, 72-73).

32. On form and matter, see the exhaustive treatment in Part IV, Section 3 (FEB, 153-219).

33. See Maskulak, *Edith Stein and the Body-Soul-Spirit*, "Chapter 3. Stein's

Ontology and Anthropology," especially 61–89; and Tyler, *Living Philosophy of Edith Stein*, "Chapter Five. Stein's Anthropology: *Seele* and Levels of the Self."

34. See also the treatment of "The Soul in the Realm of Spirit and the Spirits," SC, 114–25.

35. FEB, 245, quoting her friend H. Conrad-Martius's article "Realontologie."

36. See Part VII, Section 9, Nos. 9–10 (FEB, 459–64).

37. FEB, 460–62. In this section, Stein cites Pauline texts (1 Cor. 15:35 and 44–46). She does not cite, but surely knew, that the body-soul-spirit view of human nature is based on Paul (1 Thess. 5:21).

38. Marian Maskulak, "Edith Stein's Trinitarian Ontology," in Hans Reiner Sepp, ed., *Edith Stein: Intersubjectivity, Humanity and Being* (Nordhausen: Traugott Bautz, 2015).

39. There are also treatments of our union with the Trinity in the SC 147–53, 204.

40. "But the philosophical meaning of the logos to which our own inquiry has advanced may perhaps help us to understand the theological meaning of the Word *and, conversely*, revealed truth may aid us in our philosophical difficulties" (FEB, 107).

41. FEB, 351. This passage shows an affinity with Eckhart's view of the intradivine activity that he calls *bullitio*.

42. Stein's mystical devotion to the Holy Spirit is evident in her poem "Und ich bleibe bei euch: Aus einer Pfingstnovene," found in *Hidden Life*, 140–45, in both German and English.

43. Letter 267, *Self-Portrait in Letters*, 279; see also her remarks on the Dionysian *Divine Names* in *Knowledge and Faith*, 132–34.

44. *On the Problem of Empathy*, 11.

45. See "Chapter 5. Jesus: Empathy in Prayer," in Mosley, *Edith Stein*, 61–77.

46. There is a translation in Maskulak, *Edith Stein: Selected Writings*, 140–46. We find Stein using a formula that echoes Meister Eckhart's famous sermon on the same text (Pr. 52): "It's indeed a difficult realization for human pride to recognize that of oneself, one is nothing and has nothing" (143).

47. See, e.g., "Eucharistic Education," in Maskulak, *Edith Stein: Selected Writings*, 160–63.

48. "The Prayer of the Church," *Hidden Life*, 7–17.

49. "Love for Love: The Life and Works of St. Teresa of Jesus," *Hidden Life*, 29–66; quotation from 38.

50. Letter 102, *Self-Portrait in Letters*, 100–101.

51. See Maskulak, "Edith Stein and Simone Weil," 445–57; and Fitzgerald, "Passion in the Carmelite Tradition," 217–35, especially on Stein's notion of expiation.

52. Letter 129, *Self-Portrait in Letters*, 128. See also Letter 330.

53. Letter 148, *Self-Portrait in Letters*, 151.

54. Letter 287, *Self-Portrait in Letters*, 295.

55. "A Night Conversation," *Hidden Life*, 128–34; see Mosley, *Edith Stein*, 95–111.

56. Four are collected in "Part III. At the Foot of the Cross," *Hidden Life*, 91–104. See also the two poems on the cross in Maskulak, *Edith Stein: Selected Writings*, 225–28.

57. For Stein's view of the important figures of Carmel, including the prophet Elijah, see Mosley, *Edith Stein*, chapter 8, "The Saints of Carmel," 112–47; and Maskulak, *Edith Stein: Selected Writings*, chapter 10, "Carmelite Mysticism," 165–91.

58. Letter of summer 1937, cited in Maskulak, *Edith Stein: Selected Writings*, 251. See also Letter 174 to Fritz Kaufmann of 1934, where she says, "it is our vocation to stand before God for all" (*Self-Portrait in Letters*, 178). For more on the life of Carmel, see, e.g., Letters 182, 183, and 320 (*Self-Portrait in Letters*, 186–87, 188, 331).

59. Letter to Ingarden of November 20, 1927, in Maskulak, *Edith Stein: Selected Writings*, 234–35.

60. "Ways to Know God," 83–134.

61. Stein also talks about mystical theology in SC 104–9, 136, and 198.

62. On the relation of the symbolic theology to the "interpretation of the spiritual names of God" in the *Divine Names*, and the mystical theology of "God's self-revelation in stillness," see "Ways to Know God," 116–17, and 128–34.

63. Letter 277 (*Self-Portrait in Letters*, 286–87), written to the Dominican Callista Kopf, recognizes the difference on this question between the "Dominican" view (Fr. Garrigou-Lagrange is cited) and the "holy parents" of Carmel.

64. The most detailed discussion is "The Different Modes of Union with God" (SC, 125–36). *Ascent* 2.5 is also treated in SC, 41–42. Further discussions of union relate to *Living Flame of Love* 1.9ff. (SC, 143–45) and the *Spiritual Canticle* (SC, 179–82, and 193).

65. Stein discusses this difference in detail in the following section, "Faith and Contemplation. Death and Resurrection" (SC, 136–39).

66. There are a number of other discussions of the Trinitarian nature of the mystical marriage that cannot be taken up here; see, e.g., SC 122–25, 194–207; FEB, 457–59; *Hidden Life*, 62, 97–101; and "Retreat Reflections," in Maskulak, *Edith Stein: Selected Writings*, 259–60.

67. "Ice bleibe bei euch . . . ," *Hidden Life*, 136–37.

Bibliography

Sources

German

Stein, Edith. *Gesamtausgabe [ESGA]*. Edited by Hanna-Barbara Gerl-Falkowitz. 27 vols. Freiburg: Herder, 2000–2020.

English

The Institute of Carmelite Studies (ICS) of Washington, DC, has published English versions of many texts in *The Collected Works of Edith Stein, Sister Teresa Benedicta of the Cross, Discalced Carmelite*, although older translations are still useful. Here I list only the books used in this essay.

On the Problem of Empathy. Translated by Waltraut Stein. Washington, DC: ICS, 1989.

Life in a Jewish Family, 1891–1916. Translated by Josephine Koeppel. Washington, DC: ICS, 1986.
The Hidden Life: Essays, Meditations, Spiritual Texts. Translated by Waltraut Stein. Washington, DC: ICS, 1992.
Self-Portrait in Letters, 1916–1942. Translated by Josephine Koeppel. Washington, DC: ICS, 1993.
Knowledge and Faith. Translated by Walter Redmond. Washington, DC: ICS, 2000.
Philosophy of Psychology and the Humanities. Translated by Mary Catherine Baseheart and Marianne Sawicki. Washington, DC: ICS, 2000.
Finite and Eternal Being. An Attempt at an Ascent to the Meaning of Being. Translated by Kurt F. Reinhardt. Washington, DC, 2002.
The Science of the Cross: A Study of St. John of the Cross. Translated by Hilda Graef. Chicago: Henry Regnery, 1960. There is also a translation by Josephine Koeppel in the ICS series from 2002.

There are several anthologies of Stein's writings. Chronologically:

Graef, Hilda, ed. *Writings of Edith Stein.* Westminster, MD: Newman Press, 1956.
Batzdorff, Susanne, ed. *Edith Stein: Selected Writings.* Springfield, IL: Templegate, 1990.
Sullivan, John, ed. *Edith Stein: Essential Writings.* Modern Spiritual Masters. Maryknoll, NY: Orbis Books, 2002.
Maskulak, Marian, ed. *Edith Stein: Selected Writings.* New York: Paulist Press, 2016.

Studies

There is a substantial literature on Stein. This is a list of some books and articles I have found helpful.

Brenner, Rachel Feldhay. *Writing as Resistance: Four Women Confronting the Holocaust. Edith Stein, Simone Weil, Anne Frank, Etty Hillesum.* University Park, PA: Pennsylvania State University Press, 1997.
Courtine-Denamy, Sylvie. *Three Women in Dark Times: Edith Stein, Hannah Arendt, Simone Weil, or, Amor fati, amor mundi.* Translated by G. M. Goshgarian. Ithaca, NY: Cornell University Press, 2000.
Fitzgerald, Constance. "Passion in the Carmelite Tradition: Edith Stein." *Spiritus* 2 (2002): 217–35.
Herbstrith, Waltraud, ed., *Never Forget: Jewish and Christian Perspectives on Edith Stein.* Washington, DC: ICS, 1998.
Koeppel, Josephine. *Edith Stein: Philosopher and Mystic.* Way of the Christian Mystics 12. Collegeville, MN: Liturgical Press, 1990.

MacIntyre, Alasdair C. *Edith Stein: A Philosophical Prologue, 1913–1922.* New York: Rowman & Littlefield, 2007. An incisive philosophical account.
Maskulak, Marian, *Edith Stein and the Body-Soul-Spirit at the Center of Holistic Formation.* American University Studies 7/261. New York: Peter Lang, 2007. A good analysis.
———. "Edith Stein and Simone Weil: Reflections for a Theology and Spirituality of the Cross." *Theology Today* 64 (2008): 445–57.
———. "Edith Stein's Trinitarian Ontology." In *Edith Stein: Intersubjectivity, Humanity and Being,* edited by Hans Reiner Sepp. Nordhausen: Traugott Bautz, 2015.
Mosley, Joanne. *Edith Stein: Woman of Prayer.* Herefordshire, UK: Gracewing, 2005.
Sullivan, John, ed., *Edith Stein Symposium: Teresian Culture.* Carmelite Studies 4. Washington, DC: ICS, 1987.
Tyler, Peter. *The Living Philosophy of Edith Stein.* London: Bloomsbury, 2023. An important recent study.

CHAPTER 6

Dag Hammarskjöld (1895–1961): Mystic and Public Servant

An unusual combination. Many might think that a world-famous diplomat, Secretary General of the United Nations (1953–1961), and a central player in many of the controversies of the early days of the Cold War between the Soviet Union and the West, could not have been more than a clever statesman, skilled politician, and possibly a man of letters. Dag Hammarskjöld's posthumously published *Markings* (*Vägmärken,* 1963; perhaps better, *Waymarks*), his private journal of 1925–1961, surprised the world by revealing someone with a deep inner, even a mystical, life.[1] A kind of modern

Confessions, also comparable in some ways to the *Meditations* of Marcus Aurelius, *Markings*, which the author described as "a sort of 'White Book' concerning my negotiations with myself—and with God" (*Markings*, 7), revealed a man filled with loneliness and doubts, but also with an unwavering dedication to honesty, truth, and public service. It is one of the most remarkable mystical documents of the twentieth century.[2]

Protestant Mysticism

Hammarskjöld was baptized and confirmed in the Swedish Lutheran Church. In later life he was not an active churchgoer, but he by no means rejected the role of organized religion.[3] *Markings* often quotes the Scriptures, and it is clear that Hammarskjöld was an avid student of the Bible (he usually cited it from the versions in the Anglican *Book of Common Prayer*). He also read many Catholic mystics, especially Thomas à Kempis and Meister Eckhart, but Hammarskjöld was definitely Protestant in upbringing, and his witness as a modern Protestant mystic is important.

For over a century, due to the influence of certain German Lutheran theologians (e.g., Albrecht Ritschl, Adolf von Harnack, etc.), mysticism was considered anathema to anyone from a Lutheran-Evangelical background, let alone the Reformed Protestant tradition (Calvin had despised most mystics). Mysticism for them was a Greek infection of solid Gospel faith, deplorable in Orthodox Christianity, and almost as bad in Catholicism. How the world has changed in the last hundred years! In the 1930s, Lutheran scholars began to see how much of the dreaded "mysticism" there was in Luther, his sources, and the Lutheran tradition. The mysticism of the Radical Reformers also came in for new appreciation, and Anglican Protestants began to see that many of the greatest exponents of the Anglican tradition could be called mystics. During the twentieth century there has been a significant range of modern Protestant religious leaders and thinkers who can be said to have been mystics. Had this been a larger book, I would like to have included more of them. As it is, I will study only Hammarskjöld; but I will mention a few of the other figures who could have been written about.

Among the early figures is Andrew Murray (1828-1917), a South African cleric trained in Scotland, who wrote extensively on mysticism. Little known today, he was widely read in the second half of the nineteenth century and beyond.[4] Much better known was the Nobel Peace Prize winner, Albert Schweitzer (1875-1965), one of the premier religious figures of his day. Famous as a biblical scholar, preacher, musician, Lutheran theologian, and pioneering jungle doctor, Schweitzer was also the proponent of what has been called "an ethical mysticism" (H. Clark). His fundamental teaching on the need for "reverence for life" flashed upon him in a moment of mystical insight in September 1915, while he was on a boat on the Congo River headed toward his hospital at Lambaréné in Gabon. As he tells us in his autobiography, *Out of My Life and Thought* (156), "Lost in thought, I sat on the deck of the barge, struggling to find the elementary and universal conception of the ethical which I had not discovered in any philosophy." He goes on: "Late on the third day, . . . there flashed upon my mind, unseen and unsought, the phrase 'Reverence for Life.' The iron door had yielded: the path in the thicket had become visible. Now I had found my way to the idea in which affirmation of the world and ethics are contained side by side!" Schweitzer went on to write much about reverence for life as the foundation for a meaningful existence and the basis for a proper philosophy of civilization. Another Protestant mystic was the Swiss female visionary who wrote under the pseudonym Joa Bolendas (1917-2005), briefly discussed in my "Introduction."

Two American Protestant mystics can also be singled out. Thomas R. Kelly (1893-1941) was a Quaker missionary, educator, and philosopher who had an interest in the culture of the Far East. He taught at the Quaker colleges of Earlham and Haverford, before dying young of a heart attack. Kelly, who read widely in medieval and early modern mystical literature, left a short manuscript published posthumously as *A Testament of Devotion*, which is a call to see life from "the Divine Center," where the "Light within . . . illumines the face of God and casts new shadows and new glories upon the face of men" (3). It is short and simple, but still a powerful presentation of living in the presence of God. Finally, I would mention the pastor, preacher, and civil rights pioneer Howard Thurman (1899-1978), whose *Jesus and the Disinherited* (1978) is a classic statement of the religious grounds for racial equality. Thurman's life and writings are an example of what has been called "Prophetic Mysticism," an approach that combines an interior life nourished by the writings of the classic mystics, taken from several traditions (see his *The Way of the Mystics*), with a commitment to racial and social justice. From his childhood Thurman had enjoyed a deep sense of the presence of God in nature. It was his study of mystics under the tutelage of the Quaker scholar of mysticism Rufus Jones (d. 1948) that opened his eyes to the riches of the mystical tradition. For Thurman, mystical insight into the presence of God necessarily impels us to work for justice and reconciliation.

Dag Hammarskjöld's Life

The future UN leader was born into a distinguished family of soldiers and statesmen in Uppsala in 1905 (standard biographies are Urquhart and Lipsey). His father, Hjalmar, was a former Prime Minister of Sweden. He grew up a rather solitary child, closer to his mother than to his father and interested in botany (on the family, see Stolpe). Dag went to university at Uppsala, where he acquired a reputation as a brilliant scholar. Hammarskjöld never married, and there has been speculation about his sexuality. The accusations that he was homosexual seem to have been engineered by his predecessor as Secretary General Trygve Lie, who opposed his nomination. His closest friends always denied he was gay and he told a friend that he did not marry because he had early on been rejected by the woman he loved. After studies in literature, law, and economics at Stockholm, he began to work for the Swedish government in various ministries (Justice, the Foreign Ministry, and Finance). Hammarskjöld was immediately noted for his quick mind and his incredible work habits. He certainly had ambitions, although he also had interests in literature and the arts and was a devoted outdoorsman. Hammarskjöld enjoyed a wide circle of friends, although only a few seem to have felt very close to him. He was fundamentally a lonely person and someone given to bouts of doubt and depression (especially in the years 1950–1953).

The United Nations, founded in 1945 at the end of World War II, was designed to introduce a new era of global cooperation to avoid a future world conflagration, but almost immediately had to confront a different kind of world in which the Communist East, cut off behind what Winston Churchill dubbed the "Iron Curtain," and the Western democracies vied for supremacy without descending into total war. Another key factor in the complex political picture of the 1940s and 1950s was the end of colonialization, as more and more countries in Asia and Africa cast off the yoke that had subjugated them to the European powers. Hammarskjöld was plunged into this maelstrom in April 1953 by a telegram informing him that he had been chosen by the major countries as the new Secretary General. As a relative unknown and a citizen of a neutral nation, Hammarskjöld was one of the few capable people that both the Communist East and the Capitalist West could agree upon, but this also meant that both sides of the great divide would try to win him over to their views, or denounce him when he seemed to favor the opposition. His was an unenviable position, but one that he managed with great skill for eight grueling years before it took his life.

One can consult the several excellent lives of Hammarskjöld for the details of his work for the UN over these years, such as his skill in defusing the Suez crisis of 1956. In 1957 he was unanimously reelected to a second four-year term as Secretary General. Something must be said in more detail about the crisis that ended his life. Perhaps the worst of all the colonial states in Africa was the Belgian Congo, which the Belgian king Leopold II had run, from 1884 on as a personal fief, robbing and terrorizing its people for his own enrichment. Even after the Congo was taken over by the Belgian government in 1908, the economic rape of the country continued and little was done to educate its people. As more and more African countries rose up and threw out their European rulers in the 1950s, the Congo's time finally came with a popular uprising led by a young firebrand, Patrice Lumumba, and his ally, Joseph Kasavubu. In June 1960, the Republic of the Congo achieved independence. The Congo's vast mineral resources, however, attracted the attention of both Russia and the United States and its Western allies. Lumumba's message seemed favorable to socialism and the Western powers soon began to connive with the local Belgian population and disaffected Black leaders in the Congo to begin a civil war in which the southern province of Katanga broke away from the rest of the country. In the midst of this chaos, Hammarskjöld tried to mediate among the different armed factions to find a peaceful solution. Lumumba was captured and executed by his foes, probably with the connivance of the American CIA. The UN intervened by sending its own peace-keeping force of many thousands, and the Secretary General spent more and more time in the war-torn country. Meanwhile, the Soviet Union came to believe that Hammarskjöld favored the United States and its allies, and in 1960 the Russian Premier, Nikita Krushchev, called for his removal, and the abolition of the office of Secretary General—a demand decisively rejected by the General Assembly. The crisis dragged on. On September 17, 1961, Hammarskjöld boarded a plane at Leopoldville, the capital of Congo, intending to fly to meet Moise Tshombe, the leader of the Katangese rebels. The flight crashed during the night and all on board were killed. Was it a case of pilot error, a tragic accident? Numerous later investigations thought that this was the case, but mounting evidence regarding the convoluted series of events leading up to the crash indicates that some of Hammarskjöld's enemies (there were many) had hired rogue Belgian jets to shoot the plane down (Somaiya). Dag Hammarskjöld died for what he lived for: the cause of peace and justice in a world of conflict and duplicity.

Hammarskjöld the Mystic
Markings as Book and Self-Revelation

Dag Hammarskjöld left an array of papers and speeches (Foote, *Servant of Peace*), but he did not write much of a private nature, which is why *Markings* was such a surprising book to many. What kind of book is it? After Hammarskjöld's death, a carefully typed copy of the work was found on his night table with a letter instructing his friend Leif Belfrage to publish the work if he thought it would be worthwhile so that the public could gain a sense of his "true profile." Belfrage went ahead with the editing of the book, whose first Swedish edition appeared in 1963. Given the wide interest in the work, Hammarskjöld's friend, the poet W. H. Auden, was commissioned to translate the work into English. Since Auden did not know Swedish, he worked closely with a professor of Scandinavian literature, Leif Sjöberg. The result was a mixed bag—a fluid and readable text, but one that Swedish scholars have consistently criticized for many mistranslations. Auden's rather supercilious "Foreword" did not do Hammarskjöld any service, nor Auden either, since he blamed the umbrage taken by the Swedes to his comments for his never receiving the Noble Prize for Literature. In 1982 Bernhard Erling published an improved translation, to which he later added an extensive commentary (1987) and a valuable "Index" (290–318). Nonetheless, I will generally use the Auden version here, since it remains the most accessible text; but I will correct it in light of the comments by Erling, Aulen, and others.

Markings is a short work, containing about six hundred entries; many are short aphorisms; others are several pages long. The book is a prosimetron, that is, a work of both prose and poetry.[5] Most of the poems, including a series of 116 haikus composed in 1959, deal with nature, of which Hammarskjöld was a keen observer throughout his life. As a private journal of his inner thoughts, the entries do not mention public events or give the names of the people Hammarskjöld at times comments on. He began the work in 1925–1930 (the section entitled "So

It Was"), but the early entries are only fifteen. In 1941–1942 ("Middle Years") he took it up again with twenty-five entries. The period 1945–1949 ("Towards New Shores") has thirteen rather long entries. In 1950 Hammarskjöld began to give concerted attention to the work. Every year from 1950 to 1961 has numerous entries, although the actual number fluctuated from year to year due to his many duties. In 1956 he reflected on the possibility that this most private of books might someday be of use to others. The entry is revealing of his introspective and self-critical nature: "You ask yourself if these notes are not, after all, false to the very Way they are intended to mark out. These notes?—They were sign posts you began to set up after you had reached the point where you needed them.... And so they have remained. But your life has changed, and now you reckon with possible readers, even, perhaps, hope for them" (*Markings*, 124–25, 56:61).

What kind of a person was Dag Hammarskjöld? A good insight into his sense of self can be found in the 1953 interview, "Old Creeds in a New World," that he gave to the journalist Edward R. Murrow upon the occasion of his taking over the UN. Hammarskjöld begins with reflections on his family: "From generations of soldiers and government officials on my father's side I inherited a belief that no life was more satisfactory than one of selfless service to your country—or to humanity. This service required a sacrifice of all personal interests, but likewise the courage to stand up unflinchingly for your convictions." He continues, "From scholars and clergymen on my mother's side I inherited a belief that, in the very radical sense of the Gospels, all men were equals as children of God and should be met and treated by us as our masters" (*Markings*, 9). He says, "Faith is a state of the mind and the soul. In this sense we can understand the words of the Spanish mystic, St. John of the Cross: 'Faith is the union of God and the soul.'" Therefore, faith is not something that can be analyzed by the senses or reason. He says that when he finally reached the point of recognizing the difference between faith and reason, "the beliefs in which I was once, and which, in fact, had given my life direction while my intellect still challenged their validity, were recognized by me as mine in their own right and by my free choice" (ibid., 10). Here he comments on his indebtedness to Albert Schweitzer, whose works for him constituted "a key for modern man to the world of the Gospels," but he goes on in a surprising way by saying, "The explanation of how man should live a life of active social service in full harmony with himself as a member of the community of spirit, I found in the writings of those great medieval mystics for whom 'self-surrender' had been the way to self-realization, and who in 'singleness of mind' and 'inwardness' had found the strength to say Yes to every fate life had in store for them." He closes with remarks on another major theme of his life that he related to the mystics: "'Love'—that much misused and misinterpreted word—for them meant simply an overflowing of the strength with which they felt themselves filled when living in true self-oblivion" (ibid.). It is important to note the four values that Hammarskjöld singled out in the medieval mystics: *self-surrender, singleness of mind, inwardness,* and *love* as an overflowing of inner strength to be then directed to the outer world. Hammarskjöld's reading of the mystics may have been partial, but they were obviously of great significance for him.

The person revealed in *Markings* conforms to this picture, but these "Waymarks" add depth and nuance, especially regarding his inner difficulties. Hammarskjöld insisted on devotion to duty and complete integrity of life: "A task becomes a duty from the moment you come to suspect it to be an essential part of that integrity which alone entitles a man to assume responsibility" (100, 55:32). The fulfillment of one's duty demands total honesty with the self and with others, as well as courage and devotion to the truth. "Respect for the word—to employ it with scrupulous care and an incorruptible heart-felt love of truth—is essential if there is to be any growth in a society or in the human race" (101, 55:37). Hammarskjöld saw the fulfillment of his public duties as a form of obedience to God, a task that was to be carried forward with humility (147–48, 59:4), as well as what he called "simplicity," that is, "to experience reality, not *in relation to ourselves*, but in its sacred independence" (148, 59:5). The Secretary General was self-effacing and an enemy of all superficiality in public and private life. He recognized that he had ambition but sought to control it lest it veer into pride or self-pity (120, 56:40). Four virtues that he often spoke of—love and patience, righteousness and humility—were guideposts of his life (see, e.g., 121, 56:43–45; 129, 57:9). *Markings* is filled with introspective aphorisms. To give but one example: "What you have to attempt—to be yourself. What you have to pray for—to become a mirror in which, according to the degree of purity of heart you have attained, the greatness of life will be reflected" (32, 25–30:9).

Hammarskjöld's ceaseless self-examination is found throughout *Markings*. "At every moment you choose yourself," he says early in the book. "But do you choose *your* self? Body and soul contain a thousand possibilities out of which you can build many *I*'s. But in only one of them is there a congruence of the elector and the elected" (38, 45–46:1). But Hammarskjöld realized that self-constitution was not a private matter; it could be achieved only in relation to our duties toward others. In 1950 he notes, "Only life can satisfy the demands of life. . . . The nature of life is such that I can realize my individuality by becoming a bridge for others, a stone in the temple of righteousness. Don't be afraid of yourself, live your individuality to the full—but for the good of others" (62, 50:42). Slightly later, echoing Immanuel Kant, he begins an entry: "'Treat others as ends, never as means.' And myself as an end only in my capacity as a means: to shift the dividing line in my being between subject and object to a position where the subject, even if it is in me, is outside and above me—so that my *whole* being may become an instrument for that which is greater than I" (64, 50:52; see also 133, 57:29).

Hammarskjöld's deeply introspective nature had its shadow side. As Gustaf Aulen has pointed out, Hammarskjöld wrestled all his life, but especially in the trying years of 1950–1953, with three problems: self-centeredness, intense loneliness, and the seeming meaninglessness of life (Aulen, 13–22). An entry from 1952 summarizes: "What I ask for is unreasonable: that life shall have a meaning. What I strive for is impossible: that my life shall acquire a meaning. I dare not believe, I do not see how I shall ever be able to believe: that I am not alone" (86, 52:20). Hammarskjöld's unremitting self-examination led to much criticism of himself and his motivations, as well as criticism of other people, though they are never named. His friend Sven Stolpe, in the memoir he wrote about Hammarskjöld, says, "In fact it is impossible to utter any criticism of Dag Hammarskjöld which he himself has not phrased more sharply in the diary. He whips himself with scorpions" (69). Hammarskjöld's self-doubt is found even in one of his late haikus from 1959: "Do you create? / Or destroy? *That's* / For your ordeal-by-fire to answer" (158, 59:86). Above all, as already noted, Hammarskjöld was tormented by a loneliness that sometimes led to depression and even thoughts of suicide (e.g., 85, 52:19). In his years of trial he once noted, "Loneliness is not the sickness unto death (John 11:4). No, but can it be cured except by death? And does it not become the harder to bear the closer one comes to death?" (86, 52:24). In 1955 he observes, "Alone beside the moorland spring, once again you are aware of your own loneliness—as it is and always has been. As it always has been—even when, at times, the friendship of others veiled its nakedness" (104, 55:46). Loneliness, however, has a positive side, as he pointed out in 1952: "Pray that your loneliness may spur you into finding something to live for, great enough to die for" (85, 1952:18). In 1958, he poignantly asks God, "Did you give me this inescapable loneliness in order that I should more easily be able to give you everything?" (139, 58:9, Erling trans., 217).

As with many mystics and religious figures, the thought of death was constantly with Hammarskjöld, not so much as something to be feared, but as the goal that would complete his life of obedience to God (Svolpe, 92–97). In 1951 he observed, "The pulley of passing days drags us inexorably forward. A relief to think of this is that there is no detour around it. . . . When days and years are fused into a single moment, its every aspect illuminated by the light of death, measurable only by the measure of death" (67, 51:1). In 1955 he notes, "In the old days, Death was always one of the party. Now he sits next to me at the dinner-table: I have to make friends with him" (97, 55:18). A series of five aphorisms on death occurs in *Markings* of 1956, beginning, "Do not seek death. Death will find you. But seek the road that makes death a fulfillment" (136, 56:42; see also 56:43–46). There is a form of dying before death that Hammarskjöld fears more than physical death. In 1950 he said, "God does not die on the day we cease to believe in a personal deity, but we die on the day when our lives cease to be illumined by the steady radiance, renewed daily, of a wonder, the source of which is beyond all reason" (64, 50:51).[6]

A final question about *Markings* concerns its sources. Hammarskjöld was a keen student of the Bible, and *Markings* cites scripture often (Aulen, 50–57, 69–70, 122–24). In his 1953 interview with Murrow, he paid tribute to Albert Schweitzer, whose lectures he heard and whom he credits for enabling him to see the Bible from a "modern perspective." By this he means that Schweitzer insisted on the humanity of Jesus as a person confronted with the problems of life and not some kind of quasi-docetic Redeemer who always knew what was going to happen to him and remained removed from the doubts and fears of the human condition. This is quite clear in Hammarskjöld's comments on Jesus, especially about his commitment to the trial and uncertainty of the cross (see below). Hammarskjöld's life was a form of *imitatio Christi*, a following of the virtues displayed by Jesus. The Secretary General loved the Psalms and cites them twenty-nine times in *Markings*, especially those Psalms that gave voice to his own trials and tribulations but that also reflect confidence in God. (A study of his use of the Psalter would be welcome.) Only a few other Old Testament texts are used, and none from the Song of Songs, whose erotic mysticism was far from the Swede's austere temperament. In the New Testament, the Synoptic Gospels occur often (Matthew 25x; Mark 7x; Luke 14x) and John is cited thirteen times. It is perhaps surprising that Paul is cited only thirteen times, given his importance in Protestant theology.

Hammarskjöld noted the importance of the mystics, especially the medieval mystics, in his life. Who were the mystics that Hammarskjöld read and pondered? (Aulen, 36–50). We know that they included *The Imitation of Christ* in an old French translation which he was accustomed to carry with him. *The Imitation* is quoted seven times in *Markings*, and, as Jos Huls has shown, some of these quotations occur at key places in the book, for example, in Hammarskjöld's reflections on the day he was sworn in as Secretary General on April 7, 1953.[7] Meister Eckhart is used more than any other mystic in *Markings*, about a dozen times, sometimes with direct quotations, at other times in paraphrase.[8] One of the most telling uses of Eckhart comes in Hammarskjöld's sole reference to the Eckhartian theme of the Birth of the Word in the soul: "'Of the Eternal Birth'—to me, this now says everything there is to be said about what I have learned and have still to learn" (124, 56:58). He follows this with a quotation from the Dominican's German Sermon 101. According to his biographer Roger Lipsey, Eckhart's writings were "among the presiding documents of his maturity" (Lipsey 2016, 66). The relation between Eckhart and Hammarskjöld deserves more attention than it has thus far received. *Markings* also cites John of the Cross several times and Pascal once. Hammarskjöld probably would have been familiar with Jan van Ruusbroec and John Tauler, although neither name is found in *Markings*. Most Lutherans would have known the *Theologia Deutsch*, because it had been edited and much praised by Luther himself. (Strangely, Luther's name never appears in *Markings*.)[9] Hammarskjöld also cited some non-Christian mystics (Rumi, Chinese figures, etc.), so, like many moderns, he was open to the worldwide dimensions of mystical insight. Furthermore, Hammarskjöld was interested in modern mystical texts, as shown by the fact that he was working on a Swedish translation of his friend Martin Buber's *I and Thou* at his death. According to the recollections of Sture Linnér, the Swedish chief of mission in the Congo, in his last conversation with Hammarskjöld as he boarded the plane that fateful afternoon, the Secretary General had spoken of how Buber reminded him of the medieval mystics, for whom "Love . . . was a surplus of power which they felt completely filled them when they began to live in self-forgetfulness" (Lipsey 2016, 552–53). Hammarskjöld was not a scholar of mysticism, but the mystics did much to nourish his thought. Nevertheless, I would agree with Gustaf Aulen that "throughout the years Hammarskjöld developed a position of remarkable independence. He did not simply repeat the insights of those who stood as his teachers" (147).

Foundations of Hammarskjöld's Mystical Thought

In what sense was Hammarskjöld a mystic? This is a question that has been much discussed in the literature on the Secretary General, but even those who feel uncomfortable with the term "mysticism" seem unable to avoid speaking of Hammarskjöld as a "mystic," though they often try to qualify that he was not one of those "mistaken" mystics they do not approve of. My sense is that in the new millennium we have gone beyond these sterile debates and that we can hail Hammarskjöld as a special, but still recognizable, representative of the new forms of mysticism that emerged in the twentieth century. This is especially true regarding his insistence that the only way to achieve mystical sanctification is through action. In order to understand the character of his mysticism, I will try to summarize the major themes of *Markings* under what has long been noted as a central motif of his life—saying YES to destiny. I will examine *what* the yes means in terms of three questions: *To whom* is Hammarskjöld saying yes?, *By whom* is he saying yes?, and *How* does he say yes?

(A). A number of important texts in *Markings* center on the theme of saying Yes. The most noted comes in a retrospective entry from Pentecost of 1961 (139, 61:5) when Hammarskjöld wrote as follows: "I don't know Who—or what—put the question, I don't know when it was put. I don't even remember answering. But I once did answer *Yes* to Someone—or Something—and from that hour I was certain that existence was meaningful and that, therefore, my life, in self-surrender, had a goal. From that moment I have known what it means 'not to look back' (Luke 9:62) and 'to take no thought for the morrow'" (Matt. 6:34). He goes on, "Led by the Ariadne's thread of my answer through the labyrinth of Life, I came to a time and place where I realized that the Way leads to a triumph which is a catastrophe, and to a catastrophe which is a triumph, that the price for committing one's life would be reproach, and that the only elevation possible to man lies in the depths of humiliation." What is more, he says that as he followed the way, "I learned, step by step, word by word, that behind every saying in the Gospels, stands *one* man and *one* man's experience. Also behind the prayer that the cup might pass from him and his promise to drink it (Matt. 26:39). And also behind each of the words of the cross." This passage brings together a number of important themes: not only the life-altering significance of the Yes, but also the meaning of existence itself, the necessity of following the Way, the paradoxical union of triumph and catastrophe, exaltation and humiliation, and finally Jesus as the exemplar of dedication and sacrifice.

Hammarskjöld writes as though the Yes was a single event, and some have pointed to his accepting the position at the UN in 1953 as the best candidate. It is true that *Markings* for 1953 contains a number of references to saying Yes, such as, "To say Yes to life is at one and the same time to say Yes to oneself. Yes—even to that element in one which is most unwilling to let itself be transformed from a temptation into a strength" (89, 53:14; see also 87, 53:1; and 88, 53:12). But these references lack the crucial notion of saying Yes to the unnamed Someone or Something. Several references from 1951 seem closer to the mystery of the Someone/Something. For example, in 51:47 (pp. 77-78), Hammarskjöld speaks of having overcome his fears "at the frontier of the unheard-of." He continues, "Here ends the known. But, from a source beyond it, something fills my being with its possibilities. Here desire is purified and made lucid: each action is a preparation for, each choice a Yes to the unknown" (see also 80, 51:60). There are also entries from 1955 (96, 55:10), 1956 (110, 56:7), and 1957 (135, 57:37) that make use of the Yes formula. The last of these is striking: "*Yes* to God: yes to destiny: yes to yourself. This reality can wound the soul, but it has the power to heal it." This shows that the Yes is an answer to multiple addressees: God, destiny, self, life, and whatever is conceived of as ultimate. So it seems that the Yes that was so important for Hammarskjöld was more an ongoing and repeated process than a single event, which is why he does not try to pinpoint it specifically in 1961 (see Aulen, 22-31, 117; Erling, 267-68). What was decisive was that Hammarskjöld had given his unconditional assent to a higher power.

Who is the "Someone," or "Something"? Obviously God, and we should remember that Hammarskjöld was accustomed to speaking about God both in anonymous language and in personal language (Aulen, chapter 4, especially 68-78). With regard to anonymous or impersonal language, the Secretary learned from the medieval mystics, such as Eckhart, that abstract terms like the "One" and the "Unheard-of" were fitting instruments to express the unknowability of the divine mystery. The "Unheard- of" (Swedish: *det oerhörda*) seems to be his own invention and occurs seven times in *Markings*. Sometimes it seems to refer to anything unknown or unusual, especially in the phrase "at the frontier of the unheard-of" (81, 51:62; 83, 52:6; 132,

57:25). At other times, it refers to the mystery of God and our union/identity with God. For example, "Then I saw that the wall [between us and God] had never been there, that the Unheard-of is here and this, not something and somewhere else, that the 'sacrifice' is here and now, always and everywhere—'surrendered' to *be* what, in me, God gives of Himself to Himself" (90–91, 54:5; see Erling, 107). Or two later entries from 1954: "The 'Unheard-of'—to be under the hands of God" (93, 54:20); and, "So long as you abide in the 'Unheard-of, you are beyond and above—to hold fast to this must be the First Commandment of your spiritual discipline" (94, 54:25). It seems that it is in the experience of the "Unheard-of" that we become one with God.

Hammarskjöld also uses the "One" to refer to God, and here the dependence on Eckhart is clear. Entry 28 for 1955 (p. 99) talks about "being *only* under God," which the Secretary says is a daily necessity that brooks no division of allegiance. He continues with a direct quotation from Eckhart's Sermon 83, one of the Dominican's most striking texts: "'How, then, am I to love God?,'" someone asks. The answer: "'You must love Him as if He were a Non-God, a Non-Spirit, a Non-Person, a Non-Substance: love Him simply as the One, the pure and absolute Unity in which there is no trace of Duality. And into this One, we must let ourselves fall continually from being into non-being. God help us to do this.'" A cluster of references to the One is found in entries for 1957 that indicate Hammarskjöld may have been rereading Eckhart at that time. Entry 16 speaks of stepping outside of the "self." He says, "To step out of all this and stand naked on the precipice at dawn—acceptable, invulnerable, free, in the Light, with the Light, of the Light, One, real in the One. Out of myself as a stumbling block, into myself as a fulfillment" (130, 57:16). This is a key text for Hammarskjöld. Two other texts on the One occur shortly thereafter. A reflection on his status as being always alone prompts the observation, "The answer—the hard straight brutal answer: in the One you are never alone, in the One you are always at home" (132, 57:22), while in the next entry he says, "The intense blaze of your anxiety reveals to what a great extent you are still fettered, still alienated from the One. However, don't worry about *this or that* [my italics], but follow the Way of which you are aware, even when you have departed from it."[10] Finally, Entry 47 of 1957 (p. 137) talks about his "self-effacement of personality in the One. One result of 'God's union with the soul' [see John of the Cross] is a union with other people which does not draw back from the ultimate surrender of the self."

Speaking of God as the "One" is also found in the New Testament (e.g., Matt. 23:8-9; John 8:41 and 50; Gal. 3:20, etc.), but the Bible more often addresses God in personal terms as "Thou." Hammarskjöld used personal forms of address to God frequently, often citing the Psalms. He was also influenced in this regard by his reading of Martin Buber. *Markings* contains a number of moving personal prayers to God couched in "Thou" language.[11] For example, in 1956 he adapts the Our Father in a strophic form: "Hallowed be Thy name / *not mine,* / Thy kingdom come, / *not mine,* / Thy will be done, / *not mine.* Give us peace with Thee / Peace with men / Peace with ourselves, / And free us from all fear" (123, 56:55). Even more striking is the prayer from July 19, 1961, where he begs for the gifts of mercy, righteousness, and humility to meet God "in the silence." He goes on, "Give us a pure heart that we may see Thee, / A humble heart that we may hear Thee, / A heart of love that we may serve Thee, / A heart of faith that we may live Thee." He ends: "Thou whom I do not know, but whose I am. / Thou whom I do not comprehend, but who hast dedicated me to my destiny. / Thou—."[12]

Some of the most intriguing of Hammarskjöld's prayers are Trinitarian in nature, and it is significant that he speaks of the Trinity mostly in prayer form. The earliest example is Entry 19 from 1954 (p. 93) in a chiastic form: "Thou who art over us [= Father], / Thou who art one of us [= Son], / Thou who art—also within us [= Holy Spirit], / May all see Thee—in me also [= Holy Spirit], / May I prepare the way for Thee [= Son], / May I thank Thee for all that shall fall to my lot [= Father]. May I also not forget the needs of others, / Keep me in Thy love / As Thou would that all shall be kept in mine" (see Erling, 113; and Ryan, 227-29). Comparable is the prayer of 1956: "*Before* Thee, Father, / In righteousness and humility, / With Thee, Brother, / In faith and courage, / In Thee, Spirit, / In stillness. *Thine*—for Thy will is my destiny, *Dedicated*— for my destiny is to be used and used up according to Thy will" (109, 56:1; see also 95, 55:7). The third of these passages on the Trinity (not a prayer) also comes from 1956. After a reference to Eckhart's "habitual will" as a way of attaining "peaceful self-unity," Hammarskjöld rather surprisingly continues: "—looking straight into one's own heart—(as we can do in the mirror-image of the Father) / —watching with affection the way people grow—(as in imitation of the Son) / —coming to rest in perfect equity (as in the fellowship of the Holy Spirit). The unity of the ultimate experience corresponds to the unity of ethical experience. Even the Confucian world has its 'trinity' of life's way" (117, 56:32). What Hammarskjöld is drawing out of Eckhart here is that the habitual interior will in which God is united with us has a Trinitarian structure, both in mystical union ("the ultimate experience") and in all ethical action, as recognized by the Confucian tradition.[13]

Hammarskjöld, without being a theologian, had many penetrating things to say about God in the course of *Markings*. He had read Rudolph Otto's classic *The Idea of the Holy* (1916), a book that shaped much twentieth-century theology. Human awe before God is well expressed in an early entry in *Markings*: "On the bookshelf of life, God is a useful work of reference, always at hand but seldom consulted. . . . But when we are compelled to look ourselves in the face—then He rises above us in terrifying reality, beyond all argument and 'feeling,' stronger than all self-defensive forgetfulness" (37, 41–43:23). Three entries from 1953 deal briefly with God and our relation to him. The first (88, 53:8) is a quotation from *The Imitation of Christ* II.10.23 on giving back to God for all the benefits he has given us. The following two are brief aphorisms on our total dependence on God: "I am the vessel. The draught is God's. And God is the thirsty one" (88, 53:9); and, "In the last analysis, what does the word 'sacrifice' mean? Or even the word 'gift'? He who has nothing can give nothing. The gift is God's—to God" (ibid.; 53:10). Besides the emphasis on how all we possess has been given us by God, Hammarskjöld returns again and again to the fact that God unites himself to us in a tight, even perhaps identical union, on which we will see more below.

(B). The second question noted above was, By *whom* do we say "Yes"? Who gives us the power and the agency; who is also the model for radical obedience? The answer is Jesus Christ. Hammarskjöld dwells mostly on Christ as model and our life as an *imitatio Christi*. He also speaks of the Holy Spirit as power of "God in us," the power of sanctification, but he would not have forgotten the biblical message of the Spirit as the Spirit of Christ. Christ appears only about a dozen times in *Markings*, but in important ways. At the end of the entries for 1945–1949 Hammarskjöld has a meditation on his desire to make a contribution to life, as well as his many failures. He says, "You asked for burdens to carry—And howled when they were placed on your shoulders. . . . The sacrificial act and the sacrificial victim are opposites, and to be judged as such." Then he makes the surprising comment, "O Caesarea Philippi: to accept condemnation of the Way as its fulfilment and presupposition, to accept this both when it is chosen and when it is realized" (50, 45–46:13). Caesarea Philippi was the town where Jesus accepted Peter's designation of him as Messiah and began teaching the disciples about his coming Passion and their need to take up the cross and follow him (Matt. 16:13–26; Mark 8:25–37). Hammarskjöld already saw his life in terms of taking up his cross. Longing for the cross appears in a number of other entries (e.g., 63, 50:44; 88, 53:11; 158, 59:81-82).

Hammarskjöld's other references to Jesus are often disconcerting—they do not belong in any sense to the usual Jesus-piety. Among the most noted is the long meditation on Jesus at the Last Supper as he prepared for the Passion, whose outcome he did not know. Jesus here is the "adamant young man, . . . alone as he confronted his final destiny." Hammarskjöld emphasizes Jesus's commitment to an outcome he could not know—"The *end* might be a death without significance—as well as being the end of the road of possibility." Was he truly "the Lamb who takes away the sins of the world," who sacrificed himself for others, or was he a victim of "sublime egocentricity"? Hammarskjöld sees the dilemma of Jesus as one that he too is called to face—"In the end, the vista of future loneliness only allows a choice between two alternatives: either to despair in desolation, or to stake so high on the 'possibility' that one acquires the right to life in a communion beyond the individual."[14] Despite his uncertainty about the future, Jesus had absolute faith in God, which is what makes him Hammarskjöld's model: "For the sacrificed—in the hour of sacrifice—only one thing counts: faith. . . . Would the Crucifixion have had any sublimity or meaning if Jesus had seen himself crowned with the martyrdom? . . . And we must forget all about it if we are to hear his commands" (130, 57:13). Jesus's commitment to fidelity unto death must be ours, as Hammarskjöld sets out in an entry of 1956, where he cites Blaise Pascal. "The third hour," he says. "And the ninth.—That is *now*. And *now*—that *is* now! 'Jesus will be in agony until the end of the world. We must not sleep during that time' (Pascal). We must not—And for the watcher the far-off is present—also present in his contact with mankind among whom at every moment Jesus dies in someone who has followed the trail marks of the inner road to the end: love and patience, righteousness and humility, faith and courage, stillness" (111, 56:10).

Hammarskjöld also sees Jesus as a model in his everyday life, as he reflects on Jesus's "lack of moral principles" as shown in his eating with publicans, sinners, and harlots (134, 57:36). Finally, there is a controverted passage from 1955, where Hammarskjöld speaks about someone who chose a unique path of sacrifice. I summarize the text: "He broke fresh ground—because, and only because, he had the courage to go ahead without asking whether others were following or even understood. He had no need for the divided responsibility in which others seek to be safe from ridicule, because he had been granted a faith which required no conformation . . . : a union in self-surrender without self-destruction. . . . How different from what the knowing ones call Mysticism" (100, 55:30). Some have interpreted the text as a self-reference, but this seems to me very unlikely and would indicate that Hammarskjöld might, indeed, have thought of himself as a kind of Swedish World-Messiah. No, the passage refers to Jesus, who was the model whom he sought to imitate, while always falling short. Jesus was also the true mystic who realized his union with God in service to humanity.

(C). My third question about Hammarskjöld's Yes asks, *How* did he answer the summons? The answer to this involves many of the aphorisms in *Markings*, which is not a theoretical treatment of mysticism, but practical reflections on his desires, his occasional successes, and his many failures to live out his call. Like Augustine, Hammarskjöld was always conscious of his failures but was convinced that *confessing* them, to God, to himself, and to others, was part of his vocation. In my comments on his character above, I have already touched on many of the values, virtues, and practices he mentions in describing a life of service; here I will try to give a summary of these and touch on a few points not mentioned so far.

It should be obvious from many of the entries already cited that the image of the "Way," or journey, is a characteristic motif in *Markings*. The Way is both the temporal journey through life and the journey within the soul. A poem from 1950 puts it as follows: "The longest journey / Is the journey inwards / Of him who has chosen his destiny, / Who has started upon his quest / For the ground (Swedish: *botten*) of his being / (Is there a ground?)" (65, 50:54). The journey within is also the right road ahead, as he said in an early entry: "Never look down to test the ground before taking your next step: only he who keeps his eye fixed on the far horizon will find his right road" (32, 25–40:5). A number of the dreams that Hammarskjöld recounts and seeks to understand involve traveling on a road (e.g., 76–77, 51:44 and 45). In 1952 he begins the year by citing a Swedish hymn, "Soon night approaches," which he uses at the outset of six other years. It is a hymn to Jesus as the good shepherd guiding his sheep along the right path. He comments, "How long the road is. But for all the time the journey has already taken, how you have needed every second of it in order to learn what it is leading—past" (82, 52:1). The road leads constantly "forward" and never allows us to halt because we know "the last steps before the summit . . . decides the value of all that went before" (125, 56:62). We do not choose the way: "It is not we who seek the Way, but the Way which seeks us. That is why you are faithful to it, even while you stand waiting, so long as you are *prepared* and act the moment you are confronted by its demands" (107, 55:60; see also 175, 62:12). The journey motif often occurs in relation to "destiny," a frequent term in *Markings*, as seen above in 50:54. We often think we choose our destiny, but like the Way, it is also given to us—"Thy will is my destiny" (109, 56:1), and "Yes to God: yes to destiny: yes to yourself" (135, 57:37).[15]

The two most important forces that empower and guide us along the way of destiny are faith (mentioned 34x) and love (33x). (Hope comes up only infrequently.) Faith is not a purely intellectual virtue but, as in Luther, is total confidence in God and his saving power—saying Yes to God. An early entry says, "The road to self-knowledge does not pass though faith. But only through the self-knowledge we gain by pursuing the fleeting light in the depth of our being do we reach the point where we can grasp what faith is. How many have been driven into outer darkness by empty talk about faith as something to be rationally comprehended, something 'true'" (37, 41–42:24). Faith is internal and integral, not something that can be detached and made objectively observable. In condemning the "pride of faith," which reveals a "split personality" that looks at faith from without, Hammarskjöld says that this stance "negates that unity born of a dying-unto-self, which is the definition of faith" (97, 55:15). Frans Maas says that, for Hammarskjöld, "Faith means being able to reside in the perspective of beyond. Faith as night, as God's silence, is painful and uprooting, but at the same time it is the union of God and the soul" (Maas, 89).

Gustaf Aulen explains that the Secretary General had two conceptions of faith, one biblical, and the other from the mystics, especially John of the Cross (58-68). The biblical definition is derived from how the Psalms (e.g., Ps. 139:9–10, cited in 94, 54:28) describe being "in," or "under," or "led" by the hand of God. That faith indicates our total dependence on God is evident from a number of entries. For example, this seems to be the reason why Hammarskjöld describes faith as both humble and proud: "Except in faith, nobody is humble. . . . And except in faith, nobody is proud. . . . To be in faith both humble and proud: that is, to *live*, to know that in God I am nothing [i.e., be humble], but that God is in me (Gal. 2:20)"—and to take pride in that fact (88, 53:13). Faith is not derived or dependent on anything, but is a reality dependent solely on God. "We act in faith and miracles occur. In consequence, we are tempted to make miracles the ground for our faith. The cost of such weakness is that we lose confidence in faith. Faith *is*, faith creates, faith carries. It is not derived from, nor created, nor carried by anything except its own reality" (125, 56:63; see Erling, 183).

It was in early 1954 that Hammarskjöld first mentioned John of the Cross as the source for what Aulen calls his mystical notion of faith. He says, "'Faith is the union of God and the soul' (St. John of the Cross). Faith *is*: it cannot, therefore, be comprehended, far less identified with the formula in which we paraphrase what it is. '—*en una noche oscura*.' The Dark Night of the Soul—so dark that we may not even look for faith. The night in Gethsemane when the last friends have fallen asleep . . . , and God *is silent* as the union is consummated" (91, 54:7). The formula is repeated later several times, as in the entry from 1956, where he says, "To have faith—not to hesitate. Also: not to doubt. 'Faith is God's union with the soul.' In that case, certainty of God's omnipotence *through* the soul: with God all things are possible, *because* faith can move mountains (Matt. 17:19)" (115, 56:25). It has been pointed out that John of the Cross actually does not totally identify faith with loving union, or marriage, with God, but sees it primarily as the necessary *means* to union along with the other theological virtues of hope and charity (e.g., *Ascent of Mount Carmel* II.9.1). Nevertheless, John does say, "The greater one's faith the closer is one's union with God," so Hammarskjöld, who shied away from the language of marriage and its notion of an erotic union (the Auden translation fudges this), is not incorrect. His notion of the irreducibility of faith shows that he could never conceive of it as a means of any kind.[16]

The other fundamental force needed to follow the road to our destiny is love (Aulen, 76–78, 106–7).[17] Love is fundamentally an attribute of God and is another name for God's goodness and benevolence. God creates us out of love and calls us to return that love to him and to other humans. Hence, Hammarskjöld counsels, "To love life and persons as God loves them—for the sake of their infinite possibilities, to wait like Him, to judge like Him without passing judgment, to obey the order never to look back (Luke 9:62)" (112, 56:13). Nevertheless, God does not compel us to love: "Man's freedom is a freedom to betray God. God may love us—yes—but our response is voluntary" (91, 54:10). The same freedom pertains to our love of others—to love someone is not to control the person; love has to be disinterested: "When you have reached the point where you no longer expect a response, you will at last be able to give in such a way that the other is able to receive and be grateful. When Love has matured and, through a dissolution of the self into light become a radiance, then shall the Lover be liberated from dependence on the Beloved, and the Beloved also made perfect by being liberated from the Lover" (78, 51:48; see also 105, 55:51). He cites the Muslim mystical poet Rumi: "The lovers of God have no religion but God alone" (95, 55:1). In some passages, love is presented as the ultimate value: "Beyond obedience, its attention fixed on the goal—freedom from fear. Beyond fear—openness to life. And beyond that—love" (115, 56:19). Our solipsism, greed for power, and death wish can be overcome only by one power, the power of love that needs to be directed to other humans. "Love, which is without an object, the outflowing of a power released by self-surrender, but which would remain a sublime sort of superhuman self-assertion, powerless against the negative forces within you, if it were not tamed by the yoke of human intimacy and warmed by its tenderness" (116, 56:26). Making one person good by our love and being willing to sacrifice oneself for mankind are not, however, alternatives, "but two aspects of self-realization, which mutually support each other, both being the outcome of one and the same choice" (ibid.). "Life will judge me," says Hammarskjöld, "by the measure of the love *I myself* am capable of" (129, 57:9; see also 140, 58:10).

There are a number of other motifs that appear often in *Markings* and that Hammarskjöld obviously thought of as central to his journey. Some of these can be paired, because they suggest each other, such as self-emptying and sacrifice, courage and obedience, stillness and silence, and righteousness and sanctification. Others, such as purity of heart, forgiveness, and liberation, have their own individual valence. Obviously, they cannot all be taken up here, but a few comments need to be made on some of them.

Hammarskjöld's reading of the medieval mystics helped to convince him of the need for *self-surrender*, as he noted in his 1953 interview. He tied this in with the concept of "sacrifice," an essential word in his vocabulary (Aulen, 79–81). In speaking of self-surrender, self-emptying, self-effacement, and the like, Hammarskjöld does not generally use the Eckhartian terminology of detachment and releasement, but he certainly thought that letting go of the ego was necessary for a life of dedication. In 1950 he speaks of "[t]he security of the consciousness's reposing harmony when emptied of all content.—This happiness is here and now, in the eternal cosmic moment. The happiness in you—but not yours" (51, 50:3; trans., Erling). In a passage on Jesus already noted, he speaks of his "union in self-surrender without self-destruction, where his heart was lucid and his mind loving" (100, 55:31). In another place he says, "God desires our independence—which we attain when, ceasing to strive for it ourselves, we 'fall' back into God"

(105, 55:52). "Falling into" God is also descending into the self: "Only when you descend into yourself and encounter the Other, do you then experience goodness as the ultimate reality—united and living—*in* Him and *through* you" (139, 58:8). This can also be described as taking the "risk" of self-surrender: "To reach perfection, we must all pass, one by one, through the fulfilling death of self-surrender. And, on this side of it [i.e., in the selfish life], he will never find the way to anyone who has passed through it" (42, 45–46:5). Self-denial is therefore essential. In a brief entry Hammarskjöld notes, "—with faith and courage. No—in *self-denial*, faith and courage" (119, 56:38). Aulen says that Hammarskjöld's "way of loving service is a combination of self-surrender and self-realization" (99).

The way of self-surrender is the way of sacrifice, a frequent theme in *Markings* (appearing some twenty times). Sacrifice is connected with purity of heart (see Matt. 5:3): "We are not permitted to choose the frame of our destiny. But what we put into it is ours. He who wills adventure will experience it—according to the measure of his courage. He who wills sacrifice will be sacrificed—according to the measure of his purity of heart" (63, 50:46). It also involves disinterested love—"Our love becomes impoverished if we lack the courage to sacrifice its object. Our will to live only survives so long as we will live without a thought as to whether it is our own or not" (64, 50:50). Sacrifice is also linked with faith. Hammarskjöld says, "For the one being sacrificed—who is also making the sacrifice—only one thing counts: faith—alone among enemies and skeptics" (130, 57:13). More deeply considered, however, it is not *we* who make the sacrifice, but God in us, as we read in an entry from 1953 cited above: "In the last analysis, what does the word 'sacrifice' mean? Or even the word 'gift'? He who has nothing can give nothing. The gift is God's—to God" (88, 53:10). It is on the level of sacrifice that the decisions about all life's questions are made (136, 57:47). These decisions involve courage and love, "the two interrelated responses of the sacrifice as an active contribution conditioned by the personality's self-chosen annihilation in the One. 'God's union with the soul'" (136–37, 57:47; Erling trans.). In a rare sexual reference, Hammarskjöld compares the creative act of sacrifice with the fulfillment of sexual orgasm (140, 58:10). Sacrifice, then, is a vicarious act willed by God and done in the service of others and without hope of our own reward. Its prime model is Jesus (Aulen, 79–81, 83–85, 87–89).

Many of the passages already cited have shown how important terms like courage and purity of heart are for Hammarskjöld's notions of self-surrender and sacrifice. Another related term, though not used as often, is obedience (see, e.g., 114, 56:21). Two other sets of paired terms deserve some attention: righteousness and sanctification, and stillness and silence.

Righteousness and the related word "justice" appear about twenty times in *Markings*. Righteousness belongs to God. An early self-reflection says, "He bore failure without self-pity and success without self-admiration," not caring how others judged him. He continues, "A Pharisee? Lord, you know he has never been righteous in his own eyes" (33, 25–50:15). Nevertheless, Hammarskjöld had a hunger both for fellowship and righteousness—"a fellowship founded on righteousness and a righteousness attained in fellowship (Matt. 5:6)" (62, 50:42). Hammarskjöld seeks the righteousness that the Father both bestows and acknowledges (e.g., 94, 54:23; 109; 56:1). In Entry 33 for 1956 (p. 118) Hammarskjöld lists righteousness among the four necessary virtues that depend on God: "With the love of Him who knows all, / With the patience of Him whose now is eternal, / With the righteousness of Him who has never failed, / With the humility of Him who has suffered all the possibilities of betrayal" (see also 121; 56:43). In a fairly long entry for 1957, Hammarskjöld makes a rare reference to original sin. He says, "*We can reach the point where* it becomes possible for us to recognize and understand Original Sin, that dark counterpoint of the evil in our nature—that is to say, though it *is* not our nature, it is *of* it." He goes on, "Life in God is not an escape from this, but the way to gain full insight concerning it. . . . The experience of religious reality . . . forces the 'Night Side' out into the light. It is when we stand in the all-seeing eye of righteous love that we are able to see, dare to acknowledge and consciously suffer because of this" (128, 57:6). Sanctification, on the other hand, appears only twice in *Markings*, but in important contexts. In speaking of the "mystical experience" (108, 55:65), Hammarskjöld says, "In our era, the road to sanctification passes through the world of action." In Entry 28 for 1957 (p. 133), he ties sanctification to self-effacement: "Sanctification—either to be the Light, or to be self-effaced in the Light, so that it may be born, self-effaced so that it may be focused or spread wider."

Stillness and silence have always been important to the mystics, so we should not be surprised that Hammarskjöld refers to them often, sometimes together, sometimes separately. I will cite just a few passages (see Aulen, 60–62). Strangely enough, stillness for Hammarskjöld at times has a relation to birds, such as in his meditation on a seagull (48–49; 45–50:11) and his dream of birds (76–77, 51:44). In Entry 12 for 1956 (p. 111), Hammarskjöld cites Eckhart (Sermon

12), and also includes a brief cryptic saying about stillness that might reflect the Dominican's teaching: "Understand—through the stillness, Act—out of the stillness, Conquer—in the stillness." This is confirmed by Entry 56:58 (p. 124), which refers to Eckhart on the Eternal Birth and quotes a passage from Sermon 101 on "silent stillness." (This is the only appearance of the Birth of the Word in the soul in *Markings*.) Silence and solitude were values for Hammarskjöld all during his life. An early entry says, "Every deed and every relationship is surrounded by an atmosphere of silence. Friendship needs no words—it is solitude delivered from the anguish of loneliness" (32, 25–50:10). An introspective meditation apparently inspired by Jean Cocteau's play *Orphée*, closes with a poetic injunction: "To preserve the silence within—amid all the noise. To remain open and quiet, a moist humus in the fertile darkness where the rain falls and the grain ripens" (83, 52:8). A poem from 1958 provides this image: "Silence shatters to pieces / The mind's armor, / Leaving it naked before / Autumn's clear eye" (141, 58:11).

Two final themes can be briefly considered: forgiveness and freedom. Forgiveness is mentioned only eight times, but is important. We cannot forgive ourselves, but we can forgive others: "'To forgive oneself'—? No, that doesn't work: we have to *be forgiven*. But we can only believe this is possible if we ourselves can forgive" (133, 57:30). Hammarskjöld says that forgiveness is the answer to a child's dream that what was broken gets made whole. "The dream," he continues, "explains why we need to be forgiven, and why we must forgive. In the presence of God, nothing stands between Him and us—we *are* forgiven" (110, 56:10). God is always forgiving: "So shall the world be created each morning anew, *forgiven*—in Thee, by Thee" (138, 58:1). Still, we continually need to ask for forgiveness, as the moving late poem from 1961 makes clear: "Almighty . . . Forgive my doubt, my anger, my pride. By Thy mercy abase me, by Thy strictness raise me up" (178, 61:16). Forgiveness is related to freedom/liberation, a frequent theme in *Markings* (twenty references). The entry for Easter 1960 says, "Forgiveness breaks the chain of causality because he who 'forgives' you—out of love—takes upon himself the responsibility for the consequences of what you have done. Forgiveness, therefore, always involves a sacrifice. The price you must pay for your own liberation through another's sacrifice is that you in turn must be willing to liberate in the same way, irrespective of the consequences to yourself" (163, 60:1; see Erling, 254). Freedom is part of human destiny: "To become free and responsible. For this alone was man created, and he who fails to take the Way which could have been his shall be eternally lost" (62, 50:42). Freedom is essential for the ability to say "Yes"—"To be free, to be able to stand up and leave *everything* behind—without looking back (Luke 9:62). To say *Yes*—" (88, 53:8). Finally, it is in freedom that we are one with God. Entry 13 in 1954 (p. 92) says, "Thou who hast created us free, Who sees all that happens—yet art confident of victory. Thou who at this time art the one among us who suffers the uttermost loneliness, Thou—who art also in me, May I bear thy burden when my hour comes, May I—."

Dag Hammarskjöld's View of Mysticism

What follows is a summary of what we have seen, but also an attempt to show why Hammarskjöld is, indeed, aptly characterized as a mystic. Hammarskjöld used the terms "mysticism" and "mystical experience" only once each in *Markings* (Erling's "Index" is here unreliable), but many other passages can be deemed mystical.[18] The key texts mentioning mysticism come from 1955. I have already noted Entry 30 from that year (p. 100), where the Secretary General reflects on Jesus as having been given "a union in self-surrender without self-destruction," and notes, "How different from what the knowing ones call Mysticism." Obviously, he has in mind the notion of mysticism as found in the "knowing ones," who identify it with visions, unusual psychological phenomena, and the like, rather than "the faith that requires no confirmation." The second text is found in Entry 65 of 1955 (p. 108), where he gives a description of the mystical experience that needs to be quoted in full. He says,

> The "mystical experience." Always: *here* and *now*—and in that freedom which is one with detachment in that stillness which is born of silence. But—this is a freedom in the midst of action, a stillness in the midst of other human beings. This mystery is a constant reality in the one who, in the midst of this world is free from self-concern, a reality that grows peaceful and mature before the receptive attention of assent.

The passage closes with the aphorism already noted: "In our era, the way to sanctification necessarily passes through the world of action." The appearance of many of the themes already discussed above should be noted in this passage—freedom, stillness, silence, action, self-emptying, mystery, sanctification and action, and assent (the Yes). The text shows that Hammarskjöld had a profound sense of mysticism. Finally, the Secretary General also seems to be talking about mystical experience without using the word in 1956 when he says that "the ultimate experience is one" (117, 56:30).

Hammarskjöld often talked about union with God, as noted above. In this connection he loved to cite John of the Cross about faith effecting union with God. We have already discussed two of these passages (91, 54:7; 115, 56:25), and there are three others (96, 55:9; 137, 57:47; and 139, 58:7). The final text is especially noteworthy: "In the faith which is 'God's union with the soul,' you are *one* in God, and God is wholly in you, just as, for you, He is wholly present in all you meet. With this faith, in prayer, you descend into yourself to meet the Other, in the steadfastness and light of this union, and see that all things stand, like yourself, alone before God." Once again, Hammarskjöld demonstrates a deep understanding of mystical union.

Union language is also found in other entries that do not specifically mention John of the Cross.[19] A good example is Entry 47 for 1957 (pp. 136-37). Especially noteworthy are the passages where Hammarskjöld uses formulae that express a deep union, even a kind of identity, between God and the soul—"Not I, but God in me" (87, 53:6, reminiscent of Gal. 2:20). There are eight or ten of these, so it is not a minor aspect of his thought. Two more come from early in 1953, as when he speaks of his sacrifice or gift as God's giving to God (88, 53:10), and then says, "To be, in faith, both humble and proud: that is, to *live*, to know that in God I am nothing and that God is in me" (ibid., 53:13). Three more such entries come from 1954. Entry 54:5 (pp. 90-91), again speaking of sacrifice, says that it is an offering "here and now, always and everywhere—'surrendered' to *be* what in me God gives of Himself to Himself." Entry 54:13 (p. 92) addresses God: "Thou—who art also in me, May I bear Thy burden, when my hour comes." Finally, Entry 54:19 (p. 93), the long prayer to the Trinity quoted above, speaks of union with the Trinity.

In his last years, Hammarskjöld continued to use such formulae. The mutuality of God and the self is evident in Entry 56:13 (p. 112): "From this perspective, 'to believe in God' is to believe in yourself, as self-evident, as 'illogical,' and as impossible to explain: if I can be, then God *is*." Entry 57:4 (p. 127) again employs the expression, "Not I, but God in me!" I already noted the passage from 1957 where Hammarskjöld speaks of divesting the self: "To step out of all this and stand naked on the precipice of dawn—acceptable, invulnerable, free in the Light, with the Light, of the Light. One, real in the One. Out of myself as a stumbling-block, into myself as a fulfilment" (130, 57:16). Here, being bathed in the divine Light (a frequent symbol in *Markings*; see, e.g., 133, 57:28), the person can become "One in the One." Finally, Entry 58:7 (p. 139) speaks of faith as God's union with the soul (without mentioning John of the Cross), but also emphasizes our complete unity with God—"You are one in God, and God is *wholly* in you, just as for you He is wholly in all you meet." All human beings are one with God, if they could just realize it.

Dag Hammarskjöld had a deep appreciation of nature, and *Markings* is filled with beautiful passages about the natural world, both in prose and in poetry (Aulen, 26–27). In some of these entries we can talk about a form of nature mysticism, that is, a desire to merge with the universe. For example, there are a series of entries at the end of 1951 (76–80, 51:44–61) that reflect aspects of nature at different times of the year, some in the mountains of Lapland, where Hammarskjöld loved to hike and climb (e.g., 51:56–58, and 60–61). These entries mix acute natural observations with dream imagery. Frans Maas has seen in these accounts a description of the mystical experiences Hammarskjöld enjoyed during that year (Maas, 82–87). Perhaps the most arresting of the nature moments is Entry 51:50 (p. 78), which begins with a picture: "So rests the sky against the earth. The dark still tarn in the lap of the forest. As a husband embraces his wife's body in faithful tenderness, so the bare ground and trees are embraced by the still, high, light of the morning." Then, he speaks of his desire to share "in this embrace, to be united and absorbed. A longing like carnal desire, but directed toward earth, water, sky, and returned by the whispers of the trees, the fragrance of the soil, the caresses of the wind, the embrace of water and light" (see also 51:56–57 and 60–61). The sense of merging is even stronger in an entry from 1952: "When the sense of the earth unites with the sense of one's body, one becomes earth of the earth, a plant among plants, an animal born from the soil and fertilizing it. In this union the body is confirmed in its pantheism" (84, 52:9).

I will close this treatment of the mysticism of Dag Hammarskjöld with an enigmatic text involving a dream of uniting with God and other souls in infinity (see Aulen, 120; Erling, 142). Here is the passage (105, 55:55):

> In a dream I walked with God through the deep places of creation; past walls that receded and gates that opened, through hall after hall of silence, darkness and refreshment—the dwelling-place of souls acquainted with light and warmth—until, around me, was an infinity into which we all flowed together and lived anew, like rings made by raindrops falling upon wide expanses of calm dark waters.

Notes

1. For the translation of *Markings* I use the version of W. H. Auden and L. Sjöberg, cited by page, but I also employ the numbering system for individual entries given by B. Erling (e.g., 112, 56:13 means p. 112 and the thirteenth entry for 1956). For full titles and publication information for the titles cited by author or short title, see the bibliography at the end of the essay.

2. The best study of *Markings* is by Gustaf Aulen. Also important is the new translation and commentary by Bernhard Erling. Other studies include those by Henry Van Dusen, Sven Stolpe, and the essay of Roger Lipsey (2011).

3. Aulen, 138–44. Further evidence is in Hammarskjöld's address to the World Council of Churches meeting in Evanston, Illinois, in August 1954. For full titles and publication information for the works cited by author or short title, see the bibliography at the end of the essay.

4. See De Villiers, "Mysticism in a Melting Pot," 94–111.

5. One of the unusual stylistic characteristics of *Markings* is its frequent use of dashes (–), which indicate pauses in thought and sometimes changes of direction.

6. For further reflections on death, see *Markings*, 35, 47, 51, 57, 58, 68, 69, 70, 75, 83, 107, 119, 140, 170, 172, etc.

7. Huls (69–81) discusses the passage in *Markings*, 88, 53:8, using *De imitatione Christi* II.10.23 about being founded on God. Two other passages are discussed in Huls's article: *Markings*, 95, 55:3, using *De imitatione* III.35 passim, on purity of intention; and *Markings*, 98, 55:21, using *De imitatione* II.10.1, on being created to labor. In addition, *De imitatione* is cited on 103, 55:53; 108, 55:66; 110, 56:8; and 123, 56:57.

8. Eckhart is explicitly mentioned in *Markings*, 117, 56:30. Eckhart texts are used without naming him on 88, 53:1; 99, 55:28 (a direct citation from German Sermon 83); 111, 56:11-12; 118, 56:34; 124, 56:57-58; 132, 57:23; 134, 57:33; and 138, 58:2-3. A few other uses of Eckhart are plausible, but a number of the mentions of "Eckhart" found in the Auden translation are spurious. Hammarskjöld read Eckhart in the 1934 modern German translation of G. Büttner (a copy is in his library). Aulen has some reflections on Hammarsköld's use of Eckhart, and there is an article by Ria van den Brandt on how Eckhart's conception of the will influenced Hammarskjöld.

9. On the relation of Luther and Hammarskjöld, see Aulen, 124–30.

10. *Markings*, 132, 57:23. This passage has generally not been recognized as Eckhartian in background, but I take the contrast between God as *ein* and created things as *dis und das* as clearly based on an essential teaching of the Dominican Meister.

11. *Markings* also contains entries on the nature and necessity of prayer; see, e.g., 34, 41–42:3; 50, 50:29; 97, 55:16.

12. *Markings*, 176, 61:13. This powerful prayer is treated by all the commentators; see Aulen, 122; Van Dusen, 202; Erling, 275. For other personal prayers to God, see *Markings*, 92, 54:13; 110, 56:7; 137, 57:52; and 138, 58:1.

13. Hammarskjöld drew his knowledge of Eckhart's "habitual will" from the Dominican's treatise *Talks of Instruction* 21 (DW 5:281). On this passage, see Aulen, 48–49; and Erling, 166–67.

14. *Markings*, 72–73, 51:29–32 (see Aulen, 52–54; Erling, 67–68). This passage

was part of the ammunition that Hammarskjöld's Swedish critics used after his death to accuse him of a "Messiah-complex," a canard long since refuted. The passage features a variety of biblical references (John 1:29; 13:34; Mark 11:1-10; and Matt. 17:20).

15. For more on "destiny" and "fate" (the same Swedish word, *öde*, serves for both), see Aulen, 92-95, and such passages as *Markings* 71, 51:27; 116, 56:27; 124, 56:59; 127, 57:1; and 132, 57:24. Erling lists fourteen appearances of the term (66).

16. Maas argues that John of the Cross and Hammarskjöld are not as far apart as it might seem (88-90).

17. Faith and love, humility and righteousness, often appear together in Hammarskjöld; e.g., 176, 61:13. On humility, see especially 148-49, 59:5.

18. For discussions of Hammarskjöld as mystic, see Aulen, 113-24; Svolpe, 66, 85-89, 99; and Lipsey 2011, 98-100.

19. On union in Hammarskjöld, see Aulen, 41-42, 64-66, 69-70, and 149-50.

Bibliography
Sources

Hammarskjöld, Dag. *Markings*. Translated by W. H. Auden and Leif Sjöberg. London and Boston: Faber & Faber, 1964. The standard translation.

Erling, Bernhard. *A Reader's Guide to Dag Hammarskjöld's* Waymarks. St. Peter, MN, 1982 (translation), 1987 (commentary). An improved translation and valuable guide. Available at: http://www.daghammarskjold.se/wp-content/uploads/2014/08/rg_to_waymarks.pdf.

Foote, Wilder, ed. *Servant of Peace: A Selection of the Speeches and Statements of Dag Hammarskjöld, Secretary-General of the United Nations, 1953-1961*. New York: Harper & Row, 1962.

Studies

Aulen, Gustaf. *Dag Hammarskjöld's White Book: An Analysis of* Markings. Philadelphia: Fortress Press, 1969. The best treatment.

Brandt, Ria van den. "Schicksalmässiges und Schöpferisches Wollen: Dag Hammarskjöld und Meister Eckhart." *Studies in Spirituality* 5 (1995): 220-31.

Huls, Jos. "A Conversation beyond the Border: Dag Hammarskjöld & Thomas à Kempis." *Studies in Spirituality* 20 (2010): 67-99.

Lipsey, Roger. "Dag Hammarskjöld and *Markings*: A Reconsideration." *Spiritus* 11 (2011): 84-103. A useful introduction.

———. *Hammarskjöld: A Life*. Ann Arbor: University of Michigan Press, 2016. An important recent biography.

Maas, Frans. "Dag Hammarskjöld: 'The dissolution of the self in pure

light.'" In Maas, *Spirituality as Insight: Mystical Texts and Theological Reflection*, 52-97. Leuven: Peeters, 2004.
Ryan, Thomas. "Wisdom as Loving Knowledge in Dag Hammarskjöld's *Markings*." *Spiritus* 17 (2017): 228-45.
Somaiya, Ravi. *The Golden Thread: The Cold War and the Mysterious Death of Dag Hammarskjöld*. New York: Twelve, 2020.
Stolpe, Sven. *Dag Hammarskjöld: A Spiritual Portrait*. New York: Scribner, 1965.
Urquhart, Brian. *Dag Hammarskjold*. New York: Knopf, 1972. The major biography.
Van Dusen, Henry. *Dag Hammarskjöld: The Statesman and His Faith*. New York: Harper, 1967.

Other Protestant Mystics

Clark, Henry B. *The Ethical Mysticism of Albert Schweitzer: A Study of the Sources and Significance of Schweitzer's Philosophy of Civilization*. Boston: Beacon Press, 1962.
De Villiers, Pieter. "Mysticism in the Melting Pot: Andrew Murray, a Mystic from Africa on the World Stage." *Spiritus* 16 (1916): 94-111.
Kelly, Thomas R. *A Testament of Devotion*. New York: Harper, 1941.
Robinson, Timothy. "'Resisting Whatever Separates One from the Ground of Being': Howard Thurman's Prophetic Appropriation of the Christian Mystical Tradition." In *Mysticism and Contemporary Life: Essays in Honor of Bernard McGinn*, edited by John J. Markey and J. August Higgins, 127-44. New York: Crossroad, 2019.
Schweitzer, Albert. *Out of My Life and Thought: An Autobiography*. New York: Holt, Rinehart & Winston, 1949.
———. *Essential Writings*. Selected by James Brabazon. Maryknoll, NY: Orbis Books, 2005.
Thurman, Howard. *The Way of the Mystics*. Edited by Peter Eisenstadt and Walter Earl Fluker. Maryknoll, NY: Orbis Books, 2021.

CHAPTER 7

Simone Weil (1909–1943): Dialectical Mysticism

Simone Weil, whom Gabriel Marcel called "a pilgrim of the Absolute," was a fascinating figure. Since the post–World War II appearance of her writings, she has attracted considerable attention from philosophers, political scientists, students of religion, cultural critics, feminists, literary scholars, and others. Weil was a philosopher by training and a number of books have been devoted to what is often called her "religious philosophy."[1] Although she was not trained in theology, her writings have important implications for contemporary theology. She was also a social and political theorist. Further, Weil has been described as a modern "mystic," a vocation she expressed interest in, although it was not a term she claimed for herself.[2] Nonetheless, I would agree with those who have termed her a mystic, and this aspect of her life and writings is what I will focus on here—although obviously her mysticism has to be framed in light of the main lines of her thought.

Weil's life was one of rigorous honesty, striving to attain the truth, dedication to the service of others, compassion, solidarity with the oppressed, selflessness, opposition to repressive structures, and an overpowering love for God, to the extent that some have described her as a saint.[3] Whatever misgivings one may have about her (see below), Weil has been a spiritual beacon for many. While many investigators place their focus primarily on her speculative and political theories, my approach will be somewhat different. I present this analysis of Weil the mystic with the caveat that she was a complex and many-sided person, and no single lens is adequate to provide the full picture of Weil's genius.

Simone Weil: The Person

Life and Mystical Experiences

Simone Weil was born in Paris on February 3, 1909, from Alsatian Jewish parents, Bernard, a doctor, and Selma.[4] Reflecting on her life in the *Notebook* written in New York in 1942, she makes the paradoxical statement: "You could not have wished to be born at a better time than this, when everything has been lost."[5] Weil's parents were thoroughly assimilated Jews, and she grew up knowing nothing of Judaism. She had an older brother André (b. 1906), who became a world famous mathematician. Simone was a gifted student who sailed through the French Lycée system, attending several schools. At the age of fourteen she says she fell into a fit of "bottomless despair" and was tempted to suicide because she could not equal her brother's intellectual accomplishments. After several months she was rescued from this, when "I suddenly had the everlasting conviction that any human being, even though practically devoid of natural faculties, can penetrate to the kingdom of truth reserved for genius, if only he longs for truth and perpetually concentrates all his attention upon its attainment."[6] The desire for truth and concentration of attention (*attente*) were to be hallmarks of her life. She was admitted to the University in 1925, and from 1925 to 1928 studied with the philosopher "Alain" (Emile-Auguste

Chartier), who remained an influence throughout her life. In 1928 she passed first in the entrance exam for the École Normale Supérieure, the premier French graduate program. She received her degree in 1931 with a thesis on Descartes. Simone Weil was at the top of the emerging group of young French intellectuals of the early 1930s.

It was at this time that Simone began to show her independence. Promising professors were generally sent off to teach in local Lycées for a few years to hone their teaching skills and work on their philosophical projects, before further advancement on the road to academic success in the universities. Simone's path was different. From her early years, she had expressed deep sympathy with "the downtrodden of the earth," that is, the poor, the oppressed, and all who were subject to what she came to call *malheur* (inadequately translated as "affliction"). Teaching first at a female Lycée in Le Puy (1931), and then in Auxerre (1932) and Roanne (1933), she not only innovated new forms of pedagogy[7] but also became active in support of workers' rights. Although never a Marxist or a Communist (she admitted to learning much from Marx, despite his errors),[8] Simone's support for radical left, especially Anarchist, causes led to her becoming known as the "Red Virgin," a reputation that led to her dismissal from several academic posts. Simone's solidarity with workers was more than just theoretical. In 1934 and 1935 she put her beliefs on the line by taking leave from teaching and working in factories near Paris on the assembly lines in order to get some idea of the actual life experience of the modern proletariat. Her reflections led to an essay, "Factory Work" (*Reader*, 53–72). There was a further stage in her politico-social activism. In 1936 war broke out in Spain between the elected Republican government (a coalition of left-wing parties) and the right-wing insurgency led by General Francisco Franco. With her deep sympathy with the left, in August 1936, Simone volunteered to fight for the Republican cause, although it is difficult to imagine what a physically clumsy intellectual could have contributed beyond a solidarity expressed by her death. She was rapidly disabused about the war. In a letter written to Georges Bernanos, a French Catholic novelist she admired, she says that she soon lost any desire "to participate in a war which, instead of being what it had appeared when it began—a war of famished peasants against landed proprietors and their clerical supporters—had become a war between Russia on the one hand and Italy and Germany on the other" (*Reader*, 75). Fortunately, she did not have to remain long in Spain, since she was repatriated after a serious accident caused by her own clumsiness.

Then, the unexpected. Weil had shown little interest in religion thus far. Her few writings had been about political and social issues. Suddenly, religion became a major topic, and it is hard to know why, despite the studies, psychoanalytic and otherwise, that have been devoted to the topic. I will look at her own testimony about how the sense of God gradually entered her life, largely taken from the "Spiritual Autobiography," a letter she wrote in 1942 for her friend and spiritual advisor, Fr. Joseph-Marie Perrin, O.P. (1905–2002). Here she recounts some events of the late 1930s in which she gradually became aware of God's presence.

On vacation with her parents in Portugal in 1935, she testifies to the state of intense *malheur* and fatigue she had been left in by her experience working in the factories. She says that she has internalized this state of abjection and slavery into her life: "There I received forever the mark of a slave, like the branding with a red-hot iron the Romans put on the foreheads of their most despised slaves. Since then I had always regarded myself as a slave" (*Waiting for God*, 67). One evening, however, she had the opportunity to listen to the wives of the poor fishermen of a village as they inspected the boats and sang an ancient hymn. "Nothing can give any idea of it," she says. "I have never heard anything so poignant unless it were the song of the boatmen on the Volga. There the conviction was suddenly borne in upon me that Christianity is preeminently the religion of slaves, that slaves cannot help belonging to it, and I among others" (ibid.). The second experience happened at Assisi in 1937, when she visited the church of Santa Maria degli Angeli, where St. Francis had prayed. Here she attests that "something stronger than I was compelled me for the first time in my life to go down on my knees" (*Waiting for God*, 67–68). (A similar experience was later to mark the conversion of Etty Hillesum; see chapter 9.) The third event took place in 1938, when she spent ten days during Holy Week at the monastery of Solesmes, attending the liturgy of the modern home of Gregorian chant. Despite a terrible headache (she often suffered from these), Simone says that by supreme concentration she "was able to rise above this wretched flesh, . . . and to find a pure and perfect joy in the unimaginable beauty of the chanting and the words." She goes on: "This experience enabled me by analogy to get a better understanding of the possibility of loving divine love in the midst of affliction. It goes without saying that in the course of these services the thought of the Passion of Christ entered into my being once and for all" (ibid.).[9]

These three experiences of a gradual sense of the divine were followed by two events that can be called properly mystical. During her time at Solesmes she met a young English Catholic man whose "truly angelic radiance" after he received communion gave her the "first idea of the supernatural power of the sacraments." He also told her about the English Metaphysical poets of the seventeenth century. Reading them, Simone discovered George Herbert's poem "Love," deeply Eucharistic in nature. She learned it by heart and often recited it during her headaches, "concentrating all my attention on it and clinging with all my soul to the tenderness it enshrines." What follows is revealing: "I used to think I was merely reciting it as a beautiful poem, but without my knowing it the recitation had the virtue of a prayer. It was during one of these recitations that, as I told you, Christ came down and took possession of me" (*Waiting for God*, 68–69). In her reflections on this event, Simone says that she had never even considered the possibility here below of a real person-to-person contact with God. She had vaguely heard of such things, but the apparitions ascribed to Francis in the *Fioretti* had put her off, just as the miracles in the Gospels. "Moreover," she goes on, "in this sudden possession of me by Christ, neither my senses or my imagination had any part; I only felt in the midst of my suffering the presence of a love, like that which one can read in the smile on a beloved face" (ibid.). She says that she had never read any mystical works, because she never felt the need to. Rather, "God in his mercy had prevented me from reading the mystics, so that it should be evident to me that I had not invented this absolutely unexpected contact" (ibid.). Simone says that her love was convinced of Christ's presence, while her intelligence still wrestled with the question out of a "pure regard for truth." (Simone was later to insist that it is only love, not intelligence, that can gain God.) Christ as the truth (John 14:6), she says, wants us to prefer truth to him (a statement similar to passages in Meister Eckhart),[10] so that, "If one turns aside from him to go toward the truth, one will not go far before falling into his arms" (ibid.).[11]

Further on in the "Spiritual Autobiography" Simone talks about the role of prayer in her spiritual progress. She says that she had never prayed in the sense of addressing words to God, either mentally or verbally. But last summer (1941), she goes on, doing Greek with her friend "T" (Gustave Thibon), she went through the "Our Father" word by word in Greek. She began to say it over and over, often repeating it while working in the vineyard. Once each morning she strove to recite it "with absolutely perfect attention," even starting over if her mind wandered. "The effect of this practice is extraordinary," she says, and "surprises me every time" (*Waiting for God*, 71–72). At times the recitation transports her from her body "to a place outside space where there is neither perspective nor point of view." This is an infinity beyond ordinary perception, a "second or sometimes third degree" of infinity, where "there is silence, a silence that is not an absence of sound but which is the object of a positive sensation, more positive than that of sound" (ibid.). "Sometimes," she says, "during this recitation or at other moments, Christ is present with me in person, but his presence is infinitely more real, more moving, more clear than on that first occasion when he took possession of me" (ibid.). Simone says that she would never have been able to tell Fr. Perrin all this had she not been going away with the conviction that she would soon be dead, which turned out to be the case. She says that the whole matter does not really concern her—"It concerns God. I am really nothing at all" (ibid.). Perhaps God sent her the experience by mistake, she muses, or perhaps it only happened because God likes to use "castaway objects, waste, rejects." Nevertheless, Simone's love for the Our Father continued, as can be seen in her several commentaries and remarks on the prayer.[12]

By the last years of the 1930s Simone had become deeply involved with Christianity and was experiencing states of mystical awareness. At the same time, events in Europe were rapidly moving ahead toward the outbreak of World War II. After the fall of France in 1940, Simone and her family moved to Vichy, the capital of the collaborating French government, where they thought Jews might be safer. In October they went to Marseilles, where Simone tried to find a new teaching position but was turned down because of her status as a Jew. In November she wrote a troubling letter to the Minister of Education ("What is a Jew?"), in which she claims, "I myself, who profess no religion and never have, have certainly inherited nothing from the Jewish religion. . . . I would say that if there is a religious tradition which I regard as my patrimony, it is the Catholic tradition. In short, mine is the Christian, French, Greek tradition. The Hebraic tradition is alien to me" (*Reader*, 80). Note that Simone does not protest against an unjust law, but instead unjustly tries to get herself exempted. This alienation from her Jewish heritage was expressed in stronger, sometimes hateful, terms throughout her writings. Simone Weil's contrast to the other two Jewish female mystics considered here, Edith Stein and Etty Hillesum, could not appear in starker terms.

In Marseilles, Simone attended meetings of the "Young Christian Workers Movement," whose views on social and political reform were much in line with her own. She also became associated with the journal *Cahiers du Sud*, in which she published several articles anonymously. The most important event of 1941 was her meeting with Fr. Perrin, the learned and tolerant priest who became her friend and a kind of spiritual director. She confided to Perrin her desire to once again take up the life of an ordinary worker, this time with agricultural work. He put her in touch with his friend Gustave Thibon (1903–2001), a farmer and also a philosopher and devout right-wing Catholic. Despite their significant intellectual and personal differences, Weil and Thibon became close friends. Simone got her wish to engage in backbreaking work in the vineyards in September and October 1941. All during these years she was writing essays, often on religious topics,[13] and making massive entries in her *Notebooks*. The situation for Jews in Vichy France was now as bad as in German-occupied France, so the Weil family left Marseilles in May. After two weeks in a refugee camp in Casablanca, they were able to sail for New York on June 7, 1942. Before she departed, Simone left her *Notebooks* with Thibon. They became the source for most of what we know about her thinking.

The *Notebooks* contain a mysterious mystical account that cannot be precisely dated but seems to come from mid-1942.[14] It can be described as a kind of medieval dream vision of Christ. The account begins abruptly: "He came into my room and said: 'You poor wretch, who understand nothing and know nothing—come with me and I will teach you things you have no idea of.' I followed him." The mysterious visitor takes her into a church and commands her to kneel. She demurs because she has not been baptized. "He said: 'Fall on your knees before this place, with love, as before the place where truth exists.' I obeyed." Then the visitor led her up to a garret with an open window, where the two engaged in conversation, along with occasional others. Several days pass. "Sometimes he paused and took some bread from a cupboard, and we shared it. That bread truly had the taste of bread. I have never found that taste again. He poured wine for me and for himself, which tasted of the sun and of the soil on which that city was built." This Eucharistic moment is followed by unspecified further days of conversation, but the visitor teaches her nothing, despite his promise. Finally, "One day he said to me: 'Now go away.' I threw myself down, clung to his knees, begged him not to send me away. But he flung me out towards the stairs." In great sorrow, she walks through the streets, realizing that she does not know where the house was. She never even tries to find the house, because, as in the case of the experiences she wrote about in her "Spiritual Autobiography," she says, "I saw that he had come for me by mistake. My place is not in that garret." Nevertheless, the experience remains with her as a token of the love of God, even for Simone, the wretch cast out of the garret. The vision closes with the following poignant lines: "I well know that he doesn't love me. How could he love me? And yet there is something deep in me, some point of myself, which cannot prevent itself from thinking, with fear and trembling, that perhaps, in spite of everything, he does love me." Simone's sense of her own worthlessness (a hallmark of her life) had been somewhat assuaged.

Simone and her family arrived in New York on July 7. Her one desire was to return to Europe as soon as possible to work for General Charles de Gaulle (who thought she was insane) and the Free French government located in London. Simone remained in New York for several months. She took the opportunity to compose an extensive *New York Notebook*. In November she sailed to Liverpool, but was detained for some time because of her service in the Spanish Civil War. Finally, she was allowed to undertake a kind of ill-defined role as a writer and advisor for the Free French. This led to the writing of the only book she ever finished—*The Need for Roots*, a visionary plan for the spiritual rejuvenation of France after the war.[15] She also worked on various position papers for the French government-to-be, including one on the suppression of the Jews.[16] Simone's major concern now was the totally illusory idea of being parachuted back into France to help the Resistance.[17] During the past few years her health had been in decline, due not only to her debilitating headaches but also to her increasing abstention from eating (she was probably an anorexic). Now that she was no longer under the supervision of her parents, her abstention became more severe. She somehow conceived the idea that she should not eat more than the average French citizen was being allowed under occupation. She was literally wasting away. One gets the impression that Simone, in her stubbornness and self-will, may have been beginning to lose touch with reality. In April 1943, she had to enter the hospital, where it was discovered that she was not only severely malnourished but also was suffering from tuberculosis. This was curable, but the cure involved medication and also eating a rich diet. To the chagrin of her doctors, Simone refused. She lingered on for a few months, eventually sinking into a coma and dying on August 22.

During her few months in New York, Simone entered what she called an "Example of prayer" into her *Notebook*.[18] It is an almost terrifying plea for total abjection. We may surmise that it reflects the kind of mentality that she increasingly had come to adopt in her final months. Some earlier mystics (e.g., Marguerite Porete and Madame Guyon) had left similar expressions of the desire for mystical annihilation, but Simone's plea goes beyond these in its stark concreteness. She begins,

"Father, in the name of Christ grant me this. That I may be unable to will any bodily movement, or even attempt at movement, like a total paralytic. . . . That I may be unable to make the slightest connection between two thoughts, even the simplest, like one of those total idiots who not only cannot count or read but have never learned to speak." She goes on, "That I may be insensible to every kind of grief and joy, and incapable of any love for any being or thing, and not even for myself, like old people in the last stage of decrepitude. Father, in the name of Christ grant me all this in reality." Then the prayer reverses, perhaps reflecting Simone's thought that it is not *her will for total abjection* that counts, but God's will to do whatever he wants with her. She prays, "May this body move or be still, with perfect suppleness or rigidity, in total conformity to thy will. May my faculties of hearing, sight, taste, smell and touch register the perfectly accurate impress of thy creation. May this mind, in fullest lucidity, connect all ideas in perfect conformity with thy truth. . . . May this love be an absolutely devouring flame of love of God for God." But then the prayer has another reversal expressing again her *own* desire for total annihilation: "May all this be stripped away from me, devoured by God, transformed into Christ's substance, and given for food to the afflicted men whose body and soul lack every kind of nourishment. And let me be a paralytic—blind, deaf, witless and utterly decrepit." Simone closes her "Abjection Prayer" with a repeated plea for transformation in the name of Christ, although she asks "with imperfect faith," begging the Father to "rend this body and soul away from me to make them things for your use, and let nothing remain of me, forever, except this rending itself, or else nothingness." She also comments that words of this frightening nature come not from her own will, but from the dictation of the Holy Spirit, and can be consented to only by "a violence exerted upon the entire soul by the entire soul."

The coroner's report on Simone Weil's death listed suicide as a cause. This seems a mislabeling. Simone always expressed opposition to suicide (e.g., *First and Last Notebooks*, 404), and, however misguided her bizarre asceticism had become, one doubts that she intended to kill herself. Rather, as her brother André noted, she seems to have decided to leave her fate in God's hands. If he wanted her to live, she would survive; if not, she was equally happy to perish.[19] In death, as in life, Simone Weil remains a difficult, perhaps even an "impossible" person, both inspiring and troubling. It may be best to leave judgment to her friends J.-M. Perrin and G. Thibon: "It is for God alone to fathom the mystery of this soul and her destiny."[20]

Simone Weil as a Problem

Simone was a totalist in the sense of someone who could never admit the slightest compromise once she had made up her mind—she was not only intransigent but also often inhuman, to foes, to friends, and especially to herself. Without the ability to see shades of color, for her everything was either pure white or total black. This had both a good and a bad side. Her uncompromising nature helps explain some of her most noble actions and deepest insights, as well as her most troubling defects. These defects were part and parcel of her stubbornness—once she had decided on an issue, she seemed unable (or unwilling) to consider an alternative view. It is ironic that someone who insisted that her goal was the total destruction of her own will proved to be so self-willed.

The paradox of this "coincidence of opposites" in Simone's character has provided difficulties for her interpreters. The treatment by her closest friends, Fr. Perrin and Gustave Thibon in *Simone Weil as We Knew Her*, which praises her genius of mind and splendor of person, while still wrestling with her errors and limitations, provides a balanced judgment. The power of her insights and the witness of her person have attracted a large number of admirers, many of whom seem to shy away from any consideration of her personal and intellectual failures. Her brother André once complained that Simone, who fought against idolatry all her life, was in danger of being treated as an idol. Some scholars who have been attracted to Simone have also tried to confront the problems of her life and thought (e.g., Coles; Zaretsky).[21] These difficulties are perhaps most evident in her deeply biased view of Judaism, which has been rejected by even her most fervent disciples.[22] How such an intelligent person could come to hold such positions has been studied by psychologists like Robert Coles, as well as Jewish philosophers and writers (e.g., Martin Buber, Emmanuel Levinas, John Oesterreicher, and others). There is no easy explanation.

Simone Weil's hatred of Judaism is on display across her writings, so it would be needless to quote numerous passages.[23] Let me cite just one disturbing text from the *Notebooks* (575-76). She begins, "The Jews—that handful of uprooted individuals—have been responsible for the uprooting of the whole terrestrial globe. The part they played in Christianity turned Christendom into something uprooted from its past [she means the Greeks!].... An uprooted Europe went about uprooting the rest of the world by colonial conquest. Capitalism and totalitarianism form part of this progressive development of uprooting.... The Jews are the poison of uprooting personified." Some of her interpreters have considered this kind of language as springing from a form of self-hatred, but I do not think this is the whole story. Weil's anti-Judaism is not just a species of self-hatred; it is also rooted in her inability to take a balanced view of things, especially peoples and periods she did not like for reasons that she could never clarify, despite her constant repetition of a few tired tropes and historical errors. Her view of history, like her general view of life, had to be black and white. Despite how much she talked about history, there have been few major thinkers who showed less historical sense when they chose not to.[24] This is another of the paradoxes of Simone Weil, who once said, "Loss of the past, whether it be collectively or individually, is the supreme human tragedy" (*Need for Roots*, 202). Why then did she turn out to be such a poor historian? Simone, of course, read some ancient texts with great attention and analyzed their meaning with remarkable insight (e.g., her essay on the *Iliad*); but her broad view of history was too often based on scanty information, bizarre writings she had run across, and her scorn for "evidence."[25] To detail the many problems with what Simone has to say about history is not the purpose of this essay. One does not read Simone Weil (I hope) to gain much information about the meaning of the past.[26]

This brief consideration of some of the deficiencies of Simone Weil's thought, however, would be remiss if it concluded that she has too many problems to be considered an important resource for contemporary thought. With all her baggage, she still affords us a prism to pursue essential philosophical, theological, and spiritual questions. As Gustave Thibon put it, "It has to be remembered that she does not provide us with a solution but a question: not a reply, but an appeal; not a conclusion, but a need."[27]

Writings and Sources

Simone wrote much but published little during her life.[28] This speaks wonders of the friendship and trust she had in Perrin and Thibon that she left the great bulk of her writing to them and allowed them to judge whether and in what form it should be published. Thibon edited and introduced *La Pesanteur et la grâce* in 1947, translated as *Gravity and Grace* in 1952. The two other works that English readers have most often turned to in exploring her thought are *Waiting for God*, first translated in 1951, and *The Need for Roots*, translated in 1952. A number of other works appeared subsequently in English.[29] The undigested heart of her thought, however, was in her large *Notebooks*. Translations of all five of these are now available in English.[30] There is a significant body of other works available only in the French critical edition.

There has been considerable discussion of the influences on Simone's thought, especially the philosophical texts. I cannot take up this literature here. She has also attracted many labels—a Gnostic, a Marcionite, a Manichaean or Cather, a quasi-Protestant, and the like. These labels seize on one or another aspect of her oeuvre, but miss much else. Many people have called her a Platonist, given her positive remarks about the philosopher as *the* original mystic and her frequent citations and analyses of his corpus.[31] Weil certainly learned much from Plato; nonetheless, as Lissa McCullough argues, Weil's dialectical mode of thinking is not Plato's. In conclusion, it seems unhelpful to try to put labels on such an original and idiosyncratic thinker.[32]

I do want to say more about her mystical sources, which are also limited. Her major resource is John of the Cross, whom she cites fairly often. She gives John high praise when she says, "The supreme and mystical state of contemplation is infinitely more mysterious still, and yet St. John of the Cross wrote treatises on the method of attaining such a state" (*Need for Roots*, 180). She is not interested in analyses of John's writings but uses his images, especially that of the Dark Night, to buttress her own apophatic approach. Nonetheless, since both the Spanish Carmelite and the Jewish philosopher contain profound treatments of the need to strip the soul of all attachments in striving for God, there are major parallels in their thought.[33] Teresa of Avila gains praise, but only as an ecstatic.[34] Simone liked Francis of Assisi, using him as model for her ideals of abjection and poverty. She mentions Catherine of Siena, and also Thérèse of Lisieux, whom she criticizes. Simone's relation to Eckhart is complicated. She notes him by name only twice, but we know she read him.[35] There are a number of intriguing analogies or parallels between Eckhart and Weil. Among the most obvious is the similarity between Eckhart's view of mystical "noughting" (he even uses the German term *entwerden*—"unbecoming") and Weil's "decreation." Both Eckhart and Weil stress mystical annihilation, although in different ways due to their divergent outlooks. Further, like Eckhart, Simone held that creation was an eternal event, not a temporal one (e.g., *Notebooks*, 222, 529, etc.). She also has something like Eckhart's "Birth of the Word" in the soul, although she expresses it in terms of the "divine seed" (language that Eckhart also employs).[36] Weil speaks of true love as being "without any prospect in view" (*Notebooks*, 276), which is like Eckhart's insistence that the annihilated soul lives "without a why." Despite these and other intriguing analogies, I would not call Weil an Eckhartian.

Simone Weil's Dialectical Thought

A. Foundations

I described Simone's Weil's thought above as one of a "dialectical mysticism," that is, as constructed in terms of contrasts, oppositions, and paradoxes. Almost all of the major themes of her thought share to some degree in this dialectical development. In that sense, her mysticism *is* her dialectical thinking as rooted in her experience of God.

1. Opposition and Contradiction[37]

Simone Weil seems to have always thought in terms of oppositions, not analogies. Leslie Fiedler makes the point: "Simone Weil's writing as a whole is marked by three characteristic devices: extreme statement or paradox; the equilibrium of contradictions; and exposition by myth [like Plato]."[38] Oppositions, contradictions, and contrasts abound in her writings—good and evil, being and appearance, reality and imagination, gravity and grace, force and justice, Creator and creature, absence and presence, atheism and theism, the necessary and the good, and many more.[39] She held, however, that "every separation represents a bond" (*Notebooks*, 497); hence we can say that every opposed term has some aspect of its alternate truth within it.[40] In the *Notebooks,* she states, "All veritable good involves contradictory conditions, and is therefore impossible. He who keeps his attention really and truly fixed on this impossibility, and acts accordingly, will do good. In the same way, every truth contains a contradiction" (410). Contradiction is humanity's essential characteristic: "Each assertion that we make implies the contrary assertion; all our feelings are mixed up with their opposites. The reason is that we are made up of contradiction, since we are creatures, and at the same time God, and at the same time infinitely other than God.... Contradiction is our wretchedness, and the feeling of our wretchedness is the feeling of reality" (*Gateway to God*, 54–55). Hence, Weil does not seek to unite the opposites in terms of any facile synthesis, but heightens the contrast between them until they explode into the annihilation of our usual ways of looking at the world and thus give rise to another way of considering ("looking," rather than "eating") reality.[41] Gustave Thibon grasped this when he said, "Contradiction is the criterion of reality.... Only imaginary things have no contradiction in them.... [W]e must receive the two branches of contradiction just as they are and allow ourselves to be torn asunder by their distance. And it is in this tearing, which is as it were a reflection of the creative act which rends God, that we rediscover the original identity of necessity and goodness."[42] This rediscovery of identity on a new and unimagined level is what I mean by Simone's "dialectic." If the "sign of contradiction" marks the whole of Simone's thought, this helps explain why she was so opposed to Aristotle and his straightforward logic.

2. God and the Good: "God alone, and absolutely nothing else, is worthy of our interest" (Waiting for God, 126)

In beginning to explore the oppositions/contradictions that mark existence, it is best to start with God. God is the Absolute Good. There are two kinds of good, she says, "The word good has not the same meaning when it is a term of the correlation good–evil as when it describes the very being of God" (*Gravity and Grace*, 89). She later explains, "There are two goods of the same denomination but radically different from each other: one which is the opposite of evil and one which is absolute. The absolute has no opposite.... That which we want is the absolute good" (*Gravity and Grace*, 144–45). Hence, David Tracy has claimed, "The primacy of the impersonal desire for the Good is ... the key to all Weil's social theory and philosophy."[43] But the Absolute Good is not directly present in this world characterized by opposition. It is only negatively present, namely, in our desire for the Good that is the negative presence of the Good that does not exist in this world. In our blindness we do not recognize that "in our world ... the attributes of God appear to us as negation ... and that possession appears disguised as desire. What we call desires are what in reality constitutes possession" (*First and Last Notebooks*, 317).

God in Godself lies beyond all oppositions as totally hidden and unknowable, but we can surmise from our experience that, if there is both good and evil in the world, God must in some way be at the root of this opposition. Simone's view here about God's "responsibility" for evil, while shared by some other traditions (including Kabbalistic mysticism, of which she appears to have known nothing), seems at odds with Christian theology.[44] The ordinary believer will probably be taken aback by statements such as: "The order of the universe is beautiful, even including evil, which, as a part of the world, has a terrible beauty. We feel it" (*First and Last Notebooks*, 329). The relation between good and evil in the world, however, is a dialectical one, so that *both* good and evil have to be brought together to fully understand reality. Hence, Simone can make statements like: "We have to learn to love God through evil."[45] This does not mean that we should commit evil, but that we need to recognize and embrace the reality of evil found in affliction and all forms of suffering and make them our own. Simone explains, "We must love God through and beyond evil as such; love him through and beyond the evil that we hate, while hating the evil; love him as the author of the evil that we are in the process of hating" (*Notebooks*, 340). Another text from the *Notebooks* puts it this way: "In order to find the One [i.e., the Good], we have to exhaust duality, to go to the very extreme of duality. This means crucifixion" (436). The cross is the higher transfiguration of both good and evil, as we will see in more detail below.[46] This view is close to that of the fourteenth-century mystic Marguerite Porete (whose *Mirror of Simple Souls* Simone read in her final year; see *First and Last Notebooks*, 205, 361). Porete held that on the way to annihilation the "simple soul" needed to identify herself with sin and wretchedness (e.g., chap. 40). The exact mechanism by which this embrace of duality and fusing of good and evil takes place is spelled out in detail by Weil—only aspects of which can be touched on in what follows.

Weil discusses many of the other transcendental attributes, such as Being, Truth, and Beauty, but there is a sense in which the Good has priority. As she says, "Truth is sought not because it is truth, but because it is good" (*Gravity and Grace*, 107). Just as God as Absolute Good is the source of the opposed categories of particular good and evil here, God as Being grounds the reality of all things in the world. Paradoxically, Weil says that God and our love for God must be both personal and impersonal (i.e., objective). "The love of God," she holds, "ought to be impersonal as long as there has not been any direct and personal contact with God; otherwise it is an imaginary love. Afterward it ought to be both personal and impersonal again, but this time on a higher level" (*Waiting for God*, 200). In a striking aphorism she says, "God is attention without distraction" (*Reader*, 425), that is, total focus. God is also the connecting bond of all: "God is essentially mediation. God is the unique principle of harmony" (*Intimations of Christianity among the Greeks*, 176).[47] Of course, God's incomprehensibility as Absolute Good has led to many false views of God. Indeed, Simone (like Eckhart and others) thought that most views of "God" were inaccurate, misleading, and dangerous. This is why she said that there are two kinds of atheism: the bad form, which denies the existence of the Absolute Good, and the good form, which is a purification of the idea of God that takes place in the "Dark Night" of faith (*Gravity and Grace*, 103–4; *Notebooks*, 126–27). Her focus for readings of the bad *God* was (alas) once again Jewish, the Jehovah of the Hebrew Bible and the later Jewish tradition, which she considered a creation of false human imagination, especially in the way he was conceived of as operating according to an "interventionist" view of providence, that is, a God who interferes in the processes of nature and history to favor his "chosen people." This interventionist view of God, of course, is found in many ancient and traditional religions, but has been criticized by a number of thinkers before and after Weil.

3. God: Creation and Redemption[48]

Simone Weil's view of creation, not unlike her theology of good and evil to which it is tied, is also unusual from the perspective of Christian theology. How God created the world is one of the fundamental issues in Christian thought. The answer, since at least the second century C.E., has been that God created the world *ex nihilo*, ruling out any other preexistent principle that could compete with divine sovereignty. But what was the meaning of *ex nihilo*? The majority viewpoint has been that the *nihil* referred to was pure negation, not a state of some kind of "pre-existing possibility." Creation is the absolute beginning of the dependence of the universe on God. There was, to be sure, a minority view in which the *nihil* was identified with God himself, the unknowable source of all he chose to make. Simone Weil created a variant of this position in which God as "No-thing" creates the universe not by "acting" but by withdrawing, or abdicating, his Being from some "space" in order to allow other things to be. This withdrawal "rends" or "tears" God apart and separates God from God; it is the original tragic disruption that explains why both good and evil (i.e., distance from God) characterize the world. In that sense creation is *the* original sin. But why does God create at all? Simone's answer is not unlike that of most other Christian theologians—he does so out of his Goodness. Again, however, the way she frames this is unique: Divine Love as a form of "Madness." She says, "'Madness of love.' The creation is a very much greater act of madness still than the Incarnation" (*Notebooks*, 262). "Creation is renunciation by love" (*Intimations*, 183). Some interpreters have postulated that Simone may have known the sixteenth-century Kabbalist Isaac Luria, who has a roughly similar view about creation as withdrawal, but there is no evidence for this. She was an original apophatic theologian and mystic.

The God who creates and is manifest in the world is the Christian God who is a Trinity of Persons—Father, Son, and Holy Spirit. Simone has much to say about the Trinity, but once again, in a novel way. For her, "The Trinity and the Cross are the two poles of Christianity, the two essential truths: the first, perfect joy; the second, perfect affliction" (*Reader*, 456–57). Both truths are necessary, but being in the world places us "infinitely far" from the Trinity, since we are stationed at the foot of the cross. The root of God as Trinity is God as love.[49] A passage from "The Love of God and Affliction" is revealing:

> God produces and knows himself perfectly.... But, before all things, God is love. Before all things God loves himself. This love, this friendship of God is the Trinity. Between the terms united by this relation of divine love there is more than nearness there is infinite nearness or identity. But through the Creation, the Incarnation, and the Passion, there is also infinite distance. The interposed density of all space and time sets an infinite distance between God and God.[50]

The Trinity, although beyond all creation and unknowable in itself, has an effect in this world. The three Persons are revealed in the three essential mysteries—Creation, Incarnation, and Passion (*First and Last Notebooks*, 130; *Waiting for God*, 126). At times Simone also relates the three Persons to the triad of Creation, Incarnation, and Inspiration by the Spirit (*First and Last Notebooks*, 352, 360, 379). The Trinity is the transcendental source for all interpersonal dialogue and friendship. Dialogue starts in God: "The dogma of the Trinity is necessary so that there may not be a dialogue between us and God, but between God and himself in us. So that we may be silent."[51] Hence, "[p]ure friendship is an image of the original and perfect friendship that belongs to the Trinity and is the very essence of God" (*Waiting for God*, 208). Simone knows of some of the analogies for the Trinity found among Christian theologians, though she notes these only in passing. In several places, however, she tries to spell out her own understanding of such Trinitarian models. One is in the *Notebooks*, where she has some rather undeveloped musings on relations in God, "who alone can be related to himself," that is, to know and love himself in the "fullness of being" (263–64). But she turns this into a message about humans: "In the case of a man who loves and beholds God, it is God who loves and beholds himself through him; in this sense the Holy Spirit dwells in him." Here the Father is the Creator, the Son is incarnate in the order of the universe, while "[t]he Spirit is not related to the world. But it constitutes the 'I' of the perfect man. It is the de-created 'I'."[52]

A second text (*First and Last Notebooks*, 133-34) also concerns the relations in the Trinity, but puts these in the wider perspective of three relations: (1) God's relation to himself, which is the Trinity; (2) God's relation to the world in the conduct of events, which she associates with the Father's abdication; and (3) God's relation to his creatures in the inspiration he gives to thinking creatures, which is the Holy Spirit. In her *Intimations*, she has remarks on the Trinity as thinking subject, as friendship, as well as the harmony of the one and the many.[53]

The fact that Creation is a withdrawal of God—his absence—sets up an unusual relation between God and the world, one of an inverse dialectic that is not unlike what can be found in Eckhart. From the viewpoint of God as Absolute Goodness and Being, the world is really nothing, a mere shadow reality. If, however, we reverse our perspective and consider God from the viewpoint of the created reality we know, then God is Nothingness. Thus, there are two forms of Nothingness (a view also found in other mystics): "The fullness of being is identical with Nothingness for the purpose of abstract thought; but not so when one is fleeing Nothingness and directing one's steps toward being. There is a Nothingness from which we flee and a Nothingness toward which we go" (*Notebooks*, 232). A passage later in the *Notebooks* lays this out in more detail. "The good represents for us a Nothingness, so no one thing is in itself good. But this Nothingness is not a non-being, not something unreal. This Nothingness is at least as real as we ourselves are. For our very being is itself nothing more than this need for the good" (491). Weil says that we cannot lay hold of this good, but only try to love it gratuitously. Everything we experience "is necessity, defiled by force, and consequently unworthy of love." If we desire only the Absolute Good and reject all the imaginary goods offered us by creatures, "then . . . , being turned toward that which we cannot possibly conceive, a revelation of it comes to us—the revelation that this Nothingness is really the fullest possible fullness, the main spring and principle of all reality. Then we can truthfully say that we have faith in God" (492).[54]

God's withdrawal, his limiting of his freedom by creating the universe, is the realm of necessity.[55] Weil says that creation is "God's chaining himself down by necessity" (*Notebooks*, 191). Since God is absolute power, the laws that govern the universe, both physical and spiritual, are an expression of his will and therefore "necessary." They are the "force," or "gravity," to which all created things are subject.[56] This is God conceived of as impersonal. "Creation," she says, "is composed of the descending movement of gravity, the ascending movement of grace, and the descending movement of the second degree of grace" (*Gravity and Grace*, 3-4). Hence, "All the *natural* movements of the soul are controlled by laws analogous to those of physical gravity. Grace is the only exception" (ibid., 1). Grace is the action of divine love breaking into the world. If necessity rules the world, then all that happens here below is an expression of God's will and is to be loved as such. Therefore, says Simone, "Divine Providence is not a disturbing influence, an anomaly in the ordering of the world; it is itself the order of the world; or rather it is the regulating principle of this universe. It is the eternal Wisdom, unique, spread across the whole universe in a sovereign network of relations."[57] This view of Providence grounds the *amor fati* (love of world order, or destiny) that Weil often spoke about (e.g., *Need for Roots*, 288-90). The necessity that is "the veil of God" (*Notebooks*, 266) may appear to us as force, might, or compulsion, but in reality this is not the case. Every force is limited by another force, so it is obedience, not force, that rules the universe—"Obedience is the very essence of the brute force inherent in Necessity itself. Everything that hurts me, everything that weighs upon me, is obedient to God. Everything that smiles upon me also" (*Notebooks*, 600). She says that there are two forms of obedience: "We can obey the force of gravity or we can obey the relationship of things. In the first case we do what we are driven to by the imagination which fills up empty spaces. . . . If we suspend the filling up activity of the imagination and fix our attention on the relationship of things, a necessity becomes apparent which we cannot help but obeying" (*Gravity and Grace*, 43). Thus, necessity and its seeming opposite freedom are brought together by obedience.[58]

This second reversing dialectic of the God-world relation clarifies one of Simone's initially puzzling statements: "Contact with human creatures is given us through the sense of presence. Contact with God is given us through the sense of absence. Compared with this absence, presence becomes more absent than absence" (*Notebooks*, 239-40). This means that, prior to the gift of supernatural grace, we can know God only by grasping his absence from the world, but this sense of absence is actually far more powerful than any experience we can have of the presence of mere created realities. The presence of God's absence is the "void," and the various forms of voiding are central to Weil's apophaticism (Nava, 47-61). The dialectic of presence and absence continues past this life: "At death some disappear into the absence of God and others disappear into the presence of God. We cannot conceive this difference" (*Reader*, 425). Such texts are founded in a fundamental opposition, as we read in another passage: "Everything is upside down in our world of sin. What is negative appears as positive, and what is authentically and fully positive appears to us as negative. This constitutes a criterion. What appears to us as positive never is, cannot possibly be, positive. Thus, good doesn't ever consist of doing good, but of not doing evil" (*Notebooks*, 433). To be sure, Weil realized that the world is also the realm of intermediate realities, the mediation she called *metaxu*, a term taken over from Plato. These realities, such as family, country, calling, and so on, are neither good nor bad in themselves; they are meant to be used as means to reach God. In *Gravity and Grace* she says, "The *metaxu* form the region of good and evil. No human being should be deprived of his *metaxu*, that is to say of those relative and mixed blessings (home, country, traditions, cultures, etc.) which warm and nourish the soul and without which, short of sainthood, a *human* life is not possible" (133). But this temporal realm is not an end in itself. "The temporal," she says, "having no meaning except by and for the spiritual, but not by being mixed with the spiritual—leading to it by nostalgia, by reading beyond itself. It is the temporal seen as a bridge, a *metaxu*" (134).[59]

The implications of Creation as the withdrawal of God have important ramifications, notably in what they say about how we are redeemed and "return" to God. We are meant to save God from Godself by doing away with the "tear" in the world. But how? By bringing together particular good and evil, without, however, merely negating the one or the other. This, however, is impossible for us, caught as we are in this divided universe. We have no possibility of "ascending" to the former world; redemption is possible only by the "descent" of Divine Love into this world in the person of the Second Person of the Trinity, and by his uniting afflicted, sinful, wretched humanity with his divine nature. That uniting, however, is not just realized in the Incarnation of the God-man in Jesus of Nazareth, but needs to be pushed to the necessary extreme moment of the cross, when Jesus testified to his total distance from his Divine Father and his identification with the wretchedness of evil, crying out, "My God, my God, why have you forsaken me?" (Matt. 27:46; Weil's favorite biblical text). Note that in the Gospel the Father does not answer Jesus's anguished cry. He is silent—the divine silence that both expresses the mystery of God and gives the lie to all easy theodicies. A text in the *Intimations* says, "The cry of the Christ and the silence of the Father together make up the supreme harmony."[60]

At that moment the original split of Creation, the split of God becoming man in the Incarnation and the split between Jesus and his Father on the cross are not "healed" in any traditional sense, but are manifested as the model for human existence. Simone summarizes: "Creation and original sin are only two aspects, which are different for us, of a single act of abdication by God. And the Incarnation, the Passion, are also aspects of this act. God emptied himself of his divinity and filled us with a false divinity. Let us empty ourselves of it. This act is the purpose of the act by which we were created."[61] This sets up a mutual reciprocity of forgiveness between God and man revealed in Christ's Passion that Simone puts strongly: "God's great crime against us is to have created us, is the fact of our existence. And in our existence is our great crime against God. When we forgive God for our existence, he forgives us for our existing" (*Reader*, 400). If the crucifixion is the ultimate manifestation of the distance between the Father and the Word made man, it is also paradoxically the realization of their love: "Christ on the cross, abandoned body and soul. In that condition he alone could love the Father. The Father could love him alone in that condition" (*First and Last Notebooks*, 328). The centrality of the cross in Weil's thought is pervasive and powerful.[62] It helps explain one of her most troubling statements: "Every time I think of the crucifixion of Christ I commit the sin of envy" (*Waiting for God*, 83). Simone was not the first woman mystic to have desired to become a co-redeemer through suffering.

But what of Christ's resurrection? Basically, Weil thinks it was a mistake, another view that puts her far from traditional Christianity. Her fundamentally negative view of the God–world relation can only admit Christ as a "loser," the rejected and tortured slave who died on the cross and revealed the essential paradox founded in Creation. Conceiving of Christ as a "winner," one rewarded by his Father for his obedience and suffering, was something beyond her. Several passages make this clear. A rather ugly text in *The Need for Roots* (269) casts scorn on the "old women everywhere who are only too ready to believe no matter what tales about dead people returned to life," and goes on to say, "Surely those who are called blessed (John 20:29) are they who have no need of resurrection in order to believe, and for whom Christ's perfection and the Cross are in themselves proof." (So much for poor old women!) She makes the same point in her 1942 "Letter to a Priest": "If the Gospel omitted all mention of Christ's resurrection, faith would be easier for me. The Cross by itself suffices me" (*Gateway to God*, 116). A passage in her "The Pythagorean Doctrine" goes further in saying that the crucifixion of Christ almost opened the door that separated Father and Son from the created realm, but, "[t]he door half opened. The resurrection closed it again" (*Intimations*, 195). Earlier in *Intimations* she says,

"The death on the Cross is more divine than the Resurrection, it is the point where Christ's divinity is concentrated. Today the glorious Christ veils from us the Christ who was made malediction." (142-43). Although other passages express a somewhat more positive view of the resurrection,[63] Weil was uncomfortable with the Risen Christ.

4. Attention, Affliction, Decreation, Love, and Work

Simone Weil's thought is of a piece, despite the fact that she expressed it in fragments, essays, partial treatments, and some contradictions. Given her form of presentation, excerpting particular themes is misleading. Nevertheless, this is what most interpreters have been compelled to do. These five themes are of central importance for how the soul is meant to conduct itself in this life—attention, affliction, decreation, love, and, perhaps surprisingly, work.

Attention is more than just paying attention, though it includes that; it is an attitude of life, a "receptive waiting" directed eventually to God.[64] In *Waiting for God* she says, "Attention consists in suspending our thought, leaving it detached, empty, and ready to be penetrated by the object" (111). Later she goes so far as to say, "Attention animated by desire is the whole foundation of religious practices. That is why no system of morality can take their place." We must wait and attend on God until he comes down to us in grace, but, paradoxically, the subjective genitive (*attente de Dieu*) can also be used objectively to describe God's waiting for us, because God is attention without distraction. "God and humanity," she says, "are like two lovers who have missed their rendezvous. Each is there before the time, but each at a different place, and they wait, and wait, and wait" (*Reader*, 424-25). We wait for God and God waits for us—another example of the reciprocal relations that Weil sees between God and the human. Attention is "looking at what saves us" (*Waiting for God*, 193); it is an exercise not in "eating," or possessing (something possible only in heaven), but in emptying the self to be able to see what we need to see in order to be saved. Mere human will, natural and sinful, is incapable of being truly attentive; it is possible only as an exercise of the power of desire, the desire for God that is already marked by grace. As she says in *Waiting for God*, "Religion on the contrary [as opposed to will] corresponds to desire and it is desire that saves" (195). Attention involves emptying, and is therefore a form of decreation; it is also ecstatic in taking the subject out of itself. It should be conceived of not in terms of an active effort to look as hard as we can, but as a passive receptivity to what reality gives us to see"

(*Waiting for God*, 111–12). It is a form of "non-acting action."[65] "Attention," according to Weil, "taken to its highest degree, is the same thing as prayer. It presupposes faith and love. Another form of freedom is bound up with it . . . , namely grace" (*Notebooks*, 205).

Maleur, generally rendered as "affliction," is among the characteristic themes of Simone's vocabulary and is closely tied to the traditional mystical category of suffering.[66] Suffering is the more general theme, but at times Simone seems to use the two terms interchangeably.[67] In her essay on "The Love of God and Affliction," however, she distinguishes between "simple suffering" and the affliction that is inseparable from physical suffering, but still distinct in that it "takes possession of the soul and marks it through and through with its own particular mark, the mark of slavery."[68] Simone has sometimes been seen as almost masochistic in her desire for suffering, but that is too strong. At the outset of the *First Notebook* she says, "I believe in the value of suffering, so long as one makes every [legitimate] effort to escape it" (3). Suffering as both interior and exterior seems a universal feature of created being. Simone distinguishes three kinds: needless suffering, expiatory suffering, and redemptive suffering. God inflicts all three; humans only the second (*Notebooks*, 222). Later she distinguishes two kinds of suffering: "Suffering is either to move towards the Nothingness above or towards the Nothingness below" (*First and Last Notebooks*, 117). The good suffering moving above is aimed at annihilation in God (i.e., decreation), while the bad suffering is directed to annihilation into the Nothingness that is hell (*Notebooks*, 463; *First and Last Notebooks*, 142). *Malheur* expresses the epitome or core of suffering as it reaches the level of insupportability, humiliation, desolation, and isolation—Jesus on the cross is always Weil's model. In her essay "Human Personality," Weil says, "Human thought is unable to acknowledge the reality of affliction. To acknowledge the reality of affliction means saying to oneself: 'I may lose at any moment, . . . anything whatsoever that I possess, including those things that are so intimately mine that I consider them as being myself.' . . . To be aware of this in the depths of one's soul is to experience non-being. It is the state of extreme and total humiliation which is also the condition for passing over into truth" (*Reader*, 332). In an extended discussion in *On Science, Necessity, and the Love of God*, Weil sets out four essential notes of *malheur*: first, it is a state that possesses the soul and brands it as a slave; second, it involves physical suffering, but the internal suffering is worse; third, it brings with it ignominious shame; and fourth, it induces self-hatred and guilt (170–75). *Malheur* is indeed terrible, but if we can learn to see it as a mark of God's love (even though it seems to drive us away from God), it is truly salvific. Again, contradiction has to be embraced and transcended.

Malheur might be described as the foremost agent of *décreation*, another term for which Simone Weil is known. Decreation is a form of mystical annihilation, a theme that goes back at least as far as the thirteenth century, but Weil's decreation has its own special notes.[69] (She also uses "annihilation" and related terms like "detachment" frequently.)[70] Decreation is the fulfillment of creation. Just as God's self-denial in creation is the foundation of the world, we have to deny and empty ourselves in order to return to him in decreation. "We participate in the creation of the world by de-creating ourselves" (*Notebooks*, 309; *Waiting for God*, 145). Weil goes further—God has to empty himself of his divinity. He has abandoned himself in the Creation, the Incarnation, and the Passion, and we have to cooperate with him in this process. This means that decreation is not just a reversion to Creation; rather, it completes the act of Creation that is also the act of Incarnation and crucifixion—we become one with Christ decreating himself before the Father. In the *Notebooks,* we read, "None goes to God the creator and almighty without passing through God EMPTIED OF HIS DIVINITY. . . . We have to *empty God of his divinity to love him*. . . . Man is only able to be one with God by uniting himself to God *stripped of his divinity*" (283–84). In the crucifixion, Christ was utterly deprived of his divinity—"My God, my God, why have you abandoned me!" Thus, we need to remember that decreation is not the result of our own efforts: "Evil is the distance between the creature and God. To abolish evil means to decreate; but that is something that God is able to do only with our cooperation." Thus, "Destruction [i.e., the negative Nothing] is the extreme opposite of decreation" (*Notebooks*, 342). As a result, true love of God and union with him are possible only through the coming together of our own emptiness in decreation and God's self-emptying of his divinity. This kind of uniting of Nothing with Nothing (*nihil cum nihilo*) was not unknown in earlier mystical authors (e.g., Eckhart; the anonymous author of the *Evangelical Pearl*; etc.), but Simone seems to have arrived independently at her own version.

Shot through most of the above discussion has been the power of *love* as the force that not only characterizes God ("the mad Lover"), but that also is what alone can restore us to God (intelligence, important as it is, cannot operate on this level). Weil's doctrine of love, natural and supernatural, is complex. Here I can give just a few comments. What is love? First, we can say that it is devotion to truth, the lodestone of Weil's thought: "Pure and genuine love always desires above all to dwell wholly in the truth, whatever it may be, unconditionally" (*Need for Roots*, 253). Pure or chaste love is directed to the present reality of what we love, while imaginary love is directed to an imaginary future pleasure (*Gravity and Grace*, 55–61). "[I]f we desire only that a being should exist, he exists. What more is there to desire? The beloved being is then naked and real, not veiled by an imaginary future" (ibid., 58). Both pure love of God and love of neighbor are expressions of attention—"The soul empties itself of all its own contents in order to receive into itself the being it is looking at, just as he is, in all his truth" (*Reader*, 51). Pure love of creatures is associated with love of God: "Pure love of creatures is not love of God, but love which has passed through God as through fire" (ibid., 57). In another passage such a love seems to partake of what Weil calls supernatural love: "Supernatural love touches only creatures and goes only to God. It is only creatures which it loves (what else have we to love?), but it loves them as intermediaries. For this reason it loves all creatures equally, itself included" (ibid., 55).

Weil distinguished between implicit forms of loving God and the explicit form. Her well-known essay "Forms of Implicit Love of God" (*Waiting for God*, 137–215) discusses three (actually four) forms of implicit love (love of neighbor, appreciating the beauty of the world, and love of religious practices—"the three things here below in which God is really though secretly present"). These three, to which she later adds love of friendship, partake of supernatural love and constitute an upward movement of the soul toward God. They lead to the explicit love where God comes to possess the soul. "After God has come in person, not only to visit the soul as he does for a long time beforehand, but to possess it and transport its center near to his very heart, it is otherwise. The chicken has cracked its shell; it is outside the egg of the world. These first loves continue; they are more intense than ever, but they are different" (209).[71] Simone seems to distance herself from such experience of explicit love when she says, "But his love in all these forms has become a movement of God himself, a ray merged in the light of God himself. That at least *is what we may suppose*" (ibid.; my emphasis). Weil therefore has a threefold movement of love—detachment from creatures, ascent to God, and re-descent in order to bring the love of God to creatures. *Notebooks* describes pure love for creatures as "a love which detaches itself completely from creatures in order to ascend to God and then redescends from God linked with the creative love of God" (616). Such supernatural love is not *our loving God*, but God loving himself in us: "It is not for me to love God. Let God love himself through me as a medium" (*Notebooks*, 363; see also 193, 330-31; and *Waiting for God*, 133-34).

In other texts, Weil compares the union with God at the height of the ascent of love to a virgin who "sleeps with God" and proves the reality of the encounter by becoming pregnant in her practice of supernatural virtues (e.g., *First and Last Notebooks*, 146).[72] Weil references the mystical marriage theme in a few places (e.g., *Notebooks*, 248), and, given her personal asexuality, also has a surprising defense of the legitimacy of erotic language in mystical texts. In *Notebooks* she says, "To reproach mystics with loving God by means of the faculty of sexual love is as though one were to reproach a painter with making pictures by means of colors composed of material substances. We haven't anything else with which to love" (472).[73]

The love of God necessarily is also the love of neighbor. Weil says that "in the secrecy of the highest level the love of God and the love of one's neighbor are one love" (*First and Last Notebooks*, 179). The redescent of love and the practice of the supernatural virtues look to the need of one's neighbor (e.g., *First and Last Notebooks*, 123-24) and are often framed in terms of compassion. Compassion is our reaction to affliction, both in ourselves and in others. This is why Simone can say, "Affliction is truly at the center of Christianity. Through it is accomplished the sole and two-fold commandment: 'Love God,' 'Love your neighbor'" (*Reader*, 461-62). Christ felt compassion for himself on the cross ("My God, my God . . ."), and the Father had silent compassion for him. "This self-compassion is what a pure soul feels in affliction. A pure soul feels the same compassion for the affliction of others" (*First and Last Notebooks*, 94; see also 209, 284). In her meditation "On the Father's Silence," she says, "One can only love one's neighbor with a compassionate love. It is the only just love. . . . Compassion makes love equal for everybody" (*Reader*, 434). Compassion is often linked with gratitude, as in *Waiting for God*: "Only the absolute identification of justice and love makes the coexistence possible of compassion and gratitude on the one hand, and on the other, of respect for the dignity of the affliction in the afflicted" (140; see also 146, 148, 151, 162, 205).

Simone Weil's thought has a special role for *work* as a necessary aspect of the path to God. Many traditional forms of mysticism had distinguished between contemplative love of God and active love of neighbor, the division between *theōria* and *praxis* (understood by Christians as love of neighbor). Any such dichotomy is totally alien to Weil, who found all work—even the hardest physical labor—important for attaining God. As Alexander Nava has shown, the two sides of Weil's writing, the social-political and the theoretical-religious, are not far apart but are intimately united. Thus, "[t]he union of justice and love in this conception of the Christian life is a key dimension of the mystical-prophetic thought of Simone Weil" (Nava, 131). One of the few things for which Weil criticized her beloved Greeks was that they lacked an appreciation of the role of work, which for a Greek was the provenance of slaves (*Gravity and Grace*, 157). For Christians, however, Christ's life as a working man, and especially his death as a slave and outcast, redeemed labor as integral to human activity.

Weil's mysticism of work is founded on her theology of the cross and her view that daily work partakes of Christ's affliction, both personally and collectively (Nava, 22). Therefore, true mysticism is "this-worldly" and open to all. In *Need for Roots,* Weil argues, "A contemporary true form of greatness lies in a civilization founded upon the spirituality of work," following up with an even stronger statement: "A civilization based on a spirituality of work would give to Man the very strongest possible roots in the wide universe, and consequently be the opposite of that state in which we find ourselves now, characterized by an almost total uprootedness" (97–98). At the end of the book, she summarizes, "It is not difficult to define the place that physical labor should occupy in a well-ordered social life. It should be its spiritual core" (302). Physical labor is a social value only because it is a spiritual one. Simone ties it to obedience, the recognition of our role in the necessity of the created universe: "Physical labor willingly consented to is, after death willingly consented to, the most perfect form of obedience" *(Need for Roots*, 295). In the section on "The Mysticism of Work" in *Gravity and Grace*, 157–60, she is even more emphatic, wondering why, "There has never been a mystic, workman or peasant, to write on the use to be made of disgust for work" (157–58). Above all, Weil, like many twentieth-century mystics, breaks down all artificial distinctions between prayerful contemplation of God and human activity, even of the most difficult and oppressive nature. Acceptance, obedience, and silence in the face of oppression are forms of mystical praxis, as she says in *Notebooks*: "Detachment, indifference. . . . One says to oneself: I no longer have any incentives; how am I to act? Why am I to act? But therein lies the miracle of the supernatural. Silence all the motives, all the incentives within yourself, and you will nevertheless act, impelled by a source of energy which is other than the motives and the incentives" (247). This aspect of Weil's thought and its relation to what has been called the "Prophetic-Tragic" dimension of her thought have been studied by Tracy and Nava, and I invite readers to pursue this further in their writings.

B. Applications of Weil's Thought

The implications of Simone Weil's highly original religious philosophy are many. Here I will discuss only two: her view of Catholicism, and what she has to say about mysticism in an explicit fashion. I emphasize *explicit* treatments here, because I agree with Nava that the whole of Weil's thought can be considered mystical in the broad sense.

1. Simone Weil's View of Catholicism

Much ink has been spilled over whether Simone should have been baptized a Catholic.[74] She certainly was strongly attracted to Catholicism and thought about the possibility of baptism. My view is that she rightly decided that she could *not* become a Catholic and also that no priest should have agreed to baptize her, at least in the state of mind she displayed down to the end of her life. In order for her to be baptized, either she would have had to deny herself, or the Catholic Church would have had to deny itself. Simone could not have been baptized in the actual Church as *Catholic*, but only in the Church of her imagination (I use the term in her sense), a kind of secret quasi-Manichaean sect.

There can be no doubt of Weil's feeling of affinity for Catholicism. In her "Letter to Bernanos," she said, "I am not a Catholic, although . . . nothing that is Catholic, nothing that is Christian, has ever seemed alien to me" (*Reader*, 74). In her letter "What is a Jew?," she put it this way: "I would say that if there is a religious tradition which I regard as my own patrimony, it is the Catholic tradition" (*Reader*, 80). Her praise for many aspects of Christianity (by which she always meant Catholicism) is unstinting. "The tremendous greatness of Christianity," she said, "comes from the fact that it does not seek a supernatural remedy against suffering, but a supernatural use of suffering" (*Notebooks*, 386–87). Her experiences of Christ, noted above, make it legitimate to see her as a kind of "Christ-mystic." For her Christ, "[t]he Lamb slain since the foundation of the world" (Apoc. 5:6 and Luke 11:50), a passage she loved to cite, is at the center of creation and history. His crucifixion as an afflicted slave infinitely distant from his Father, is also, paradoxically, the true meaning of human life. In her "Last Text" of 1943, she lists the Christian doctrines she believes. "I believe in God, the Trinity, the Incarnation, the Redemption, the Eucharist, and the teaching of the Gospels." Nevertheless, she says that she does not believe in them in the sense of taking over what the Church says on these matters, "but that, through love, I hold on to the perfect, unseizable truth which these mysteries contain" (*Gateway to God*, 62).

On the other hand, Simone Weil remained highly critical of the Church as an institution, just as she was opposed to all bad "collectivities." Christianity was a form of totalitarianism (*Notebooks*, 505) to be identified, along with Israel and Rome, as manifestations of the "Great Beast" (*Notebooks*, 620). Catholicism had manifested its totalitarianism by its rejection and persecution of heretics, the Crusades, the Inquisition, its role in colonization, and much else. These, of course, are all parts of the story of Catholicism that cannot be denied and that most Catholics today would also reject. In her black-and-white view of history, however, Simone could never forgive the Church her sins (Coles, 120). Weil was particularly incensed by the Church's use of the *anathema sit* formula that excluded some positions from Christian teaching. In her "Last Thoughts" to Fr. Perrin she says, "The love of those things that are outside the visible Christianity keeps me outside the Church" (*Reader*, 111).[75] She believed that the Church did have authority to distinguish between right and wrong beliefs, but not the right to *exclude* them. Weil loved the *idea* of Catholicism and the Church's sacramental practice. (She was a great devotee of Christ's real presence in the Eucharist, something that I cannot go into here.) But she rightly described herself as "remaining outside the Church, on the threshold" (*Notebooks*, 340). A few texts in her writings hint at hopes for some modified form of Catholicism as the coming universal religion, but these are utopian dreams.[76]

2. Simone Weil's View of Mysticism in Particular

Weil's thought has been described as a form of "Religious Metaphysics." I see no reason why it should not also be called a "Mystical Metaphysics." Along with her general view of reality and essential mysticism, briefly outlined above, she also had much to say about mysticism and mystics in a particular way.

In discussing the three ways of dealing with the problem of good and evil, Simone says that the third way "is the mystical way. Mysticism means passing beyond the sphere where good and evil are in opposition, and this is achieved by the union of the soul with the Absolute Good."[77] She often speaks about "mysticism" in general and the "mystics," without naming names. She values mysticism highly: "Mysticism should provide the key for all knowledge and all values" (*First and Last Notebooks*, 98). For her, the mystics fulfill the ideal of life devoted to truth: "What is really marvelous, as in the case of the mystics and the saints, is not that they have more life, . . . but that in them truth should have become life" (*Need for Roots*, 249). She recognized that mysticism is rooted in the question of the experience of God (*First and Last Notebooks*, 195). But what makes a mystic for Weil? In the essay "Human Personality," she stresses the annihilative (decreative) core of mysticism: "The whole effort of the mystic has always been to become such that there is no part in his soul to say 'I'" (*Reader*, 318). The same message occurs in the *Notebooks*: "Man is only able to become one to God by uniting himself to God stripped of his divinity" (284). God and man both must be divested of their being to be united.[78]

Mystical contemplation is based on the experience of God and faith. In a puzzling passage in the *Notebooks,* she says, "Faith . . . is a conjecture by analogy based on supernatural experiences" (438). Thus, "those who have acquired the privilege of mystical contemplation . . . , *suppose* that, since God is mercy, the created world is a work of mercy—*pistis*, belief. . . . It is for this reason that mysticism is the only source of the virtues." Contemplation is also linked to love: "The eye of the soul for the contemplation of the divine is love" (*Notebooks*, 240). The mysteries of the faith should not really be approached by way of affirmation and negation, she says, but only through contemplation (*Notebooks*, 245). Weil mentions contemplation in a number of other places.[79]

Weil also speaks about the relation of mysticism and ecstasy. Again in the *Notebooks,* she says, "The highest ecstasy is the attention at its fullest. It is by desiring God that one becomes capable of attention" (515). In *Need for Roots*, she connects ecstasy with physical phenomena, such as levitation. She withholds judgment whether or not such lifting up from the ground is true, but says, "It doesn't much matter. What is certain is that if the mystical ecstasy corresponds to something real in the soul, it must be accompanied in the body by phenomena which are not observable when the soul is in a different state" (267).[80] This text should not be taken to mean that Weil thought that special mystical states, such as visions, stigmata, and the like, were the essence of mystical consciousness. Like most of the major mystics, she thought of them as peripheral and often misleading. This is at the root of her distinction between two kinds of mysticism: the spurious mysticism always searching for special experiences, and the true mysticism of attention and direct consciousness of God. In *Waiting for God*, she talks about the different forms of vices that search "for a state where the beauty of the world will be tangible." She goes on, "The mistake lies precisely in the search for a special state. False mysticism is another form of this error. If the error is thrust deeply enough into the soul, man cannot but succumb to it" (173–74; for more on spurious mysticism, see *Need for Roots*, 158). In her *Seventy Letters*, she makes an unusual distinction between "people who merely experience states of ecstasy," and those "who devote themselves almost exclusively to the study of these states, who describe and classify them, and, insofar as it is possible, induce them" (No. 39, 123). Then she makes a surprising statement: "It is the latter who are generally called mystics; and that is why St. Francis is not, I believe, regarded as such." The second, true, sense of mysticism she connects with "Gnostics, Neo-Platonists, . . . and gymno-sophists." This position shows a radical misunderstanding of Christian mysticism.

The misunderstanding, alas, fits well with two other aspects of Weil's view of mysticism. The first is the claim that the mystical tradition is one and the same across all religions from the beginning. In one place she says, "It is obvious also that the morality which proceeds directly from mystic thought is one, identical, unchangeable. This can be verified by turning to Egypt, Greece, India, China, Buddhism, the Moslem tradition, Christianity and the folklore of all countries" (*Gateway to God*, 30 [note no Judaism]; see also 112). The second is her notion that the religion of the mystics is *not* the religion of the Church, something she often repeats. In one place she says that, although it appears that Christianity is "one social organism," in actuality, "there were two separate religions—that of the mystics and the other one" (*Gateway to God*, 108). *The Need for Roots* is full of such claims. Speaking of how "the Roman conception" of religion infected and ruined Christianity, she says, "The truly Christian inspiration has fortunately been preserved by mysticism. But apart from pure mysticism, Roman idolatry has defiled everything—yes, idolatry" (277). She goes on, "In the mystic traditions of the Catholic Church, one of the main objections of the purifications through which the soul has to pass is the total abolition of the Roman conception of God. So long as a trace of it remains, union through love is impossible" (*Need for Roots*, 278; see also 262, 280). In the *Notebooks*, she also repeats the claim that Christian mysticism was destroyed by Rome (251–52). Of course, other thinkers have also asserted that all mysticism is one and that mysticism alone is the true religion—the *real* Christianity. But these assertions are highly questionable, to say the least.

Conclusion

Simone Weil remains a bone of contention. Of her brilliance as a thinker there can be no question. Of the inspiration of her life in sacrifice for the poor and oppressed, no one can doubt her status as a model. Her view of reality is among the most original of the twentieth century. In an important sense, Weil can be seen as representing a powerful, if idiosyncratic, retrieval of the tradition of apophatic mysticism. She also taps into much else in the history of mysticism, such as identification with the desolation of Christ on the cross. I believe, however, that there are serious issues about some aspects of her thought, especially her views on the nature of Christian mysticism.

Notes

1. See especially McCullough; also useful is Vető. Full titles and publication information for works cited by author or short title can be found in the bibliography at the end of the essay. For a short overview, see David Tracy, "Simone Weil and the Impossible: A Radical View of Religion and Culture," in Tracy, *Filaments: Theological Profiles. Selected Essays, Volume 2* (Chicago: University of Chicago Press, 2020), 375-89.

2. On Weil as a mystic, see Nava. Many other commentators also speak of her as a mystic.

3. On Weil as an example of a "new form of saintliness," see Davy, 80-84. Weil herself wrote about the need for a modern sanctity in "Letter VI. Last Thoughts," in *Waiting for God*, 98-99.

4. The best life remains that of her friend Simone Pétrement.

5. *First and Last Notebooks*, 47.

6. From her "Spiritual Autobiography," which is Letter IV in *Waiting for God*, 61-83, and is also found in the *Reader*, 10-26; quotation from *Waiting for God*, 64.

7. Weil's essay on reforming education, "Reflections on the Right Use of School Studies with a View to the Love of God," can be found in *The Simone Weil Reader*, 44-52 (hereafter *Reader*).

8. For Simone's attitude to Marxism, see the essays in *Oppression and Liberty*.

9. Weil uses similar language in *Notebooks*, when she says of God, "He enters into us. He alone is able to enter into us" (326).

10. See, for example, German Sermon (Pr.) 26, as translated by M. O'C. Walshe: "The truth is such a noble thing that if God were able to turn away from truth, I would cling to truth and let God go; for God is truth, and all that is in time, and that God created, is not truth" (Sermon 11 in Walshe, *The Complete Mystical Works of Meister Eckhart* [New York: Crossroad, 2009], 95).

11. Weil closes this account with a typical universalistic summary, saying that after the event she was convinced that Plato was a mystic, that the *Iliad* "is bathed in Christian light," and "that Dionysius and Osiris are in a certain sense Christ himself" (*Waiting for God*, 70).

12. See "Concerning the Our Father," in *Waiting for God*, 216-27, as well as *Notebooks*, 309-10; *First and Last Notebooks*, 296, 360; and *Gravity and Grace*, 41. For a discussion of Simone on the Our Father, see Hein Blommestijn, "The Mystical Realism of Simone Weil," *Studies in Spirituality* 16 (2006): 181-203.

13. Several of these essays were gathered into *Waiting for God*; for example, "The Love of God and Affliction" (117-36), along with the addendum found in *Reader*, 453-68; and "Forms of the Implicit Love of God" (116-215).

14. The account appears at the end of *Notebooks*, vol. 2, from 1942 (638-39),

and is also found as the "Prologue" to the *New York Notebook* in *First and Last Notebooks*, 65–66.

15. On *The Need for Roots*, see Springsted, *Simone Weil and the Suffering of Love*, 102–23.

16. Pétrement, 509.

17. Simone's other concern was equally illusory—the formation of a group of front-line "suicide" nurses to attend the French forces fighting the Germans.

18. *New York Notebook* in *First and Last Notebooks*, 243–44.

19. "Appendix," in *Gateway to God*, 145.

20. Perrin and Thibon, "Introduction," *Simone Weil as We Knew Her*, 10.

21. Coles has some pretty harsh comments on Weil, speaking of her "deadly pride" (26), and calling her work "a mix of ruthless logic and wild illogic" (119).

22. For a summary of some of the treatments of Weil's bizarre view of Judaism, see Brenner, chapters 5–6. While Weil did express admiration for some of the books of the Hebrew Bible (e.g., *Waiting for God*, 160; and *Need for Roots*, 285), the brunt of her animus is directed against the theocratic kingdom of Israel and its successors.

23. For her, Israel and Rome were always the manifestation of the "Great Beast," the oppressive collectivities that enslaved people, promoted worship of the False God, and constructed societies based on blood lust and war. For some texts on Israel and Rome as the Great Beast, see *Notebooks*, 482, 504, 564, 574–75; *First and Last Notebooks*, 120; and especially "The Great Beast," in *Selected Essays*, 89–144.

24. Weil's lack of historical sense has been noted by many commentators; see, e.g., Thibon, *Simone Weil as We Knew Her*, 139; and T. S. Eliot, "Preface," in *Need for Roots*, viii–x.

25. In a revealing text, André Weil tells of a discussion he once had with his sister in which he asked her for evidence for one of her strange historical claims. She replied, "I don't need any evidence. It is beautiful, therefore it must be true" ("Appendix," in *Gateway to God*, 143).

26. Among Weil's historically dubious positions are: (1) her view of the Jews; (2) her supposition about an ancient primordial revelation descending down through many channels (a kind of *prisca theologia*); (3) her identification of the Gnostics, Manichaeans, and Cathari as the true descendants of early Christianity; and (4) her misunderstanding of the Middle Ages. The list could go on.

27. *Simone Weil as We Knew Her*, 17.

28. Vető, discusses three periods in her writing (5–7).

29. For example, *Intimations of Christianity among the Early Greeks* (1957); *Selected Essays, 1934–1943* (1963); *Seventy Letters* (1965); *On Science, Necessity and the Love of God* (1968); *Oppression and Liberty* (1973); and *Lectures on Philosophy* (1978).

30. The *Pre-War Notebooks (1933–1939)*, the *New York Notebook (1942)*, and the short *London Notebook (1943)* are available in *First and Last Notebooks: Supernatural Knowledge* (1970). The large *Notebooks (1942–1943)* are found in *The Notebooks of Simone Weil*, 2 vols. (1956).

31. On Weil's relation to Plato, see the papers in Doering and Springsted.

32. McCullough has a good discussion of the influences on Weil (213–25), although I cannot agree with her contention that Weil is best identified as a "quasi-Jansenist."

33. For a treatment of these, see Nava, 49–58.

34. Letter 39: "I admire Saint Teresa but I think she would be even more admirable if she had never written" (*Seventy Letters*, 123).

35. In the "Spiritual Autobiography" (*Waiting for God*, 79), she cites Eckhart as one of the "friends of God" who repeat "words they have heard in secret amidst the silence of the union of love," even when they are "in disagreement with the teaching of the Church." Eckhart, of course, would have disagreed with this assessment. In *First and Last Notebooks* she cites Eckhart on the uncreated power in the soul (136). The interesting reading list contained in the *New York Notebook* (77-78) includes Eckhart in a wide range of sources from the Platonic tradition.

36. On the divine seed being born in us, see *First and Last Notebooks*, 287-88.

37. See the section "Contradiction," in *Gravity and Grace*, 89-93.

38. Fiedler, "Introduction," in *Waiting for God*, 29-33; quotation from 29.

39. For a study, see McCullough, "Chapter 1. Reality and Contradiction" (12-50).

40. An illustration of this can be found in her dictum: "Case of two contradictories: God exists; God doesn't exist. Where lies the problem? No uncertainty whatever. I am absolutely certain that there is a God, in the sense that I am absolutely certain that my love is not illusory. I am absolutely certain that there is not a God, in the sense that I am absolutely certain that there is nothing real which bears a resemblance to what I am able to conceive when I pronounce that name" (*Notebooks*, 127).

41. Fiedler speaks of this as an "equilibrium of truths," which "honors contradictions" ("Introduction," in *Waiting for God*), but I think that does not go far enough. Simone does not merely want the reader to remain on the level of truths we already know, but to transcend them by recognizing *both* their truth and their falsity as insufficient. Weil always contrasted "looking," that is, the good way of cherishing things, with "eating," or attempting to make things our own (e.g., *First and Last Notebooks*, 286).

42. Thibon, "Introduction," in *Gravity and Grace*, xxv.

43. Tracy, "Simone Weil and the Impossible," 396.

44. McCullough notes that Weil's view of evil is "the most potentially scandalous and offensive aspect of Weil's religious thought" (150).

45. *Gravity and Grace*, 75; see also, e.g., *Notebooks*, 340, 505, etc.

46. See McCullough, 230-34.

47. Mediation is an important notion that Simone developed out of Plato; see Springsted, *Christus Mediator*.

48. McCullough, "Chapter 3. God and Creation" (85-122).

49. God as love is a frequent theme in the *Notebooks*; see, e.g., 193, 206, 274, 333, 344, 401; see also *First and Last Notebooks*, 102-3, 179; *Waiting for God*, 133; etc.

50. *Reader*, 445-46.

51. *Reader*, 434-35, from *First and Last Notebooks*.

52. In the "de-created I," the soul's eye becomes God's eye: "But when the individual has become effaced, without the organ having lost its virtue, the soul then becomes the organ of God's vision. The Spirit is this vision" (*Notebooks*, 344). This is much like Eckhart (see German Sermon 12).

53. *Intimations*, 166-70; see also 93-94.

54. Faith is an important theme in Weil that cannot be pursued in depth here, but note the following text: "Faith is the experience that the intelligence is

lighted up by love" (*Notebooks*, 240). There are useful considerations on faith in McCullough, passim.

55. McCullough, "Chapter 4. Necessity and Obedience" (123–70).
56. Springsted, "Force," in *Simone Weil*, 15–35.
57. *Need for Roots*, 285. See the whole discussion of Providence here (279–85).
58. In *Waiting for God*, Weil says, "If a reasonable creature is absolutely obedient, he becomes a perfect image of the Almighty as far as this is possible for him" (179).
59. For more on *metaxu*, see *Notebooks*, 48–49, 102, 188, 233, 258, etc.
60. *Intimations*, 199; see also *Science, Necessity, and the Love of God*, 197–98. God's silence, a major theme in mysticism, has an important role in Weil that cannot be pursued here; see McCullough, 117–22.
61. *First and Last Notebooks*, 140. The notion that Creation, Incarnation, and Passion are three aspects of God's single act of abdication is found in many other texts, e.g., *First and Last Notebooks*, 120; *Waiting for God*, 126, 145; *Gateway to God*, 70. See McCullough, 111–12.
62. There are a host of texts on the cross in Simone, e.g., *Waiting for God*, 127, 136; *Gateway to God*, 79–83; *Notebooks*, 191, 258, 411, 414–15, 429, 564; *First and Last Notebooks*, 183; *Reader*, 425–28, 452–53, 455–56, 463–64; etc.
63. At times Weil hints at decreation as a kind of resurrection without tying it to Christ (e.g., *Notebooks*, 61, 213). In *First and Last Notebooks*, she speaks of the resurrection as Christ's "pardon to those who killed him" (69) and says that "the joy [of Easter] . . . is the joy that soars above pain and perfects it." See also the "Letter to Joë Bousquet" (*Reader*, 92–93).
64. On the different forms of attention, see Nava, 61–73.
65. See, e.g., *Gravity and Grace*, 39. For a study, see Vetö, "Chapter 7. Non-Acting Action" (128–52). This concept has interesting analogies to Madame Guyon.
66. Much has been written on affliction; for an introduction, see Springsted, *Simone Weil*, 29–31, 42–66, and passim.
67. E.g., "Affliction," in *Gravity and Grace*, 72–77.
68. "The Love of God and Affliction," in *Waiting for God*, 117. The whole of this essay (*Waiting for God*, 117–36, and *Gateway to God*, 77–91) is essential. For more on affliction, see *Notebooks*, 232, 272, 311–13; *Gravity and Grace*, 86; etc.
69. See McCullough, "Chapter 5. Grace and Decreation" (171–212); Vetö, "Chapter 1. The Notion of Decreation" (11–40); and Nava, 40–44, and 58–61.
70. E.g., "God created me as a non-being which has the appearance of existing, in order that through love I should renounce this apparent existence and be annihilated by the plenitude of being" (*First and Last Notebooks*, 96).
71. Weil also uses the image of the bird (= Love) cracking the egg of the world to release the spirit into the silence of infinity ("Letter to Joë Bousquet," in *Reader*, 87, 89).
72. For more on marriage and sexual imagery for union with God, see *First and Last Notebooks*, 244–46; and *Science, Necessity, and the Love of God*, 111, 118. See also Nava, 73–77.
73. *Notebooks*, 474. Weil goes on, however, to distinguish between the true mystic who turns "the faculty of love and desire" based on sexual energy toward God and the false mystic who turns it toward an imaginary object he calls God. For more reflections on sex and mysticism, see *Notebooks*, 530, 582.
74. Persistent rumors circulate about a friend baptizing her when she was

close to death; see Pétrement, who concludes, "It appears therefore that she did not think of herself as having been baptized" (524).

75. In New York, Weil wrote an unfortunate "Letter to a Priest" (Fr. Coutourier), listing no fewer than thirty-five objections, which for years "have formed a barrier between me and the Church." The letter combines serious objections and difficulties with bizarre views and strange historical interpretations.

76. See *Waiting for God*, 98-99; *First and Last Notebooks*, 299, and the discussion in McCullough, 234-39.

77. "A War of Religions," in *Selected Essays*, 214.

78. Union or merging language is found in some other places, e.g., *First and Last Notebooks*, 339. Weil also speaks of "being transformed into Christ," or "being made similar to God," e.g., *First and Last Notebooks*, 224, 265, 297, 310.

79. On contemplation, see, e.g., *Notebooks*, 81, 449, 480; *First and Last Notebooks*, 133; etc.

80. This passage may help explain the text where Weil notes some similarity between mysticism and mental pathology (*Notebooks*, 311-12).

Bibliography

Sources

French

The critical edition is *Oeuvres complètes*. 16 vols. Paris: Gallimard, 1988-2006.

English

I mention only works used in this essay.

First and Last Notebooks. Translated by Richard Rees. London: Oxford University Press, 1970. Reprint, Eugene, OR: Wipf & Stock, 2015.

Gateway to God. Translated by David Raper. London: Fontana, 1974. Reprint, New York: Crossroad, 1982.

Gravity and Grace. Translated by Emma Craufurd. London: Routledge & Kegan Paul, 1952.

Intimations of Christianity among the Greeks. London: Routledge, 1957.

The Need for Roots: Prelude to a Declaration of Duties toward Mankind. Translated by Arthur Wills. New York: Putnam's Sons, 1952.

The Notebooks of Simone Weil. Translated by Arthur Wills. 2 vols. London: Routledge & Kegan Paul, 1956.

Oppression and Liberty. Translated by Arthur Wills and John Petrie. Amherst: University of Massachusetts Press, 1973.

On Science, Necessity, and the Love of God: Essays. Edited and translated by Richard Rees. London: Oxford University Press, 1968.

Selected Essays, 1934-1943. Translated by Richard Rees. New York: Oxford University Press, 1962. Reprint, Eugene, OR: Wipf & Stock, 2015.

Seventy Letters. Translated by Richard Rees. New York: Oxford University Press. Reprint, Eugene, OR: Wipf & Stock, 2015.

Waiting for God. Translated by Emma Craufurd. New York: Harper & Row, 1951.

Anthology

The Simone Weil Reader. Edited by George A. Panichas. New York: McKay, 1977.

Studies

Brenner, Rachel Feldhay. *Writing as Resistance: Four Women Confronting the Holocaust. Edith Stein, Simone Weil, Anne Frank, Etty Hillesum.* University Park: Pennsylvania State University Press, 1997.

Coles, Robert. *Simone Weil: A Modern Pilgrimage.* Reading, MA: Merloyd Lawrence, 1987.

Davy, Marie-Magdaleine. *The Mysticism of Simone Weil.* Boston: Beacon Press, 1951.

McCullough, Lissa. *The Religious Philosophy of Simone Weil: An Introduction.* London: I. B. Tauris, 2014.

Nava, Alexander. *The Mystical and Prophetic Thought of Simone Weil and Gustavo Gutiérrez: Reflections on the Mystery and Hiddenness of God.* Albany: State University of New York Press, 2001.

Perrin, J. M., and G. Thibon. *Simone Weil as We Knew Her.* London: Routledge & Kegan Paul, 1952.

Pétrement, Simone. *Simone Weil: A Life.* New York: Pantheon, 1976.

Spingsted, Eric O. *Christus Mediator: Platonic Mediation in the Thought of Simone Weil.* American Academy of Religion Academy Series 41. Chico, CA: Scholars Press, 1983.

———. *Simone Weil and the Suffering of Love.* Cambridge, MA: Cowley, 1986.

Tracy, David. "Simone Weil and the Impossible: A Radical View of Religion and Culture." In Tracy, *Filaments: Theological Profiles. Selected Essays. Volume 2,* 375–89. Chicago: University of Chicago, 2020.

Vető, Miklós. *The Religious Metaphysics of Simone Weil.* Albany: State University of New York Press, 1994.

Zaretsky, Robert. *The Subversive Simone Weil: A Life in Five Ideas.* Chicago: University of Chicago Press, 2021.

Collections

E. Jane Doering, and Eric O. Springsted, eds. *The Christian Platonism of Simone Weil.* Notre Dame, IN: University of Notre Dame Press, 2004.

CHAPTER 8

Henri Le Saux (Swami Abhishiktānanda) (1910–1973): Mysticism beyond East and West

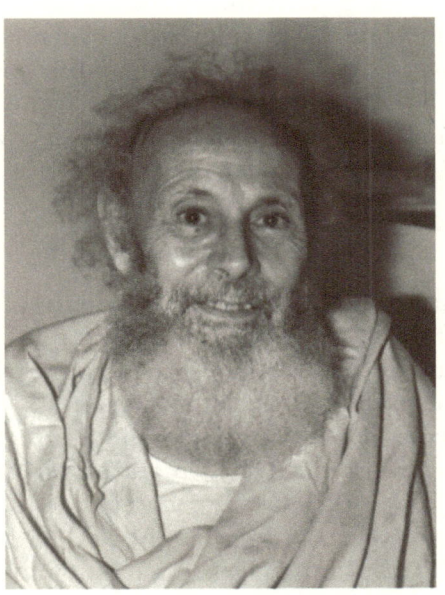

Mystics are by definition seekers—hunters after God, as Meister Eckhart once put it. God in his infinite incomprehensibility seems to elude human effort of full attainment in this life, and even in the life to come, according to mystics. And yet, the French monk Henri Le Saux, living in India under his Hindu name, Abhishiktānanda, or more correctly Abishikteśvarānda ("Bliss of the Anointed One"), wrote in his *Diary* under January 3, 1956, "Mysticism is essentially the attainment of the absolute."[1] *Can* God really be attained in this life? And *how* might God be attained, given the variety of mystical paths found in the world religions? Abhishiktānanda wrestled with these issues throughout his life, and thus he emerges as a central figure in modern mysticism due to his dual commitment to pursue God both through the Catholic monastic mysticism in which he was formed, and through the Hindu advaitan (non-dual) mysticism he embraced in India when he took on the life of a *sannyasī*, an ascetic wanderer.[2] The interior search for God on which the mystic embarks often involves physical dislocation. More difficult is the mental or religious dislocation that happens when someone, like Le Saux, feels called to pursue God in a religious world different from that in which he grew up. Such a person (a "trans-border" mystic, we might say) seems to be a modern phenomenon. Can one be a Buddhist and a Christian mystic at the same time? Or a Hindu and a Christian mystic? Isn't there a contradiction in trying to belong *equally* to two diverse traditions? There are no definitive answers to these questions. There are, however, witnesses such as Abhishiktānanda, who help us to think about how it might be possible to be both a Christian monk and a Hindu mystic.

An Extraordinary Life

Henri Le Saux was born at St. Briac in Brittany on August 30, 1910, the eldest in a family of seven children.[3] His family was pious, and it was in no way unusual that he entered the seminary in 1921. While in the seminary he experienced a call to the monastic life and was accepted into the Benedictine monastery of Sainte-Anne de Kergonan in June 1929. Here he was ordained in 1935, and settled down to life devoted to both liturgy (he was the Master of Ceremonies of the community) and scholarship as librarian and teacher. About 1934 he began (in a fashion inexplicable even to him) to feel an attraction to India. As he later put it, "India's religious genius is such that, through its worship and the very structure of its temples, through its myths and equally through every aspect of human life, it constantly recalls you to what is essential, and ceaselessly invites you to discover in the depths of your being the ultimate mystery of yourself" (*Guru and Disciple*, 41). After his mother's death in 1944, he felt free to pursue his longing to go to India, making requests both to the abbot of his monastery and through letters sent to Catholic authorities in India. He finally obtained permission and, in July 1948, set sail for India. He arrived in August, where he joined another French priest, Fr. Jules Monchanin (1895–1957), who had come to India in 1939 hoping not only to serve Indian Catholics but also to work to integrate Christianity and Hinduism.[4] Fr. Monchanin was a noted philosopher and theologian, widely respected in the French Catholic world. Few could understand his desire to "bury" his talents as a parish priest in southern India (Tamil-Nadu). He and Fr. Le Saux shared a desire to found a coenobitical monastery, or *ashram*, that would combine Catholic and Hindu monastic practices, living in full poverty and with a deep commitment to the contemplative life. On the Feast of St. Benedict in 1950, now dressed as Hindu monks, they set up some modest huts for their *ashram* on the bank of the River Kavery. They called it "Shantivanam" ("Forest of Peace"). Here they took new names to express their new life—Swami Abhishiktānanda and Swami Parama Arubi Anandam ("Supreme Formless Bliss").

Shantivanam was an impressive symbol, but not originally a success. The founders' hopes to attract fellow-minded European monks who would adopt the Hindu lifestyle, and above all to attract Indian applicants, proved futile. This was partly due to the conflicts between the two men. They respected, even admired, each other, but they had fundamentally different temperaments, as Abhishiktānanda recognized from the start. Swami Parama was brilliant but disorganized. For all his commitment to contemplation, Abhishiktānanda was more practical and goal-driven. Furthermore, an intellectual/spiritual gulf soon emerged. Swami Parama was deeply enamored of Hindu life and religious culture, but he drew back from the forms of full adoption of Hinduism that Abhishiktānanda began to embrace. Abhishiktānanda, on the other hand, accused Monchanin of being too "rational," too "Greek," too "hesitant" regarding what needed to be done to incorporate Christ in India.[5] The tensions and the ups-and-downs of the fortunes of Shantivanam continued from 1950 through 1957, when Swami Parama was taken ill and had to return to France for an unsuccessful operation. He died on Thursday, October 10, 1957.

Abhishiktānanda had already begun to feel the pull of adopting a more eremitical monastic life, one modeled on the wandering Indian ascetics. He was resident only sporadically at Shantivanam after 1952. Although he never became indifferent to the fate of the *ashram*, he more and more felt that he could not fulfill his vocation to be a Hindu monk in the fullest sense at Shantivanam (*Diary*, 148). Fortunately, there were other Catholic monastics, both Western and Indian, who were interested in combining Hindu and Catholic traditions. Abhishiktānanda became friendly with an English Benedictine, Bede Griffiths (1906–

1994), who had come to India in 1955 and set up an *ashram* at Kerala that combined Trappist and Hindu observances.[6] Fr. Bede spent time at Shantivanam and eventually, in 1968, Abhishiktānanda gave Shantivanam to Bede and the Cistercian Fr. Mahieu. They took over the site and developed it, until in 1980 it was incorporated into the Camaldolese Benedictine congregation as the Hermitage of the Holy Trinity. Although changed over the decades, the *ashram* founded by Monchanin and Le Saux still continues its work of striving to combine Christian and Hindu religious traditions.

Swami Abhishiktānanda's own spiritual journey, only partly tied to Shantivanam, followed a complicated path over the years from 1952 until his death in 1973. We have three forms of evidence for his story. The first comprises the works he wrote for a public audience about his experiences and thoughts. The most engaging of these are the three short accounts of his pilgrimages and encounters with Indian sages.[7] In addition, there are a number of mystical treatises of varying length.[8] Abhishiktānanda was an inveterate letter writer with a wide circle of friends in France and India, so his letters serve as a second major resource for his life and mystical teaching.[9] Finally, there is what he wrote only for himself, the *Spiritual Diary* that he kept from his arrival in India in 1948 until his death. The document is problematic. When Abhishiktānanda left the last of these notebook to his disciple Marc Chaduc in 1973, he told him: "They should not be taken literally. When an idea comes to me, I pursue it as far as possible, wherever it may lead. These are vectors of free-floating research. They are not for publication. You can destroy them all. They can only be understood on the basis of the interior *experience* which was his own and from within which these 'vectors' welled up in him with an infinite glow" (*Diary*, 282). Marc made excerpts and then threw the notebooks in his possession into the Ganges. In 1976, two of Abhishiktānanda's closest friends asked Marc for permission to edit and publish what was left, and the silent hermit seems not to have objected. The Swami's friend Fr. Raimon Panikkar (1918–2010) selected and edited the notebooks under the title the *Ascent to the Depth of the Heart*, first published in French in 1986. Reading what remains of the *Diary* is fascinating but also disconcerting. The book is filled with moving and profound mystical passages but is often repetitious, obscure, and contradictory. It also has the flavor of self-absorption, which may be excusable in a personal work, but that can often be grating for an outsider.

On the basis of this wealth of material, we can turn to a fuller account of Abhishiktānanda's later life. As early as December 1951, he was feeling the tension between his "Hindu side" and his "Catholic side." Writing to a friend at Christmas, he says, "The further I go, the more I feel the gulf between me and my Hindu brothers and my Church. I am like someone who has one foot on one side of the gulf, and the other on the other side. I would like to throw a bridge across, but I do not know where to fasten it, the walls are so smooth" (Stuart, 50). The first major turning point in his path took place through the mediation of Fr. Monchanin. In 1949, Monchanin had taken Le Saux to visit the famous ascetic and mystic Sri Ramana Maharshi (1879–1950), who lived at Tirrunvanamalai at the foot of the holy mountain, Arunāchala.[10] Le Saux was not initially impressed, but as their brief stay went on he began to see the Maharshi as the kind of authentic Hindu guru that he had longed to meet ("the unique Sage of the eternal India," he called him).[11] Although he visited Ramana only a few times, he felt that this mystic had become his spiritual teacher par excellence, the one who could lead him to a true "Awakening." Abhishiktānanda also felt the pull of the mountain Arunāchala itself, "the linga of Shiva," one of the most sacred sites of Hinduism.

In March 1952, Abhishiktānanda returned to Arunāchala, this time to live for five months as a *sannyasī*, an ascetic hermit in the caves that dot the mountain. (He returned for another four months in 1953.) This was a "mind-blowing" experience. It is not easy for those who have not had a similar encounter with a "sacred place" to appreciate the effect the holy silence of "The Flame-Crowned Mountain" had on the Swami. The short account he wrote of his encounter with the Maharshi and subsequent stay on the mountain, *The Secret of Arunāchala*, testifies to the power of these events. The Maharshi had died, but Abhishiktānanda was able to consult with many of his disciples as he sought to penetrate deeper into "the mystery of the heart," the central point of the Maharshi's teaching.[12] One of these disciples eloquently summarized Ramana's teaching about divesting the self, recalling how the Master upbraided a disciple who was praising a great meditator by saying, "What advantage is there in meditating for ten hours a day, if in the end that has only the result of establishing you a little more deeply in the conviction that you are meditating? Do not meditate—Be! Do not think that you are—Be! Don't fuss about being—you *are!*" (*Secret*, 75). Above all, it was the mountain itself that was drawing and teaching Abhishiktānanda: "I began to understand what had long before been said to me about the attractive power of Arunāchala and his [Shiva's] Mountain. If Ramana himself was so great, how much more so must be this Arunāchala which drew Ramana to himself, how much more so his mystery? . . . That was how the call of the Mountain came to me, the first of Arunāchala's spell-binding wiles—the calls and wiles of a lover."[13] During this time Abhishiktānanda met another of Ramana's disciples, "Harilal" (H. W. L. Pooja), who gave him instruction in the advaitin teaching on the "Self," or *ātman* (*Secret*, 81–97). In June of 1952, while living in a cave on the mountain, Abhishiktānanda seems to have had the early mystical experience recounted in his *Diary*.[14]

The years 1953 to 1956 were difficult for Abhishiktānanda, as revealed especially in his *Diary*. He was increasingly torn between the Catholic and the Indian sides of his identity and could not seem to find any resolution.[15] He speaks of "blowing up" the institutional Church (e.g., *Diary*, 139, 141, 144, 307), and he confesses on July 29, 1956, "My best times have been lived as a Hindu! Vedanta gave me what the Church never did! So?" (*Diary*, 154). At times he worried that he was losing his faith (e.g., *Diary*, 120–21). In 1955 he seems to have experienced a kind of psychological breakdown,[16] during which he consulted with an Indian Jungian psychologist, Dr. V. Mehta, who "channeled" messages from Jesus to him advising him to leave the practice of Catholicism, advice he wisely did not follow.[17] He began to realize that the torture of living between two worlds was teaching him something about the need for absolute surrender. On September 5, 1955, he confessed, "'Surrender' both my desire to remain a Christian, born of an instinctive fear, and my desire to live completely as an advaitin Hindu which I often think I am. In total surrender to the mystery. Free and naked at the heart of the abyss, hanging there" (*Diary*, 124). This seems to be an early expression of the insight that I argue became more and more central to Abhishiktānanda's path: the recognition that *both* Christianity and Hinduism had legitimacy as *symbols*, but were secondary to the *experience* of encountering the depths of the mystery that could never be expressed in words, creeds, or rites. Mysticism ultimately goes beyond both East and West.

Abhishiktānanda's faith in the institutional Church (the "neolithic Church," as he called it) grew shaky, but he did not abandon his devotion to Jesus as the teacher of the inner way: "In revealing the secret of his being, Jesus revealed the secret of every being. . . . Jesus revealed 'his' secret only so that each one after him, with him, may discover his own secret within himself. . . . Jesus taught the way to reach it [*ātman*], the way of the Beatitudes, the way of love" (*Diary*, 157, for Nov. 8, 1956). In these years of trial, the Swami continued to enjoy powerful religious and mystical experiences. For example, in July 1955 he visited the Hindu temples at Elephanta near Bombay, and he says he was "thunderstruck" by the statue of the three-headed Shiva. He continues, "When I saw it, I simply had to hold on to a pillar for support. . . . Late yesterday evening I stayed for a long time gazing at it, and in the ensuing darkness allowing myself to be bathed in its influence."[18]

These years of inner trial also saw a second major spiritual turning point in Abhishiktānanda's inner path: his meeting with Srī Gnānānanda (ca. 1880–1960), the sage of Tirukoyilur. Abhishiktānanda's time with the Maharshi had been brief, but he was able to spend more time with Gnānānanda (February–March 1956, and a later two-week period). In the "Preface" to the account of his time with the guru he says, "The path he teaches is basically one of total renunciation, whose final result is that no place is left for the ego to show itself. Anyone who doubts this should make a trial of the path of *dhyāna* [meditation] which he teaches!"[19] Recounting his first meeting with Gnānānanda, he tells of how he questioned the guru about whether supreme Reality was *dvaita* (dual) or *advaita* (non-dual). The immediate response was: "What is the use of such questions? . . . The answer is within you. Seek it in the depths of your being. Devote yourself to *dhyāna*, meditation, beyond all forms, and the solution will be given to you directly." Similarly, when Abhishiktānanda asked about initiation rites, he was told, "Initiations—what is the use of them?" If the disciple is not ready, they are empty words; if he is ready, they are not needed. "He went on: 'So long as you perceive the world, it is ignorance, not-knowing, *a-jnāna*. When nothing of the world is any more perceived, it is wisdom, *jnāna*, the only true knowledge'" (*Guru and Disciple*, 8–9). Abhishiktānanda had found another true guru, and he had also realized that "the mystery of the guru is actually the mystery of the spirit's own depth," because guru and disciple are one "in the sphere of original non-duality" (*Guru and Disciple*, 12; see also the whole of chap. 9).[20] At times Gnānānanda's teaching on the necessity for radical releasement is reminiscent of Meister Eckhart. Speaking of the desire for God, the guru said, "There are the people who want everything except God, others who want everything and also God, others who want only God, and yet others who, having recognized themselves in God, are no longer capable of any desire, even for God" (*Guru and Disciple*, 86). Later in 1956 (November 5 to December 8) Abhishiktānanda undertook a thirty-two day silent retreat at Kombakkonam.[21] It was a powerful experience both of inner anxieties and moving spiritual insights. He began the retreat with poignant queries to God: "If I am, how can You be? You, my brother, my friend, the unknown, my God?—If I were not, how could You be?" (*Diary*, 155–56). Some of his finest mystical passages come from the

Diary pages on this retreat, but again the torture of his dual allegiance breaks in: "How could the mystery I bear within me be two? It is sometimes called Jesus and sometimes Arunāchala. You give the impression of laughing at my anguish, and of playing with me a cruel game of hide-and-seek" (November 15, *Diary*, 162). He struggles to reformulate the doctrine of the Trinity on the basis of the "heart of being," but admits, "Even so, what a struggle it is to remain Christian! All the other problems are forgotten, these days; but that one, the fundamental problem, keeps coming back" (*Diary*, 165; see also 170–71, 175, 188). At the end, he said that, while he had received no "decisive enlightenment," and had experienced his "psychic and physical limits," it was yet "*a milestone in my life*" (*Diary*, 195).

Swami Abhishiktānanda, often now referred to as "Swamiji," was gradually turning his attention to northern India, the Hindu shrines there, and especially the sacred river, the Ganges. His first trip to the north was made in 1957, the year of Monchanin's death. It was not until 1959 (May to October) that he was able to visit the Himalayas and the area of the source of the Ganges, where he, like many other *sannyasī*, sought to build a hut for meditation and to bathe in the sacred river. In early 1961 he was back in the Himalayas and was able to begin building a hermitage (*kutiya*) at Gyansu near Uttarkashi. Due to his writings and many contacts, Swamiji was becoming well known and was often invited to give retreats and attend meetings, such as the Nagpur conference of Hindus and Christians (December 28, 1963 to January 4, 1964). A notable event of 1964 was the pilgrimage he made with his friend the Indian-Spanish priest Raimon Panikkar to the sources of the Ganges at Gangotri in June–July of that year.[22] He and Panikkar celebrated Mass at Gomukh, the place where the Ganges issues from the glacier. He then made a three-week silent retreat. Writing to his sister (June 28), he said, "Now I am alone, and I am keeping total silence for three weeks. . . . I have not brought a single book with me. A complete fast of the mind, while praying inwardly with my brother sadhus, slowly murmuring the OM which says everything. Not allowing myself to locate God anywhere outside me, but recognizing that within as well as without there is only He alone. . . . Nothing is left but He who says: I AM!" (Stuart, 162–63).

The Swamiji said goodbye to southern India in August 1968. His final years from 1968 to 1973 were spent mostly at his hermitage at Gyansu, although he continued to travel, give talks, and to try to find and train disciples, as a guru should.[23] Despite the rigors of his hut in the Himalayas and his declining health, Abhishiktānanda tried to spend six to eight months in solitude and meditation there, being drawn deeper into the meaning of *advaita*. Inspired by the writings of Panikkar (e.g., *The Hidden Christ of Hinduism*) and his conversations with the Japanese Dominican Shigeto Oshida, he became more bold about suggesting that the Jesus of the Gospels is *one* of the ways (the Christian way) to recognize the mystery of the unknown God. In a letter from January 1971, he put it as follows: "Our Cosmic Christ, the all-embracing Iśvara, the Purusha of the Veda/Upanishads . . . we cannot escape to give him such a full dimension. . . . Yet, why then only call him Jesus of Nazareth? Why say that it is Jesus of Nazareth whom others unknowingly call Shiva or Krishna?, and not rather say that Jesus is the theophany for the Bible-believers, of that unnameable mystery of the Manifestation" (Stuart, 244; see also 230).

One of the other key developments of these last years was that the Swamiji finally acquired his first true disciple, the person who would enable him to complete his vocation as a guru. A young French seminarian from Bourg, Marc Chaduc, who had been writing him for several years, arrived in India in October 1971. The two immediately hit it off and Abhishiktānanda began intensive spiritual training of his disciple. Already on November 8, while walking on the banks of the Ganges, guru and disciple experienced what Marc later referred to as "the irruption of the mystery of Being between—at the heart of—us two," something that left Abhishiktānanda "shattered." This moment of *advaita* was a sign of their true master–disciple relationship (Stuart, 255–56). A crucial event in their later relations came on the night of the Feast of the Ascension (May 11, 1972). Abhishiktānanda's partial account of this experience in the *Diary* is difficult to follow, but it was a shared mystical meeting of three persons—"There is Jesus, M., and myself." Mixing Christian and Hindu vocabulary, he ends mysteriously: "Sudden emotion at the discovery of the abyss between God-Brahman and myself. The '*unbearable*' emotion when I realized that there was no abyss. The abyss is an illusion! Ah! An illusion to want to cross over it! And M. said to me: 'Even an illusion to say that there is no abyss!' Then simply panic-stricken" (*Diary*, 350).

The Swamiji's last pieces of spiritual wisdom come mostly in the letters he wrote to Marc (see Stuart, 293–98) and in the many papers (including the *Diary*) left to him.[24] After overseeing Marc's consecration (*diksha*) as a Hindu hermit on June 30, 1973, Abhishiktānanda suffered a major heart attack at Rishikesh on July 14, 1973. Had not a European friend spotted his body on the ground, he probably would have died. As it was, he survived for five months, dying on December 7.

During these months, Abhishiktānanda reflected on his heart attack in letters, coming to see it as the final stage in his long pilgrimage. In his *Diary* he says, "After some days there came to me, as if it were a marvelous solution to an equation: I have found the Grail." He now wished to live a life "at the service of this Awakening." Although he did yet know how, he claims that "it was very clear to me that there has been a fundamental break in my life" (*Diary*, 386). In his last letters, he also uses the "Holy Grail" (an image from his Breton upbringing) to describe how his "near-death" experience had granted him the breakthrough to eternity. He put this in typically provocative terms: "The Christ I might present will be simply the I AM of my (every) deep heart, who can show himself in the dancing Shiva or the amorous Krishna! And the kingdom is precisely this discovery . . . of the 'inside' of the Grail! . . . The awakening is a total explosion. No Church will recognize itself or its Christ afterwards" (Stuart, 311).[25] Here, once again, Abhishiktānanda suggests that the "Awakening" is something that is deeper and more primordial than its highest historical manifestations in Christianity and Hinduism. In death, as in life, the Swamiji continues to challenge the contemporary Catholic Church and what he thought was its too-narrow view of salvation and mystical contact with God.

Abhishiktānanda's Mystical Teaching

Part of the difficulty in writing about the Swamiji as a mystical teacher is the problem of determining what he really held. Many mystics evolve in their views; Abhishiktānanda seems to have gone further. Especially in his *Diary*, he floated contradictory ideas back and forth, as he admitted. Should we then look to some of his treatises, especially *Saccidānanda*, as a kind of summary? But this work, like others, went through many revisions after it was first drafted in 1962 in his hermitage in the Himalayas. It may not represent his final thoughts. Given the contradictions in both his writings and his life, I can only try to give a "rational," or "theological" account of his views—something that would probably have been anathema to him, given his rejection (although qualified) of "Greece," "reason," and "theology," as inadequate to capture the depth of the Real.

Another issue in trying to give a theological account of Abhishiktānanda is that he insisted that only experience could give the reader any clue to what he was talking about. In the "Preface" to *Guru and Disciple* he reflects on the issue of the commonality of "the fundamental Christian experience and the genuine Vedantin experience," despite the incompatibility of their expressed formulations. He says, "In fact, it is clear that, at the level of pure ideas, at the speculative level, no solution of the dilemma is possible. The experience of Jesus, which underlies all genuine Christian experience, is existential in character, just as is the experience of the Indian *jñānī* [enlightened one]. . . . But no concept could ever capture these experiences in any definition, still less transmit them" (*Guru and Disciple*, xv). In *Saccidānanda* he says, "Deep experience can be recognized only by the heart, for it is only in the depths of the heart, the 'cave' of the Upanishads, that man is truly himself" (194). In a letter of 1971 he puts it this way: "Only he who has reached the 'depth' can understand one who speaks from the 'depth.' A smile, a freedom, which those who do not know completely misunderstand" (Stuart, 243). The appeal to inexpressibility is not a new message for mystics, but one can still ask—why did Abhishiktānanda write so much, and *theologically*, about what was best left unsaid? The paradox of mysticism.

I will sketch out the Swamiji's basic teaching under only a few of many possible headings. The essential question here is, What is the mystery? Ancillary questions concern issues such as, How do we prepare for attaining the mystery?, What is the goal of the spiritual path?, and How is the mystery expressed in various religious traditions?

The Essential Question

When we ask, What is the mystery that Abhishiktānanda was pursuing?, we can use the customary labels of "the Real," "Being," "the Self," and even "God," all of which he spoke much about. I think, however, it may be more helpful to begin with the expression *advaita*, that is, "not-two," "identical," "not-divided."[26] The word is omnipresent in the Swamiji's writings as the major religious insight of the Vedantin tradition enshrined in the Upanishads that he loved to recite and chant.[27] What is *advaita*? Speaking of the undividedness of the god Shiva and the linga in which he manifests himself, Abhishiktānanda says, "For this, *advaita*, non-duality, is the only appropriate word. Not monism, not dualism; but that sheer mystery in which man, without understanding it at all, rediscovers himself in the heart of God" (*Guru and Disciple*, 42). In a *Diary* entry of April 1964, he says, "*Advaita* is not an intellectual discovery—but a fundamental spiritual attitude. Much more the impossibility of saying two than the affirmation of One. What is the use of saying One in your thought, if you say two in your life? Not to say two in your life, that is love" (271). Intellectually, the advaitin refuses to say *either* that God and creatures are one *or* that they are two, "since the *mystery of being* transcends all numeration, as it does all thought" (*Saccidānanda*, 88 n. 1). Of course, puzzled outsiders may worry that such language compromises the distinction between Creator and creature, but they fail to recognize that it is not in *language* or *thought* that the issue can be grasped, but only in *experience*. Abhishiktānanda might well have appealed to a story told of his teacher, the Maharshi, who was once asked about the distinction and who replied, "Who asks this question? God does not. You do. So find who you are and then you may find out whether God is distinct from you."[28] In a later *Diary* entry (May 20, 1971), Abhishiktānanda summarizes: "The advaitin experience is not an idea, a theory, with which other ideas, for example Christian theology, would eventually have to be harmonized. It is a new consciousness, a new level of consciousness, in which all ideas are seen as if for the first time" (326).

Abhishiktānanda saw *advaita* as central to Hindu religious teaching, but he also argued that it enabled him to understand the core of the message of Christianity, that is, Jesus's non-dual experience of his Father as expressed in the *Abba*-cry of the Gospels (e.g., *Saccidānanda*, 110). Furthermore, in Indian terms at least, "one can very well call the Holy Spirit 'the advaita of God,' the mystery of the non-duality of the Father and the Son, and in the final consummation, the inexpressible communion of all in one" (*Saccidānanda*, 95). Swamiji even suggested that some Christian mystics, such as Eckhart, Tauler, and Ruusbroec, had enjoyed the experience of non-duality.[29]

Ultimate Reality, which the Upanishads refer to as *Brahman, Atman, Sat*, as well as through the formula *tat tvam asi* ("That Thou Art"), is most often called "God" in Christian theology.[30] Abhishiktānanda spoke much about God, especially in the tropes of negative theology. God is a "hidden God"; God is a "desert";[31] God lives in "solitude." Anything we say about God is more like lying than truth-speaking.[32] If *advaita* frames the fundamental experience of God for Hindus, Swamiji was at times open to exploring non-duality in the more Western form of the coincidence of divine transcendence and immanence.[33] Nevertheless, when he expounded on the Christian view of God in terms of *advaita*, he usually invoked the *properly* Christian teaching on God as Trinity. (In this he forms a notable contrast to Teilhard de Chardin, who used little Trinitarian language; see chapter 4 above.) Trinitarian contemplation is the proper form of Christian *advaita*. A passage from August 30, 1963, is a good example. Meditating on the Trinity is recognizing that "the mystery of the twofold gaze which constitutes me before him" actually has eternal value, because it is inscribed in the depth of God (*Diary*, 260). "Meditation on the Trinity itself, in its mystery, is the specifically advaitin contemplation, in which the soul has disappeared at the level considered to be its own and only the level of God continues to exist. The Trinity is this mystery of God and myself in its divine and eternal reality." This is why Abhishiktānanda's great hope was to be able to bring together the Indian advaitin "experience of the Self which is at the center of every Indian theological and spiritual tradition" with the advaitic Christian "contemplation of the blessed Trinity at the very source of the soul." He felt that this would effect "a mystical renewal of the whole *Catholica*" (*Saccidānanda*, xv). In another place he puts it as follows: "The Christian experience of the Saccidānanda is the Trinitarian culmination of the advaitic experience which redeems time and multiplicity from their 'kenotic' condition, as it was understood in the Greek tradition; or, in Vedantic terms, from their quasi-illusionary condition as *māyā*. It rediscovers them, hidden in the depths of God's Being, in his Love, and realizes their essential value" (*Saccidānanda*, 129). In the section that he devotes to the two forms of advaitic experience (*Saccidānanda*, 195–98), he begins by saying, "The Christian cannot but rejoice and give thanks to the Lord that the Vedantic experience of the Self leads on to the Trinitarian experience of Saccidānanda. But at the same time he cannot overlook the fact that his conviction of this depends on faith alone" (195).

The Swamiji has many discussions of the three Persons—the Trinity was central to his spiritual life and teaching. He was familiar with the Trinitarian theology of the Greek Fathers, Augustine, and the early Councils, although he felt that the traditional formulations were not very useful in the modern world. His core teaching on the communicative nature of the Trinity is quite orthodox and is well expressed in the following passage: "The mystery of the Holy Trinity reveals that *Being* is essentially a *koinōnia* of love; it is communion, a reciprocal call to *be*; it is a being-together, being-with, *co-esse*; its essence is a coming-from and a going-to, a giving and receiving. All that is, is communion, extending from the Father, the source of all, to the Spirit, the consummation of all, and transmitted by the Son and everything that was created in the Son."[34] The Father is the unnamed mystery. Everything that we can think or say about the Father is accessible to us only through our experience of the Son and the Spirit. Sections of part 2 of *Saccidānanda* explore the relation of the Son to the Father, a relation that has also been communicated to us.[35] The Son made flesh in Jesus Christ is "[t]he *grund*, which is the depth of myself, in the depth of everything."

Hence, he can go on to say, "Jesus is that mystery that '*grounds*' me, that '*sources*' me, in the abyss, in the bottomless *guhā* [cave]—the mystery (as we say) of the Father—and *extends me*, pours me out . . . into all that is."

This mystery is very much the historical Jesus, not just the Cosmic Christ. "This same mystery is Jesus, who awakens me, springing up from the Father-Source and poured out in the Spirit, offered naked on the Cross, . . . all outpouring, all gift, all Eucharistic bread, broken and given, in order to be given, to be eaten and become the other." But the mystery is expressed in advaitin terms: "Jesus is this mystery of advaita in which I can no longer recognize myself *separately*. This "emptiness of all self" is "the kenosis of Christ!"[36] The experience of God as Trinity is no less Spirit-centered. In *Prayer*, the Swamiji says, "The mystery of the divine life is also the universal and all-pervading presence of the Holy Spirit of God. The Holy Spirit is in us, as he is in God, the mystery of unity, the mystery of non-duality. He is in us as coming from the Father, as sent to us from the Father, as pouring out in us the eternal love of the Father and the Son" (13-14). The presence of the Spirit in the hearts of believers makes them all one: "In the Spirit each one lives in the very depths of the other person—in the same way as the Father and the Son live from each and in each other, their 'circumincession' in theological language."[37]

This is a fully orthodox account of the Trinity, but, insists Abhishiktānanda, it is not final. As he says elsewhere in the *Diary*, "The Trinity is the interpretation by the Greek intellect of the impact of the experience of Jesus in his depth on the Jews and Hellenistic Christians. It is time to erect the Trinity at the heart of being" (November 1956, 165; see also 260, 278). A later passage clarifies the insufficiency of this historical understanding of the Trinity. "The Helleno-Christianity in which we are still living is only one historical form of the living experience of Jesus. The trinitarian and christological formulations of the early Councils are only one form—among an indefinite number of forms—of communicating the divine mystery to oneself and one's brethren. Jesus did not teach any philosophy, any more than the Buddha did." Then he goes further: "The Trinity [is] the way in which God appears to human beings in the circle of believers in Jesus. The Trinity only exists in relationship to us. No formula can express the mystery of Being. The Trinity is always at the level of the *devas* [personified divine beings or powers]." This is why Abhishiktānanda insisted that the real Trinity is not an "idea" but "an experience of my own consciousness" (*Diary*, 357). The very last entry in the *Diary* (September 12, 1973, 388) says, "The Trinity is the ultimate mystery of oneself. But in the very depth of this discovery of the Self-Trinity there lies the paradox: in the mystery of the non-source, who still speaks of the Source? It is only at the level of the Source, of the trickle of water springing up, that we speak of what is beyond. In the beyond there is no beyond. It simply is."

Swami Abhishiktānanda found resources in Hindu traditions to begin the creation of a new form of Trinitarian theology. He did not argue that there was a "hidden" Trinity in Hinduism. Rather, as he once put it, "It is only the revelation of the Trinity that allows us to go beyond Hinduism" (*Diary*, 224), that is, the consciousness of Reality given to Jesus and explicated in Hellenic terms by the Fathers could be seen in a new (perhaps deeper?) way by invoking the experience of Vedantic Hinduism. Two forms of language were singled out to help in this endeavor: the formula *sat-cit-ananda*; and the sacred mantra *OM*, which he saw as related to the biblical *ABBA*.[38] In September 1952, we already find Abhishiktānanda reflecting on how the Upanishads and the Bible "agree in suggesting the truth [about God]: the 'I am who I am' . . . of Exodus; 'one without second,' says the Upanishad." Seen from the angle of being (*sat*), God is aseity, "Pure Being in itself" (the Father). From the angle of consciousness (*cit*), we see the non-distinction between subject and object," what Christ meant when he said, "I and the Father are one" (John 10:30). "From the angle of *ānanda* [bliss]," we find "the non-distinction of the enjoyer and the enjoyed, of the lover and the beloved" (*Diary*, 54), that is, the Holy Spirit. These terms can never provide more than "a 'clue' to the heart of the Trinity," no more nor less than Augustine's speculations on the three Persons. "God is *sat, cit, ānanda*. All our concepts remain inadequate. We cannot say in reality that God knows himself, loves himself, enjoys himself" (ibid.). Both Augustine's investigations and the Swami's use of the Hindu formulae are secondary human formulations. The reality of the experience of the mystery goes beyond the mysticism of the West *and of the East.*

Abhishiktānanda's penchant for describing the Trinity as *saccidānanda* (the consonants change in the one-word form) is evident throughout his works. Along with the major treatment in the treatise of that name, chapter 15 of *Prayer* is another important source ("The Heart of the Trinity," *Prayer*, 174–81). Less well known is the fact that the Swami saw the *OM* mantra (more correctly *AUM*) as also helpful for understanding the Christian theology of God as Trinity. In the Upanishads, *AUM* is the primordial phoneme and also points to *Brahman* as signifying the ineffable abyss of the divine mystery.[39] The chapter Abhishiktānanda devotes to the *OM* in *Prayer* is revealing.[40] He starts

(110-11) by saying that the *OM* is formed of three elements: A and U, united with the diphthong O, and then M, three letters with a single sound. "This symbolizes, as they say, all the existing or imaginable triads in the universe." He continues, "It is also sometimes said that *OM* is not composed of only three parts, but of four, the fourth being the silence in which the *OM* finally disappears." *OM* covers a lot of ground, pertaining both to Creation, the eternal Word (*Vāc*), and the beginning of God's self-manifestation. "*OM* is also at that center of the soul from which arises the awareness of being oneself. All the words that our lips could possibly utter, . . . are already contained in this primordial *OM*" (111-12). It is the first sound that each person hears when coming into life and the last in death. He says that it has been seen both as a kind of foreshadowing of the Trinity, as well as the Word proceeding from the Father's silence, but that even in Christian interpretation, "it is always in the first place the symbol of God's ineffability, the very last step in our ascent towards him that is capable of outward expression" (113). "If we treat of *OM* as multiple," he says, "it is only so in the same way that Being itself at the level of manifestation is multiple" (114). Furthermore, "*OM* is the word which, being at the horizon of meaning, gives its full truth to everything" (115). Abhishiktānanda contends, however, that because the *OM* mantra is so deeply anchored in Hindu mystical experience, it should not be recommended to all Christians (116).

There are also many excellent Christian mantras, of which the "holy name of Jesus" as used in the Orthodox "Jesus Prayer," is a good example. Le Saux's own preference is for the prayer "Abba, Father!" used by both early Christians (e.g., Rom. 8:15; Gal. 4:5), and by Jesus himself in the Passion (Mark 14:36; Luke 23:46). The use of this mantra will help Christians not only to conform more and more to Christ but also to enter into the inner life of the Trinity. "More than any other prayer, *Abba, Father!* will enable them to share in the interior life of the Father and the Son, in their endless mutual Gaze in the unity of the Holy Spirit. *Abba, Father!* will be their ceaseless response to 'Thou art my beloved child!' (Matt. 3:17),[41] which the Father addresses to them in the only Son for all eternity" (119). *Abba* is the last articulate word that can be uttered by the creature because it leads directly "to the unfathomable abyss of the Father." Hence, he concludes, "ABBA is the mystery of the Son, *OM* the mystery of the Spirit. But nothing is able to signify the mystery of the Father in himself," who is made known only in the manifestations of Son and Spirit. "The Father is that last, or fourth part of the *OM*, which is pure silence" (120).

Abhishiktānanda's teaching on the Son as the Second Person in the

Trinity is clear, and everything that is said about the Son is true of Jesus, the God-man. What needs some further comment is his personal attitude toward Jesus. Jesus is the "true Self," and therefore is the necessary model for our own awakening to the inner self. The person of Jesus and our inner self become one when viewed from the Source that is attained in the *advaita* experience.⁴² Hence Abhishiktānanda can say, "The mystery of Jesus is the mystery of the Self, the presence of Jesus is the presence of the Self, to the Self" (*Diary*, 93), or, "You will only become yourself by becoming Christ" (*Diary*, 259). This is because Jesus is the "Free Person" (Stuart, 287, 294), the one who is identical to the divine "I am" (Stuart, 310–11, 314–15). He is the presence of God among us (*Diary*, 327–28) and, as such, is also the Supreme Guru (*Guru and Disciple*, 13).

Christ as the true self reveals the final component in addressing the question, What is the mystery?, namely, What is the Self, specifically the human Self? In Hindu teaching, *Brahman*, or Reality, and *Atman*, the Self, are inwardly identical, and only outwardly distinguished. Abhishiktānanda's teacher, Ramana Maharshi, had a rich doctrine of the need for self-inquiry in order to go beneath the everyday "I," or pseudo-self, to attain the self of pure consciousness. As he once put it, "The mind turned outwards results in thoughts and objects. Turned inwards it becomes itself the Self."⁴³ Swamiji accepts this teaching, if in a modified way. A key to his modification, as I see it, is his treatment of the Christian theme of humans being made in the "image and likeness of God" (Gen. 1:27).⁴⁴ The notion of humans as *imago dei* shows not only the mutual relation of God and human, as a number of Christian mystics had taught, but also their non-duality, an understanding of the *imago* that has affinities with Meister Eckhart, although the Swami does not mention him in this regard.

In his *Diary*, Abhishiktānanda often speaks of the need for the mind to turn within to seek the true Self and God as the Absolute. For instance, an entry for July 24, 1952, says, "The peaceful one [*sānta*] takes refuge in the center of himself and closes the circle round himself. . . . Closing the circle round himself, he lives in himself, living *secum, ātmanishtha*. But at this summit—or in this center—where one discovers oneself as Absolute, it is truly God who is encountered in the form of Self. . . . God in the clarity and bareness of his Absolute, which alone is able to reveal to us the way to enter our own Absoluteness. . . . One simply IS" (*Diary*, 51–52).⁴⁵ Numerous later examples can be cited regarding the need to move into the center where God and the true Self are manifested as not-two.⁴⁶ Late in the *Diary*, he expresses this succinctly: "If God were not an *I*, how could I myself be an *I*? At the root of my *I*, there is ultimately the *I* of God. And so if God is I, I am the Thou that he says to *himself*—that he says to me" (337).

Abhishiktānanda saw the non-duality of God and the self as the heart of the biblical teaching of the human as *imago dei*. In *Saccidānanda* he says, "Only to the extent that man enters into himself does he find God, and equally the extent of his entering into God is the measure to which he finds himself. Truly to find God, man has to descend to that level of his being at which he is nothing but the image of God, to the place where, at the very source of his being, nothing exists except God" (87). This position is spelled out in detail in chapter 14, "The Image of God" (163-74), which says that man is not an image of God in some way *outside* God, but is himself the inner *imago*, because "the Son reveals himself in me and lives in me, because the divine generation and the divine life are operative in me to my very depths" (165). God's presence in me and to me is nothing else but his presence to himself as *Saccidānanda* (167-72). The non-duality of God and the human as image means that humans share in the same freedom that characterizes the divine nature (*Saccidānanda*, 118-24). Apophatically speaking, man is as much a mystery as God: "Man's unknowable being is of the same order as God's, for man comes from God and has been created in his image. His is the 'beyond all' of Being itself."[47] There is a remarkable text from April 16, 1956, in which the Swami expresses the advaitin identity of God and true self through a series of mystical paradoxes about seeking God and the self (*Diary*, 150). These eighteen aphorisms are too long to be detailed here. They begin with the command, "Seek God until you find him beyond all thought of him and feeling of him," but soon add, "And to seek God, seek also yourself." As long as we are still aware of ourselves, we are not aware of God—"You are as far from God as God is far from you. God is as close to you as you are close to yourself." This is rooted in the following fact: "Your own mystery is the mystery of God. And (it is) a mystery of God even deeper than the mystery of God in himself—so the poor reason will stammer."

Ancillary Questions

How Do We Attain the Mystery? Abhishiktānanda's mysticism was more practical than speculative. Despite the depth of his thought, he insisted that it was only *experience*, not theology, that could gain the Real. In order to be open to the experience of non-duality, one had to embrace a devout way of life and various kinds of spiritual practice. For himself, this was the way of the ascetic hermit, the *sannyasī*, but he by no means thought that this form of life was necessary for all,[48] although some of the spiritual practices of the eremitical life, such as ascesis, emptying, solitude, and silence, would have to be practiced to some degree by all. Some of the practices and virtues necessary for the experience of God were pure gifts. For the Christian, the most prominent was faith, about which Abhishiktānanda has a good deal to say. He held that "[f]aith, in short, is to recognize that we are face to face with our God, to realize the presence of that fundamental love which makes us to be, and opens up in God immeasurable abysses of grace and mercy" (*Prayer*, 17). Note that this definition has nothing to do with doctrine or theology but is founded on experience. He says that such a conception of faith is as true of the Upanishads as it is of Christianity. Therefore, "[f]aith, prayer, and contemplation are simply the recognition of the presence of the Spirit in everything, everywhere, and at every moment."[49] As we might expect, Swamiji also says much about the importance of solitude and silence. Silence, of course, is a crucial aspect of the advaitin experience, and Abhishiktānanda learned much about it during his time as a hermit on Arunāchala.[50] He also has reflections on silence in *Prayer* (e.g., 51-57, 117-20) and in *Eyes of Light* (39-47). In *The Secret of Arunāchala* (130-31) an aged abbot instructed him about the three kinds of silence: the first form of those who remain silent out of dislike of fellow men (a type of egoism); the second of those who bind themselves to silence by a vow; and the true silence "of the one who has plunged so deeply within that it is well-nigh impossible for him to abandon it for conversation with others." Another practice about which the Swamiji has some comments is something often discussed in Christian mysticism, the practice of the presence of God.[51]

Abhishiktānanda wrote a fine short book on *Prayer*, perhaps the most accessible of his treatises. In it he discusses meditation (*dhyāna*), contemplation, action and contemplation, other styles of prayer,[52] as well as the purpose of prayer. There is no question that he thought of prayer as an (perhaps *the*) essential practice for attaining the Absolute. A full analysis of his views on prayer cannot be given here, but this treatise needs to be considered in light of some important passages on prayer in his other writings, such as in Stuart, *Life* (251-52), where he distinguishes between how liturgy and *advaita* exist on two different planes, as well as a text in the *Diary* for July 5, 1956, where he discusses three different kinds of "meditation." This passage seems to take meditation in a wider sense than it has in *Prayer*.[53]

What More Can We Say about the Goal? As is evident from what has already been said, what Christianity calls mysticism is closest to what the Hindu tradition spoke of as pure awareness of self, a consciousness in which all distinction between the self and divine Reality vanishes. As Abhishiktānanda put it in *Prayer*, "*the experience of self*, as India calls it, is the greatest of human acts, and without it no human act can be regarded as complete" (78-79). He calls this "the substratum of any genuine mystical experience. It can even be said that in it mystical experience is found in its pure state, no matter what forms it may happen to assume when manifested in the human psyche." Thus, "[i]t is only at the center of our being . . . that we can at least have a glimpse of the central mystery of God in himself." All of this sounds very Hindu, but then the Swami invokes the Christian Trinitarian character of the experience: "In the experience of which we are speaking, God appears at that very point where awareness (*cit*) is identical with being (*sat*) in the infinite bliss (*ānanda*) of the Spirit, who is unique (*a-dvaita*, not two) in the Father and the Son, and equally so in God and man, being in indivisible *Saccidānanda*." So, the goal of the mystical journey, for Abhishiktānanda at least, continues to be a Hindu experience of the self that, on deeper analysis, reveals the Christian Trinity to the believer.

In his early works and in the first parts of his *Diary* the Swami had much to say about the pure awareness of the self that he had learned from the Maharshi and Srī Gnānānanda. He cites the Maharshi: "You have to take the leap into the beyond . . . in the beyond, you find the Real. Only when everything has been left behind, . . . you can find the vision which has no beginning and no ending, the vision of Being, of the Self" (*Arunāchala*, 93). His other teacher Harilāl, a disciple of Ramana, pushed him hard to put off his Christian prayers, worship, and contemplation, declaring, "For anyone who has seen the Real, there is neither Christian, Hindu, Buddhist, or Muslim. There is only the ātman, and nothing can either bind or limit or qualify the ātman." He continued: "There is only the ātman. God is the ātman, the Self of all that is. *I* am the ātman. *You* are the ātman. Only the Self exists, in itself and in all" (*Arunāchala*, 84-85). And yet Abhishiktānanda never abandoned his Catholic faith and practice, especially saying Mass.

According to *Guru and Disciple*, "The 'I' is not truly known so long as it is not known in itself; no more can God be known, so long as he is not known in himself. . . . No one will ever reach his own self except through himself and in the very depth of himself" (78). Furthermore, "So long as I distinguish within me the I which is within, I am not yet truly 'within'. . . . When at least that has been realized, then that which seeks and that which is sought vanish together.... The final task in the spiritual quest is to resolve this ultimate distinction, that between the goal and the path, between the goal and him who is moving towards it" (79). In his last years, Abhishiktānanda seems to have focused more and more on the "I am" formula to express the disappearance of the distinction. "The awakening to God is inseparable from the awakening to the self. The first statement of the (prophetic) message is not God is (in the beginning, *en archē*), or that God said to me, but that *I am*" (*Diary*, 329). The *I am* is Christological: "Jesus explodes, but nothing replaces him.... Jesus reveals to us the shining of Brahman everywhere. He is that pure light.... This whole mystery is Jesus, the 'I AM' *ego eimi*; my name is 'I am'" (*Diary*, 347; see 376, 385). The *I am* is also Trinitarian and relational, even for us: "The Trinity, the experience of the other as 'oneself.' Going out of one's limit-self. Discovery of oneself in the other.... It is the sense that I am not other to anyone or to anything whatever, that *I am*" (*Diary*, 342). This leads to the new sense of freedom Abhishiktānanda felt at the end of his life: "I know that *ego eimi* [I am]. Do not ask me anything else—whether forever in my personal being or not, I know nothing about that, I am not concerned with it at all" (*Dairy*, 359).

What about the Religions? Throughout his life, Abhishiktānanda experienced the gulf between Catholicism and Hinduism on a deeply personal level. He often spoke of the difficulty of remaining Catholic, although this seems to have lessened with age. He was convinced that the Hindu religious experience was superior to that of the Jews and Greeks at the origins of Christianity. For example, in February 1962, he wrote in his *Diary*: "The religious experience of India is unquestionably superior to Jewish and Hellenic religious experience. And so it allows us to reach a greater depth of the Christic message, an interpretation, a verbal expression that is perhaps more genuine, more real, and more complete. But Christians are not ready for that" (245). He always spoke of Christianity (and indeed Hinduism) in terms of *mythos* and *symbol*, by which he meant not things that were "untrue," but things that were secondary manifestations of the *experience* of the Real. He did admit that dogmas and theological formulations could serve a useful function in preparing the mind for real religious experience (e.g., Stuart, 246); but at other times he is quite negative, insisting that the "myths" are to be left behind. In one place, for example, we read, "The myth of the Church is left behind, as is the myth of Christ. They have been marvelous guidelines, but by being turned in on themselves they have lost their elemental force as myths *'appealing to the depths of the human heart'*. And the myth can no longer be recovered. The christic and ecclesial myths are now exploding [that word again!] into symbols that are more powerful, more universal" (*Diary*, 373; see also 149). Statements like these seem to move Swamiji beyond recognizable Christianity.[54]

But what did Abhishiktānanda think was coming? His hopes for his own contributions to the future seem to have faded as he reflected on the failure of Shantivanam and his lack of success in attracting many real disciples (aside from Marc). He did think that his writing could at least *begin* to build bridges between Hinduism and Christianity. In the most positive of these works, *Saccidānanda*, he set out a fourfold understanding of the stages of revelation that may provide a clue to his thoughts about the future (98–100). He says that God has revealed himself by ever more inward and hidden stages through history. "First, there was cosmic revelation: God manifested through the forces of nature, and even more through the inner motions of the heart." This was the stage of Hinduism, which set "the stage for God's manifestation 'in person.'"[55] The second stage was the revelation of God himself "in his transcendence, his majesty and his holiness" to the Hebrews. "After this, in terms of chronology comes the revelation of the Son. The Father opened his heart, and in its depths he showed mankind the Son of Man." But the mystery of God's epiphany was still not complete. "The New Covenant had finally to be accomplished in the revelation and descent of the Spirit," which "aims at opening up the innermost center of the heart." The revelation of the Spirit began at Pentecost, and continues on in the growth of the Church, a growth whose fulfillment *needs* India. "As the Spirit reveals himself in that 'cave of the heart' which so deeply fascinates India, he progressively enables the soul to perceive the mysteries still unrevealed in herself and in him." For millennia, the sages of India have contemplated Being in its inner mystery; therefore, more than any other men, they should be "splendidly qualified to plumb the depths of the 'unoriginate' I, which is the Father, and of the 'Self' which is the Spirit." This will happen only in the "fullness of time," when at last India comes to know Jesus. He concludes, "Then, sharing in the 'filial' consciousness of Jesus, she will experience in the Spirit the ultimate depths of God. This awakening of India to the mystery of the Father in the Spirit will surely be a major turning-point for the Church in her ascent towards her 'parousiac fullness,' and in her growth towards the perfect maturity of the Lord in her (Eph. 4:13)."

Notes

1. *Diary*, 135. For full titles and publication information of works cited by author or short title, see the bibliography at the end of the essay.
2. On the problematic of Christian *sannyāsa* and Le Saux's role, see Tyler.
3. An important account is Stuart, *Swami Abhishiktānanda*. There is also a life by Du Boulay.
4. Fr. Le Saux wrote an appreciation of Monchanin, *Swami Parama Arubi Anandam (Fr. J. Monchanin) 1895-1957: A Memorial*, which includes some of his writings, especially the important essay comparing Eastern and Western mysticism, "The Quest of the Absolute" (142-46). Monchanin's writings are available in English as *In Quest of the Absolute*.
5. For some examples of these tensions, see *Diary*, 138, 140, 142, etc. For more on the problems between Monchanin and Le Saux, see Stuart, 52, 87-89, 98, 102-3, etc.
6. Bede Griffiths himself was a noted mystical author, as seen in his two autobiographical works, *The Golden String* (1954) and *The Marriage of East and West* (1982). For an introduction, see Matus.
7. These are: *The Secret of Arunāchala*; *Guru and Disciple*; and *The Mountain of the Lord*.
8. The most popular of these, available in several languages, was the short tract *Prayer*. Two other important writings were the longer essay, *Saccidānanda*, and the late treatise, *The Eyes of Light*, essays on religion in India.
9. See especially Stuart, but there are several other collections.
10. On Ramana Maharshi and his place in modern advaitin Hinduism, see R. Balasubramanian, "Two Contemporary Exemplars of the Hindu Tradition: Ramaṇa Maharṣi and Śri Candraśekharendra Sarasvati," in Sivaraman, 361-78.
11. Abhishiktānanda summarizes the Maharshi's teaching in *Saccidānanda*, chaps. 2 and 3 (19-41).
12. On the "mystery of the heart," see, e.g., *Secret*, 14, 21, 25, 86, etc.
13. *Secret*, 23. The book is filled with hymns to Arunāchala, some by Ramana, others composed by Abhishiktānanda himself (e.g., 24-25, 29, 36-37, 53-55, 58-59, and 104). For his account of the traditional history of the sacred mountain, see 50-52 and 133-34.
14. *Diary*, 43-45. Later, writing to a friend in France, he said, "This Arunāchala is strange. . . . Never in my life have I felt so much at peace, so joyful, so near to God, or rather, one with God, as on this mountain" (Stuart, 57).
15. For some expressions of his inner turmoil in 1953, see *Diary*, 59-60, 74-75; for 1954, *Diary*, 85; for 1955, *Diary*, 120-21; for 1956, *Diary*, 142-43.
16. On the crisis of mid-1955, see Stuart, 82-84.
17. On the consultations with Dr. Mehta, see *Diary*, 107-14.
18. Stuart, 81. See also *Diary*, 106.
19. *Guru and Disciple*, xvii. For more on meditation, see "Chapter 8. The One Essential" (65-81).
20. In a letter of August 26, 1969, Abhishiktānanda reflects on his two masters: "I had the grace of meeting Ramana and Gnānānanda . . . and it was surely at their feet that I learned something of the Upanishads. . . . We need a Master . . . who will have passed through—or rather passed beyond—the shattering confrontation of the Gospel . . . with the Vedantin experience" (Stuart, 218).

21. On the retreat, see Stuart, 99-100; and *Diary*, 155-95.

22. Abhishiktānanda told the story of this adventure in the third of his short "spiritual journey" books, *The Mountain of the Lord* (1966).

23. On the Gyansu period, see Stuart, 205-322; and *Diary*, 297-389.

24. Mystery surrounds the fate of Marc Chaduc, who vanished in 1977. Panikkar suggests that he might have performed the rite of *jala-samādhi*, or throwing his body into the Ganges ("Introduction," in *Diary*, xxvii). Equally strange is the disappearance of Abhishiktānanda's foremost female disciple, the Carmelite nun of Lisieux, Sr. Thérèse, whom he counseled for years and eventually managed to get settled in India as a recluse. She vanished into the Himalayas in 1976.

25. There is much rich material on these final months in the *Diary*, 385-88; and Stuart, 306-22.

26. See *Saccidānanda*, chap. 4, "The Advaitic Dilemma" (42-55). For a helpful selection of texts on *advaita*, see Du Boulay, *Essential Writings*, 56-74. Everyone who has written on Le Saux recognizes the importance of *advaita* for his thought; for a more detailed study, see Pierre Loudat, "A propos de Henri le Saux et de l'Advaita," *Studies in Spirituality* 7 (1997): 178-215.

27. For introductions, see two essays in Sivaraman: John G. Arapura, "Spirit and Spiritual Knowledge in the Upanishads" (64-85); and K. T. Pandurangi, "Vedanta as God-Realization (Madhva)" (299-318).

28. Cited in Balasubramanian, "Two Contemporary Exemplars," 369.

29. *Saccidinānda* praises "Eckhart, Tauler, and Ruysbroeck, who express their inner experience in terms which approach those of Plotinus, and even Parmenides, and who are therefore the best introduction for the western Christian to a true understanding of Hindu mystical experience" (74 n. 8).

30. On "That Thou Art," see Arapura, "Spirit and Spiritual Knowledge in the Upanishads," 22-26.

31. It would be interesting to compare Abhishiktānanda's teaching on God and the desert with that of Eckhart. See especially the passage from February 6, 1965: "If in the desert there were still God and myself, it would not be the desert. In the desert I have lost myself. . . . God is not in the desert. The desert is the very mystery of God which has no limits, and nothing to either measure him or locate him, and nothing to measure myself or locate myself in him, in relation to him" (*Dairy*, 277).

32. But see the interesting remark in *Diary*, 216: "There are no false gods, there are only false ideas of God. . . . Every idea of God is false in that it is imperfect, and there is no idea of God, even if it is false, that fails to express God, at least to a very slight extent."

33. See, e.g., *Saccidānanda*, 129-32.

34. *Saccidānanda*, 135; see also 224. Sometimes Abhishiktānanda explores the mystery of the Trinity in terms of seeing/knowing: "The Trinity. The infinitude of the See-er, the infinitude of the Seen, infinitude itself. But when at the heart of this infinitude all relationship vanishes, when there is no longer a see-er, then where is the Trinity?" (*Diary*, 361).

35. *Saccidānanda*, part 2: "Jesus and the Father" (78-83); "The Return to the Father" (83-85); and "Divine Sonship" (104-9).

36. All these texts are taken from a meditation for Christmas 1971 in *Diary*, 336-37.

37. For some other important texts on the role of the Holy Spirit, see *Diary*, 39–40, 46, 102, etc.

38. There are a number of other Hindu terms that can also be related to the Trinity; see *Diary*, 299, 301, etc.

39. Arapura, "Spirit and Spiritual Knowledge in the Upanishads," 77–79.

40. *Prayer*, "Chapter 10. OM! ABBA!" (110–20); see also *Saccidānanda*, 64–65, 174, 181–82 n. 1, 186, 189–91; and *Diary*, 80, 283, 301–2.

41. Jesus's baptism, as recounted in all four Gospels, plays an important role in Abhishiktānanda's thought as signifying the moment when Jesus receives full consciousness of his non-dual relation to the Father (e.g., *Diary*, 285–86). On the *ABBA*, see also *Diary*, 377.

42. A daring text comes from October 28, 1955: "The Christ, whom I first knew in his historical life in Jesus, and then in his epiphany in the Church, at the end of time (of my time) has appeared to me in the form of Bhagavān Srī Ramana.... Not the Bhagavān that I have venerated and before whose image his disciples prostrate, but the Bhagavān that I am in all reality at the source of myself" (*Diary*, 129).

43. Balasubramanian, "Two Contemporary Exemplars," 370–77; quotation from 374.

44. Admittedly, this theme is not found across his works but is strong in *Saccidānanda* (e.g., 69, 87, 163–74, 119, 121), as well as *Prayer* (e.g., 49, 55, and 78–82, which does not explicitly mention *imago*). See also *Diary*, 327.

45. Here the Swami mixes Western and Eastern mystical terms. *Secum* ("with himself") is a term ascribed to St. Benedict in Gregory the Great's *Dialogues* 2.3, while *ātmanishtha* is a term from the Upanishads meaning "firmly fixed in the self."

46. See, e.g., *Diary*, 78, 80, 92–93, 94, 115, 264, 267, 329–30, 374–75.

47. *Saccidānanda*, 4. Here too Abhishiktānanda shows remarkable similarity to earlier Christian mystics like Gregory of Nyssa, Eriugena, and Eckhart.

48. Stuart, 291, says, "He who renounces both *sannyasa* and non-*sannyasa* is the true *sannyasi*."

49. *Prayer*, 23. For more, see *Saccidānanda*, 198–201, on the mystery of faith; and *Diary* 122–24 on the "abyss of faith."

50. See *Arunāchala*, 26, 28–30, 36, 85, etc.

51. Stuart, 268: "Salvation comes from a deepening sense of the presence of God." See also *Prayer*, 1–3, 5, 27, 42–43.

52. The other styles of Christian prayer discussed (85–109) are: *lectio divina*; corporate reading of prayer; liturgical prayer; the Jesus Prayer; and in the Hindu vein, *Yoga* (68–73).

53. See *Diary*, 150–51, which describes the three forms of meditation as concerning (1) the content of consciousness (Western mystics); (2) the states of consciousness (the Yogis); and (3) advaitic identity with God.

54. Another troubling statement comes from October 22, 1967: "The Church and religions are tied to the neolithic era which is coming to an end. They will only last long enough to prepare human beings for taking total control of themselves. Today's atheism is necessary for the religious evolution of the human being" (*Diary*, 296). It would be easy to find a number of other such statements. On Abhishiktānanda's thought as moving beyond Christianity, see Tyler, 314–16.

55. For more on Hinduism and the "Cosmic Covenant," see *Saccidinānda*, chapter 5 (52–61).

Bibliography

Works by Abhishiktānanda

I cite only works in English that I have used.

Ascent to the Depth of the Heart: The Spiritual Diary (1948–1973) of Swami Abhishiktānanda (Dom Henri Le Saux). Selected and introduced by Raimon Panikkar. Delhi: ISPCK, 1998. [Cited as *Diary*.]
Guru and Disciple: An Encounter with Srī Gnānānanda Giri, a Contemporary Spiritual Master. Delhi: ISPCK, 1990.
Prayer. Norwich: Canterbury Press, 2006.
Saccidānanda: A Christian Approach to Advaitic Experience. Delhi: ISPCK, 1974. Reprint, 1997.
The Eyes of Light. Denville, NJ: Dimension Books, 1983.
The Secret of Arunāchala: A Christian Hermit of Shiva's Holy Mountain. Delhi: ISPCK, 1979. Reprint, 1997.
The Mountain of the Lord. Pilgrimage to Gangotri. Delhi: ISPCK, 1999.
Swami Parama Arubi Ananda (Fr. J. Monchanin) 1895–1957. A Memorial. Shantivanam, India, 2007.

Anthology

Du Boulay, Shirley, ed. *Swami Abhishiktānanda: Essential Writings.* Modern Spiritual Masters. Maryknoll, NY: Orbis Books, 2006.

Studies

Du Boulay, Shirley. *The Cave of the Heart: The Life of Swami Abhishiktānanda.* Maryknoll, NY: Orbis Books, 2005.
Loudot, Pierre. "A propos de Henri le Saux et de l'Advaita." *Studies in Spirituality* 7 (1997): 178–216.
Matus, Thomas, ed. *Bede Griffiths: Essential Writings.* Modern Spiritual Masters. Maryknoll, NY: Orbis Books, 2006.
Monchanin, Jules. *In Quest of the Absolute: The Life and Work of Jules Monchanin.* Edited and translated by J. G. Weber. Cistercian Studies Series 51. Kalamazoo, MI: Cistercian Publications, 1977.
Sivaraman, Krishna, ed. *Hindu Spirituality I: Vedas through Vedanta.* World Spirituality 6. New York: Crossroad, 1989.
Stuart, James, ed. *Swāmī Abhishiktānanda: His Life as Told through His Letters.* Delhi: ISPCK, 2000.
Tyler, Peter. "Swami Abhishiktānanda and the Possibility of Christian Sannyāsa." *Studies in Spirituality* 27 (2017): 295–321.

CHAPTER 9

Etty Hillesum (1914–1943): Witness to Universal Love

Some readers may wonder about the inclusion of Etty (Esther) Hillesum in this collection of mystics of the twentieth century, especially not only because she was Jewish, but also because her life seems at odds with the usual picture of a mystic. Of the five women studied here, three were Jewish, and two of them died as victims of the Holocaust (*Shoah*).[1] Edith Stein was a convert to Catholicism, but she remained proud of her Jewish heritage as she went to her fate at Auschwitz. Etty Hillesum never expressed any interest in conversion to Christianity and was strongly committed to sharing the fate of her people. She hoped to be a witness who would survive the horror of the *Shoah*, but only her voice remains. On July 27, 1942, as she packed her belongings to go to the transition camp for Jews at Westerbork, she wrote the following in her *Diary*: "And yet there must be someone to live through it all and to bear witness to the fact that God lived, even in these times. And why should I not be the witness?"[2]

For Etty's unconventional life we are almost totally dependent on the large *Diary* that records the months stretching from March 1941 to October 1942, as well as some letters from her final year of life. The *Diary* gives an honest portrayal of a self-centered young woman in inner turmoil, as well as one who was unabashedly promiscuous. But the book is also a conversion account. The history of mysticism features many conversion stories, as found, for example, in Augustine's *Confessions* and in the life of Charles de Foucauld (see chapter 1). Etty's story, however, subverts usual conversion narratives in many ways, although it too centers on a gradual transition from a life given over to sexual *erōs* to the gradual realization and practice of a universal love directed to the world and to all humans, even the persecutors who were responsible for her death. Etty never rejected the importance of physical love, but she came to see it from a different perspective. Obviously, Etty Hillesum raises important questions about the nature of love—human love for God, God's love for humans, human sexual love, and human love for all who are made in the image and likeness of God. This is why Etty's writings, not fully available until 1986, have been so much read, pondered, and commented upon over the past generation.

Many who set out to read Etty may find her endless introspection at times tedious, and her direct accounts of her sexual desires and encounters off-putting. Nevertheless, throughout the *Diary* her search for truth and meaning in her life is always clear, and the focus of her attention on helping God and others emerges ever more strongly as the circumstances of her life under Nazi oppression grow worse. A long entry for July 11, 1942 (*Diary*, 484–88), can provide an illustration. Etty muses on how she and God must carry on, saying, "And if God does not help me to go on, then I shall have to help God." She fears for the future in anticipation of life in the labor camps, but still finds a measure of "cheerfulness and inner peace." She says that she has "dropped the pretense that I'm out to help others. I shall merely try to help God as best I can, and if I succeed in doing that, then I shall be of use to others as well." Many accuse her of indifference and passivity, she says, because she does not go into hiding to avoid the clutches of the Nazis. "I don't feel in anybody's clutches," she retorts; "I feel safe in God's arms." She concludes the entry: "We must forget all our big words, begin with God and end with Death, and we must become as simple as pure spring water."

It is this kind of total honesty and full surrender to God that has attracted so many readers to Etty Hillesum. Among these is Pope Benedict XVI, who spoke of her in an Ash Wednesday audience in 2012. Benedict saluted her as an example of finding God in a secular age and in unlikely places, noting, "At first far from God, she discovered him looking far within her and she wrote, 'There is really a deep well inside me. And in it dwells God. Sometimes I am there too. But more often stone and grit block the well, and God is buried beneath. And then he must be dug out'" (26.08.41, 91). Benedict continues, "This frail and dissatisfied young woman, transfigured by faith, became a woman full of love and inner peace." He concludes, "We may not be surprised to discover modern-day mystics and unconventional instances of contemporary sanctity that fall outside the framework of traditional hagiography."[3] We must be careful, however, not to canonize Etty or to make her into what she was not—a kind of Christian martyr or saint. But we can still read and admire her as someone who found God and sought to bring God to others in word and deed.

Etty Hillesum sits on the margins of the religious traditions of Judaism and Christianity. She was not raised in an observant Jewish family, but she did find an important resource in the Hebrew Bible, especially the Psalms, in her final years. Under the influence of her therapist, Julius Spier (1887–1942), and her pious Christian friend Henny Tideman ("Tide"; 1907–1989), she began reading the New Testament, especially the Gospels of Matthew and John, as well as the letters of Paul. She also read some classic Christian mystics (Augustine's *Confessions*, *The Imitation of Christ*, and Meister Eckhart). Although she did not identify with any particular religion, she could truly say, "I feel that I am one of many heirs to a great spiritual heritage. I shall be its faithful guardian. I shall share it as best I can" (18.7.42, 521). She was the very definition of a nondenominational mystic.

Etty's relation to Christianity was complex. She was influenced by the message of Jesus (especially the Sermon on the Mount), but the figure of Jesus, especially the crucified Jesus, plays no part in her *Diary* (as contrasted with Simone Weil; see chapter 8). Still, there are aspects of Christianity that helped form her mystical spirituality. For example, her impetus to kneel in prayer was not a traditional mode of Jewish praying, as she recognized (10.10.42, 547). She also often cites Paul's hymn to love in 1 Corinthians 13 as the perfect expression of the love she aspired to in practice.[4] On October 13, 1942 (*Diary*, 549), she makes the astonishing statement: "When I suffer for the vulnerable, is it not for my own vulnerability that I really suffer? I have broken my body like bread and shared it out among men (see Matt. 26:26). And why not? They were hungry and they had gone without for so long—." Finally, there is the intriguing conversation she had with her friend and former lover Klaas Smelik in September of 1942, in which she explains how in the time of persecution each person must "turn inward and destroy in himself all that he thinks he ought to destroy in others." Klaas replies in astonishment, "But that—that is nothing but Christianity!" Etty coolly answers, "Yes, Christianity, and why ever not?" (23.09.42, 529).

Etty was accustomed to entering quotations from her readings into her *Diary* and there are a number from the New Testament (seven from Matthew's Gospel). Nonetheless, Etty's main resource was the prose and poetry of Rainer Maria Rilke (1875-1926), whom she quotes about 120 times as she meditates on the meaning of her life.[5] As she once put it, "You can never 'get away' from Rilke once you have read him properly. If you can't carry him with you all your life, there is no point in reading him" (20.2.42, 247; see also *Diary*, 275, 281, 322, 337, 447, 533). She was also interested in Russian literature, especially Dostoevsky and Tolstoy. Under Spier's influence, she became familiar with depth psychology and copied out many passages from C. G. Jung in the *Diary*. Etty was eclectic in her reading and spiritual searching. It is precisely because she was marginal, non-institutional, unplaceable, surprising, and yet open, universally loving, and positive, that she has such a strong appeal to many contemporary seekers for deeper meaning in their lives.

A Short Dramatic Story

Aside from her *Diary* and some letters, we know little about Etty Hillesum and her early life, though some of her friends who survived the *Shoah* left accounts of her. What we have in the *Diary* is a form of confession in the Augustinian manner, in which the narrative of a life, partly realized in dialogue with God, has the character of a paradigmatic *exemplum*, as David Burrell pointed out.[6] In one of the last entries in the *Diary*, she sums up her journey: "What a strange story it really is, my story: the girl who could not kneel. Or its variation: the girl who learned to pray" (10.10.42, 547). Along with a life story as *exemplum*, there is in Etty's *Diary* a kind of drama in which a large cast of characters interact with her as she shapes her inner journey. Perhaps a skilled dramatist could fashion Etty's narrative into a moving play. Etty herself desired to be a great writer, to produce novels to rival Dostoevsky; but all she has left us is this moving personal story. Since she wrote nothing of an expository nature, I think it best to explore her mystical teaching as it is presented in the *Diary*, that is, by an investigation of the last few years of her short life—from March 1941, when the text begins, to September 7, 1943, when her last letter-fragment was thrown from the train that was transporting her to her death at Auschwitz.

First a few facts about her earlier life. Etty was born on January 15, 1914, in Middelburg in Zeeland. Her father, Louis Hillesum (1880–1943), a classics professor, was raised in an Orthodox family, but had given up the practice of Judaism. Her mother, Rebecca Hillesum-Bernstein (1881–1943), was born in Russia but had fled to the Netherlands in the pogrom of 1907. Etty harked back to her mother's heritage and thought of herself as more Russian than Dutch. She later studied Slavic languages and gave tutoring lessons in Russian. Her parents were not well matched and fought a good deal. Etty was quite critical of them but became very protective of her family during the Nazi persecution and in the concentration camp. There were two other children, Jacob (Jaap) born in 1916 and Michael (Mischa) born in 1920. Both were very talented, Jaap as a doctor and Mischa as a pianist. Both were also psychologically fragile and spent time in mental institutions. It was a troubled family, and this helps to explain some of Etty's interior doubts and struggles, as well as her many physical ailments (headaches, digestive problems, etc.).

In 1924, the family moved to Deventer, where Louis served as the head of the Gymnasium. As a child Etty developed a habit of voracious reading that stayed with her. In 1932 she graduated from high school and went to Amsterdam to study law, where she took a BA in 1935 and an MA in 1939. However, she later showed little interest in law. Etty was involved in left-wing political issues at the university, and it was here that she became sexually "adventurous," as she put it. Early on, she had a passionate but brief affair with a fellow student, Max Knapp. In 1934 she had a six-month affair with the married Klaas Smelik, a writer and leftist activist, who later edited her writings. They remained friends and Etty became close to his daughter Johanna (b. 1916). In 1937 Etty went to live as a housekeeper at the large house of the widower Hendrik Wegerif ("Pa Han"; 1879–1946). She soon entered into a sexual relationship with him and they lived as "husband and wife" for five years. Etty, who described herself as "a sensual young woman" (22.2.42, 259), says at the beginning of the *Diary*, "I am accomplished in bed, just about seasoned enough that I should think to be counted among the better lovers." She goes on to say that, while physical love suits her to perfection, "yet it remains a mere trifle, set apart from what is truly essential, and deep inside me something is still locked away" (8.3.41, 4). It is clear that her relation with "Pa Han" did not prevent her from taking other sex-partners in "one-night stands," because after meeting Julius Spier she admits, "All the adventures and transient relationships I have had have made me utterly miserable, tearing me apart. But I have always lacked the strength to resist, and my curiosity always got the better of me" (19.3.41, 33; see also 24.3.41, 48). Etty's *Diary* is filled with erotic reveries and sensual accounts, including her attraction to other women (e.g., 25.9.41, 104; 2.3.42, 319; and 11.6,42, 407); but she, perhaps paradoxically, insisted that sex was secondary, even unimportant.[7] In later parts of the *Diary*, she says that prayer is a far more intimate act than sex (e.g., 22.11.41, 148). Etty continued to struggle with her sexual urges, or "confounded eroticism" (*Diary*, 55), noting, "It is difficult to be on equally good terms with God and the lower parts of your body" (4.8.41, 70). Etty was also conflicted about marriage. At times she had thoughts about devoting her life to perfect love of one man—the romantic ideal of the time. But she recognized that this was not for her, given her temperament and her developing ideal of love for all people. Speaking of Spier at one point, she says, "And though there will be brief moments when I shall long to be bound to him for life, I must always remember that I want to go through life alone" (27.2.42, 258). Perhaps in part due to her inner fragility and especially the psychological problems of her brothers, she definitely did not want to have children. One of the most troubling passages in the *Diary* is the description of her self-induced abortion (6.12.41, 168-69).

Etty's Spiritual Journey

Etty Hillesum's search for deeper meaning in her life may well have been active for some years, but we have no record of what form it took before early 1941, when she began the *Diary*. The story is one of personal transformation, a passage from fragmentation to integration. Etty at times described her starting point as "chaos." On October 12, 1941, she says, "Perhaps it is my task in life, my sole task, to put some order and harmony into the chaos which is myself" (*Diary*, 130). She often expressed this hoped-for harmony in terms of bringing together her physical and spiritual sides (e.g., 7.8.41, 75).

Etty's struggle with her inner chaos took place against the background of the Nazi persecution of the Jews. The Germans had taken over the Netherlands in August 1940, and had begun to restrict Jewish life almost immediately. More and more restrictions, persecutions, imprisonments, and eventually deportations to the death camps followed. Although references to the political situation are relatively rare in the first year of the *Diary*, where Etty was obsessed with her own inner turmoil, by 1942 and especially 1943, the specter of the *Shoah* looms large in the narrative. Her discovery of God and her vocation to universal love was her response to the increasing horrors that surrounded her and eventually led to her death.

Many friends enter into the dramatic narrative of the *Diary*. The most important, and the most ambiguous, is the psychotherapist and "chirologist" Julius Spier, who was the major influence on her conversion.[8] In a letter she wrote to him on August 9–10, 1941, she says, "You are, in fact, the first person to whom I have ever related personally, whom I have tried to emulate" (*Dairy*, 84). After his death on September 15, 1942, she says, "You taught me to speak the name of God without embarrassment. You were the mediator between God and me, and now you, the mediator, have gone, and my path leads straight to God" (15.9.42, 516). A little later she describes him as "my great friend, the one who had attended the birth of my soul" (24.9.42, 531). It is hard to know what to make of Spier. Was he an unrecognized genius? A sincere religious seeker, despite his faults? A charlatan who enjoyed having sexual relations with his clients? Probably a bit of each. It is worth citing Etty's final evaluation of Spier shortly after his death: "All the good and all the bad that can be found in a man were in you—all the demons, all the passions, all the goodness, all the love—great discerner, great God-seeker, and God-finder that you were. You sought God in every human heart that opened up before you . . . , and found a little bit of him in each one " (15.9.42, 515).

Julius Spier was a German Jew who had been successful in business before deciding to become trained in the new discipline of depth psychology, which he studied under the famous Carl Gustav Jung (1875–1961). Spier pioneered what he called "psychochirology," that is, the interpretation of persons' hands to reveal their character and inner psychological states. Jung thought enough of Spier and his approach to write him a letter of recommendation, which launched him on his career in Berlin in 1930. Spier read widely in a number of religious traditions; he also prayed and meditated. His fascination with Christianity may be gauged by his once telling Etty, "I have such strange dreams, I dreamed that Christ himself came to baptize me" (15.9.42, 517). Spier's method of therapy, however, included things unacceptable today in psychological practice, such as physical wrestling with female clients to release their "inner tensions." These wrestling bouts often induced sexual arousal. Spier, like Etty, had had many affairs and assignations. As a result of his perilous situation as a Jew in Berlin, the "psychochirologist" decamped to Amsterdam in 1939, although not before becoming engaged to one of his Jewish patients, Hertha Levi, who fled to England in the face of the Nazi threat. Spiers's therapy and "magnetic personality" (as admirers noted; others demurred) attracted many, not least Etty Hillesum. He soon formed a "Spier-kreise," or circle, in Amsterdam, consisting mostly of women who used his therapy and also hung on his words. This included Etty and a number of her closest friends, such as Henny Tideman, Dicky de Jonge, Adri Holm, and Liesl and Werner Levie. All of this seems very strange today, but psychotherapy was far less regulated at that time.

Etty was introduced to Spier on February 3, 1941 (she always referred to him as S. in the *Diary*). Initially resistant, she soon became a devoted follower. It seems that it was at Spier's suggestion that she began a *Diary* to record her inner states—the only reason that we know anything about Etty Hillesum today. The relation between the two was complicated, involving therapist and patient, teacher and pupil, friend and friend, and lover to lover. Etty had sexual relations with Spier a number of times, although she did not want to marry him and encouraged him in his hopes to be reunited with his fiancée in London. Despite the large role that Spier occupies in the *Diary*, however, the story is Etty's—her deepening sense of the reality of God gradually enabled her to gain a more realistic sense of the significance of Spier's intervention in her life, as is evident in her moving account of his deathbed (*Dairy*, 514–17).

The *Diary* consists of eleven "Exercise Books" written between March 8, 1941, and October 14, 1942, although the seventh is lost. It is known that Etty continued writing her books when she was definitively consigned to the camp at Westerbork (October 1942 to September 1943), but these have been lost. There are, however, some letters from this time. Several of them provide searing accounts of what life was like in the camp (see especially Letters 23 and 64).

The *Diary* is a day-by-day account of Etty's life, but it is possible to structure this diffuse material into periods that reflect her inner journey (although scholars disagree on exactly how to determine the periods). I would suggest that the first period comprises the year after her meeting Spier, as reflected in books 1–4 (March 1941 to February 1942). This is primarily a time of inner turmoil and gradual progress to greater self-awareness. Etty's self-discovery, however, like Augustine's, is also a discovery of God. The second period (books 5–9) involves the early months of 1942 (March–June), when one gets a sense of growing spiritual maturity in Etty, although it is hard to find any dramatic single point of conversion. She still wrestles with her inner demons and her relationship with Spier. Soon, however, her inner development and her increasing recognition of the threats to the Jews coalesce into a new and final stage in her journey. On July 3, she writes, "Something has crystallized. I have looked on our destruction, our miserable end, which has already begun in so many small ways in our daily life, straight in the eye and accepted it into my life, and my love of life has not been diminished." Later in the same entry she reflects on her relation to Spier and says, "I feel a new period is beginning in our lives, more serious and more intense, in which we shall concentrate on the essentials" (3.7.42, 463-64). This last stage of Etty's journey can be seen in books 10–11 of the *Diary* (July to October 1942). These books also contain many prayers. This stage of spiritual maturity was lived out for another year during her incarceration at Westerbork, for which her letters bear some testimony, since the *Diary* for this time has been lost.

It would be quite possible to present Etty Hillesum's spirituality through an analysis of the major themes of her thought. I would suggest that there are at least five of these. The first is her thinking about God and her relationship to God, or what we can call her mysticism proper (the term and its equivalents occur fourteen times in her writings).[9] The word "God" is found over four hundred times in the *Diary*, and Etty's notion of God has a number of distinctive features, especially what she has to say about the relationship of God and human persons and her notion of God's "frailty" and "vulnerability."[10] A second major theme deals with prayer and contemplation, as well as her practice of kneeling as a reaction to the presence of God in her life.[11] A third theme is Etty's reflections on the meaning of life as a good and meaningful gift from God, both in the present moment and in the time to come.[12] Also obvious is the fourth theme, that of love. The role of universal love as compassion for all and her concomitant refusal to hate even the persecutors is one of the most striking aspects of her witness.[13] As Patrick Woodhouse put it, "Perhaps the most remarkable thing about Etty Hillesum was that what she experienced did not embitter or dull her heart. And, because that was where her faith came from, still she believed."[14] Etty experienced love both as *erōs* and *agapē* (to use Christian categories) during her life.[15] The notion of love is tied up with another important theme in the mystical tradition—the meaning of suffering. The suffering of her people in the *Shoah* and her own sharing in this form the context of her teaching on universal love.[16] These themes will emerge in more concrete detail from the following overview of the *Diary*.

The first period of the *Diary*, the year from March 1941 to February 1942, brings Etty before our eyes in all her honesty, confusion, and promise. It begins with a letter to Spier of March 8, in which she confesses her strong erotic feelings for him, as well as boasting of her accomplishments in bed, as we have seen. Nevertheless, she also admits, "at times I am nothing more nor less than a miserable, frightened creature, despite the clarity with which I can express myself" (8.3.41, 4). This is the Etty Hillesum who, seven months later, can still pray, "Oh Lord, make me a little less complicated" (8.10.41, 127). In these early months of her journey several important issues already emerge. Among these is the impulse to fall on her knees as a mark of her receptivity to a "new feeling for life." On March 16 she tells how, while sitting on the dustbin on the terrace, as she often did, she got a clear sense of the difference "between then and now." In the past she had sought to subject what she saw to herself and interpret it; now, "I just let it happen to me" and allow it to give her more strength. She continues, "As I sat there in the sun, I bowed my head unconsciously to take in even more of that new feeling for life. Suddenly I knew deep down how someone can sink impetuously to his knees and find peace there, his face hidden in his folded hands" (*Diary*, 25–26).[17] This new feeling of receptivity is not yet specifically related to God and Etty does not yet physically sink to her knees, but her attitude has begun to change. In September 1941, Etty questioned her religious friend Tide about whether she knelt when praying (25.7.41, 106), and in the same month she recounts her own actual kneeling: "This afternoon I suddenly found myself kneeling on the brown coconut matting in the bathroom, my head hidden in my dressing gown." She says kneeling doesn't come easily to her and she feels embarrassed, "because of the critical, rational, atheistic bit that is part of me as well." She continues, "And yet so often I have a great urge to kneel down with my face in my hands and in this way to find some peace and listen to the hidden source within me" (24.7.41, 103). The source is not yet named God.

By late November she begins to talk about herself as "the girl who could not kneel." Speaking about the things that are inside her but are hard to bring out, she says that she "still has a lot of false shame to get rid of," and then goes on, "And there is God. The girl who could not kneel but learned to do so on the rough coconut mat in an untidy bathroom. Such things are often more intimate than sex" (22.11.41, 148). In December, she twice mentions how she kneels by her bed now almost automatically (14.12.41, 181; 31.12.41, 212). In the latter text she says, "I listen in to myself; allow myself to be led, not by anything on the outside, but by what wells up from deep within. It's still no more than a beginning, I know. But it is no longer a shaky beginning, it has already taken root." In April 1942, she has become more direct about the relation of kneeling to God living within her: "A desire to kneel down sometimes pulses through my body, or rather it is as if my body had been meant and made for the act of kneeling." She continues, "When I write these things down I still feel a little ashamed, as if I were writing about the most intimate of intimate matters. Much more bashful than if I had to write about my love life. But is there anything more intimate as man's relationship to God?" (3.4.42, 320). There are many later references to "the girl who could not kneel," or its variant, "the girl who learned to pray" (10.10.42, 547). As Marja Clement put it, "Kneeling for Hillesum was the most intimate of all intimacies."[18]

Another theme that appears early in the *Diary* is the notion of the "center of life, or the soul," the core of the person that cannot be ceded to another (see *Diary*, 29, 58, 60)—"And man himself must be a small center in which the inner and the outer worlds meet. These two worlds are fed by each other, you must not neglect one at the expense of the other" (60). The center of the person comes up often in the later Exercise Books. As she put it, "When you lose your own center, everybody and everything goes out of kilter and seems unreal" (*Diary*, 118).[19] Eventually, the "center" seems to merge, or be subsumed, into the God who lives within her. Already in August 1941, she speaks of "regaining contact with myself, with the deepest and best within me, which I also call God" (10.8.41, 83). Some texts in the *Diary* could be read as if Etty's notion of God is a purely immanent one, a projection of her inner self; but a wider and deeper reading shows that God is also the transcendent other, the biblical "Thou."[20]

If Etty's kneeling seems to be spontaneous, the *Diary* also notes that she has begun setting aside more formal times for prayer by mid-1941. On June 8, she says that she is devoting a half-hour each morning to turning within. "I think I'll do it anyway: I'll turn inward for half an hour each morning before work, and listen to my inner voice. Lose myself. You could call it meditation. I am still a bit wary of that word. But anyway, why not?" She wants to turn her "innermost being into a vast empty plain," so that "something of 'God' can enter you, and something of 'Love,' too" (*Diary*, 56–57). The turn to meditation was facilitated by Spier, who told her that meditation is beautiful, so that she resolved to ask him, "How does one meditate? Can I learn to do it too?" (*Diary*, 58–59). Also in June of 1941, Etty is already realizing the need to abandon her own little ego to work for other people, to move from the purely personal to what she calls the "supra-personal" level (*Diary*, 66–67). On July 4, she prays, "Oh God, take me into your great hands and turn me into your instrument, let me write" (*Diary*, 68). So, the First and Second Exercise Books (March to October 1941; 3-133) already reveal some key themes of Etty's developing mystical life.

Exercise Book 3 (October–December 1941, 134–69) is revelatory about aspects of Etty's developing sense of responsibility for the world and her notion of universal love. The book starts out by reflecting, "It is a slow and painful process, this striving after true inner freedom," because "there is no help or assurance or refuge in others." This is especially true for a woman, who is supposed to lose herself in one man. Etty goes further, "My heart runs quite wild, but never just for one person. For all mankind. I believe this heart of mine is very rich indeed" (21.10.41, 134). She was to learn much more about love for all mankind in the months to come. In the end of November she has some thoughts about her commitment to life and her need for God's help. On November 24 (*Diary*, 153), she speaks to God, "Look, God, I'll do my best. I shall not withdraw from life. I shall stay down here and try to develop any talents I may have. . . . But give me a sign now and then and let some music flow from me." The next evening, while cycling home, she utters a prayer, "God, take me by your hand, I shall follow you dutifully and not resist too much. I shall evade none of the tempests life has in store for me. I shall try to face it all as best I can. . . . I shall follow wherever your hand leads me and try not to be afraid.[21] I shall try to spread some of my warmth, of my genuine love for others, wherever I go. But we shouldn't boast of our love for others. We cannot be sure it really exists." She says she sometimes imagines that she longs for seclusion in a nunnery, "But I know that I must seek you among people, out in the world." She concludes, "I vow to live my life out there to the full" (25.11.41, 154). Which, indeed, she did.

Another reflection on love is connected to a visit she made to her family and the feeling of deep affection she experienced for her father on that occasion. This leads her to meditate on the suffering to come that hangs over them all and the meaning of love. She feels she has a "higher sort of love" living in her. Sometimes she thinks that this may be "sentimental," but she rejects that: "I have two great feelings deep inside me: love, an inexplicable love, which perhaps cannot be analyzed because it is so primitive, for creatures and for God or for what I call God; and compassion, a boundless compassion that can sometimes bring tears to my eyes" (30.11.41, 161). This is an important text, not only because it shows that Etty was aware of the unusual character of her view of God ("what I call God"), but also because of its distinction between the deep inner *love* she has for God and creatures and her universal *compassion*, that is, the affective sharing she has for the feelings of others.[22] The theme of active love comes up again on December 3 (*Diary*, 165), when she kneels and prays, "Oh, Lord, let me feel at one with myself. Let me perform a thousand daily tasks with love, but let everyone spring from a greater central core of devotion and love."

Exercise Book 4 goes from December 8, 1941, to January 25, 1942, thus rounding out the first year of Etty's acquaintance with Spier. Etty's deepening sense of God's presence within her appears in a prayer from December 12: "Oh God, I thank you for having created me as I am. I thank you for the sense of fulfilment I sometimes have. That fulfilment is after all nothing but being filled with you" (12.12.41, 175; see also 15.1.42, 231; and 23.1.42, 234-35). She feels a growing sense of confidence, because, "Feeling safe and secure in your hands, oh God, I am no longer cut off quite so often from that deep undercurrent within me." As she becomes freer and freer, she is "learning not to inhibit the growth of anything, be it a person, or a day, or a book, or God himself, or me" (21.12.41, 197). Etty's sense of *her* responsibility for God, one of the unusual characteristics of her thought, is becoming more pronounced. This comes to the fore in an entry for January 9, 1942 (*Diary*, 223), where she thanks God for strengthening "the inner center regulating her life" and then speaks of her collaboration with God: "I think I work well with you, God, that we work well together. I have assigned an ever larger dwelling space to you, and I am also beginning to become more faithful to you. I hardly ever have to deny you anymore." Nor does she deny her own inner life out of a sense of shame. Etty thus has a sense of mutuality with God, a conviction that she and God work together and that she (and others) are called to help God out in fulfilling his many tasks. One of the most striking expressions of her mutuality with God and others comes late in the *Diary* on September 17, 1942 (*Diary*, 519), when she says, "Truly, my life is one long hearkening unto myself and unto others, unto God. And if I say that I hearken, it is really God who hearkens inside me. The most essential and the deepest in me hearkening unto the most essential and deepest in the other. God to God." Etty may not as yet have read Meister Eckhart, but this passage is not far from the Eckhartian notion that "the eye with which I see God is the same eye with which God sees me" (Eckhart's German Sermon 12).

During these months, Etty also reflects more and more on the meaning of suffering, noting the difference between going in search of suffering, which is a kind of masochism, and accepting it as it comes: "Nor need we go in search of 'suffering,' but whenever it thrusts itself upon us, we must not avoid it. And it thrusts itself upon us at every step, but life is beautiful for all that" (15.12.41, 183).[23] Etty's optimism, her sense of the goodness and beauty of life in the midst of the suffering of Nazi persecution, will be tried from time to time, but never yielded to despair.

In Books 4 and 5 of the *Diary*, Etty continues to wrestle with her confusing love life with its commitment to two old men, Julius Spier and "Pa Han"—"the 55-year-old and the 62-year-old" (*Diary*, 224). That part of her life is still in chaos. "My body," she says, "still has its own way much of the time, is not yet at peace with my soul. Yet I firmly believe in that oneness" (11.1.42, 225). In a discussion with Spier, she testifies to her split personality with regard to sex: "Isn't it odd, on the one hand I'm terribly shy and almost chaste and on the other hand I am quite shameless" (24.1.42, 239). She continues to describe her praying during February and March of 1942. Her practice of *hineinhören*, or "hearkening to her inner self," at times is so constant that she gives up formal prayer for praying within (20.2.42, 246, and 250). Such "listening" is a major aspect of her mysticism (see, e.g., 17.9.42, 519).[24]

Etty's prayer also reaches out to others. During the joy of listening to a Beethoven concert, she prays for all those in the frozen concentration camps, asking God to give them strength and the memory of former good times in their lives (22.2.42, 252). The noose was tightening for Etty and the Jews of the Netherlands. On February 25, she was among the Jews summoned to Gestapo Hall to be questioned. A young Gestapo officer threatened her, but she did not feel fear or indignation, but rather "real compassion" and wondered if the officer had an unhappy childhood or was let down by his girlfriend. "Despite all the suffering and injustice," she says, "I cannot hate others." She continues, "I felt very strongly that morning that you cannot take your hate out on individuals, no one person is to blame, the system has taken over, an ominous structure capable of crashing down on top of us all, on top of the interrogators as well as on the interrogated" (27.2.42, 259).[25] In another text Etty muses on the role of suffering in her life and thanks God for being able to experience it, because it enables her "to understand and to sympathize with my fellow men a little more" (2.3.42, 262). She also meditates on how she must learn to carry many other people within her, allowing them a place to flourish and unfold (13.3.42, 281). In a later prayer she says how hard it is to comprehend how people made in God's image can do such terrible things to each other.[26] She still says, "I try to face up to your world, God, not to escape from reality in beautiful dreams . . . —and I continue to praise your creation, God, despite everything" (29.5.42, 384).

Exercise Book 6 takes up just a month (March 27 to April 30, 1942, 303–61). Etty continues to desire to have a mature spiritual relation to Spier, but also has sex with him a number of times. On March 28 (*Diary*, 307), she reflects on why war exists and finds its root in the fact that "I and my neighbor and everyone else do not have enough love." She says that although she is sad from time to time, she tries not to cling to such moments, but to allow them to pass through her like a river so that she can say, "Yes, life is beautiful and I value it anew at the end of every day, even though I know that the sons of mothers . . . are being murdered in concentration camps." Even these mothers must learn to bear their sorrows and adhere to the love precept: "Do not relieve your feelings through hatred, do not seek to be avenged on all German mothers, for they, too, sorrow at this moment for their slain and murdered sons" (28.3.42, 308). Difficult as it may be in practice, this was always Etty's response to the evil she found around her. During this month she continues to record her prayers to God (see *Diary*, 328, 329, 335), but she spends much of the time pondering her relation to S., admitting to herself that, with their commitments to other people, they still take a great number of liberties with each other, "something the average person would be unable to cope with" (30.4.42, 356). There seems to be a bit of elitism and false conscience here.[27]

Book 7, which would have dealt with early May, has never been found, and Book 8, extending from May 18 to June 5, 1942, is short (*Diary*, 363–94). It testifies to the growing sense of threat that Etty feels (*Diary*, 364; and later, 443, 455–56, etc.), but does not add appreciably to the themes of her mysticism. The final three books of the *Diary* are the culmination of her journey and contain many passages essential to her message. Book Nine also covers only one month (June 5 to July 3; *Diary*, 395–462), despite its length. In the entry for June 19, there is an important passage that provides insight into Etty's view of mysticism, despite her infrequent use of the word. She distinguishes two kinds: "We try to save so much in life with a vague sort of mysticism. Mysticism must rest on crystal clear honesty, can come only after things have been stripped down to their naked reality. My goodness, how obvious everything will be then" (19.6.42, 426). Thus, Etty knew the negative, or ambiguous and vague uses of the term, but here and elsewhere (see *Diary*, 75–76, 198, 269) she holds out for a positive sense, which we find expressed also in a statement her brother Mischa later made to Henny Tideman and to which Etty agreed. Mischa said, "Henny, I too believe—I know—that there is another life after this one. I even believe that some people can see and experience that life together with this one. It is a world in which the eternal whispers of the mystics have been made living reality, and in which common, everyday subjects or sayings have taken on a higher meaning" (27.9.42, 534). Among those "eternal whisperers" was Meister Eckhart, whom we know Etty was reading at Westerbork.[28]

In the middle of Book 9, there is an important passage that enriches our understanding of Etty's view of God. She confesses feeling that she has had a privileged life as "a loner, who can fly as high and as fast as I like." But then, as often, she relates this self-worth to God: "It means gathering together all the strength one can have, living one's life with God and in God and having God dwell within"—a theme we have already seen. Then, in a parenthesis, she reflects on a question apophatic theologians have often asked—Is God a useful term? She says, "I find the word 'God' so primitive at times, it is only a metaphor after all, an approach to our greatest and most continuous inner adventure; I'm sure I don't even need the word 'God'.... Is God real, or is 'God' a name for what is within?" She wonders, "And, at night, when I sometimes have the inclination to speak to God and say very childishly, 'God, things cannot go on like this with me ...,' it is nevertheless as if I were addressing something in myself, trying to plead with a part of myself" (22.6.42, 439-40). Etty may be distinctively modern in the way she addresses the problem of "God's" reality, but this was not a new issue for many mystics, who often warned against customary uses of the term "God" as in danger of idolatry. In early July, as the weight of fear for the fate of the Jews descends painfully in her, she asks Spier: "Isn't it almost godless to keep having faith in God at times like these? And isn't it almost frivolous to go on finding life so beautiful?" (2.7.42, 459). Nevertheless, a few days later, on July 7, Etty testifies to the power of faith within her: "There are moments when I can see right through life and the human heart, when I understand more and more and become calmer and calmer and am filled with a faith in God that has grown so quickly inside me that it frightened me at first but has now become inseparable from me."[29] This ongoing involvement with God within never deserted her. In her last letter to Henny Tideman (August 18, 1943; *Diary*, 640), she says, "Sometimes I try my hand at turning out small profundities and uncertain short stories, but I always wind up with just one single word: God. And that says everything, and there is no need for anything more."

The increasing threats to the Jews led Etty to take a step that has been criticized by some. On July 14, 1942, through the urging of her brother Jaap, she applied for a position in secretarial work on the Jewish Council that the Nazis had set up to organize the Dutch Jews for transport to the East. She did not like this work, but she thought it would help her protect her family and allow her to give concrete assistance to fellow Jews. Etty's attitude toward the evil of the *Shoah* was one of constant loving opposition, not of active resistance. It remains controversial, then and now. By July 16 Etty was already working for the Council, and on July 30 she went to work at Westerbork, the transit camp, to help in the "Social Welfare Section" for Jews who were being readied for transport to the death camps. As a member of the Jewish Council, she had the possibility to return to Amsterdam for personal and health reasons, so she spent a number of extended periods back in the city, especially when she became ill (e.g., August 14–21, 1942; September 15–November 20, 1942; and December 5, 1942–June 5, 1943).

The entries for Books 10 and 11 in the *Diary* (July 3 to October 13, 1942; *Diary*, 463–550) are a remarkable witness to Etty's mature sense of God's presence in her life, something that was now inseparable from her compassionate love for all people. Book 10 starts out with a series of reflections. Etty asserts the goodness that exists in all people, Germans as well as Dutch, despite the evil that some commit. "Yes, we carry everything within," she says, "God and Heaven and Hell and Life and Death and all history. The externals are simply so many props; everything we need is within us. And we are to take everything that comes: the bad with the good, which does not mean that we cannot devote our life to curing the bad" (3.7.42, 463).[30] This is not fatalism, but an acceptance of the sacrament of the present moment, especially in the face of death. Shortly later she notes, "By 'coming to terms with life' I mean: the reality of death has become a definite part of my life; my life has, so to speak, been extended by death, by my looking death in the eye and by accepting it" (ibid., 464). Her reflections for the day end with a reminder to pray for a German soldier who had shown kindness to a Jewish girl. "German soldiers suffer as well," she says. "There are no frontiers between suffering people, and we must pray for them all" (ibid., 465).

In her current weakened state, Etty was convinced she would not last long in the labor camp, but even if she died in three days, "I should lie down and still not find life unfair" (4.7.42, 468). She knows that one thing is certain: "We must help to increase the store of love in this world. Every bit of hate we add to the surfeit of hate there is, renders this world more inhospitable and uninhabitable" (ibid., 471). On a visit to Amsterdam, she sees Spier again and reads the Bible with him, recognizing that they had reached a new, more peaceful stage in their relationship. She knows that he is dying of lung cancer, so, "All that matters now is to be kind to each other with all the goodness that is in us. And every encounter is also a farewell" (6.7.42, 475). More and more Etty recognizes that she has to forget her own worries to be of assistance to those she loves, and to go on wherever God has placed her. Above all, don't blame God: "I am ready for everything, for anywhere on this earth, wherever God may send me, I am ready to bear witness in any situation and unto death that life is beautiful and meaningful and that it is not God's fault that things are as they are at present, but our own" (7.7.42, 480–81). Etty sees that her attitude may seem like defeatism to some, but she claims that it is not; her equanimity springs from "that radiant feeling inside me, which encompasses but is untouched by all the suffering and all the violence" (9.7.42, 483). These excerpts from early July demonstrate the inner peace she had finally attained.

Etty's attitude toward God does not change, but deepens in these months. Again she expresses her sense that she must help God—"And if God does not help me to go on, then I shall have to help God" (11.7.42, 484). She says that she always feels safe in God's arms. In the labor camp they might well break her body, "Yet all this is as nothing to the immeasurable expanse of my faith in God and my inner receptiveness." The persecutors "cannot rob us of anything that matters." To those who urge her to go into hiding because she still has so much to give, she responds that she can help her friends and other people no matter where she may be. "It is sheer arrogance," she says, "to think oneself too good to share the fate of the masses. And if God himself should feel that I still have a great deal to do, well then, I shall do it after I have suffered what all the others suffer. . . . And if I should not survive, how I die will show me who I really am" (ibid., 487). Sunday, July 12, records a moving prayer that once again emphasizes God's weakness, frailty, and need for our assistance: "Alas, there doesn't seem much You yourself can do about our circumstances, about our lives. Neither do I hold You responsible. You cannot help us, but we must help You and defend your dwelling place inside us to the last" (12.7.42, 488-89). The perhaps surprising notion that it is we who must come to the aid of a weak and vulnerable God is surely connected with living in the midst of the horror of the *Shoah*. It also turns up in the poetry of the Romanian Jew Paul Celan (1920-1970), whose poem "Tenebrae" of 1957 is an elliptical meditation on the *Shoah*. There have been many evocations in mystical literature of the absence of God. Celan heightens this by making absence God's "sin," as the voices of those being slaughtered insist that they are near God, but God is not listening, so that God should *pray to them* and come near: "Near we are, Lord / near and graspable / . . . Pray, Lord, / pray to us, / we are near . . . / Pray, Lord / We are near."[31]

Much of the remainder of Book 10 consists of prayers and thoughts about prayer. Spier tells her on the telephone, "We shall have to pray hard tonight." She sends him a note, saying, "We have to pray every minute now, not just tonight. It's as if something within me has been compressed into constant prayer, something keeps praying inside me, even when I laugh or make jokes" (14.7.42, 490). Etty writes with searing honesty about her moments of near despair, when she was "unfaithful to God," but she always springs back. "When I pray," she tells us, "I never pray for myself; always for others, or else I hold a silly, naïve, or deadly serious dialogue with what is deepest inside me, which for the sake of convenience I call God" (15.7.42, 494). Her attention to God is almost constant. For example, "Have you any other plans for me, oh God?" (16.7.42, 496); and "I need to talk to you so much, oh God" (19.7.42, 496).[32] On July 20, her morning prayer begins, "Oh God, times are too hard for frail people like myself." Nevertheless, she prays that she will be able to carry on into the new age to come. "Somewhere in me I feel so light, without the least bitterness and so full of strength and love. I would so much like to help prepare for the new age and to carry that which is indestructible within me intact into the new age, which is bound to come, for I can feel it growing inside me, every day" (*Diary*, 497). Many of her prayers are for God to give her the strength and constancy to carry on as conditions worsen. At times she feels the urge to kneel down even in the midst of a crowd. She continues to look for meaning in all the suffering she sees: "If all this suffering does not help us to broaden our horizon, to attain a greater humanity by shedding all trifling and irrelevant issues, then it will all have been for nothing" (24.7.42, 504). On July 27 she is oppressed with sadness and numbness, but still expresses hope: "And yet there must be someone to live through it all and to bear witness to the fact that God lived, even in these times." She knows that she must not give up, no matter how hard life is. She must "try to bear it and try to save a little piece of God" (*Diary*, 506). In order to do that she has to concentrate on the present: "I have learned one important thing today: wherever you happen to find yourself, be there with your whole heart" (*Diary*, 508). At the end of July she intends to read through her notebooks and she reflects that, "We [Jews] have had more than enough time to prepare for our present catastrophe: two whole years. And the last of these has proved to be the most crucial of my life, my most beautiful year. And I know for certain that there will be a continuity between the life I have led and the life about to begin. Because my life is increasingly an inner one . . ." (*Diary*, 511–12).

Entries for August and the first half of September are lacking, so that Book 11 begins on September 15, the day of Spier's death and her reflections on the meaning of his life (*Diary*, 514–17). She starts the account with one of her most moving prayers (*Diary*, 514), thanking God for how much he has given her, both what was beautiful and what was hard to bear. She says, "To think that one small human heart can experience so much, oh God, so much suffering and so much love, I am so grateful to you, God, for having chosen my heart, in these times, to experience all the things it has experienced." In this new state she will find patience through her old method of talking to herself. She adds, "And talking to you, God. Is that all right? With the passing of people, I feel a growing need to speak to You alone. I love people so terribly, because in every human being I love something of You." Etty's grasping and anxiety-making *erōs* seems to have finally attained the equanimity of agapeic love.[33] Spier's death has released her from false and selfish love: "I stood beside his bed and found myself standing before one of your last mysteries, my God. Give me a whole life to comprehend it." Heaven lives within her, because she has learned to "accept everything from your hands, oh God, as it comes" (*Diary*, 515). Her gratitude to God leads her to a renewed dedication to life: "I shall live on with that part of the dead that lives forever, and I shall rekindle into life that of the living that is not dead, until there is nothing but life, one great life, oh God" (16.9.42, 518).

Although it may seem strange, Etty says that she has learned to love Westerbork, because her two months behind barbed wire "have been the two richest and most intense months of my life, in which my highest values were so deeply confirmed" (17.9.42, 520). The final entries in

Book 11 are full of expressions of gratitude to God. Her dialogues with God continue to explore the mutual need of God and the soul to help each: "At difficult moments like these, I often wonder what you intend with me, oh God, and therefore what I intend with you" (24.9.42, 531).[34] She recognizes that her own life still needs work. On September 25 (*Diary*, 533), she writes, "If one wants to exert a moral influence on others, one must start with one's own morals. I keep talking about God the whole day long, and it is high time that I lived accordingly. . . . A soundless voice . . . tells me what to do and forces me to confess: I have fallen short in all ways, my real work has not even begun." Still in Amsterdam under doctor's care, she longs to go back to Westerbork and be with her people in their suffering. She playfully tries to bargain with God (*Diary*, 538, 541, 542), but recognizes, "Not *my* will, but thy will be done" (Matt. 26:39). She even prays for suffering, if God will give her the power to bear it (*Diary*, 541, 545). One of her last entries turns to St. Augustine and the *Confessions* that she had been reading for several years. "I am going to read Saint Augustine again. He is so austere and so fervent. And so full of devotion in his love letters to God. Truly those are the only love letters one ought to write: love letters to God" (9.10.42, 546). Etty Hillesum's *Diary* contains her love letters to God. The very last line of her *Diary* also testifies to her constant loving concern for others: "We should be willing to act as balm for all wounds" (13.10.42, 550).

On July 5, 1943, the special privileges of those who worked for the Jewish Council were revoked and Etty had to remain in the camp thereafter. Despite the efforts of many to prolong her stay, a special order from the German High Command in the Hague ordered the whole Hillesum family on to the transport train on September 7. Etty managed to throw a poignant note out of the car. She says that sitting in the railroad car waiting to depart, she had opened her Bible, and found the consoling text, "The Lord is my high tower" (Ps. 18:3). She continues, "We left the camp singing, father and mother firmly and calmly, Mischa too. We shall be traveling for three days. Thank you all for your kindness and care" (7.11.43, 659). One imagines that these were Jewish songs or hymns. Her parents were soon murdered; Etty survived until November 30, 1943.

Conclusion

That, in brief, is Etty Hillesum in all her chaos and confusion, in the vagaries of her erotic life, but also in her love for all people, even those who destroyed her. It discloses a spiritual adventurer with an intense sense of God in her life and a conviction that she needs to help God so that he can help her and others. Perhaps the best homage we can render to this remarkable woman is to follow her example and fall on our knees in gratitude to God for the goodness of life.

Etty Hillesum is an arresting, even moving, figure. I have also argued that she is a modern mystic, if of a distinctive kind. She was not raised in any religious tradition and hence did not have any of the usual forms of preparation for experiencing mystical states. Two factors precipitated the transformation of this "girl who could not kneel" into a true mystic. The first was the growing persecution of the Jewish people by the Nazi regime. The second was the influence of an unlikely spiritual guide in the person of Julius Spier, who helped awaken her inner search for God. The menacing shadow of the *Shoah* made Etty confront the mystery of evil in its starkest form. She came to realize (or better, it was given to her to realize) that it was love alone that had the power to overcome such evil. The love that God poured out in her heart (Rom. 5:5) brought her to a deep inward experience of God and eventually to a state of almost constant prayer. But this love also had an external effect. Etty realized that she could not hate anyone, not even the Nazi persecutors. Through her concern and service to her fellow victims in the camps at Westerbork and later at Auschwitz she became a model of the universal power of love.

Notes

1. On the four noted Jewish women authors of the time of the Holocaust (Edith Stein, Simone Weil, Anne Frank, and Etty Hillesum), see Brenner. For full titles and publication information of the works cited by author or short title, see the bibliography at the end of the essay.

2. The critical edition of the *Diary (Dagboek)* and Etty's letters, primarily in Dutch, but with some German, was edited by K. A. D. Smelik in 1986. The full English version, also by Smelik, appeared in 2002 (see bibliography). I will cite the *Diary* by date of entry (day, month, year) and page of the translation. This passage is: 27.07.43, 506.

3. Benedict XVI, as cited in Rosenberg, 173–74.

4. There are five references to 1 Corinthians 13: *Diary*, 28.11.41, 157; 27.02.42, 256; 23.9.42, 534; 2.10.42, 541; and Letter 23 (591).

5. As Patrick Woodhouse puts it, "Etty Hillesum read Rilke not just for pleasure but for survival, the survival of her sanity and her soul" (290).

6. Burrell, "Assessing Statements of Faith."

7. In some accounts Etty is honest about using a man only as an instrument to satisfy an attack of lust. See the unpleasant seduction described on January 2, 1942 (*Diary*, 213–14).

8. Pleshoyano, 43-74.

9. For an overview of Etty's spirituality and mysticism, see Maas, 112-45. See also Fulvio Cesare Manara, "Dimensions of Mystical Experience in the Thinking and Behavior of Etty Hillesum," in Smelik et al., *Ethics and Religious Philosophy*, 49-67, which studies all the appearances of "mystics/mysticism" in her writings; Francesca Brezzi, "Etty Hillesum, An 'Atypical' Mystic," in Smelik et al., *Spirituality in the Writings of Etty Hillesum*, 173-90; and, in the same volume, Ria van den Brandt, "Etty Hillesum and Her Catholic 'Worshippers': A Plea for a More Critical Approach to Etty Hillesum's Writings," 215-31.

10. On Etty on God, see Klaas A. D. Smelik, "Etty Hillesum and Her God," in Smelik et al., *Spirituality in the Writings of Etty Hillesum*, 75-102; Woodhouse, "Chapter 2. Discovering God" (29-54); and van den Brandt, *Etty Hillesum*, 89-96.

11. Marya Clement, "The Girl Who Could Not Kneel," in Smelik, *The Lasting Significance of Etty Hillesum's Writings*, 139-55.

12. On Etty's hopes for the future, see Manja Pach, "Let's Talk about Hope: Etty Hillesum's Future-Perspective—'We May Suffer, but We Must Not Succumb,'" in Smelik, *Spirituality in the Writings of Etty Hillesum*, 351-63.

13. McDonough, 179-202; see also McDonough, "Etty Hillsum as Moral-Theological Guide: From Fear to Love's Givenness and At-Riskness," in Smelik et al., *Ethics and Religious Philosophy*, 90-118; van den Brandt, *Etty Hillesum*, 119-30; and Woodhouse, "Chapter 3. Refusing to Hate" (55-75).

14. Woodhouse, 126.

15. Maria Clara Lucchetti Bingemer, "The Journey of Etty Hillesum from Eros to Agape," in Smelik et al., *Ethics and Religious Philosophy*, 68-89.

16. Rosanna E. Navarro Sanchez, "Suffering, Silence, and Wisdom in the Life of Etty Hillesum," in Smelik, *Lasting Significance of Etty Hillesum's Writings*, 293-303.

17. There are a number of similar texts about the desire to kneel in the face of natural beauty, e.g., 4.7.41, 68.

18. Clement, "Girl Who Could Not Kneel," 154.

19. For more appearances of the center, see *Diary*, 120, 223, 246, 423, etc.

20. Smelik, "Etty Hillesum and Her God," 85-86, and 96; and Meins G. S. Coetsier, "'You-Consciousness'—Towards Political Theory: Etty Hillesum's Experience and Symbolization of the Divine Presence," Smelik et al., *Spirituality in the Writings of Etty Hillesum*, 103-24.

21. There are many other texts on accepting suffering, e.g., 2.12.41, 163.

22. For more on compassion, see Davies, who discusses Etty on 22-27; and McGinn, "The Compassion of the Mystics" (forthcoming). There are many texts on Etty's universal love for all, e.g., 66-67, 88, 134, 252-53, 262, 276, 291, 302, 310-11, 475, 483, 487, 493, 526, 629, 635, etc.

23. For a summary of Etty's view of suffering, see Bingemer, "Journey of Etty Hillesum," 81-84.

24. On *hineinhorchen* and *hineinhören* in Etty, see Clement, "Girl Who Could Not Kneel," 144-47.

25. Not hating the enemy is a constant theme in the *Diary*; see, e.g., 21-22, 307-8, 329, 435, 492, 503, 590-91, etc.

26. The fact that all humans are made in the image and likeness of God (Gen. 1:26-27) is the root of Etty's conviction that we must love everyone, good and evil (see also *Diary*, 157, 641, 644).

27. Etty also reflects on the lack of conventional morality in her relation with Spier on 23.5.42, 372-73. She later quotes Spier as saying, "In the erotic sphere I may be polygamous, but deep down, in my innermost self, I am monogamous" (*Diary*, 377)! Later entries continue to reflect her ambivalence. On the one hand, she harbors a growing sense that casual sex is wrong (27.6.42, 448), but in the same entry (*Diary*, 451) she asserts the freedom of every person "to develop his own relationships based on unique laws." Etty seems to have been still confused about the role of sex in her life.

28. A passage from a letter to Hes Hijmans of August 24, 1942, says, "This morning, I read Meister 'Eckehardt,' the mystic, for a while and scrubbed W.C.s." The letter is not in *Etty*, but is cited in Manara, "Dimensions of Mystical Experience," 60-61.

29. *Diary*, 7.7.42, 481. For other passages on faith, see, e.g., 258, 432, 490, 532 ("Yes, you see, I believe in God"), and 545. Note also her famous saying, "I believe in God and I believe in man" (20.6.42, 434).

30. Etty believed that "[e]verywhere things are both very good and very bad at the same time. The two are in balance, everywhere and always" (Letter 58, in Smelik, *Etty*, , 637-38).

31. Translation of John Felstiner, *Selected Poems and Prose of Paul Celan* (New York: Norton, 2001), 102-3. There is a study of Hillesum and Celan, although it does not mention this poem: Ulrich Lincoln, "The Mystery of Encounter: Poetry and Faith after Auschwitz in the Work of Paul Celan and Etty Hillesum," in Smelik, *Lasting Significance of Etty Hillesum's Writings*, 241-52.

32. That her later life at Westerbork continued to be one of constant prayer is evident from Letter 61 to Henny Tideman (August 18, 1943), already cited above. Its major theme is dialogue with God: "My life has become an uninterrupted dialogue with you, oh God, one great dialogue. . . . At night, too, when I lie in my bed and rest in you, oh God, tears of gratitude run down my face, and that is my prayer" (Smelik, *Etty*, 640).

33. For more on the transformation of erotic love, see the entry for 18.9.42, 525.

34. Etty's conviction of our need to care for God was with her to the end, as we can see from one of her last letters written on September 2, 1943, where she says, "And if we just care enough, God is in safe hands with us despite everything" (Smelik, *Etty*, 657).

Bibliography

Writings

Etty: De nagelaten geschriften van Etty Hillesum, 1941–1943. Edited, introduced, and annotated by K. A. D. Smelik. Amsterdam: Balans, 1986. The standard edition.

Etty: The Letters and Diaries of Etty Hillesum, 1941–1943. Edited by Klaas A. D. Smelik. Translated by Arnold J. Pomerans. Grand Rapids: Eerdmans, 2002. This is the complete English version used here.

An Interrupted Life: The Diaries, 1941–1943, and, Letters from Westerbork. Edited by Jan G. Gaarlands, with a Foreword by Eva Hoffman. Translated by Arnold J. Pomerans. New York: Henry Holt, 1996. An earlier and incomplete translation. Nonetheless, since this is only half the size of the full version, it may be a good place to start reading Etty.

Studies

Brandt, Ria van den. *Etty Hillesum: An Introduction to Her Thought.* Münster: LIT, 2014.

Brenner, Rachel Feldhay. *Writing as Resistance: Four Women Confronting the Holocaust. Edith Stein, Simone Weil, Anne Frank, Etty Hillesum.* University Park: University of Pennsylvania Press, 1994.

Burrell, David. "Assessing Statements of Faith: Augustine and Etty Hillesum." In Burrell, *Faith and Freedom: An Interfaith Perspective,* 245–57. Challenges in Contemporary Theology. Oxford: Blackwell, 2004.

Davies, Oliver. *A Theology of Compassion: Metaphysics of Difference and the Renewal of Tradition.* London: SCM Press, 2001.

Downey, Michael. "A Balm for All Wounds: The Spiritual Legacy of Etty Hillesum." *Spirituality Today* 40 (1988): 18–35.

Maas, Frans. "Etty Hillesum, 'In me is the earth and in me is heaven,'" In Maas, *Spirituality as Insight: Mystical Texts and Theological Reflections,* 112–45. Leuven: Peeters, 2004.

McDonough, William. "Etty Hillesum's Learning to Live and Preparing to Die: *Complacentia Boni* as the Beginning of Acquired and Infused Virtue." *Journal of the Society of Christian Ethics* 25 (2005): 179–202.

Pleshoyano, Alexandra. "Etty Hillesum: For God and with God." *The Way* 44 (2005): 7–20.

Rosenberg, Randall. "The Metaphysics of Holiness and the Longing for God in History: Thérèse of Lisieux and Etty Hillesum." In Rosenberg, *The Givenness of Desire: Concrete Subjectivity and the Natural Desire to See God,* 157–83. Toronto: University of Toronto Press, 2017.

Woodhouse, Patrick. *Etty Hillesum. A Life Transformed.* London: Bloomsbury-Continuum, 2009. A good introduction.

Collections

Smelik, Klaas, ed. *The Lasting Significance of Etty Hillesum's Writings.* Amsterdam: Amsterdam University Press, 2019. Contains a full bibliography (421–82).

Smelik, K. A. D. et al., eds. *The Ethics and Religious Philosophy of Etty Hillesum: Proceedings of the Etty Hillesum Conference at Ghent University,*

January 2014. Supplements to the Journal of Jewish Thought and Philosophy 28. Leiden: Brill, 2017.

Smelik, K. A. D., et al., eds. *Spirituality in the Writings of Etty Hillesum: Proceedings of the Etty Hillesum Conference at Ghent University, November 2008*. Supplements to the Journal of Jewish Thought and Philosophy 11. Leiden: Brill, 2010.

Smelik, Klaas, Gerrit Van Oord, and Jurjen Wiersma, eds. *Reading Etty Hillesum in Context: Writings, Life, and Influences of a Visionary Author.* Amsterdam: Amsterdam University Press, 2018.

CHAPTER 10

Thomas Merton (1915–1968) and the Renewal of Contemplation: A Reflection

I start with a story. Years ago I was invited to give a series of lectures on Cistercian mysticism at Gethsemane Abbey in Kentucky, Merton's home monastery. While wandering the grounds near the monastery one afternoon, I ran into a young couple who seemed to be searching for something. I asked if I could help and they said that they had been traveling nearby and heard that there was some famous "holy man" buried here and thought they would come to visit the grave. I said, "Oh, maybe you were thinking of Thomas Merton." "Yes, we think that was the name." So, I pointed out Merton's grave, which had had to be moved outside the monastery enclosure walls, because so many visitors had "violated" the sacred space of the enclosure to visit the grave. They seemed to be happy to have found what they were looking for.

Thomas Merton himself would have been horrified to have been considered a "holy man," and, given some incidents in his life, there is little danger that he will be put forward for canonization. Still, there is no figure in twentieth-century American Catholicism who has a reputation to equal that of Thomas Merton, or Father Louis as he was known within the abbey. It is said that more Ph.D. dissertations have been written on Merton than on any other figure in modern American Catholicism. The literature on Merton is immense. But Merton himself may have written more than what has been written about him—four thousand letters, according to some; a lifetime of journals, which take up at least a dozen volumes; books and articles past counting. He was a compulsive writer.[1]

This amount of production is bound to be uneven, and critics have used this fact to dismiss Merton as a mere religious journalist. This is not fair (even to religious journalists). In spite of some ephemera, it is hard to deny that as a spiritual writer, social critic, and man of letters, Thomas Merton not only had real genius, but also has had an immense effect on many readers. A number of Merton scholars have described him as a "spiritual master" and, indeed, even a mystic.[2] Merton himself said that he felt he had a real calling to "a deep mystical life."[3] In this chapter I will try to lay out a case why Merton should be considered a mystic on the basis of what must necessarily be a partial look at an immense corpus of writings that I do not pretend to have totally read, but that I have delved into for many decades.

The Heart of Merton's Mysticism

Merton used the word "mysticism" sparingly in his book titles.[4] His volumes often bore titles about "contemplation," "inner experience," "the silent life," "solitude," and the like. It was not that he avoided the term "mysticism," which appears in a number of his writings, but I think that Merton, who had a vast, if not always direct or systematic knowledge of the history of Christian mysticism, realized that "mysticism" was a modern term (seventeenth century), and that what he really wanted to do was to retrieve the ancient tradition of contemplative prayer that, correctly understood, begins in Scripture; it was developed in the Fathers of the early Church, enriched in the Middle Ages, expanded in the Late Middle Ages, put to the test in the early modern period, and marginalized in the eighteenth and nineteenth centuries. His efforts to renew the contemplative tradition were often addressed to monks and other religious, but, as he matured, it became clearer that he meant the message for all. In Merton's contribution to Pope Paul VI's request for a "message of contemplatives to the world" (August 21-22, 1967), he wrote, "The contemplative life should not be regarded as the exclusive prerogative of those who dwell in monastic walls. All men can seek and find this intimate awareness and awakening which is the gift of love and a vivifying touch of creative and redemptive power" (*Hidden Ground of Love*, 159).

Contemplation and mysticism are intimately related for Merton. As he once put it, "contemplation means mysticism" (*Introduction to Christian Mysticism*, 148), although in other places he recognized certain distinctions between the two closely related words (e.g., *Mystics and Zen Masters*, 203-4). He continually emphasized the importance of mysticism and the mystics. For example, in a 1963 letter to the English writer on mysticism E. I. Watkin, he says, "There is no question that the mystics are the ones who have kept Christianity going, if anyone has" (*Hidden Ground of Love*, 583). Merton also recognized the necessary connection between mysticism and theology. At the beginning of *An Introduction to Christian Mysticism*, he laments the separation of theology from "spirituality" and says, "Without mysticism there is no real theology, and without theology there is no real mysticism." The course, he tells his students, is designed to "help us to ... live our theology" (16).

Merton was aware that contemplation was an ambiguous, often-misused word (*Inner Experience*, 60-61, 63; *Contemplation in the World of Action*, 249-50), but it is the best word we have. In his writings, early and late, Merton gave many brief descriptions of contemplation and the contemplative life, which do not greatly differ.[5] Perhaps the best place to begin exploring his view of the nature of contemplation is in the first three sections of his 1962 book *New Seeds of Contemplation*, where he circles around the topic, probing both what it is and what it is not. Among these many explorations, one that I find telling is his insistence that contemplation is not mere "consideration of abstract truths about God" or even "affective meditation" on belief, but "is awakening, enlightenment and the amazing intuitive grasp by which love gains certitude of God's creative and dynamic intervention in our lives" (5). Contemplation, therefore, "is the experiential grasp of reality as *subjective*," not a matter of possessiveness but a moment in which our "existential depths . . . open out into the mystery of God" (8–9). This awakening to the mystery of the God who cannot be known is not something that we can choose to do of ourselves; it is "God Who chooses to awaken us" (10).

During the course of the years he wrote on the topic, Merton's view of contemplation broadened. Contemplation, he eventually insisted, is not just a particular kind of spiritual activity, but is a whole way of life. As "the highest expression of man's intellectual and spiritual life," contemplation supersedes or, more correctly, subsumes "every other form of intuition and experience—whether in art, in philosophy, in theology, in liturgy or in the ordinary levels of love and belief" (*New Seeds*, 1–2). Hence, Merton grew increasingly critical of views that saw contemplation as an inner retreat from the world and apostolic/political action, as well as any notion of Christian contemplation as a purely intellectual speculation in the manner of Greek philosophical *theōria*.[6] True *contemplatio* is ineluctably tied to right action and to love. In his prefatory remarks to Merton's *Introduction to Christian Mysticism*, Patrick F. O'Connell puts it this way: there is "clear evidence that for Merton contemplation and action, an interest in mysticism and a passion for social justice, were not alternative but correlative, both essential ways of being faithful to God's will for humanity" ("Introduction," lii). In his desire to highlight the union of contemplation and action for Christians in the modern world, Merton grasped the truth that Karl Rahner enunciated when he said that "[t]he Christian of the future will either be a mystic [= contemplative], or will not be a Christian at all."[7]

Other figures of mid-twentieth-century Catholicism, of course, also labored to revive the contemplative/mystical tradition. Merton knew and worked with many of them. Where he was distinctive, however, was not only in his efforts to retrieve the broad tradition of Christian teaching on contemplation (little known at the time in English-speaking Catholicism), but also in his conviction that the revival of Christian contemplation would be most fruitful when conducted in the context of an engagement, or dialogue, with the contemplative traditions of the other great world religions: Hinduism, Buddhism (especially Zen), Judaism, Islam, and the like. In a 1961 letter to Dona Luisa Coomaraswamy, he praised her late husband, Ananda, as an example of someone who was able to combine the spiritual traditions of the Orient and the Christian West. He says, "This kind of comprehension, is, it seems to me, quite obligatory for the contemplative of our day, at least if he is in any sense a scholar." He went on to call for a "movement" of people who would be "able to unite in themselves and experience in their own lives all that is best and most true in the various great spiritual traditions" (*Hidden Ground of Love*, 126). In his dialogue with the Buddhist scholar D. T. Suzuki at the end of *Zen and the Birds of Appetite*, he says, "I feel that in talking to him I am talking to a 'fellow citizen,' to one who, although his beliefs in many respects differ from mine, shares a common spiritual climate. This unity of outlook and purpose is supremely significant." Merton's ecumenical outreach, particularly with regard to Zen, is evident in two books from the 1960s: *The Way of Chuang Tzu* (third century B.C.E. Taoist philosopher), and *Zen and the Birds of Appetite*.[8] Perhaps the most moving statement of his conviction of the need for dialogue to realize the inner harmony of the various contemplative traditions comes from the informal talk he gave to an interreligious group in Calcutta in October 1968, where he concluded, "And the deepest level of communication is not communication, but communion. It is wordless. It is beyond words, and it is beyond speech, and it is beyond concept. Not that we discover a new unity. We discover an older unity. My dear brothers, we are already one. But we imagine that we are not. And what we have to recover is our original unity. What we have to be is what we are" (*Asian Journal*, 308).

In the 1960s Merton became a lightning rod for criticism because of his prophetic stance against racism, nuclear war, and other social evils; he was equally controversial in conservative Catholic critics due to his ecumenical view of contemplation. For Merton, however, the awakening to God that is the essence of mystical contemplation is inseparable from the call to take a stand against the evils of the day. Merton, therefore, can be seen as an example of the "mystical-prophetic" strain in Christianity.[9] While it is never easy to place the productive and wide-ranging figure of Thomas Merton under a single heading, I am suggesting that one way to see his contribution to contemporary religious life is as a foremost representative of the "renewal of contemplation."

Merton's Moments

Like many Christian mystics, Thomas Merton was suspicious of the special gifts and paranormal experiences that so many modern Catholics mistakenly thought constitute the essence of mystical contact with God. Of course, in some cases the highest forms of mystical grace (Merton sometimes used the traditional term "infused contemplation") could be accompanied by visions, ecstasies, and other unusual gifts, like the stigmata; but Merton was too good a student of Eckhart, Teresa, John of the Cross, and others to confuse the cake with the icing. Like these Christian mystics, as well as the Zen masters he studied, he saw mysticism as a growing direct consciousness of God's presence realized in love; a new, sometimes shattering, awareness of the reality of God; a breakthrough to a level of being, which, while always present, is often overlooked.

Merton analyzed the nature of contemplative prayer in detail, as we will see below. At times, but only rarely, he spoke of his own special moments of what we can call mystical awareness. A few places in his expositions of prayer seem to reflect his inner experience without speaking in the first person. Two of these occur in his book on praying the Psalms, *Bread in the Wilderness* (1953). The first is in the section "Transformation in Discovery," where he talks about the change that is sometimes worked in us by the Holy Spirit as we sing the Psalms. He says, "The peculiar mystical impact with which certain verses of the Psalms suddenly produce this silent depth-charge in the heart of the contemplative is only to be accounted for by the fact that we, in the Spirit, recognize the Spirit singing in ourselves" (75). A later section on "Dark Lightning" speaks of an experience that goes beyond the "veiled contemplation" of living faith. According to Merton, "But it also happens—and this is rarer—that under the pressure of a very great love, or in the darkness of a conflict that exacts a heroic renunciation of our whole self, or in an ecstasy of a sudden splendid joy that does not belong to this earth, the soul will be raised out of itself. It will come face to face with the Christ of the Psalms. In an experience that might be likened to a flash of dark lightning, a thunderclap on the surface of the abyss, 'its eyes will be opened and it will know Him and He will vanish from its sight' (Luke 24:31)." In this moment that belongs to eternity, not time, "the whole soul is transfixed and illumined by the tremendous darkness which is the light of God" (119). Is this Merton speaking of his inner prayer life?

An early directly autobiographical account is found in his monastic journal, *The Sign of Jonas*. The book tells of the young monk's life at Gethsemane in the years from the time of the writing of his popular autobiography, *The Seven Storey Mountain*. The title is based on Jesus's reference to his resurrection as being "a sign of Jonas the prophet" and his three days in the belly of the whale, because, says Merton, "I feel that my own life is especially sealed with this great sign, . . . because like Jonas himself I find myself traveling toward my destiny in the belly of a paradox." The "Epilogue" of the book, "Fire Watch, July 4, 1952," portrays Merton serving as the night "Fire Watcher," walking through the monastery all night to guard against the danger of a possibly disastrous conflagration. The ascent and descent of the journey of the "Watcher" is an image of the course of the spiritual life, using the figures of Jonas and Isaiah's text on the night watchman (Isa. 21:11). In the course of his journey, Merton reflects on how he wrestles with God in prayer: "God, my God. God Whom I meet in darkness, with You it is always the same thing! Always the same question that nobody knows how to answer! I have prayed to You in the daytime with thoughts and reasons, and in the nighttime You have confronted me, scattering thought and reason." He complains that the result of all this questioning has come to nothing: "You have listened and said nothing, and I have turned away and wept with shame." Toward the end of the account, as Merton ascends the monastery's church tower, something changes as he recognizes the presence of God in nature at the approach of dawn. The text becomes allusive—is it a dialogue projected within the self, or a true conversation with God? "You, Who sleep in my breast are not met with words, but in the emergence of life within life and wisdom within wisdom. You are found in communion: Thou in me and I in Thee and Thou in them [his monastic brothers] and they in me, dispossession within dispossession . . . I am alone. Thou art alone. The Father and I are one" (*Sign of Jonas*, 342, 351).

A second Mertonian moment occurred in 1964 on a trip to Louisville, a neighboring city, on some monastery business. "In Louisville," says Merton, "at the corner of Fourth and Walnut, in the center of the shopping district, I was suddenly overwhelmed with the realization that I loved all these people, that I was theirs and they were mine, that we could not be alien to one another even though we were total strangers. It was like waking from a dream of separateness, of spurious self-isolation in a special world. . . . The whole illusion of a separate holy existence in a dream." Later he says, "This sense of liberation from an illusory difference was such a relief and such a joy that I almost laughed out loud." To recognize himself as "a member of a race in which God Himself became incarnate" is to see "the secret beauty" of all humans in the eyes of God. In language that may reflect Meister Eckhart he notes, "At the center of our being is a point of nothingness which is untouched by sin and by illusion, a point of pure truth, a point or spark which belongs entirely to God" (*Conjectures of a Guilty Bystander*, 156–58).[10] Note that if the "Fire Watch" moment of awareness centers on a oneness with God that includes unity with his monastic brethren, the Louisville insight is one of unity with all people, as seen from God's perspective. These two moments show that Merton increasingly saw the division between the sacred and the secular as an illusion.

At the end of his all-too-short life Merton was allowed to go off, as he had long desired, to visit Asian monastic sites and to meet with monks of East and West to discuss the future of monasticism. He traveled a good deal in India, Sri Lanka, and Thailand, and wrote about it all in his posthumous *Asian Journal*. While gazing on the great Buddha figures at Polonnaruwa in Ceylon (now Sri Lanka), he had another revelatory moment. He says, "Looking out at these figures I was suddenly, almost forcibly, jerked clean out of the habitual, half-tied vision of things, and an inner clearness, clarity, as if exploding from the rocks themselves, became evident and obvious." He continues, "I don't know when in my life I have ever had such a sense of beauty and spiritual validity running though one aesthetic illumination. . . . I know and have seen what I was obscurely looking for. I don't know what else remains but I have now seen and have pierced through the surface and have got beyond the shadow and the disguise" (*Asian Journal*, 233–36). Once again, this is a sudden awareness, aesthetic in character, of the inner oneness that reflects the core of mysticism. Although Merton always taught that mystical union is essentially Christological and Trinitarian, these three "moments of illumination" are revelatory of the general psychology of his mystical life.

Life and Letters

Due to his immense letter production and extensive journals, we probably know more about Thomas Merton than almost any other twentieth-century American Catholic religious figure. On this basis, many biographies have been written, and a host of other books have investigated aspects of his life. Merton would, of course, have publicly eschewed all this attention, but one can wonder if such rejections were really the whole truth. One of the paradoxes of this complex man was the way in which he expressed a strong desire to retire into the anonymity of the eremitical life at the same time that he cultivated ever-wider public attention, both through his writings on political and social issues and through his extensive correspondence. In the 1960s Merton wrote increasingly sharp attacks on the American government for its policies on war and racial justice, as well criticisms of the apathy and indifference of the leadership of American Catholicism.

In order to contextualize his teaching, it will be helpful to give a brief survey of the major events of Merton's life, along with some notes on the most important of his writings.[11] His popular spiritual autobiography, *The Seven Storey Mountain*, begins with the memorable sentences:

"On the last day of January 1915, under the sign of the Water Bearer, in a year of a great war, and down in the shadow of some French mountains on the borders of Spain, I came into the world. Free by nature, in the image of God, I was nevertheless the prisoner of my own violence and my own selfishness, in the image of the world into which I was born" (3). Although Merton was later cool toward the book with its world-denying piety and triumphalist Catholicism, *The Seven Storey Mountain* was what unexpectedly catapulted him to fame.

Merton's father, Owen, was a painter from New Zealand; his mother, Ruth Jenkins, was an American art student. They married in 1914 shortly before the outbreak of World War I. Tom (as he was originally called) was born at Pardes in southern France, but the family fled to the United States in 1916. Tom's mother died of stomach cancer in 1921 when he was six. Tom lived for a time with his maternal grandparents on Long Island, but in 1925 he joined his father in France. From 1928 until 1933 he lived in England with his father, attending the school at Ripley Court. In 1929 he entered the Oakham Public School, where he studied until 1933. In January of 1931, his father died of a brain tumor and Tom was left an orphan. In October 1933, he began his studies at Clare College, Cambridge, but the young orphan stayed there for only a year. Totally adrift in his personal life, he spent the year drinking and womanizing and was forced to withdraw from school after making a young woman pregnant. Back in the United States, in January 1935, he entered Columbia University, where he studied English, taking a master's degree in 1939 with a thesis on William Blake. The Columbia years were decisive in Merton's personal and intellectual evolution. He made a circle of talented friends and mentors, read widely, and began to develop an interest in religion and even mysticism.[12] Although he still led a rather wild student life, Merton became more and more convinced of the emptiness of life without God, so in September 1938, he went to the local parish of Corpus Christi and asked to be received into the Catholic Church, which took place on November 16.

Thomas Merton the Catholic was still unsure about his future. He thought of continuing studies for a Ph.D. and also of becoming a Franciscan priest. In 1940 and 1941 he taught English at the Franciscan University of St. Bonaventure in Olean, New York, but a retreat he made at Gethsemane in Holy Week of 1941 convinced him to join the Trappists (Order of the Cistercians of Strict Observance). On December 10, he entered the monastery as a postulant and was given a new name in religion, Louis. The Cistercians at that time were scarcely a contemplative order, so Merton's natural contemplative bent was not comfortable with the regime of discursive meditation and the emphasis on severe asceticism at Gethsemane. He persevered, however, under the guidance of Abbot Frederic Dunne, whom he came to revere. Although for a number of years, Merton thought seriously of transferring to a more eremitical order, such as the Carthusians or the Camaldolese, in the long run he realized that his call was to the Trappists. During his early years in the monastery (1941–1947), Merton received permission to continue his writing and soon was allowed to publish some volumes of poetry, beginning with *Thirty Poems* (1944). Even more surprisingly, he also was encouraged to write the account of his life and conversion, what became *The Seven Storey Mountain*, published in 1948. Thomas Merton, the monk and writer, burst into public notice in the late 1940s. Meanwhile, in March 1947, he had made his final vows as a Cistercian and was ordained a priest on May 26, 1949. In November of that year he began to give introductory courses on mystical theology to the novices. In June 1951, he was named Master of Scholastics, and in 1955 he became the Master of Novices. Merton's role in shaping the young monks of the order was of great importance.

How shall we take stock of Merton's career as a writer? Fortunately, he has given us some help here in his later reflections on his works. Writing to an anonymous Sister J. M. on June 17, 1968, six months before his death, Merton surveys what he has published to that point in terms of three periods.[13] The first is from his conversion in 1938 down to his ordination in 1949, the period of *The Seven Storey Mountain*. Characteristic of this period of monastic isolation are his early books of poetry, as well as *Secular Journal, Seven Storey Mountain*, and *Seeds of Contemplation*. Regarding this "first fervor stuff," Merton says it was "highly unworldly, ascetical, intransigent, and somewhat apocalyptic." He feels uncomfortable with its "rigid, arbitrary separation between God and the world, etc."[14] "The second period," he continued, "was a period in which I began to open up again to the world, began reading psychoanalysis..., Zen Buddhism, existentialism and other things like that, also more literature." Important books from this period (1949–1959) are *No Man Is an Island, The Sign of Jonas, Thoughts in Solitude*, and *The Silent Life*. Merton says that the fruits of this reading did not really appear until the third period, beginning with *Disputed Questions* in 1960, and including works like *New Seeds of Contemplation* (1962), *The Way of Chuang Tzu* (1965), and *Conjectures of a Guilty Bystander* (1966). Merton allows that many conservative people still get a lot out of his early books. He says that there are thus two Mertons: "one ascetic, conservative, traditional, monastic; the other radical, independent, and somewhat akin to beats and hippies and to poets." He concludes somewhat pessimistically: "Looking back on my work, I wish I had never bothered to write about one-third of it—the books that tend to be (one way or another) 'popular' religion. Or 'inspirational.'"

The years between 1950 and 1966 in Merton's life as a monk are paradoxical. On the one hand, his constant stream of books, as well as many articles, led to increasing fame and attracted a host of correspondents. There seem to have been very few people of importance in the religious world of the time, and even in the political world, who did not write to Merton, or to whom he did not write. On the other hand, he was restricted to the monastery. The new abbot of Gethsemane, James Fox, was temperamentally very different from Merton and the two did not get on. Abbot Fox consistently refused Merton the opportunity to travel, even to religious gatherings, something which sorely chafed him and prevented many opportunities for enriching contacts.

For many Catholics like myself growing up in the 1950s Merton's writings of that time, such as *The Sign of Jonas, Bread in the Wilderness, No Man Is an Island, The Silent Life,* and *Thoughts in Solitude* were touchstones of new possibilities in the spiritual life, however much he later judged them transitional works. The 1960s, as noted above, saw Merton emerge as an important social observer and a critic of the accepted forms of middle-class American life. His interests in societal issues (e.g., as illustrated in his longtime friendship with Dorothy Day and Catherine de Hueck Doherty) were increased by his stance against the Vietnam War and his association with Catholic peace advocates, like Fr. Daniel Berrigan. Between October 1961 and October 1962, he wrote over a hundred letters supporting nonviolence, later collected as the "Cold War Letters." Merton's engagement in racial justice questions brought another circle of friends and correspondents. Ditto for his increasing interest in other religious traditions, as many letters to Orthodox Christians, Buddhists, Hindus, Jews, and Sufis show. Of course, Merton also wrote to a host of Catholics, from popes (John XXIII, Paul VI), to cardinals, bishops, priests, and a variety of theologians (e.g., Jean Daniélou, Karl Rahner, Hans Urs von Balthasar). Very many of his letters were to other monks, missives of spiritual counsel and often letters about monastic renewal in light of the ongoing Second Vatican Council (1962-1966). A special case was Merton's friendship with the great Benedictine scholar Jean Leclercq (1911-1993). Merton first wrote to Leclercq in January 1950, and the two began a lively exchange that lasted until Merton's death.[15] They were even able to meet in person several times when Leclercq was invited to speak at Gethsemane.

An important aspect of the life of Merton the monk was his growing desire to live a life of deeper solitude as a hermit.[16] The Cistercians were prime examples of the coenobitical life in community, but earlier ages had allowed for special permission for hermits. Merton sought to revive the practice and was eventually successful. As early as 1953, he had been allowed to spend some hermit-time in a shed on the monastery grounds, and these periods multiplied until August of 1965, when he received permission from Abbot Fox to move to a small hermitage he had set up at some distance from the main building at Gethsemane. The solitude and opportunity for greater silence to be gained in a hermitage represent a key aspect of Merton's spiritual teaching.

A crisis in Merton's life came in 1966. He had long suffered from ill health, including back problems that grew increasingly worse after he moved to the hermitage. Finally, in March he underwent a serious back operation in Louisville to correct the problem. While recuperating, he was tended to by a young student nurse, whom he refers to in his writings as M. They fell in love. The story is too well known to be detailed here.[17] For the next eight months or more Merton was conflicted, self-justifying, and sometimes dishonest to his superiors and to the young woman. Like Augustine's account in his *Confessions* of his love for his concubine and the mother of his son, Merton tried to be honest about the good and the bad in this event. He had probably never had a love relation with a woman before, admitting that in his early life he had only used women selfishly. Now he discovered that he had the capacity to love and be loved. But, given his commitment to the monastic and eremitical life, he gradually realized how inappropriate the affair was and it faded from his life in 1967 and 1968. Reading his expressions of deep affection and tortuous self-justifications over these months makes Merton into a more believable human figure, though readers will have to judge for themselves how this incident affects their view of Thomas Merton.

As he recovered from the inner turmoil of his love for M., Merton continued his extensive writing on both public and private matters through 1967 and 1968. Many visitors came to see him at his hermitage and his constant letter-writing did not decrease. Abbot Fox retired and also became a hermit, and on January 13, 1968, Flavian Burns was elected as the new abbot of Gethsemane. Abbot Burns relaxed the ban on Merton's traveling and he was able to visit monastic houses in California and New Mexico, as well as to make a trip to Alaska to search for possible sites for a hermitage. To crown all this new freedom Merton was invited by Jean Leclercq to come to Southeast Asia to attend an international conference of monastic superiors. He left the United States on October 15 and went to India for the Temple of Understanding Conference in Calcutta. He then traveled around India and had memorable meetings with the Dalai Lama. Merton spent a week in Sri Lanka before going on to Singapore and then Bangkok, where the conference sponsored by the International Benedictine Organization was to take place. On Tuesday, December 10, he addressed the conference on the topic "Marxism and Monastic Perspectives." That afternoon in his room he died by electrocution due to a faulty fan. It was an unexpected and tragic end, although Merton had not expected to live a long life.

Many of Merton's books of his third period of the 1960s are collections of essays he grouped under provocative titles, which in no way lessens the impact of these penetrating, and often controversial, pieces. Some of these books, although the titles do not seem to be very mystical, contain deep insights into his views on the topic (e.g., "Rain and the Rhinoceros," in *Raids on the Unspeakable*). In November 1967, Merton established the "Thomas Merton Legacy Trust" to control his extensive literary remains. Much of this material is housed at the Thomas Merton Studies Center at Bellarmine College in Louisville, Kentucky. After his death, Merton's books continued to pour forth, edited by his friends and fellow monks, especially his last secretary, Brother Patrick Hart. Merton's journals began to appear only in 1993 after the twenty-five year period he had stipulated in the Trust. Among these posthumous books there are several that are vital to his teaching on mysticism.

Merton's Mystical Teaching

Sources

Given how much Merton wrote, I will start with comments on the specific writings of Merton that seem to me most important for his mystical teaching. I begin with *Bread in the Wilderness* (1953). This somewhat overlooked book is Merton's meditations on the Psalms as a source for both liturgical and private contemplative prayer. Dedicated to Jean Daniélou, S.J., it also is an exercise in reviving the spiritual interpretation of biblical texts after the manner of the Fathers, as the Jesuit patristic scholar had long argued for. The second book is earlier in origins but later in its mature form. In 1949, Merton put out a book called *Seeds of Contemplation*, which was an early attempt to write a general work on contemplative spirituality. He grew dissatisfied with the abstract and "Scholastic" tone of the book, so, as was typical with him, he did a complete revision under the title *New Seeds of Contemplation*, which appeared in 1962.[18] The first version, he says, had been written in isolation, when "the author had no experience in confronting the needs and problems of other men" (ix). The new version is written out of contact "with other solitudes"—younger members of his own community, and "the loneliness of people outside the monastery, with the loneliness of people outside the Church" (x). *New Seeds* is a far more existential, personalistic, and ecumenical book than its predecessor. Merton warns the reader about the misleading character of the word "contemplation," lest it be thought of "as a spiritual commodity that one can procure." Contemplation is also something that cannot be taught, "but certainly an aptitude for it can be awakened . . . by someone who knows by experience what it is, and who can make it real to those in whom it begins to awaken."[19] Merton was such a person and *New Seeds* is perhaps the best illustration of this. Several other books that Merton published during the 1950s and '60s also have important material on contemplation, notably *The Ascent to Truth* (1951), *No Man Is an Island* (1955), *Mystics and Zen Masters* (1967), and *Zen and the Birds of Appetite* (1968).

Three of Merton's most important works on mysticism appeared posthumously. Almost from the outset of his monastic career, Merton, with his good Latin, had thought about translating the Cistercian Fathers of the twelfth century into English for the benefit of monks who had no Latin. In the late 1960s, one of Merton's younger colleagues, M. Basil Pennington, drafted proposals for two series: the Cistercian Fathers Series, which would contain such translations; and a series called Cistercian Studies. Merton resisted Pennington's effort to get him deeply involved in editorial work, but he did promise to send him a manuscript on monastic prayer that he had been working on for several years. *The Climate of Monastic Prayer* was published by the new Cistercian Publications in 1969 and also, somewhat confusingly, by Herder and Herder in the same year under the title *Contemplative Prayer*.[20] Although written for monks, and reviewing the history of monastic prayer, the book was not restricted to monastics. A major part of the book deals with "meditation," by which Merton meant not the discursive meditation of the Jesuit tradition, but the ancient monastic sense of *meditatio* as "the prayer of the heart," something close to Zen meditation. Its goal is knowledge of the true self and deeper knowledge of God through existential awareness. Several other aspects of the book are worth noting. First, Merton wanted to overcome the still-lingering sense among some of a conflict between the public liturgy of the Church and personal contemplative prayer—each nourished the other, he insisted. Second, he reiterated a message he had been expressing for decades: "There is no contradiction between action and contemplation when Christian apostolic action is raised to the level of pure charity. On that level, action and contemplation are fused into one entity by the love of God and of our brother in Christ" (153; see also 84–85). Finally, he insisted that the "contemplative orientation of the whole life of prayer," what the Desert Fathers had called "the prayer of the heart," was a necessity for the entire Church in the contemporary era.

The second posthumous work had a more convoluted history. In 1948 Merton had written a brief and rather unoriginal work called *What Is Contemplation?* for a student at St. Mary's College in Indiana. In 1959 he decided to rewrite the work in substantial fashion under the title *The Inner Experience*, keeping much of the original text but making large additions. Although he called it "a respectable book," Merton thought it still needed revisions and he talked about doing these at times in the '60s. Finally, in 1968, just before he left for Asia, he made some revisions, but not major ones. In 1967, however, when the Merton Legacy Trust was drawn up, he had stipulated that *Inner Experience* was not to be published as a book. What to do? In 1983 the Merton Trust gave permission to Patrick Hart to publish a version of the work as a series of articles in *Cistercian Studies Quarterly*, and the work had also been used in some books on Merton. Finally, the Trust decided that, given the importance of this final book on mysticism, it should be fully and critically edited. The Merton scholar William V. Shannon undertook this task, and *The Inner Experience: Notes on Contemplation* came out in 2002. The book is necessary reading for anyone wishing to understand Merton's view of mysticism.

The last of the posthumous works is the third volume of a series of Merton's lectures given to the novices at Gethsemane published under the general title *Initiation into the Monastic Tradition*. This book, *An Introduction to Christian Mysticism*, comprising notes for a course taught March to May in 1961, was edited by Patrick F. O'Connell and appeared in 2008. Class lecture notes, to be sure, are not finished literary products, but this substantial work tells us a great deal about Merton's mature view of the mystical tradition and the extent of his reading. It also reveals how his growing knowledge of some mystics (e.g., Evagrius Ponticus, Maximus the Confessor, Eckhart) had broadened and enriched his own views. Merton was the first to admit that much of his knowledge of the mystics was second-hand. He had carefully read some mystics for years (e.g., the Cistercians, Eckhart, and the Spanish mystics, especially John of the Cross). For other figures and themes he relied on articles from the *Dictionnaire de Spiritualité* and major modern studies, especially in French. There are some notable omissions in the *Introduction* book, such as the French mystics, although Merton knew and appreciated Fénelon.[21] Perhaps he just ran out of time.

Themes

Silence and Solitude: The Desert

Merton wrote often about the necessity for silence and solitude.[22] As he put it, "Solitude is as necessary for society as silence is for language and air for the lungs and food for the body" (*No Man Is an Island*, 246–47). True solitude is not rejecting other people and our social obligations. "Go into the desert," he said, "not to escape other men but in order to find them in God" (*New Seeds*, 53). We might think of silence and solitude as merely preparation for contemplation, but they are really core aspects of mystical contemplation itself. While silence and solitude are exemplified by the monastic and especially the eremitical life of those who went off into the desert to find God, silence and solitude are aspects of all Christian life, and, indeed, of authentic living itself. We all need the inner desert, although as Merton remarked in *No Man Is an Island*: "The soul that has thus found itself [i.e., in solitude] gravitates towards the desert but does not object to remaining in the city, because it is everywhere alone."[23]

Merton's teaching on silence and solitude is summarized in the essay "The Philosophy of Solitude," where he says, "The vocation to solitude therefore is at the same time a vocation to silence, poverty, and emptiness. But the emptiness is for the sake of fullness: the purpose of the solitary life is, if you like, contemplation" (192). He continues, "The contemplation of the Christian solitary is the awareness of the divine mercy transforming and elevating his own emptiness and turning it into the presence of perfect love, perfect fullness." The stress on our emptiness, the inner abyss (a theme found in Eckhart and in the teaching of Chuang Tzu), is characteristic of Merton's late thought. This insight leads to an amazing discovery: "Man's loneliness is, in fact, the loneliness of God." In learning to live with his solitude, a person "finds he and God are one: that God is alone as he himself is alone. That God wills to be alone in him" (190). Christ's assumption of "*essential* solitude of man" means that human solitude "becomes mysteriously identified with the solitude of God" (188).

Inner solitude, correctly understood, is a separation that is paradoxically a "profound solidarity" ("Philosophy of Solitude," 188) with all human beings and with Christ. It is both accepting our absurdity, and an "actualization of a faith in which a man takes responsibility for his own inner life" (180). Since solitude is a concrete realization of our inner emptiness and limitations, it is closely tied to death. The sections on "The Inward Solitude" and "Silence" that end *No Man Is an Island* have meditations on this relationship, especially on death and silence. Life, Merton says, is not an uninterrupted flow of words leading to the silence of death. Rather, "[life's] rhythm develops in silence, comes to expression in moments of necessary expression, returns to deeper silence, culminates in a final declaration, then ascends quietly into the silence of Heaven which resounds with unending praise" (261). Life is therefore a meditation on the ultimate decision between life and death. This is why "[t]hose who love true life ... frequently think about their death. Their life is full of a silence that is an anticipated victory over death. Silence, indeed, makes death our servant and even our friend" (263). Both solitude and silence are necessary to the human condition, whether we realize it or not. They are rooted in the real. "Solitude has to be objective and concrete," says Merton. "It has to be a communion in something greater than the world, as great as Being itself, in order that in its deep peace we may find God." So too, "[t]ruth rises from the silence of being to the quiet tremendous presence of the Word. Then, sinking again into silence, the truth of words bears us down into the silence of God" (*Thoughts in Solitude*, 106, 108). The true solitary life bears "infinite risk," says Merton, and often involves spiritual dryness, poverty, and self-doubt. It has to have a "grain of folly." "Otherwise," he insists, "it is not what it was meant to be, a life of direct dependence on God, in darkness, insecurity, and pure faith" ("Philosophy of Solitude," 201).

Mystical Contemplation
We have already seen what I take to be the core of Merton's view of mystical contemplation. Here I will flesh out some significant details. At the beginning, it is worth noting again that, for Merton, contemplation cannot be taught and is not a method of prayer, but is rather a

stance or an attitude about the whole of life. In *The Climate of Monastic Prayer*, he says, "The contemplative way is, in fact, not a way. Christ alone is the way, and he is invisible" (125). This is why Merton always insisted that *Christian* contemplation, which is what he mostly talked about, must be Incarnational and eschatological.[24] Contemplation is impossible without freedom, so he also held, "Nothing is in fact more inimical to the contemplative life as regimentation" (*Inner Experience*, 78). But the contemplative life is not incompatible with other aspects of how we engage the world. "To praise the contemplative life is not to reject every other form of life, but to seek a solid foundation for every other human striving" (*Inner Experience*, 152).

Merton was always most interested in the existential reality of contemplation, not in constructing a complete and final theory. Nevertheless, he did write about the different forms of contemplation, and here his thinking shows an important evolution. In his early writings he stuck to a generally traditional line, especially on the difference between active, or acquired, contemplation, and passive, that is, infused contemplation. Only the latter is contemplation in the proper sense, whereas the active form is sometimes described as "quasi-contemplation." For example, in the first version of his essay, "Poetry and the Contemplative Life" (1947), Merton distinguished, in a fairly unoriginal way, three levels of contemplation. The first degree is "a kind of natural contemplation of God—that of the artist, the philosopher, and the most advanced pagan religions." The second is the contemplative life in the usual sense as "a life in which the baptized Christian . . . strives to conform his will with God's will and to see and love God in all things and thus to dispose himself for union with Him." This is active contemplation, which is a preparation for "the life of infused or passive or mystical contemplation," which is "the normal term of the Christian life even here on earth."[25] In *Bread in the Wilderness*, he talks about two levels of the "experiential recognition" of God on the basis of the story of Jesus and the disciples on the way to Emmaus (Luke 24) (117-19). As the disciples walked with Jesus but did not recognize him, their hearts were still burning within them. This signifies the common experience of "living faith," where "the ardor of love constitutes a kind of indirect experience of God" that Merton calls a "masked" or "veiled" contemplation. Contemplation proper is when the disciples' eyes were opened in the breaking of the bread, when the soul is "raised out of itself," in what Merton elsewhere calls infused contemplation.

In his later writings Merton emphasized the continuum of the contemplative life, as well as the significance of *all* the forms of contemplation. He still used the language of "infused contemplation," although the apophatic, or dark, dimension came more and more to the fore.[26] As he put it in *New Seeds* in good Dionysian fashion, "In contemplation we know by 'unknowing.' Or better, we know *beyond* all knowing and 'unknowing'" (1-2). The highest contact with God is in the darkness. A late detailed exposition of the forms of contemplation is found in *Inner Experience*. Here the category of "masked contemplation," described as "pre-experiential contemplation," appears often, but now within a schema taken over from the Greek Fathers, especially Evagrius, Gregory of Nyssa, and Maximus Confessor.[27] Beginning with reflections on the necessarily Incarnational nature of Christian contemplation in relation to Jesus (*Inner Experience*, 36-50), Merton takes up the two forms of contemplation. The first is the higher, which is "an immediate and in some sense passive intuition of the inmost reality, or our spiritual self and of God present within us." The second is the lower, "an active and mediate form . . . in which this perception is attained in some way by our own efforts" (57). Most of chapter 5 of *Inner Experience* is concerned with this active contemplation, which is often that "masked contemplation" where contemplation is hidden from the contemplative himself in his everyday acts, or in the celebration of the liturgy. Merton seeks to avoid the outmoded language of acquired and infused contemplation and proposes a distinction based on the Greek Fathers: "that between natural contemplation (*theōria physikē*) and theology (*theologia*), or the contemplation of God" (67). "*Theoria physike* is the intuition of divine things in and through the reflection of God in nature and in the symbols of revelation" (ibid.). It is a true grace from God and is therefore "mystical," but can also be described as "natural," due to its object, not its origin. Merton calls it "active contemplation," meaning "a contemplation which man seeks and prepares by his own initiative but which, by a gift of God, *is completed in mystical intuition*" (68). This is different from "*theologia*, or pure contemplation ('mystical theology' in the language of Pseudo Denis, [which] is a direct quasi-experiential contact with God beyond all thoughts, that is to say, without the medium of concepts." Merton concludes, "This supreme Christian contemplation, according to the Greek Fathers, is a quasi-experiential knowledge of God as He is in Himself, that is to say, of God as Three Persons in One Nature" (ibid.). So, Christian mystical contemplation is necessarily both Incarnational *and* Trinitarian.

On the basis of this Greek approach, chapter 6 of *Inner Experience* proceeds to a fuller discussion of "Infused Contemplation," laying out eleven characteristics of the passive, mystical darkness of unknowing

(72–78).²⁸ Finally, chapter 12 ("The Desire for Contemplation," 115–17) stresses the potential universality of all forms of mystical contemplation: "Everywhere we find expressions of some kind of spiritual experience, often natural, sometimes supernatural. Supernatural mystical experience is at least theoretically possible anywhere under the sun, to any man of good conscience who sincerely seeks the truth and responds to the inspirations of divine grace" (116).

The strong emphasis on *theōria physikē* in Merton's late view of contemplation was of considerable importance.²⁹ The influence of the Greek Fathers on his developing thinking is also evident in *An Introduction to Christian Mysticism*.³⁰ Here he devotes considerable attention to *theōria physikē*, which he says is "partly mystical and partly natural," and defines it as "the reception of God's revelation of Himself in creatures, in history, in Scripture" (123). Merton always had a quasi-mystical view of nature. Some of his best writing as poet and prose writer reflects his sensitivity to the sacred power of the natural world. Now he had found a theological category to help him recognize the Christian character of what some might have seen as only a kind of nature mysticism, fine as that is. Mostly following Maximus, he lauds *theōria physikē* as "a most important part of man's cooperation in the spiritualization and restoration of the cosmos. It is by *theoria* that man helps Christ to redeem the *logoi* of things and restore them to Himself" (124). Furthermore, because "*theoria physike* is a dynamic unity of contemplation and action, a loving knowledge that comes along with *use* and *work*" (129), it underlines Merton's continuing insistence on the necessary connection of action and contemplation. Finally, it also gave Merton a new way to analyze sacred art, long an interest of his.

Two other aspects of Merton's view of contemplation are worthy of note: the aspect that he often spoke of as "dread" (an existential term); and the role of mystical union as the goal of the contemplative life. Merton was intimately familiar with John of the Cross and his teaching on the "Dark Night" in the path to God.³¹ He also had read other mystics, such as Tauler, who spoke of the role of darkness and dereliction in mysticism. Merton seems to have used "night" and "dread" somewhat interchangeably to express this aspect of the experience of the mystical path, although "night" relates to our blinding before God's transcendent light and "dread" is tied to the emptiness and fear attendant on sin. Both *New Seeds* and *Inner Experience* have discussions of the role of this form of negation,³² but the most extensive treatment is in *The Climate of Monastic Prayer*.

Climate has a brief discussion of John of the Cross's Dark Night (section V, 60–64), and a longer treatment of "dread" in sections XVI and XVII (130–48). Merton starts out section XVI by saying, "Our 'nothingness' is then something more than the contingency of the creature. It is compounded with the *dread* of the sinner alienated from God and from himself, set in rebellious opposition to the truth of his own contingency and his own malice" (131). Merton claims that the guilt of dread, or the night, which is "a *basic antagonism between the self and God*" (132), cannot be overcome as long as we "cling to the empty illusion of a separate self." In language that echoes earlier mystics of "dereliction" (he uses the word on 135), he speaks of how even the faithful Christian "seems to lose the conviction that God is or can be a refuge for him. It is as if God were hostile or implacable or, worse still, as if God himself has become emptiness, and as if all were emptiness, nothingness, dread and night" (133). The experience of "deep dread and night," however, is not a punishment; it is a purification and a grace in which our emptiness encounters God's fullness. Hence, he gives the following definition: "Dread is an expression of our insecurity in this earthly life, a realization that we are never and can never be completely 'sure' in the sense of *possessing* a definitive and established spiritual status" (136). Merton concludes by citing passages from John of the Cross, as well as the desert father Ammonas and the Cistercian Isaac of Stella to illustrate such mystical trials.

Merton had much to say about the traditional category of mystical union.[33] One of the best of his more academic studies was, "Transforming Union in St. Bernard and St. John of the Cross."[34] The topic also came up often in his presentations of the nature of mystical contemplation. For Merton, union with God was always the goal of the mystical path. As early as 1938, while he was just beginning to become interested in Christianity through reading Etienne Gilson's *The Spirit of Medieval Philosophy* and recognizing the importance of the desire for God, he says, "I was already dreaming of mystical union when I did not even keep the simplest rudiments of the moral law. But nevertheless I was convinced of the reality of the goal, and confident that it could be achieved" (*Seven Storey Mountain*, 204). Discussions of union are frequent in his early *Ascent to Truth*, and union is also mentioned in a number of places in his history of monasticism called *The Silent Life*. Nevertheless, it is clear from his whole corpus that union with God remained a crucial theme. In his 1967 letter to Pope Paul VI about the message of contemplatives to the world he says that the contemplative asks "his brother" to penetrate his own silence and risk sharing it with the "other" in order to "truly recover the light and the capacity to understand what is beyond words and beyond explanations." This is "the intimate union in the depths of your own heart of God's spirit and your own secret inmost self, so that you and He are in all truth One Spirit" (*Hidden Ground of Love*, 158).

An important treatment of union is found in the essay "The Second Adam," where Merton distinguishes three kinds of union: our natural union with God residing in the soul as the source of our physical life; "our supernatural union with God," which is "an immediate existential union with the Triune God as the source of grace and the virtues"; and, finally, mystical union itself, "the perfect coalescence of the uncreated Image of God with our created image not only in a perfect identification of minds and wills . . . but also above all knowledge and all love in perfect communion."[35] There is no need to assemble a host of other texts on union here, but it is worth noting that the discussion of "Union with God in Activity" in *Inner Experience* (63–66) shows that Merton treated union as an analogous term, as many of the great Christian mystics before him had done (see also 26, 37–38, 50, 101). In his treatment of the higher stages of union, especially the traditional "mystical marriage," Merton tended to invoke the authority of his sources, especially Bernard, Teresa, and John of the Cross. Of course, we must remember that mystical union is just one among a range of related and overlapping terms for quasi-experiential knowledge of God. In his essay "Contemplation in a World of Action" Merton stresses the need "to renounce our selfish and limited self and enter into a whole new kind of existence" where we see things in a new light. "Call it faith, call it (at a more advanced stage) contemplative illumination, call it the sense of God or even mystical union: all these are different aspects and levels of the same realization: the awakening to a new awareness of ourselves in Christ" (*Contemplation in a World of Action*, 157–58). Another way of speaking about this new awareness is by way of the category "transcendent experience," on which Merton wrote an important essay in 1966.[36]

Concomitants of Contemplation

The sheer variety of Merton's many writings makes it difficult to separate out discrete motifs of his mysticism. Such motifs are not so much *results* of having found contemplation, as they are *spiritual values*, or concomitants, that are part and parcel of being committed to the contemplative life. Different lists could be given, but here I will briefly discuss only three of these "concomitants."

Prayer. Contemplation is a form of prayer. Throughout his career, Merton strove to show the inner unity of all types of prayer, from the simplest verbal prayers, through the official prayer of the liturgy, which was so dear to him, to the most advanced forms of mystical and contemplative prayer discussed above. One might say that prayer was the central theme of his writings. Prayer, for Merton, "means a yearning for the simple presence of God" (*Climate*, 92). Elsewhere he emphasizes that today "prayer is a real source of personal freedom in the midst of a world in which men are dominated by massive organizations and rigid institutions which seek only to exploit them for money and power" (*Hidden Ground of Love*, 159). Avoiding any attempt to set a detailed program of prayer practice ("Do this! Do that!"), Merton emphasized freedom in praying, though one that always included devotion to the liturgical prayer of the Church. To paraphrase Augustine, we might say his motto was, "Pray to God and do what you will."

But how did Thomas Merton the monk actually pray? A major part of his prayer life was liturgical, as books like *Bread in the Wilderness* and *Seasons of Celebration* show. Regarding his personal prayer practice, he was quite reticent. There is, however, an important letter in which he does speak of how he prays. Abdul Aziz was a Pakistani civil servant who had an interest in Sufism. He read Merton's *Ascent to Truth* and first wrote to him in November 1960. A long correspondence, "as one spiritual man to another," followed in which Aziz encouraged Merton's interest in Sufism and sent him books on the subject. Merton, in turn, recommended books to Aziz and opened up to him about his own spiritual life.[37] In December 1965, Aziz wrote to Merton about his personal "method of meditation," and Merton responded on January 2, 1966. "Strictly speaking," he says, "I have a very simple way of prayer. It is centered entirely on attention to the presence of God and to His will and His love. That is to say that it is centered on *faith* by which alone we can know the presence of God." He goes on, ". . . it is a matter of adoring Him as invisible and infinitely beyond our comprehension, and realizing Him as all. My prayer tends very much to what you call *fana* [absorption in God]. . . . My prayer then is a kind of praise rising up out of the center of Nothing and Silence." After a few more reflections on Nothingness, Merton notes, "Such is my ordinary way of prayer, or meditation. It is not 'thinking about' anything, but a direct seeking of the Face of the Invisible, which cannot be found unless we become lost in Him who is Invisible. I do not ordinarily write about such things and I ask you therefore to be discreet about it" (*Hidden Ground of Love*, 63–64).

Authenticity and Freedom. As one reads Merton, it is hard not to note how often he discusses the need to shuck off the old false self that we all inherit from Adam and to strive to attain the true and authentic self we gain in Christ, what he called the "inner self."[38] Attaining such authenticity is finding real freedom, not the ersatz claims regarding personal liberty so often touted in the modern world. This is not a new theme in Christian mysticism. Merton sometimes appealed to the Desert Fathers when speaking of such authenticity, as well as to other mystical writers.[39] He was keenly aware of how much of the false self remained in him, as when he speaks of "my persistent desire to be somebody" (*Learning to Love*, 215). Attaining the authentic self and real freedom is not a permanent state to be enjoyed but a task that is always being accomplished. The task begins with setting aside useless activity and illusions in order to attain self-knowledge. In *No Man Is an Island* he puts it as follows: "The deep secrecy of my own being is often hidden from me by my own estimate of what I am. My idea of what I am is falsified by my admiration for what I do." He goes on, "We cannot be ourselves unless we know ourselves. But self-knowledge is impossible when thoughtless and automatic activity keeps our souls in confusion." This does not mean that we cease all activity, but that "we have to cut down our activity to the point where we can think calmly and reasonably about our action," knowing the reasons and intentions for which we are acting and how appropriate these are to the situations at hand (*No Man Is an Island*, 125–26).

The emergence of the true "I" is tied to contemplation. "The 'I' that works in the world, thinks about itself, observes its own reactions and talks about itself is not the true 'I'. . . . Contemplation is precisely the awareness that this 'I' is really 'not I' and [is] the awakening of the unknown 'I' that is beyond observation and reflection and is incapable of commenting upon itself" (*New Seeds*, 7). Contemplation, then, allows us to lose the false self and gain the true self in God's love. The emptying-out of the "false self" is a constant theme in Merton.[40] The self-aggrandizement characteristic of the false self is given a memorable picture in his essay "Promethean Theology" (*New Man*, 23–48), which uses the myth of Prometheus, who stole fire from the gods, to illustrate the false "death-mysticism" of the person who is described as "the mystic without faith, who believes neither in himself nor in god" (27). Love is the only power that allows escape from the false self: "I who am without love cannot become love unless Love identifies me with Himself. But if He sends His own Love, Himself, to act and love in me and in all that I do, then I shall be transformed, I shall discover who

I am and shall possess my identity by losing myself in Him" (*New Seeds*, 63). Mystical renewal, then, involves "an inner transformation brought about entirely by the power of God's merciful love, implying the 'death' of the self-centered and self-sufficient ego and the appearance of a new and liberated self who lives and acts 'in the Spirit'" (*Climate*, 120). The real "I" is the liberated "I."

In his essay "The Study of Zen," Merton specifies four "needs" that must be met in order for there to be a revival of Christian consciousness today. The first is the need for an authentic community of love for our fellow men. The second is the need for "an adequate understanding of the everyday self in his ordinary life," while the third involves the "integral experience of the self on all its levels, bodily, as well as imaginative, emotional, intellectual, spiritual." The fourth need of modern man "is precisely liberation from his inordinate self-consciousness, his monumental self-awareness, his obsession with self-affirmation, so that he may enjoy the freedom from concern that goes with being simply what he is" (*Zen and the Birds of Appetite*, 30–31). The contemplative life is the way for man to be given the greatest freedom—freedom from himself and his selfish desires (*Inner Experience*, 151–54). That is why in another context Merton could say, "In humility is the greatest freedom," that is, the freedom to do the will of God.[41]

Conclusion

Mystical contemplation and its concomitant aspects formed the kind of person that Thomas Merton was—the man, the monk, the engaged activist, and the interlocutor with other faiths. Each of these dimensions could be the subject of many more comments and reflections, but in this essay I have merely tried to bring out the essential features of Merton the mystic. Merton was not one man but many—perhaps not all of them in harmony. I do not pretend to have solved the mystery of the many Mertons, but I will end with a statement that seems to bring together key aspects of his sense of his mission:

> Whatever I may have written, I think it can all be reduced in the end to this one truth: that God calls human persons to union with Himself and with one another in Christ, in the Church which is His Mystical Body. It is also a witness to the fact that there is, and must be in the Church, a contemplative life which has no other function than to realize these mysterious things and to return to God all the thanks and praise that human hearts can give to Him.[42]

Notes

1. Full titles and publication information for the books and articles by Merton and others that are cited by author or short titles are listed in the bibliography at the end of the essay.

2. This is the title of Cunningham's anthology of Merton's spiritual writings: *Thomas Merton: Spiritual Master*. A number of treatments of Merton's mysticism exist, especially Bailey, *Thomas Merton on Mysticism*; and Shannon, *Thomas Merton's Dark Path*.

3. *Learning to Love*, 157.

4. It does appear in two: *Mystics and Zen Masters* (1967); and the posthumous *Introduction to Christian Mysticism* (2002).

5. Here are four typical descriptions: (1) "Contemplation is our personal response to His [the Father's] mystical presence and his activity within us" (*Bread in the Wilderness*, 117); (2) "The union of the simple light of God with the simple light of man's spirit in love, is contemplation" (*New Seeds*, 290–91); (3) "Contemplation is the conscious, experimental awareness of the mission of the Son and the Spirit, a reception of the Word Who is sent to us not only as life but as light" (*Inner Experience*, 47; see also 33–34); and (4) "The contemplative life is then the search for peace not in an abstract exclusion of all outside reality, not in a barren negative closing of the senses upon the world, but in the openness of love" ("A Letter on the Contemplative Life," in Cunningham, *Spiritual Master*, 426).

6. See, for example, the rather critical remarks on Gregory the Great and Bernard's views of the relation of contemplation and action in *Climate of Monastic Prayer*, 70–79. See also *Contemplation in the World of Action*, 249–53.

7. Karl Rahner, *Theological Investigations VII* (New York: Herder & Herder, 1971), 15.

8. Merton's understanding of Zen, especially as filtered through Suzuki, has been the subject of much discussion. For a summary, see John D. Dadosky, "Merton's Dialogue with Zen: Pioneering or Passé?," *Fu-Jen International Religious Studies* 2 (1998): 53–75.

9. On the "mystical-prophetic," see David Tracy, *Dialogue with the Other: The Inter-Religious Dialogue*, Louvain Theological and Pastoral Monographs 1 (Louvain: Peeters, 1990), especially chapters 1 and 5. In his essay, "Problems and Prospects," *Contemplation in a World of Action* (1998), Merton says, "Without experienced guides who are completely open to the full dimension—the mystical and the prophetic dimension—of love of Christ, renewal will mean little more than the replacement of old rules by new ones and of old traditions by novel frenzies" (27).

10. Merton never wrote a separate piece on Eckhart, though he studied him for many years. His journals, especially for 1966, have many reflections on Eckhart. A telling remark is made in *Zen and the Birds of Appetite*: "Whatever Zen may be, however you define it, it is somehow there in Eckhart" (13).

11. The most detailed biography of Merton is Mott, *The Seven Mountains of Thomas Merton*. Other biographies include Furlong; Griffin; and Shannon, *Silent Lamp*.

12. See James Harford, *Merton and Friends: A Joint Biography of Thomas Merton, Robert Lax, and Edward Rice* (New York: Continuum, 2006).

13. The letter is found in *School of Charity*, 384–85. In 1967 Merton also drew a graph evaluating his books from "awful" and "very poor" to thirteen that he rated "better" (none got to "best"). This is available as "Appendix 2" in *Introductions East & West: The Foreign Prefaces of Thomas Merton*, ed. Robert E. Daggy (Oakville, ON: Mosaic Press), 1981.

14. Merton's letter has the following remark on *Seven Story Mountain*: "*Seven Story Mountain* is a sort of phenomenon, not all bad, not all good, and it's not something I could successfully repudiate even if I wanted to. Naturally I have reservations about it because I was young then and I've changed." It may be noted that the English writer Evelyn Waugh edited the English publication of the book under the title *Elected Silence*, a version that Merton himself preferred.

15. See *Survival or Prophecy? The Letters of Thomas Merton & Jean Leclercq*. If I may be permitted to quote myself, the "Intoduction" (xix) to this volume cites something I wrote for a volume of essays for Jean Leclercq in 1993: "When the history of twentieth-century monasticism comes to be written, it is hard not to think that two monks will dominate the story: Thomas Merton and Jean Leclercq."

16. Merton wrote much on monasticism and the future of the monastic life. Typical works include *The Waters of Siloe* (1949), *The Sign of Jonas* (1953), *The Silent Life* (1957), and *The Climate of Monastic Prayer* (1969). See also three important essays in the *Asian Journal*: "Thomas Merton's View of Monasticism" (305–8); "Monastic Experience and East-West Dialogue" (309–17), and "Marxism and Monastic Perspectives" (326–43).

17. Merton's anguished account of the affair is detailed in his journal for the time; see *Learning to Love,* especially 37–126. All the biographies of Merton deal with this affair; see especially Mott, *Seven Mountains*, 435–66.

18. On the differences of the two (actually three) versions of *Seeds*, see Shannon, *Merton's Dark Path*, 142–51.

19. This comes not from *New Seeds*, but from a letter to his friend Etta Gullick of June 15, 1964 (*Hidden Ground of Love*, 367).

20. Shannon, *Merton's Dark Path*, 164–69, shows how *Climate of Monastic Prayer* is actually a cobbling together (not always successfully) of two different manuscripts.

21. Merton wrote an important essay on Fénelon: "Reflections on the Character and Genius of Fénelon," in *Fénelon: Letters of Love and Counsel*, selected and translated by John McEwen (New York: Harcourt, Brace & World, 1964), 9–30.

22. See, e.g., *No Man Is an Island*, chapters 15-16; *Thoughts in Solitude*, especially the sixteen meditations in "Part Two, The Love of Solitude"; *Disputed Questions*, "Notes for a Philosophy of Solitude" (177–207); and *New Seeds*, chapters 8 and 11.

23. *No Man Is an Island*, 253. See also "Notes for a Philosophy of Solitude," 195: "The desert does not necessarily have to be physical—it can be found even in the midst of men. But it is not found by human aspirations or idealism. It is mysteriously designated by the finger of God."

24. "Contemplation and Dialogue," in *Mystics and Zen Masters*, 212–13.

25. "Poetry and the Contemplative Life," in *Figures for an Apocalypse*, 95–96.

26. As shown by Shannon, *Merton's Dark Path*. Merton's reading of the Greek Fathers, of Zen texts, and of Eckhart seems to have been a factor in the growing apophatic emphasis.

27. The schema is laid out in *Inner Experience*, chapters 4, "Christian Contemplation" (35–56); 5, "Kinds of Contemplation" (57–70); and 6, "Infused Contemplation" (71–79). "Masked contemplation" appears on 63–66, 86–87, 91, and 143–44.

28. For an earlier treatment of infused contemplation, see "33. Journey through the Wilderness," in *New Seeds*, 239–44.

29. *Theōria physikē*, however, was not a new discovery of the 1960s, because it was already mentioned in *Ascent to Truth*, 27–28.

30. *Introduction to Christian Mysticism*, "IV. Divinization and Mysticism" (58–96), "V. Evagrius—Prince of Gnostics" (96–121); "VI. Contemplation and Cosmos" (121–36); and "VII. The Dionysian Tradition" (136–54).

31. Merton's *Ascent to Truth* contains a detailed analysis of John of the Cross, but he later became dissatisfied with the work, judging that it interpreted John in too Scholastic a fashion. John of the Cross is discussed in many other works, e.g., *Bread in the Wilderness, Climate of Monastic Prayer, Inner Experience*, and various essays.

32. "32. The Night of the Senses," in *New Seeds*, 233–37; and *Inner Experience*, 75–77, 93–100, and 119–22.

33. Mystical union involves deification. Merton does not seem to have spoken of deification much in his early published works, but, under the influence of the Greek Fathers, there is an important discussion in *Introduction to Christian Mysticism*, 58–67.

34. *Thomas Merton on Saint Bernard*, Part III (161–240).

35. "The Second Adam," in *New Man*, 131–61; quotation from 140–41.

36. "Transcendent Experience," in *Zen and the Birds of Appetite*, 71–78. Here Merton surveys the language of loss, even annihilation, of self as found in Zen, Sufism, and some Christian mystics (e.g., Eckhart). He describes this as a "superconsciousness" (74).

37. Merton's side of the correspondence can be found in *Hidden Ground of Love*, 43–67. The letters have been studied by Sidney H. Griffith, "'As One Spiritual Man to Another': The Merton–Abdul Aziz Correspondence," in Baker and Henry, *Merton & Sufism*, 101–29.

38. *Inner Experience*, 5–7, 11–22, 25–27, 31, 54–55. For more on Merton's view of the self, see Carr, *Search for Wisdom and Spirit;* as well as Shannon, *Merton's Dark Path*, 155–60.

39. There are, of course, non-Christian mystics who also exhibit true authenticity and freedom, such as Chuang Tzu. Another example is the Greek philosopher Herakleitos; see "Herakleitos: A Study," in Cunningham, *Spiritual Master*, 280–93.

40. Neil Pembroke compares Weil and Merton on this key mystical issue, preferring Merton's version because it "maintains a healthy self-love" ("Two Spiritualities of Self-Emptying: Weil's 'Decreation' and Merton's Emptying Out of the False Self," *Studies in Spirituality* 25 [2015]: 267–78, here 268, 277–78).

41. *New Seeds*, 57; see also "27. What Is Liberty? (199–202).

42. Cited from Shannon, *Silent Lamp*, 96.

Bibliography

I. Works by Merton in Chronological Order

The following list contains only works used for this essay.

Figures for an Apocalypse. New York: New Directions, 1947.
The Seven Storey Mountain. New York: Harcourt, Brace, 1948.
Seeds of Contemplation. New York: New Directions, 1948.
The Waters of Siloe. New York: Harcourt, Brace, 1949.
The Ascent to Truth. New York: Harcourt, Brace, 1951.
The Sign of Jonas. New York: Harcourt, Brace, 1953.
Bread in the Wilderness. New York: New Directions, 1953.
Thoughts in Solitude. New York: Dell, 1956.
No Man Is an Island. New York, Harcourt, Brace, 1955.
The Silent Life. New York: Farrar, Straus & Cudahy, 1957.
Disputed Questions. New York: Farrar, Straus & Cudahy, 1960.
The Wisdom of the Desert. New York: New Directions, 1961.
The New Man. New York: Farrar, Straus & Cudahy, 1961.
New Seeds of Contemplation. New York: New Directions, 1962.
The Way of Chuang Tzu. New York: New Directions, 1965.
Seasons of Celebration. New York: Farrar, Straus & Giroux, 1965.
Conjectures of a Guilty Bystander. New York: Doubleday, 1966.
Raids on the Unspeakable. New York: New Directions, 1966.
Mystics and Zen Masters. New York: Farrar, Straus & Giroux, 1967.
Zen and the Birds of Appetite. New York: New Directions, 1968.

Posthumous Works
The Climate of Monastic Prayer. Cistercian Studies Series 1. Kalamazoo, MI: Cistercian Publications, 1969.
Contemplation in a World of Action. Garden City, NY: Doubleday, 1971.
The Asian Journal of Thomas Merton. Edited by Naomi Burton et al. New York: New Directions, 1973.
Thomas Merton on St. Bernard. Cistercian Studies Series 9. Kalamazoo, MI: Cistercian Publications, 1980.
The Inner Experience: Notes on Contemplation. Edited by William H. Shannon. San Francisco: HarperSanFrancisco, 2003.
An Introduction to Christian Mysticism. Edited by Patrick F. O'Connell. Kalamazoo, MI: Cistercian Publications, 2008.

Letters and Journals
The Hidden Ground of Love: The Letters of Thomas Merton on Religious Experience and Social Concerns. Edited by William H. Shannon. New York: Farrar, Straus & Giroux, 1985.

Learning to Love: Exploring Solitude and Freedom. Edited by Christine M. Bochen. Journals of Thomas Merton 6: 1966–1967. San Francisco: HarperSanFrancisco, 1997.

The School of Charity: The Letters of Thomas Merton on Religious Renewal and Spiritual Direction. Edited by Patrick Hart. New York: Farrar, Straus & Giroux, 1990.

Survival or Prophecy? The Letters of Thomas Merton and Jean Leclercq. Edited by Patrick Hart. New York: Farrar, Straus & Giroux, 2002.

Anthology

Cunningham, Lawrence S., ed. *Thomas Merton, Spiritual Master: The Essential Writings.* New York: Paulist Press, 1992.

II. Books about Merton

Bailey, Raymond. *Thomas Merton on Mysticism.* Garden City, NY: Doubleday, 1974.

Baker, Rob, and Gray Henry, eds. *Merton & Sufism: The Untold Story. A Complete Compendium.* Fons vitae Thomas Merton Series 1. Louisville: Fons Vitae, 1999.

Carr, Anne E. *A Search for Wisdom and Spirit: Merton's Theology of the Self.* Notre Dame, IN: University of Notre Dame Press, 1988.

Furlong, Monica. *Merton: A Biography.* San Francisco: Harper & Row, 1980.

Griffin, John Howard. *Follow the Ecstasy: The Hermitage Years of Thomas Merton.* Maryknoll, NY: Orbis Books, 1993.

Harford, James. *Merton and Friends: A Joint Biography of Thomas Merton, Robert Lax, and Edward Rice.* New York: Continuum, 2006.

Mott, Michael. *The Seven Mountains of Thomas Merton.* Boston: Houghton Mifflin, 1984.

Shannon, William H. *Thomas Merton's Dark Path: The Inner Experience of a Contemplative.* New York: Farrar, Straus & Giroux, 1981.

———. *Silent Lamp: The Thomas Merton Story.* New York: Crossroad, 1992.

Conclusion: Reading the Modern Mytics

Working on the history and theology of mysticism, as I have for decades, I often get asked to recount my own "mystical" experiences by those hoping to record personal witnesses to forms of more immediate contact with God. I resist these requests. This is due not only to a natural reticence to talk about private matters (Etty Hillesum said it was much easier to talk about her sexual affairs than her prayer life), but also because these petitioners may be expecting much more than they would get. How can they be so sure that those who are interested in mysticism must have a rich trove of accounts of an inner life filled with unusual things, if not ecstasies, raptures, and special revelations? Furthermore, as I have argued in this book and in other venues, to *identify* the mystical with the paranormal, let alone the uncanny and the abnormal, is a serious mistake. To be sure, there have been many mystics, both in centuries long ago and in the past hundred and more years who have, indeed, recounted gifts and experiences beyond the usual modes of consciousness. Perhaps, however, this is because these individuals have been given to see *what really is normal*, to behold and experience reality as it actually is from the perspective of God. In that sense the heightened forms of consciousness that many mystics speak of is only a tearing away of the veils of custom, selfishness, and obtuseness that prevent most of us from beholding the profound actuality of love—love of God and love of neighbor.

I think that by our reading, pondering, and meditating on the major witnesses to God we call mystics we are already participating in what I call mystical consciousness. The contemplative life necessarily involves reading (*lectio*) as the basis for the ladder of ascending practices that as long ago as the twelfth century was described as consisting of *lectio, meditatio, oratio,* and *contemplatio* (see the Carthusian Guigo II). This is perhaps more true in the twenty-first century than it was in the twelfth, when so much of our culture is tied to the word (and perhaps now the image). We need to set aside the time and cultivate the silence and attention for a careful reading of mystical texts that will "suck out their wisdom." The past generation has seen a fruitful renewal of the ancient monastic practice of *lectio divina*–slow, meditative reading that "ruminates," or "chews over" the letter of the text to get at its nourishing inner meaning. *Lectio divina* is most often practiced on the Bible, but nothing precludes it from also being applied to mystical classics, both old and new.

We need to understand that when we read the mystics it's not an issue of "them" (those wonderful mystics!) over against "us" (the peons who can only admire from afar). If only in a limited way, we are all called to embark on the mystical path. What we need is desire. As Bernard of Clairvaux (and many others) has said, "To truly desire God is already to have found him." The finding is realized on many levels—some searingly obvious and intense; others masked, unobtrusive, often dim. The intensity of these levels is not due to us and our efforts and what we may think are our successes or failures, but to the modes of the grace that God (and God alone) chooses in his Wisdom to bestow on each of us. That great theologian Thomas Aquinas expressed this truth perfectly when he said the "poor old lady" praying in the back of the church may be far more gifted with the experience of God and the sapiential wisdom that flows from this than the most learned theologian or most pious monk or nun. To be fair to the Franciscan tradition, the same holds for Thomas's contemporary, Bonaventure. Once asked by his confrere Giles of Assisi whether a simple person could love God as much as a learned one, the General responded, "An old woman can do so even more than a master in theology." Giles went away shouting, "Poor little old woman, . . . love the Lord God and you will be greater than Brother Bonaventure!"

The ten figures contained in this volume were chosen because they have nourished my own attempts to understand and practice the love that is the essence of Christian mysticism. I don't think I'm able to explain exactly how each of them did that—but I know it is the case. I think it is up to each reader to discover if they will do that for her or him. This book is meant to be an introduction to reading these modern exemplary figures, not any definitive treatment. What I have to say about them is, as I said at the outset, a "personal" view, and my own reactions may be in some cases more harmful than helpful. In any case, I firmly believe that each of them is worth reading and that is what I am encouraging in writing this book.

I have pondered over why I chose these ten figures out of a list of more than forty. I have no answer aside from a personal preference based on what seemed helpful for my own spiritual life. Four or five of them I had read extensively half a lifetime ago and was glad to return to in the past year. Another half were folk I had collected, read a bit of, and registered as important in my mental file. Over the past year and more, I have had the opportunity to reread what I read years ago, to study new texts, and, above all, to think about why I might judge these figures as exemplary mystics for our changed "modern" and "postmodern" world.

Mysticism, as an expression of how humans communicate their sense of God's presence, is a historical phenomenon—it has a past, a present, and a future. My efforts to complete my history of Western Mysticism, *The Presence of God*, have firmly convinced me of this. The mystics described in this volume are no less historical figures than are Origen, Augustine, Bernard of Clairvaux, Meister Eckhart, and the many other mystics treated in *The Presence of God* series. The twentieth-century mystics, like their predecessors, are all dead; their writings are historical artifacts. Nonetheless, we all know that some human artifacts have a long shelf life. They can become beacons for future generations to study and assimilate in order to grasp what it means to live a full human life; not just one devoted to personal satisfaction, material gain, and political advantage.

Mysticism, conceived of as giving primacy to the love of God and neighbor (sounds a lot like Christianity!), goes a step further. It insists that a full *human life* also has to be a *divine life*. We cannot reach such fulfillment on our own, if we just try a little harder to be good, do good, and to live the good. We can't do that, as Teilhard de Chardin (an optimist) and Simone Weil (a pessimist) both realized. The human situation (that is, *we*) are a mess. Only God can do what needs to be done. An important aspect of the message that the mystics collected in this volume agree upon is the utter emptiness of hubristic and utopian hopes that humanity can and will save itself. What they call out for is not just sociological, political, humanitarian, and even ecological reforms (necessary as these are), but a deeper spiritual and mystical reform as the only way to ground whatever hope is left for humanity. "We are saved by hope" (Rom. 8:24), and the mystics are great "hope-givers."

These modern mystics provide us with a range of options about how to live *sub specie aeternitatis*, or, to put it better, "under the eye of God." Of course, their messages vary in many ways—that is the genius of the mystical tradition, conceived of, as I have often said, as a great symphony with many different movements, instruments, and leitmotifs. When we listen attentively to a symphony, we are often inspired, sometimes even changed, by both the whole and the parts. We at times seem to partake of something transcendent. When we read the mystics, is it too much to think that we cannot, under their inspiration, also enter into a new and transcendent contact with the divine? That is the purpose for which this book was written.

Index of Scripture References

Old Testament

Genesis
1:26–27   65, 105, 261

Exodus
3:14   159, 252, 259

Deuteronomy
4:24   95

Psalms
General   187, 192, 273, 302, 309
17:2   105
18:1   105
18:3   105, 291
18:5   105
41:1–2   107
41:8   96
61:1–2   107
71:15   108
83:3   107
117:1   79
139:9–10   196

Lamentations
2:13   102

Proverbs
9:4   74, 75

Song of Songs
General   73, 187
1:3   79
4:9   101
6:1   103
8:7   64

Isaiah
21:11   303
24:16   150
53:3   68, 76, 77
53:66   73
66:12–13   74
66:13   75

New Testament

Matthew
3:17   97–98, 260
5:3   52, 165, 199
5:6   200
5:8   106

6:10   151
6:34   189
11:29   52
16:13–26   193
16:24   106
17:5   93, 97
17:19   197
18:2–10   74
23:8–9   192
25:40   55
26:26   274
26:39   189, 291
26:41   57
27:46   107, 227, 231, 233

Mark
8:25–37   193
10:13–16   74
14:36   260

Luke
1:35   97
1:38   151
1:51   106
2:51   53
5:11–32   73
7:47   75

Luke (cont.)		Romans		4:13	266
9:62	189, 197, 202	5:5	12, 292	4:22	106
10:39	103	8:15	260		
11:50	235	8:24	329	**Philippians**	
18:22	50	8:29	99	1:21	106, 107
19:5	107			3:16	78
19:15	76	**1 Corinthians**			
22:62	54	2:16	165	**Colossians**	
23:46	56, 57, 260	6:17	13, 92	1:15–17	115, 127
24	314	8:22–24	115	1:17	133, 161
24:31	302	12–13	70, 274	1:24	101
		13:12	94	2:6–7	106
		15:28	115, 133	2:10	115
John		15:31	105	3:11	115
1:1	161	15:54	106		
1:14	106			**Hebrews**	
4:7	64	**2 Corinthians**		1:3	108
8:41	192	3:18	104	10:7	49
8:50	192			11:1	104
10:30	259	**Galatians**		11:27	104
11:14	186	2:20	93, 105, 107, 196, 203	12:29	95
12:24	55				
13:34–35	78	3:20	192	**2 Peter**	
14:23	98	4:5	260	1:4	105
15 and 17	13	5:17	21		
15:9	98			**1 John**	
17	73	**Ephesians**		4:16	77, 92, 104,
17:21	92, 98	1	107		
18:11	107	1:4	104	**Apocalypse**	
19:30	107	1:6	87	5:6	235
20:29	228	1:10	106, 115	7:9	105
21:15–17	54	1:11–12	87, 90, 92, 94, 104	7:14–17	105
		1:21–23	115	14:1–4	105
Acts				14:8	105
17:28	133	2:4	92	14:10–11	105

Index of Subjects

Abandonment, 14, 17, 19–20, 57, 67–68, 79–81, 106–7, 152, 231, 263, 282
Abjection, 52–53, 211, 215–16, 219
Absence of God, 13–14, 54, 220, 225–26, 289. *See also* Presence of God
Abyss, 77, 94, 96, 98–99, 103–5, 107–8, 250, 253, 258–60, 263, 302, 312
Action. *See* Contemplation and action
Adoration, 38–39, 42, 51, 56–58, 79, 87, 90, 92, 95–96, 98, 100, 102, 104–5, 108, 140, 319
Advaita (non-dual), 246, 249, 251, 253, 255–56, 258, 261–63
Affliction. *See* Dereliction; *Malheur*
Angels, 18, 59, 63, 68, 161, 163–64, 167, 212
Annihilation, 52–53, 102, 105, 107, 131, 166, 199, 215–17, 219–20, 222, 230–31, 237
Anthropology, 9–10, 21–22, 99, 106, 118–19, 122, 124–25, 128, 130, 133, 137, 140, 152–53, 159–61, 163–64, 167, 171, 185–86, 220, 224, 227, 229, 234, 255, 261–62, 264, 313, 321, 329

Apophatic theology, 9–10, 12, 15, 22, 25, 135, 160, 219, 221–23, 226, 239, 256, 262, 286, 315. *See also* Cataphatic theology
Apostolic life, 58–59, 68, 70, 82, 89, 104, 300, 311
Asceticism, 11, 15, 33–34, 37–38, 40, 42, 44, 63, 81, 91, 136, 138, 216, 246–47, 262, 306
Attention, 12, 209, 212, 218, 220, 222, 226, 229–30, 232, 237, 272, 289, 319, 328
Authenticity and authentic self, 261–62, 312, 320–21
Awareness, 12, 24, 162, 169, 213, 260, 262, 264, 279, 299, 302–4, 311–12, 318, 320

Beatitude, 20, 52, 59, 98, 105, 122, 163, 165, 228, 245, 247, 250, 259, 264
Beauty, 59, 66, 93, 95, 102, 104, 153, 211, 221–22, 232, 237, 282, 284–86, 288, 290, 303–4
Being, 15, 59, 92, 95–96, 100, 106–7, 123, 126, 130–31, 156, 159–63, 171, 191, 195–96, 211, 216, 220–25, 227, 230, 232, 246, 250–51, 253, 255, 257–60, 262, 264–66, 302, 313

Bible, 8, 19, 39, 47, 56, 67, 73, 90–91, 97–98, 102, 105–6, 108, 115, 165, 169, 179, 187–88, 192, 196, 223, 253, 259, 262, 273–74, 281, 288, 298, 309, 316, 328
Birth of the Word in the Soul, 188, 201, 219
Body, 21–22, 38, 69, 102, 160, 164, 171, 185, 204, 212, 216, 237, 274, 276, 281, 284, 288, 312
Buddhism, 23, 238, 246, 258, 264, 300–301, 304, 306–7

Carmelite Order, 19, 63–67, 70, 73, 75–76, 78–79, 82, 87, 89–92, 96, 98–99, 101, 103–7, 149–51, 154–56, 168, 170
Cataphatic theology, 10, 15, 22, 132
Center of the soul, 93, 96, 98–99, 164, 232, 260–61, 264, 266, 281, 283, 303
Charity, 48–49, 53, 55, 66, 70, 78, 93, 99, 104, 127, 129, 135, 140, 197, 311
Chastity, 39, 118–19, 284
Childhood, 64–65, 68, 74, 76, 81, 92, 99–101, 103, 152–53, 160, 184, 201, 260, 284. *See also* Littleness
Christ and Christology, 3, 14, 17–19, 21–24, 37, 39, 44, 48–49, 51, 53–55, 57–58, 66–68, 70–72, 75–80, 89, 93, 97, 99–101, 103, 106–7, 115, 118, 124–31, 133, 138–40, 152, 165–67, 171, 187, 189–90, 192–95, 212, 214–16, 224, 227–28, 231, 234–35, 250, 253–54, 257–58, 260–61, 265, 273–74, 302, 304, 314, 316, 318, 320–21
Church and Ecclesiology, 4, 7, 18–19, 22, 24, 47, 58, 70, 73, 82, 101, 127, 155, 165–66, 235–36, 238, 249–50, 254, 265–66, 310–11, 319, 321
Cistercian Order, 33–34, 37–38, 49, 53, 248, 297, 305–6, 308, 310, 312
Colonialism, 40–41, 135, 181–82, 217, 236
Compassion, 82, 209, 233, 279, 383–84, 287
Confidence, 48, 57, 63–64, 71, 74–77, 80–81. *See also* Love
Consciousness, 4, 11–14, 17, 115–16, 121–24, 134, 151, 158, 162, 168, 237, 256, 258–59, 261, 264, 266, 302, 321, 327
Consolation, 67, 69, 74, 76, 78, 80, 104–5, 107, 166
Contemplation, 2–4, 6, 13, 20, 34, 42–43, 51, 55–57, 59, 79, 88, 94, 98, 104–5, 108, 140, 150, 165, 168–70, 219, 233, 237, 247, 256–57, 263–64, 266, 279, 297–301, 305, 309–10, 312–21, 327–28
  and action, 20–21, 51, 56, 82, 104, 150–51, 168, 189, 200, 202, 233–34, 263, 300, 311, 316
Convergence, 114–16, 119, 122–24, 129, 135–36, 139
Conversion, 11, 18, 23–24, 33, 35–36, 40, 43–47, 57, 66, 149–50, 154, 156–57, 211, 271–72, 277, 279, 306
Co-Redeemer, 97, 100–101, 105, 108, 228
Cosmos, Cosmogenesis, Cosmic Christ, 21, 25, 115–17, 122, 124–25, 128–29, 135, 152, 198, 253, 258, 266, 316
Creation, 21–22, 51, 58, 93, 125–27, 130, 137, 162–63, 167, 171, 197, 201, 204, 216, 219–21, 223–25, 227–28, 231, 235, 256, 260, 262, 283, 285

Index of Subjects

Cross, 14, 19–20, 42, 53, 55, 58, 66, 68, 76, 80, 82, 99, 100–102, 106, 138, 165–67, 171, 187, 189, 194, 222, 224, 227–30, 233–34, 239, 258. *See also* Passion

Dark Night, 17, 19–20, 44, 48, 66, 71, 170–71, 197, 219, 223, 316
Death, 46, 62, 64, 69–72, 91, 101, 129, 138–39, 152, 155, 160, 166, 186–87, 194, 198–99, 210, 213, 215–16, 226, 234, 246, 252, 254, 260, 272–73, 277–78, 280, 291, 309, 313, 320–21
Decreation, 219, 224, 229–31, 237
Deification, 100–101, 105, 108, 136–37, 140
Dereliction (affliction, desolation), 13–15, 19–20, 71–72, 82, 107, 166, 194, 211, 216, 222, 224, 230, 233–34, 239, 316–17
Detachment, 15, 48, 51, 79–80, 136–38, 198, 229, 231–32, 234
Devotion and devout life, 2, 17, 67–68, 76, 100, 103, 116, 140, 180, 185, 233, 250, 283, 291, 319
Dialectic, 208, 219–22, 226
Dialogue, 224, 274, 289, 291, 300–301, 303
Dignity, 41, 135, 233
Divinization. *See* Deification

Ecstasy and rapture, 3–6, 16–19, 88, 92, 101, 124, 163, 168, 212–13, 219, 229, 237–38, 301–2, 327
Ecumenism, 9, 18, 23, 135–36, 301, 310
Enlightenment, 4, 22
Epektasis, 78–79
Eroticism, 10, 187, 197, 204, 233, 276, 280, 291. *See also* Sexuality

Essence, 104, 121, 135, 151, 158–59, 161–64, 224, 226, 237, 246, 257, 276, 279, 284–85, 301, 328
Eucharist, 34–36, 38–39, 42, 44, 46, 51, 56–58, 66, 78, 81, 115, 118, 127–28, 130–31, 139–40, 165, 171, 212, 214, 235–36
Evil, 35, 42, 126, 138, 200, 220–23, 227, 231, 236, 285, 287, 292, 301
Evolution, 21, 115, 117, 120–41, 314
Experience, mystical, 1, 8–9, 11–12, 14–15, 88, 115, 150–51, 157, 168–71, 191, 200, 202, 204, 211–15, 220, 235, 237, 250, 253, 264, 286, 292, 302–4, 310, 315, 318, 327–28. *See also* Mysticism

Faith, 6, 19, 22, 35–36, 45, 47–48, 71–72, 91, 94, 96, 103–4, 106–7, 114, 122, 127–28, 153, 157–58, 160–61, 164, 166, 168–71, 179, 184, 192, 194–97, 199, 202–4, 216, 223, 225, 228, 230, 237, 250, 253, 262–64, 273, 280, 286–88, 300–302, 313–14, 318–20
Fall of humanity, 21, 104, 125–26. *See also* Sin, original
Father, God the, 14, 69, 81, 93, 97–100, 106–7, 152, 161–62, 164, 166, 171, 192, 200, 216, 224–25, 227–28, 231, 233, 235, 256–60, 264, 266, 303
Fear, 48, 63, 69, 79, 81, 190, 192, 198, 215, 250, 282, 284, 287
Freedom and free will, 42, 120, 126, 157, 159–60, 163–64, 167–68, 170, 184, 191–92, 197–98, 201–2, 225–26, 230, 255, 261–62, 265, 282–83, 303, 305, 309, 314, 319–21

Gifts, 3–5, 16–18, 47, 63, 116, 171, 183, 199, 203, 226, 262, 279, 299, 301, 315, 327
Glory, 48, 51, 68, 76, 87, 90, 92–94, 96–98, 101, 103–5, 107–8, 180
God, nature of, 12–15, 22–23, 36, 47, 64, 68, 92, 96, 99, 106, 119, 124, 129, 134–36, 138–39, 153, 155, 157, 159–60, 165, 168, 171, 187, 190–93, 196, 198–99, 201, 203–4, 213, 216, 220–23, 226–27, 229, 231–32, 250, 252, 255–56, 261–62, 264–66, 272–73, 277, 279, 280–84, 286–92, 303, 312–13, 317, 329–30
Good and goodness, 15, 21, 48, 55, 59, 64, 71, 95, 102, 137, 152, 186, 197–99, 220–23, 225, 227, 236, 277, 279, 284, 287–88, 292, 308, 329
Gospel, 17, 36, 42, 47, 49, 54, 73–74, 78, 106, 137, 151, 179, 184, 187–89, 212, 227–28, 235, 253, 256
Grace, 3, 5, 11, 44, 50–51, 56, 66–68, 71, 74, 78, 88, 92, 101, 103, 163–66, 170–71, 220, 226–27, 229–30, 262, 301, 315–18, 328
Guru, 249, 251–53, 261

Heart, 20–21, 36, 39, 43, 51–52, 57, 66, 69–70, 74–76, 78–79, 90, 97–98, 100, 102, 128–29, 131, 135, 150, 152, 165, 171, 185, 192, 198–99, 212, 218, 232, 248–49, 252–55, 258–59, 265–66, 277, 280, 282, 286, 290, 292, 302, 310–11, 314, 318, 321
  Cave of the heart (*guha*), 255, 258, 266
Heaven, 11, 13, 48, 54, 59, 64, 66–68, 71–73, 75, 78, 80–82, 93–94, 98, 101, 108, 124, 229, 287, 290, 313
Hell, 14, 19, 81, 287
Heresy, 4, 236
Hinduism, 11, 23–24, 134–35, 245–66, 300, 307
Holocaust. *See* Shoah
Holy Spirit, 3–4, 21, 93–94, 97, 99, 102, 106, 162–64, 171, 192–93, 216, 224–25, 256–60, 263–64, 266, 302, 321
Humility, 37–39, 49–50, 52–54, 58, 73–75, 99, 107, 166, 185, 192, 194, 196, 200, 203, 321
Hybridity, 23, 246, 253–55, 267, 259, 275

Illumination, 5, 70, 103–4, 128, 139, 170, 180, 187, 252, 302, 304, 318
Image of God (and Trinity), 42, 48, 55, 99–100, 103, 105–6, 161, 163–64, 261–62, 272, 285, 305, 318
Imitation of Christ, 14, 34, 36–37, 43–44, 47–59, 77, 97, 99, 107, 127, 165, 187, 194–95, 199
Immediate, 12–13, 157, 162, 315, 318, 327
Incomprehensibility. *See* Ineffability
Indifference, 52, 139, 224, 227, 273
Indistinction, 256, 259, 261, 264–65
Ineffability, 14–15, 22, 66, 98, 162, 190, 192, 245, 255, 259–60, 262
Infinity, 57, 59, 69, 77–78, 80, 82, 87, 95–97, 160, 162–63, 197, 204, 213, 219–20, 224, 245, 248, 313, 319
Intention, 12, 103, 137, 152, 320
Interiority (Introspection), 51, 59, 105, 107–8, 121–24, 128, 139, 164–65, 170–71, 178, 183–86, 195, 246, 248, 250–51, 261,

Index of Subjects

263–64, 266, 272–74, 278, 281–84, 286, 288, 290, 292, 298, 307, 312–13, 315, 320

Islam, 11, 34–35, 40, 42, 45, 55, 135, 238, 264, 300, 307, 319

Itinerary, mystical, 2, 13–14, 19–22, 39, 140, 184, 189–91, 193, 195–96, 198, 201, 233, 255, 264, 303, 316–17, 328

Jesuit Order, 35, 40, 114–21, 125–26, 131–32, 135, 140, 155, 309–10

Jesus. *See* Christ

Joy, 36, 50, 54, 68, 72, 77, 79–80, 100–101, 108, 137, 211, 216, 224, 284, 302–3

Judaism, 11, 24, 35, 55, 135, 149, 151, 153–54, 156, 167, 209, 213–15, 217–18, 221, 223, 235, 238, 265, 271–75, 277–79, 284, 286–87, 289–90, 292, 300, 307

Justice, 68–69, 79, 107, 180–81, 183, 200, 220, 233–34, 284, 300, 304

Knowledge, 7, 12–13, 16, 44, 59, 79, 106, 116, 131, 157–58, 162, 165, 168–71, 224, 236, 251, 259, 298, 311–12, 315–16, 318

Laity, 16, 18, 38, 44

Language, mystical, 13–16, 22, 132, 151, 169, 190–92, 259, 317

Littleness, 43, 63, 67, 73–76, 78, 80–82, 90

Liturgy, 11, 15, 17, 37, 95, 105, 133, 155, 211, 246, 263–64, 300, 309, 311, 315, 319

Love and desire, 12–13, 19–21, 24, 34, 36, 40, 43, 49–50, 53–59, 63–64, 68–70, 72, 74–75, 77–81, 89–90, 92–95, 100–101, 106, 108, 119, 122, 128–32, 134–37, 141, 152, 162–65, 170, 185, 188, 190–92, 194, 196–200, 209, 212, 214–16, 219, 221–33, 235–37, 250–51, 255, 259, 262, 271–72, 274, 276–77, 279–80, 282–83, 285, 287, 289–92, 299–300, 302–3, 308, 311–12, 314, 318–21, 327–29

Pure love, 4, 70, 94, 170, 231–32

Malheur, 20, 210–11, 230–31

Marriage, mystical (Christ as spouse), 54, 57, 59, 64, 68, 70, 77, 97, 99–101, 105, 168, 170–71, 197, 233, 318

Martyrdom, 24, 43, 46, 55–56, 66, 69, 74, 76, 107, 194, 275

Mary, 17–19, 53, 66, 69, 81, 100, 103, 107, 116, 151–52, 167

Matter, 22, 115–16, 118–19, 121–23, 127–28, 130–32, 138–39, 158–59, 164

Meditation, 9, 16, 34, 38–39, 47, 52, 77, 90, 93, 106, 136, 152, 156–57, 167, 193–94, 200–201, 233, 249, 251–53, 257, 263, 274, 278, 282, 285, 289, 299, 306, 309–11, 313, 319, 327–28

Mercy (divine), 2, 17, 63–64, 68–69, 74, 79–80, 82, 96, 155, 192, 201, 212, 237, 262, 312, 321

Miracle, 39, 72, 88, 196, 212, 234

Missions, 40, 44, 70–71, 73, 75, 82, 108

Monasticism, 7, 16, 24, 38, 155, 246–48, 299, 304, 306–10, 312, 317, 328

Modernism, 7–8, 117

Modernity, 5, 7, 10, 40, 62, 82, 117, 137, 168, 179, 184, 187, 209, 246, 257, 273–74, 286, 292, 300, 320, 329

Mortification. *See* Asceticism
Mystery, 3, 10, 13, 20, 90, 93, 95–98, 106, 127, 131, 163, 166–67, 190–91, 202, 216, 219, 227, 235, 237, 246, 249–53, 255–62, 264–66, 290, 292, 300, 321
Mysticism (concept of), 1–3, 10–15, 63–64, 81–82, 87–88, 95, 98, 114–16, 128–29, 131–40, 150–51, 168–71, 179–81, 184–85, 188–89, 195, 202–4, 212, 219, 234–38, 245–46, 250, 254, 259, 263–64, 272, 279, 284–86, 292, 298–302, 304, 309, 311–12, 320, 327–30
  Academic study of mysticism, 5–10
  Nature mysticism, 133, 183, 186, 200–201, 204, 303, 315–16
Mystical theology, 2, 4–5, 8, 169, 306, 315

Nazareth, life of, 34, 37, 39–40, 49–55
Negation. *See* Apophatic theology
Non-dualism. *See* Advaita
Noogenesis, Noosphere, 121, 123–25, 128, 132
Nothingness, 48, 53, 72, 74, 98, 105, 126, 203, 216, 219, 223, 225, 231, 303, 317, 319

Obedience, 13, 19, 38–39, 43, 49, 53–54, 120, 185, 187, 197–98, 200, 226, 228, 234
Omega point, 22, 115–16, 122–25, 128–29
Our Father, 2, 151, 192, 212–13

Paleontology, 115, 117–19
Pantheism, 115, 122, 127, 132–34, 139, 204
Paradox, 13–15, 24, 55, 70–71, 82, 190, 209, 217–18, 220, 222, 228–29, 255, 259, 262, 276, 302, 304, 307, 313
Passion of Christ, 18, 50, 58, 69, 97, 99–100, 105, 107, 193, 211, 231. *See also* Cross
Passivity, 137–38, 171, 229, 273, 280, 314–15
Peace, 36, 54, 59, 77, 150, 183, 192, 247, 261, 272–73, 280, 284, 288, 307, 313
Penance, 36–38, 51, 54, 168
Perfection, 2, 21, 48–49, 50, 53, 58–59, 65, 69, 75, 78, 94, 104, 106, 108, 163, 197–99, 224, 228
Phenomenology, 115, 121–22, 125, 140, 154, 156–58
Philosophy, 6–7, 9–11, 20–22, 36, 118, 133, 135, 149, 151, 154–58, 160–62, 167, 180, 208, 210, 213, 217–19, 221, 235, 247, 258, 300, 314
Political and mystical, 21, 234, 301
Poverty, 34, 37–41, 43, 49–53, 74, 78, 165–66, 219, 238, 247, 312–13
Praise, 87, 90, 92–94, 98, 103–4, 107–8, 249, 313, 319
Prayer, 2, 6, 9, 34, 37–39, 43, 45, 51, 56–57, 59, 73, 81–82, 88–90, 93, 97–98, 103, 107, 131, 136, 138, 140, 155, 165–68, 185, 189, 192, 203, 211–12, 215–16, 230, 260, 263–64, 274–76, 278–85, 287–90, 292, 302–3, 310–11, 313, 319, 327–28. *See also* Meditation
Predestination, 87, 90, 92, 95, 99–100, 103–4, 107, 152
Presence of God, 2, 11–14, 58, 88, 98, 104, 106, 114, 137, 151, 157, 169, 180–81, 201, 203, 211–13, 220–21, 226, 258, 261–63, 279, 283, 287, 302–3, 312–13, 315, 319, 329

Prophecy, 82, 169, 180, 234, 265, 301–2
Protestantism, 2, 18, 179–81, 188, 219
Providence, 223, 226
Psychology, 5–6, 8–9, 19–20, 65–66, 154, 202, 211, 218, 250, 274–78, 304, 306
Purgation, 19, 171, 222, 238, 317
Purity, 2, 21, 185, 198–99

Quietism, 4–6

Rapture. *See* Ecstasy
Reason, 9–10, 22, 47, 157–58, 161, 167, 184, 187, 218, 247, 254, 262, 280, 303, 320
Ressourcement, 6–7
Resurrection, 21–22, 129, 131, 139, 153, 228–29, 302
Revelation and revelations, 6, 17, 121, 133, 139, 157, 161, 167–68, 225, 266, 304, 315–16, 327
Righteousness, 185–86, 192, 194, 200

Sacraments, 2–3, 22, 91, 130, 165, 212, 236, 287
Salvation (and Redemption), 14, 21, 55, 105, 107, 125–27, 137, 140, 152, 165–67, 227, 229, 231, 235, 254, 299, 316
Sanyassi, 246–47, 249, 252, 262
Scholasticism, 5–7, 10, 115, 155, 310
Self-knowledge, 162, 184–87, 190–91, 196, 264, 311, 321
Sexuality, 33, 35, 118–19, 181, 199, 233, 272, 275–78, 281, 284–85, 305, 327
Shoah, 24, 151, 156, 271–72, 274, 277, 280, 287, 289, 292. *See also* Judaism
Silence and stillness, 14–15, 38, 51, 56–57, 93–96, 99, 103, 105–6, 108, 150, 168, 192,194, 196–98, 200–202, 204, 213, 224, 227, 233–34, 248–49, 251–52, 260, 262–63, 298, 302, 308, 312–13, 317–18, 328
Sin, 51, 54, 59, 63–64, 67, 71–72, 81–82, 126, 137, 167, 194, 222, 227–29, 236, 289, 303, 316–17
  Original sin, 118, 126–27, 152, 165, 167, 200, 223, 228
Son of God. *See* Christ
Spirituality and spiritual life, 2–3, 9, 21, 23, 46, 48, 50, 55, 58–59, 63, 65, 68, 73, 81, 88, 90, 93, 115, 120–22, 132, 136, 154, 164, 191, 218, 227, 234, 251, 253, 255, 257, 262, 273–74, 276–91, 298–301, 307–8, 310, 316–19, 321, 329
Stigmata, 17–18, 64, 69, 81, 88, 237, 301
Suffering, 14, 19–20, 25, 39, 41, 50, 53, 55, 65, 67–69, 71–72, 76–77, 79, 80–82, 87, 99–102, 107,126, 130–31, 136, 139, 166–67, 200, 211–12, 228, 230, 235, 274, 280, 282, 284, 288–91
Sufism. *See* Islam
Supernatural, 39, 48, 105, 127, 157, 161, 164, 169, 212, 226, 231–35, 237, 316, 318
Sweetness, 69, 71, 78–79, 94, 100, 102, 107
Symbols, mystical, 73–75, 79–80, 93–96, 169, 232, 260, 265–66

Temptation, 54, 71–72, 122, 190
Transformation, mystical, 11–12, 15, 55, 74–75, 78, 93–94, 98, 100, 102, 104–5, 107–8, 139–40, 151, 170, 190, 216, 222, 276, 292, 302, 312, 320–21

Trials, 66, 68, 71–72, 81, 101, 186–87, 251–52, 275, 279, 282, 302, 308, 317
Trinity, 3, 17, 19, 68, 76, 87, 90, 93–99, 102–3, 106–8, 160–64, 170–71, 192, 203, 224, 235, 252, 256–60, 264–66, 304, 315, 318
Truth, 5–6, 16, 47–48, 59, 70, 73–74, 81, 125, 130, 132, 139, 154–55, 157–59, 161, 165–66, 179, 185, 209, 212, 214, 216, 220, 222, 224–25, 230–32, 234–37, 259–60, 263, 265, 272, 299–300, 303–4, 313, 316–18, 321

Union, mystical, 3–4, 13–14, 17, 19–20, 39, 50, 53, 55–56, 58–59, 66, 79–80, 88, 90, 92–93, 95–98, 101–2, 106, 108, 115–16, 129, 131, 133–41, 152, 165–71, 184, 191–93, 195–99, 202–4, 231, 233, 236–38, 303–4, 313–14, 316–18, 321

Violence, 41, 68, 216, 288, 305
Virtue, 48, 53–56, 74, 104, 187, 195–97, 200, 233, 237, 262, 318

Vision and Visionaries, 3–4, 16–19, 63, 66, 88, 116, 120, 126, 129–30, 136–37, 140, 180, 202, 212, 214–15, 264, 301, 304
Vision of God, 13–14, 19–20, 96, 102, 104, 157, 224

Will of God, 38, 43, 48, 54, 65, 67, 71, 81, 90, 140, 151–53, 164, 166–67, 171, 192, 196, 199, 216, 225–26, 291, 300, 313–14, 319, 321
Wisdom, 59, 92, 134, 161, 163–64, 226, 251, 253, 303, 328
Women, role of, 4–5, 16–17, 118–19, 154–55, 157, 228, 278, 282, 308, 328
Worship. *See* Liturgy
Word of God, 78, 93, 97, 99, 101, 106, 127, 130, 152, 157, 260, 313. *See also* Christ
Work and Working, 37–38, 43, 48, 50, 53, 64, 69–70, 72, 103, 107, 127, 166, 233–34, 283, 316

Zen. *See* Buddhism

www.ingramcontent.com/pod-product-compliance
Lightning Source LLC
Chambersburg PA
CBHW030105010526
44116CB00005B/110